D0910062

Advances in the Social Sciences, 1900-1980

What, Who, Where, How?

Written Under the Auspices of the Wissenschaftszentrum Berlin
June 1982

Edited by

Karl W. Deutsch
Harvard University and Science Center Berlin

Andrei S. Markovits
Boston University
Center for European Studies, Harvard University

John Platt
Harvard University

UNIVERSITY PRESS OF AMERICA

LANHAM • NEW YORK • LONDON

Abt Books
Cambridge
Massachusetts

University Press of America,® Inc.

4720 Boston Way
Lanham, MD 20706

3 Henrietta Street
London WC2E 8LU England

Printed in the United States of America

Co-published by arrangement with
Abt Books

ISBN (Perfect): 0-8191-5172-6
ISBN (Cloth): 0-8191-5171-8

All University Press of America books are produced on acid-free paper which exceeds the minimum standards set by the National Historical Publications and Records Commission.

To the memory of
Harold Lasswell, Margaret Mead, Talcott Parsons,
and Norbert Wiener

Contents

Preface and Acknowledgments

THE IDEA OF THIS INQUIRY was born long ago, in 1968–1969, at the Mental Health Research Institute at the University of Michigan. John Platt was then associate director of that institute, as well as a professor at the university; I was a consultant at the institute, in addition to teaching at Yale; and Dieter Senghaas was then a young visiting scholar from West Germany. Together we discussed a related group of questions: Have there been real, substantial advances in the social sciences in the twentieth century? Are they continuing? What favorable conditions seem to have been associated with them in their social and institutional environment? Who made most of these advances—lonely great men, small teams, or large teams? Where were they made? How evenly or unevenly were they distributed among disciplines, countries, and institutions? How were they made? What method and approaches proved most often fruitful? How did these matters change in the course of our century?

Clearly this was a program for many scholars, working for many years, and on their way getting entangled in many controversies. Yet our curiosity drove us; we wanted to make at least a beginning; and in what now seems to me an act of plain temerity, we did. Between us, we had a fair knowledge of a broad range of social sciences, and a good many years of experience in social science research. More important, we had learned from close association with other social scientists, and we were tireless in asking and taking advice from our colleagues in other fields and other countries. The responsibility for our findings remains, of course, our own.

The result was the study by Deutsch, Platt and Senghaas [DPS] that is reproduced for the first time in a general publication as the appendix to this book. A briefer version was published in *Science* (the weekly of the American Association for the Advancement of Science) on January 5, 1971, under the title, "Conditions Favoring Major Advances in Social Science." We received both letters of praise and letters of protest. Our curiosity persisted. Even though Dieter Senghaas's interests moved into other fields, his early contributions were substantial, and John Platt and I kept looking for new advances and asking our colleagues at many universities about them.

More than a decade after the brief publication in *Science*, in June 1982, it became possible to assemble a group of knowledgeable social scientists at the International Institute for Comparative Social Research of the Science Center Berlin [Wissenschaftszszentrum Berlin—WZB] for a conference, to do three things: to assess our basic enterprise; to take a new look at our early findings; and to survey the new advances, if any, in the social sciences in the two decades between 1960 and 1980. What they said and what they found is reported in this book.

In particular, much of the spirit of the lively debates and exchanges at the conference has been captured in the summaries of the highlights, prepared by Professor Andrei Markovits, who participated in all the sessions as a member of the conference and then served as editor of its discussions. John Platt carried the majority of the editorial burden in the preparation of this manuscript for publication.

Three of the papers presented at the conference are being published elsewhere. The presentation of I. Bernard Cohen is now being published as part of a book on historical relations between the sciences, and a resumé is presented here in connection with the discussions; that of Alex Inkeles has been published under another title in *The Social Science Journal* and is being reprinted here by permission; and that of Hermann Krallmann on computer-supported decision tools for management has been published separately by the International Institute for Comparative Social Research as part of their reprint series.

This conference, together with the subsequent revisions and additions made by some authors to their contributions, is just the latest stage in an intellectual adventure that has extended over fifteen years. In one form or another, this adventure will have to be carried on, if not by ourselves, then by other scholars. It is essential that the social sciences, and those who work in them, should gain a clearer awareness of their mission and their powers. It would be unbearable if people gave up the attempt to gain communicable, reproducible, verifiable, and cumulative knowledge—which means scientific knowledge—about major aspects of their own individual and collective behavior. Such a renunciation would be a piece of intellectual suicide and a step toward the material suicide of humankind—

at a time when human beings more then ever threaten one another, need one another, and are one another's fate.

I am confident that efforts toward the greater self-awareness, self-responsibility, and cumulative fruitfulness of the social sciences will be carried on. For our own small part in this work, we are indebted to the participants of the conference, and earlier to many other colleagues, among them Hayward Alker, Jr., Gabriel Almond, David Apter, Kenneth Arrow, Samuel Beer, Paul Bohannan, Kenneth Boulding, Robert Dahl, Robert Dorfman, Carl Friedrich, Harold Guetzkow, Robert Lane, Wassily Leontief, Seymour Martin Lipset, Roy Macridis, Candido Mendes de Almeida, Richard Merritt, James Grier Miller, Frederick Mosteller, Charles Osgood, Ithiel de Sola Pool, Gardner Quarton, Anatol Rapoport, Bruce Russett, Paul Samuelson, J. Richard Savage, J. David Singer, B. F. Skinner, John Spiegel, Sidney Verba, and Harrison White.

We are further particularly indebted to Gerald Holton and Anatol Rapoport for long analyses of these problems, and to Clifford Geertz, Carl Kayzen, George A. Miller, and George Stigler for their dissenting but instructive letters. And we are indebted to colleagues who gave us valuable advice and who are now no longer with us, including Harold Lasswell, Margaret Mead, Talcott Parsons, and Norbert Wiener—but whose thoughts live on.

We owe a debt of gratitude for material and institutional support to the Science Center Berlin; the Mental Health Research Institute of the University of Michigan; the Universities of Harvard, Michigan, and Tel Aviv and their libraries and staffs; Konstanza Prinzessin zu Löwenstein, for her important administrative work on the details of the Conference; and to our always helpful secretaries, Ina Frieser and Soad Bader in Berlin, and earlier, Anne Hargreaves in Ann Arbor. At one time or another, each of these gave valuable help to an enterprise that still represents only a beginning.

Karl W. Deutsch
Cambridge, Mass., and Berlin
October 25, 1983

Analytical Table of Contents

CHAPTER 1

What Do We Mean by Advances in the Social Sciences?

Karl W. Deutsch

THIS BOOK AND THE CONFERENCE on which it is based represent an effort to find out how the social sciences have been developing in the twentieth century, and particularly in the last two decades, and what are the conditions for their sound and rapid development. About the end of the 1960s, John Platt, Dieter Senghaas, and I tried to identify substantial advances in the social sciences from 1900 to 1965, and to explore the conditions that had favored them (Deutsch, Platt, and Senghaas 1970, 1971) [DPS]. Now, a dozen years later, we are returning to the enterprise, asking a group of well-informed and thoughtful critics how our evaluations and conclusions should be changed, and what has happened since then in the social sciences. We are now calling this collection of papers *Advances in the Social Sciences, 1900–1980: What, Who, Where, How?* The *how* is the key word for us, because under the *how* we would like to find out what scientific and social conditions favor major advances in this field.

What Is a Substantial Contribution?

We are concerned with advances—*new* advances in knowledge with *substantial* impact in at least one field of the social sciences. Perhaps the first question that would produce a good deal of debate would be: What is meant by *substantial*? We tried to define it in terms of its impact on the field and its consequences for later work. I am not trying to prescribe the meanings of words that any of our colleagues might wish to use, but I think we need the word *substantial* or some word like it to distinguish the larger and more important contributions from the lesser ones, whether we make a distinction based on intuition or more careful judgment.

Alex Inkeles points out in Chapter 2 that we should have been more formal about stating our "intercoder agreement." At first, however, we were not concerned with agreement so much as with getting a broad range of instances of "advances" to examine. There were three of us with different backgrounds: John Platt, a biophysicist who was then the associate director of the Mental Health Research Institute of the University of Michigan, with a broad interest in natural and social science; Dieter Senghaas, a political scientist from Germany who was familiar with European developments in the social sciences; and myself, living partly in the world of U.S. political science but with some continuing contacts with European thought. We also, of course, went around and asked friends and colleagues wherever we could. A list of important economists and their substantial contributions was compiled with the advice of Wassily Leontief, Kenneth Arrow, and other members of the Harvard Department of Economics. Some of our evaluations must have had considerable general acceptance, because the economists we listed in 1970 later received a surprisingly large number of Nobel Prizes.

We could have used more objective tests or quantitative tests in getting a list of substantial advances. In Chapter 2 Inkeles refers to the number of textbooks that cited certain sociologists and their contributions more than five times, and he mentions three studies in which this reputational method of evaluation was used. In political science several studies have used similar reputational methods, one by Bruce Russett (1970), and another by Albert Somit and Joseph Tannenhaus (1967), where every fifth member of the American Political Science Association was asked to evaluate contributions to the field, both in 1960 and in a repeated study published in 1978.

A very recent study of political science contributions is based simply on the frequency of citations in the *Social Science Citation Index*. Of course, the frequency-of-citation method still requires judgment. For example, it might seem that Western writers and statesmen consider the late Leonid Brezhnev a great authority on politics, because they cite him so frequently. The devil was also one of the authorities—or authors—referred to most frequently by medieval churchmen. Clearly the citation method needs to be used with good sense and supported by personal judgment; using several such methods in overlap, however, permits the question of a real advance in science and of its impact to be resolved in many cases.

In the future we might become even more specific in using quantitative measures such as citation frequency or the frequency of reputational mentionings; and we could define *substantial* or at least *influential* contributors as those more than 1.0, or 1.5, or 2.0 standard deviations above the mean or median frequency, provided they meet our other criteria. Our discussions here may lead to a consensus on how to make better evaluations of advances. (See Chapters 5 and 16 and the discussion after Chapter 13.)

Of course, it is not necessary to have an exhaustive list or perfect agreement if our goal is mainly to know what conditions help to create major scientific advances. A consensus on even, say, four-fifths of the cases might still be very useful. Even if, at the margin, each of us would have added or excluded a few authors, we might still reach firm and robust conclusions if we have a fairly large common core of cases with some instructive common characteristics.

Significant Kinds of Novelty

What is *new* about new advances? The approach in the DPS papers emphasized the element of discovery or invention. It therefore gave a premium to the first people who broke through, or to those who added a substantial further gain of knowledge—even though this approach is necessarily somewhat unfair to the many workers who have added small but important pieces of understanding step by step.

In emphasizing novelty, we distinguished two kinds. The first is the novelty of finding new facts or relationships of the kind that can be formulated in an *existential statement* of the logical form, "There is . . ." or "If . . . then . . . ." Such statements are verifiable or falsifiable. Thus in chemistry we can verify and measure quite exactly whether there is or is not a fairly exact preservation of the quantity of matter during a chemical reaction. In physics, either there is an electron with certain properties, or there is not. In any field of science we need to find out to what extent new discoveries refer to verifiable reality.

A second kind of substantial contribution or novelty relates to methods. In a narrow sense, methods are *techniques*, such as techniques of observation, of measurement, or of calculation. These might be either newly invented or imported from other fields of the social or natural sciences. Quantitative content analysis, for instance, turns out to have been developed first by literary scholars. Konrad Burdach used this method early in the twentieth century to pull out concepts from a literary work of 1400 A.D., *The Ploughman from Bohemia* (Burdach 1926). Much later the method got into the arsenal of the social scientists. Other techniques have been developed in the natural sciences and in engineering before they were used for social science.

In a wider sense, methods can include new concepts and new conceptual schemes, theories, or models. In Chapter 2 Inkeles mentions Max Weber's distinction between economic class and social status—that is, a recognition of two distinct patterns, though ones that might be partly correlated. Such new *recognition patterns* are very often proposed. As we know from cybernetic machines, in order for us to recognize anything, whether it be rotten eggs or enemy airplanes, the important thing is to store the right kind of recognition pattern for comparison with the observed phenomena.

In the widest sense, new methods might include the identification of *new areas of interest.* At first there may not be a precise or even a systematic theory. However, there might be a serious argument, backed by some significant evidence, that an important new field for exploration exists that is described sufficiently well for people to know what it is, or at least what it is at the core. This argument and this evidence may then direct a great deal of attention toward the new field.

I should like here to add a note on the classic Aristotelian mode of thinking that a concept is useful only if it is sharp at the edges, so that we can say precisely where it stops, what belongs to it, and what does not. Reality is not as conveniently organized as Aristotle would have liked. What is exactly the end of a cloud? What is exactly the boundary of the atmosphere of the planet earth? The natural sciences provide many examples of phenomena that are diffuse or statistical distributions. These are dense and easily recognizable in their central region but tend to fall off toward the edges to such a degree that one may have to make a convention to decide where to cut off. In these cases there is no obvious sharp boundary. Not everything that is real is sharply bounded. When international lawyers try to determine how high up the atmosphere reaches, or where up there national sovereignty ends, they have to wrestle with exactly this problem. One proposal is to say that the nation-state reaches as far as the atmosphere is thick enough to heat a satellite to the point of destruction. Beyond that, it is no longer the nation-state (McDougal and Lasswell 1980).

One example of such a fuzzy but important area of interest would be motivation research, as represented by the work of David McClelland and others (McClelland 1961). Motivation is not very sharply bounded or separable from other psychological and social phenomena. Nevertheless, one can identify evidence relating to motives, and such an area of interest seems to me legitimate for inclusion in our discussions.

Finally, we might return to the question of whether we should include *cumulative small gains* in a field if they reach a critical level. History gives us a conveniently sharp date for the French Revolution. On July 14, 1789, a crowd stormed the Bastille. To this day, the French dance in the streets in commemoration. The Industrial Revolution, on the other hand, has no such precise date. Nevertheless, it cumulated to the point where it changed first England and then the world. The Industrial Revolution was probably no less real than the French Revolution was, and the same may be true of many gradual developments in science.

The Unity of the Natural and Social Sciences

The basic viewpoint that informs what we try to do is that of the unity of science. We have assumed that the common features of the natural and social sciences are large enough and important enough to permit a transfer of experience—to permit us to ascribe relevance to many parallel problems and decision criteria in the development of these two great fields, while still trying not to forget the significant differences between them.

These common features include, first of all, *formal rationality*. In operational terms, this means *retraceability*. A scientific argument must be stated in such a way that it can be retraced step by step by some pattern of logic or mathematics. We know now that there is more than one kind of logic and more than one kind of geometry and arithmetic in the world, but by some specifiable pattern of logic or formal reasoning it must be possible to retrace a scientific argument. That holds for the social as well as for the natural sciences.

Second, it must be possible to *confirm* at least some of the existential statements by empirical methods that are based on *standardized operations*. Existential statements that cannot be so verified may have the status of *constructs*, as the physicist Bridgman called them. They can be reached by paper-and-pencil operations. It may happen that something that is first invented as a construct later turns out to have *physical reality*. Thus the electron was first a theoretical construct in physics; eventually, more and more evidence accumulated that moved physicists to ascribe physical reality to it. Physical reality, however, means that a large number of different and mutually independent operations will give consistent results. In that sense, *reality* is a quantitative concept. The more independent operations that confirm that something is there, the more real it may be considered to be. To refute Bishop Berkeley's theory of the nonexistence of matter, Dr. Samuel Johnson struck his foot against a large stone, saying, "I refute it thus." He was using two independent tests: his eyes and his toes. Stones have turned out to answer many more tests, and the notion of science is that we can test by a plurality or multiplicity of mutually independent operations whether something exists or not.

Scientific statements in both natural and social science also have *limits of validity*. No statement in any science has unlimited validity everywhere. In his philosophical writings on domains of validity, Anatol Rapoport has educated many of us to this viewpoint (Rapoport 1960).

We may also note that theories in both natural and social sciences are replaceable by *successor theories*. Existential statements, too, may have to be revised—remember "phlogiston" in chemistry and the ether in physics—but the closer to experiential fact a statement is, the less it will change with fashion. Since Columbus discovered the Western Hemisphere, no fashion in geography, social science, or philosophy has ever denied its existence: It is there. Nevertheless, theories can be reformulated, and have been. Karl Popper conveyed the impression in some of his writings that theories not only must be "falsifiable" but that they are all eventually falsified—that is, refuted or disconfirmed in some testing domain—and that there is an endless succession of such theories going in no very clearly defined direction (Popper 1961). Rather, we have taken the view that successor theories have to include approximately as many, or more, existential statements than their predecessors did. The successor theory must account for most or all of the phenomena the predecessor did, and preferably for additional ones. This approach leads to a much narrower line of possible successions (although there is not a line but rather a tree of possibilities); and it suggests a certain direction of change, including the notion of cumulative growth.

The notion that natural and social science have all these things in common implies that, at least in principle, all these ought to be accessible eventually to the language of *mathematics*. That mathematical calculations were applicable to real stones and to architecture was demonstrated by Brunelleschi when he constructed the cupola of the dome of Florence around the year 1400 (de Santillana 1956). As late as 1900 mathematics was rejected as being inapplicable to biology, but it is now accepted in biology so thoroughly that one cannot get a doctorate in biology at any of the better universities without a knowledge of mathematics. In recent decades, economics has gone through a similar development. What Plato wrote over the door of his academy, "Let no one ignorant of geometry enter," is slowly becoming the motto of universities.

How Fundamental Are the Differences?

Historically, the unity of the natural and social sciences has been asserted time and again by major thinkers: Plato, Aristotle, Locke, Kant, Hegel, Marx, and Pareto. The opposite notion is much younger. A fundamental difference between the two sciences—the two kinds of knowledge—was asserted by Wilhelm Dilthey; later by Heinrich Rickert and by Wilhelm Windelband; and to some extent, though not nearly so radically, by Max

Weber. (For a discussion of the first three, see Collingwood [1946]). Their view was that human culture and behavior, and indeed all social and "cultural" sciences, should not be approached in a manner similar to that of the natural sciences, but by an operation called *understanding*. Understanding is a psychological operation by which a scientist tries to reproduce in his own mind and by his own emotions the supposed state of mind of others. According to this approach, the student of society should try to feel as Caesar did when he crossed the Rubicon, or as Hitler did when he gave his orders for the extermination of the Jews. An analyst should do what psychiatrists often do as they learn to understand a mentally disturbed person without becoming mentally ill themselves. That is one way to approach the science, and I should argue that this school of thought has made valuable contributions.

The followers of this view have contributed a better search for recognition patterns, but they have not succeeded in establishing a fundamental incompatibility between sciences dealing with human beings and sciences dealing with all the rest of the universe. The three contrasting features of the two areas that are often cited are not as fundamentally different as they appear. One of them is that the social sciences deal with fewer levels of systems and smaller numbers of cases than the vast sweep of the natural sciences. If we take different system levels as defined in size by the power of 10, then natural science works with something like forty-three powers of 10, from subatomic particles to metagalaxies.

The social sciences also have a wide range, however, with something like fifteen system levels, from the lowest level of intrapsychic components, and psychoactive drugs, and effects of the hormonal system; to personality components, à la Freud, a little higher up in the scale; then to individuals; and on up to groups and societies, going beyond the United Nations to the population of the globe and up to social interactions with the whole biosphere (Miller 1978).

Some might say that every area of social science is immensely complex and that any attempt to subdivide by levels, or to make a scale in parallel with the natural sciences, is simplistic and sterile. However, there are operational tests for the significance of system levels other than mere physical scale or numbers. One such test is *inclusion*: The larger level includes the smaller. Berlin is part of Germany, but Germany is not a part of Berlin. Individual personalities include psychological and psychic components, social groups and organizations include individuals, and larger organizations and communities may include smaller ones. Villages and cities are included in metropolitan areas, provinces, and states; they in turn are included in nation-states and federations. Thomas Aquinas already wrote of five levels: the family, the village, the county, the duchy, and the kingdom.

Another test of the importance of the concept of system and subsystem levels is the probability of prevailing in case of conflict or collision.

In political and military matters, the larger and more inclusive system is likely—though not certain—to prevail over any of its components. When the U.S. federal government sent troops to Little Rock, Arkansas, in 1957, it prevailed over local opposition. Many important effects of this kind in the relations between system levels are described in James G. Miller's book *Living Systems* (Miller 1978).

One could even propose a general technique based on this, for research in the natural or social sciences, by saying that if we are working on a problem on system level i, then to understand it we should go to at least one level above—as from the nation-state up to its international environment; and to one level below, to the components of the system—as down to the main social classes, interest groups, and organizations within the nation-state. With more time and a bigger budget, we can go on to the levels of $i \pm 2$, or two levels up and two levels down; and so on.

Stability of Interactions in Different Fields

It has also been argued that natural science is somehow more scientific because it deals with a larger number of cases, giving a manifold of data or statistical smoothing; but there are areas that are not very different from social science in this respect. In fields such as meteorology, seismology, planetology, or the zoology of rare species such as elephants, we may find only a few cases within any short time of observation. There are probably not more hurricanes in the world than there are local elections. If we can say something intelligent and general about hurricanes—even though in many ways every hurricane is different from every other—then we can at least look for regularities in elections. We do indeed find that elections are sufficiently similar that many predictive statements can also be made about them, often with success.

In any field where there are few cases, statistical problems or complex computational problems will create a margin of error. Electoral research by sampling generally has an error margin of about 2 percent; in exceptional cases it goes up to 10 percent. Since elections are designed to be decided often by margins of 1 percent or less, this is not satisfactory. Meteorology, however, which works with an error margin of 20 percent, is considered a "hard science" with a very useful measure of accuracy. Despite the uncertainties, it is sensible for any politician to pay attention to sample surveys that indicate within 2 percent accuracy whether he or she is falling behind or getting ahead in an electoral race. Similarly, it is worthwhile for any airline company to know within a 20 percent error margin whether its expensive airplane should be sent out over the Atlantic or whether it would be better to wait a day until the weather improves.

A second difference from the natural sciences that is often discussed is that in the social sciences the characteristics of the elements in combination change quickly. Yet even in the natural sciences, although many of the basic elements and interactions do remain stable or change slowly, there are still large cross-effects and dynamic instabilities in certain areas of study. It is amusing to note that while some people say we cannot have social science because people change too quickly, an equal or larger number of colleagues will tell us at the same time that we do not need social science because human nature always stays the same. Commonsense judgments often come in opposing pairs, and we then have to make an intuitive decision about which half of the polarity we want to believe, or at least to use at each moment.

The third and perhaps the most serious contrast between the fields is that social science is more sensitive than natural science to the interests of the researchers. What is studied and what is found depends on their expectations of social, economic, or psychological reward and also on the personality, biography, and especially the culture of the researchers. Again, however, James Conant, Thomas Kuhn, and others have shown that in the natural sciences the supposedly detached acceptance of paradigms is not at all immune from these infirmities. When people believed and wanted to believe in ruthless competition, they saw with Darwin nature red in tooth and claw. When they preferred a gentler and more human relationship, they found with Prince Peter Kropotkin nature full of symbiosis and mutual aid. One can have fairly different notions about facts of nature. There is a problem of what to consider important, and this does affect the social sciences more often, but the natural sciences are not immune to it.

The Social Sciences do Progress

Is there progress, and is it visible and verifiable? Yes, certainly. We can apply to the social sciences a generalized notion of progress similar to the biologist Julian Huxley's notion of biological progress. Huxley argued that progress in evolution—evolutionary progress—can be judged by the increasing independence of a species from its environment, and hence by the increasing range of habitats in which that species can survive. In this sense a parasite regresses; it makes no progress. Although it is true that evolution has produced more lice than lions, a louse must stay in the pelt of some host. The lion has a little more freedom of movement. The evolutionary progress of human beings means that they have more freedom of movement and a wider range of habitats than any other species known to biologists (Huxley 1942).

Scientific progress might be defined as a similar increase in range of understanding and control—an increase in what people can recognize, what they can predict, and what they can do. Recognition, prediction, and action are the first three tests of real progress in science. Recognition—an essentially qualitative operation—comes first, in natural science as well as social science.

Scientific progress, so defined, does not necessarily imply increases in wisdom. Wisdom is not knowledge, but the knowledge of which knowledge is worth having. Scientific or cognitive progress also does not automatically imply any increase in morality, beauty, happiness, or even the chances of peace or survival. Knowledge that is represented by recognition, prediction, and capacity for action is helpful in dealing with peace or survival; but obviously human motivation is deeper and more complex. Scientific knowledge in itself cannot take the place of everything else.

I would say, however, that knowledge in the social sciences can be applied to social performance in the same sense as knowledge in the natural sciences has been. Here I am particularly grateful for the ironical point made by Alex Inkeles. In Chapter 2 he gives a list of people who have said how wonderfully well the social sciences have progressed, and another list of people who argue that the social sciences have not achieved anything. In short, as in so many other fields of human endeavor, people oscillate between the attitude of the Reverend Norman Vincent Peale, who wrote *The Power of Positive Thinking*, and the attitude of the prophet Jeremiah.

Would we not have had a similar ambivalence if we had asked, What have the natural sciences accomplished? and if we had posed that question just at the time when they made their discoveries? What did Copernicus accomplish in 1534, or even half a century later, in 1584? What practical applications were made of the Copernican theory at that time? What political, economic, or social improvement did Copernicus produce? What did Kepler do? Kepler's laws of planetary motion were totally useless in terms of information relevant to the concerns of the political and economic decision makers of his day. Kepler, knowing that, wrote, "Astronomy would have often gone begging if her sister, Astrology, had not earned her bread." The decision makers wanted information relevant to their concerns, and they got it: they got horoscopes. Today we no longer supply them with horoscopes; instead, we give them strategic studies. These are highly relevant—and about as reliable and as truthful as horoscopes were.

In the nineteenth century the physicist Michael Faraday was asked by a Lord of the Treasury of what use his little prototype of a dynamo would be. He replied, "I do not know, my lord, but I am sure that someday you will tax it." He proved right. One could say the same about Charles Darwin. At the moment when *The Origin of Species* was published, what applicable results did people get from Darwinian biology? Eventually many of these ideas led to further discoveries, and also to some applications. Today we know more, thanks to genetics, about breeding and even about genetic engineering, but it took about 120 years from Darwin's and Wallace's contributions for us to reach the present level of agricultural and ecological applications.

Something similar holds for technological applications, although the typical lead times are different. Consider five examples: railroads, steamships, electric lights, automobiles, and pasteurized milk. In each case thirty-five to fifty years elapsed between the creation of the invention and the broad innovation of putting it into widespread practice. Automobiles were widespread in the United States in the mid-1920s, but they only became widespread in the rest of the world twenty to thirty years later.

Major Applications of the Social Sciences

The social sciences show a similar sequence of effective applications and similar lead times, although these times are getting shorter in more recent years. Probability began in the seventeenth century with the study of gambling, which had no applications: Not even the gamblers learned much from it. Probability-based insurance came considerably later, in the late eighteenth century, but this turned out to be a very important application. The same was true for the arguments that showed free labor to be more productive than slavery. The arguments that slavery was no good, or the scientific argument that torture was useless for getting judicial evidence, came in the middle of the eighteenth century. The abolition of these practices did not come until 50 to 100 years later in different parts of the world, and there are still relapses.

In this century the theory of games was formulated in 1928 by John von Neumann and reformulated in 1944 by von Neumann and Oscar Morgenstern, but it was not widely applied until the 1960s. In 1935 George Gallup and others developed sample surveys for attitude studies. These were then used in a simple way for election forecasts, but the major applications to electoral and other behavior came in the 1950s; and the first major campaign in the United States based on sample surveys—the Kennedy campaign—came in 1960 (Abelson, Pool, and Popkin 1964).

More recently, world models using the system dynamics method began with Forrester's work after 1969 (Forrester 1971), and the publication with the most impact came in 1972 (Meadows et al. 1972). Ten years later the approach is still hotly debated; Chapter 9 by Gerhard Bruckmann will tell us more about what has been accomplished. World models, by this showing, are only about halfway through the lead time that seems to be normal for major scientific advances today.

Probably the structure of society and most social outcomes are the result of a plurality or multiplicity of relatively weak forces and processes. The search for single causes and single models, which has been pursued for a long time, turns out to be less fruitful than once was thought. Outcomes of a particular kind seem to occur most often when "all systems are 'go' "—that is, when all the weak factors, or at least a critical number of them, point in the same direction. Step by step, more of these weak factors are being identified.

Are there a few such contributing factors, or many? We do not know their distribution or how they interact; and we do not yet have a sensitivity analysis of adequate models that might depict social, political, and economic processes. Nevertheless, it is possible to hope that if civilized humankind survives, the social sciences may be moving in that direction.

References

Abelson, R. P.; Pool, I.; and Popkin, S. L. 1964. *Candidates, Issues, and Strategies*. Cambridge, Mass.: MIT Press.

Burdach, K. 1926. *Der Dichter des Ackermann aus Böhmen und seine Zeit*. Berlin: Weidmannsche Buchhandlung.

Collingwood, R. G. 1946, *The Idea of History*. Oxford: Oxford University Press.

de Santillana, G. 1956. *The Age of Adventure*. New York: New American Library.

Deutsch, K. W.; Platt, J.; and Senghaas, D. 1970. "Conditions Favoring Major Advances in Social Science." Comm. 271, Mental Health Research Institute. Ann Arbor: University of Michigan, May. [Reprinted, slightly abridged, in Appendix.] A shorter version was also published under the same title in *Science 171* (1971): 450–459.

Forrester, J. W. 1971. *World Dynamics*. Cambridge, Mass.: Wright-Allen Press.

Huxley, J. 1942. *Evolution: the Modern Synthesis*. London: Allen and Unwin.

Lijphart, Arend. 1974. "The Structure of the Theoretical Revolution in International Relations." *International Studies Quarterly 18*(1): 41–74.

McClelland, D. 1961. *The Achieving Society*. Princeton, N.J.: van Nostrand.

McDougal, M., and Lasswell, H. D. 1980. *Human Rights and World Public Order*. New Haven: Yale University Press.

Meadows, D. H.; Meadows, D. L.; Randers, J.; and Behrens, W. W. 1972. *The Limits to Growth*. New York: Universe Books.

Miller, J. G. 1978, *Living Systems*. New York: McGraw-Hill.

Popper, K. 1961. *The Logic of Scientific Discovery*. New York: Basic Books.

Rapoport, A. 1960. *Fights, Games, and Debates*. Ann Arbor: University of Michigan Press.

Russett, B. M. 1970. "Methodological and Theoretical Schools in International Relations." In N. D. Palmer, ed., *A Design for International Relations Research: Scope, Theory, Methods and Relevance*. Philadelphia: American Academy of Political and Social Sciences, pp. 87–105.

Somit, A., and Tannenhaus, J. 1967. *The Development of American Political Science*. Boston: Allyn and Bacon.

CHAPTER 2

Advances in Sociology—A Critique†

Alex Inkeles

IN THEIR SEARCH for the conditions favoring major advances in the social sciences, Deutsch, Platt, and Senghaas (1971, hereafter DPS; reprinted in Appendix) identified sixty-two "leading achievements" generated during the first two-thirds of this century. Two criteria, they claim, were used by DPS. To qualify as an advance, its author or authors had to produce a new perception *or* new operations, and these in turn had "to have proved fruitful in producing a substantial impact that led to further knowledge."

It seems obvious that these criteria could easily lead one to list a very large number of advances for the social sciences as a whole during the years 1900–1965. It is therefore instructive to compare the list of sixty-two advances actually selected by DPS to see why other work was evidently seriously considered but finally excluded.

For one thing, the advances in the list are not what usually would

†This chapter was first presented as a paper at the Science Center Berlin Conference in June 1982, but it was published in *The Social Science Journal 20* (3), 1983, pp. 27–44, under the title "The Sociological Contribution to Advances in the Social Sciences," and is reprinted here with their permission.

be recognized as specific discoveries or proofs of empirical regularities—such as, for example, Durkheim's (1897) finding that suicide varies inversely with the degree of integration of the social group. Instead, the DPS list emphasized general perspectives such as "elite studies," or the even broader "functionalist anthropology." In the case of methods, they included "scaling theory" rather than the Guttman scale (1944) or the Likert scale (1932), and the "laboratory study of small groups" rather than Freed Bales's (1950) system of "interaction process analysis."

This approach avoids singling out one person for credit when several individuals are introducing similar ideas across the broad front, but the lists are then rather different from those one might obtain using a narrower definition of an advance.

Likewise, the DPS approach leaves little room for crediting the contributions of those who come later, even though they may produce a much greater advance in actual knowledge than did the precursors. Their list therefore stresses innovative thinking and seminal ideas more than the growth of knowledge. Take, for example, H. Murray (1938), who makes the list for his development of projective testing. I do not quarrel with this nomination; Murray should also be credited with greatly deepening our awareness of and sensitivity to the variety of basic motives. His work, however, might well be judged less important than that of David McClelland (1953), whose studies added substantially to the store of knowledge through systematic and cumulative research. He did this by applying and extending the theory of motives in an analysis of economic growth, while developing new approaches to measurement in the process. To follow what seems to be DPS's procedure is equivalent to saying that once the germ theory of disease had been propounded, Pasteur could not thereafter qualify as having made an advance by developing his inoculation against rabies, nor could Salk qualify with his vaccine for polio.

I do not expect to resolve this issue here. In what follows, however, I will nominate a classification of innovations, mainly in sociology, emphasizing my preference for cumulative contributions to knowledge. I will attempt to include the advances mentioned by DPS, but I will amplify their list by suggesting other ideas and methods that significant segments of the sociological community would claim deserve the status DPS conferred on their necessarily shorter list.

Political and Organizational Innovations

DPS claim that they omitted "more purely political and organizational achievements," such as the European Common Market and the Tennessee Valley Authority. They did include the contributions of Lenin, Mao, and Gandhi, however, because, say DPS, "they were connected with explicit theories." Yet many political and organizational achievements that they excluded were also connected with explicit theories, such as the innovations of Martin Luther King and others in the struggle for civil rights (including the consumer boycott) and those leaders of the resistance to the Vietnam War who elaborated the technique of the sit-in and the sit-down. Once started on this course, however, we cannot hope to find any obvious rule of exclusion to prevent the nomination of the offensive and even the heinous. Radicals have developed "explicit theories" to justify hijacking, taking public figures hostage, and other forms of modern terrorism. Even the destruction of the 6 million Jews of Europe was linked to explicit social theories about racial purity and national destiny.

I would urge, therefore, that this category be eliminated. This need not be done on either political or moral grounds, but rather on the ground that these presumed advances are "impacts *simply* on social practice" that do not meet, and perhaps cannot meet, DPS's second criterion: "leading to further knowledge."

Innovations Primarily Conceptual

A second category, though not much represented in the DPS list, seems peculiarly important in the development of sociological thought. This category includes conceptualizations of the social order and its component elements. Such conceptualizations greatly influence the thinking of sociologists and the exposition of their ideas, even when these concepts do not lead to any substantial amount of research systematically designed to test them. Indeed, it is a peculiarity of these schemes that by nature they are often neither testable nor falsifiable.

In this category we must place the dominating ideas and concepts of the founders of the field, which continue to reverberate through all the standard tests, generation after generation. Taken together, they make up a large part of what is often called, pejoratively, "armchair sociology," or, more favorably, "grand theory." Here we may place the fundamental distinctions between associational types, such as Tönnies's *Gemeinschaft und Gesellschaft* (1887) and Durkheim's (1897) differentiation of systems as embodying mechanical and organic solidarity, and his *conscience collective*. These may have been omitted from the DPS list because their main contributions were before 1900.

Any list of such profoundly influential conceptual distinctions also must heavily represent Max Weber. Bendix (1968) has said of Weber that "he tried to provide a more secure foundation for sociology and history by specifying the meaning of ideas and concepts." The most influential among these were: his classification of the bases of authority or domination as traditional, charismatic, and legal; his distinctions of economic class and social status; his definition of bureaucracy; and his explication of the ethic of action embedded in religions, as in the "Protestant ethic."

Other candidates for the development of dominant concepts in sociological thought would include the following:

- Robert Michels (1911) for the concept of oligarchy in organizations, especially as formulated in his "iron law."
- Pitirim Sorokin (1937–1941) for his distinction among cultures as sensate and ideational.
- Vilfredo Pareto (1916) for his ideas about the character of the different actors in stratification systems and the resultant circulation of elites. (DPS cited Pareto, Mosca, and Lasswell for "elite studies.")
- Georg Simmel (1908), who was among the first to use what later became the ubiquitous concept of the social "role."
- Charles H. Cooley (1902) for his conception of the self, especially the idea of the "looking-glass self."
- George Herbert Mead (1934), especially for his concept of "taking the role of the other." (In DPS, Cooley and Mead appear linked to Dewey and W. I. Thomas as the innovators of "pragmatic and behavioral psychology.")
- Thorstein Veblen (1899) for his concept of "conspicuous consumption" as an attribute of class behavior and competition for status.
- William Ogburn (1922) for the concept of "cultural lag," which had earlier been developed by Veblen.
- W. I. Thomas (1923) for his elaboration of the idea of the differential "definition of the situation" as the determinant of social behavior.

There are several more recent authors of concepts that seem to have a similar ability to get themselves woven into the fabric of expositions of basic sociology and textbooks:

- Robert Merton (1949) with his paradigm for the analysis of deviance, and his conception of "theories of the middle range."
- Talcott Parsons (1937, 1951) for his pattern variables.
- Erik Erikson (1950) with his conception of identity and his seven stages of development.
- David Riesman (1950) who identified the types of modern man as inner-, outer-, and other-directed.
- Louis Wirth (1938) for his conception of urbanism as a way of life.
- Dennis Wrong (1961) for his image of "the oversocialized conception of man."

- C. Wright Mills for his image of the white-collar class (1951), his conception of the power elite (1956), and his view of the sociological imagination (1959).

Among all these, the names of Weber, Pareto, Mead, Cooley, Ogburn, Thomas, Merton, and Erikson are also on the DPS list, though sometimes for different reasons. It is appropriate to compare Read Bain (1962), who found twenty-four names that were cited five or more times in at least four of the ten leading introductory sociology texts in use between 1958 and 1962. This exercise, repeated by Oromaner (1968) for texts used between 1963 and 1967, yielded twenty-three names. Seven of the names cited in both periods were on the DPS list: Burgess, Cooley, Merton, Parsons, Stouffer, Warner, and Weber. Nine others not on the DPS list, or a total of sixteen, were on the textbook lists in both time periods. (This consensus broke down after 1967, as noted later.)

Gratifying as such agreement may be, it is not the main point. What I find distinctive about the sociological enterprise is the relative importance of individuals whose main contribution has been to introduce a purely conceptual ingredient into the sociological perspective, even though no systematic line of research developed to render the concept operational.

These seminal thinkers had important intellectual influences on later workers, but their notable conceptions live almost in the realm of abstract ideas. Thus we have no studies systematically measuring the degree to which communities or other structures differentially embody *Gemeinschaft* rather than *Gesellschaft* relationships. No array of societies has been scored for solidarity as organic or mechanical; Parsons's pattern variables have not been systematically measured; we have no tests of inner- and other-directedness, nor any actual measurements of the distribution of these qualities in populations. There has been no systematic investigation of "taking the role of the other." No one has devised a method for identifying "foxes" and "lions," and then tested whether Pareto's ideas about their circulation are correct.

There are, of course, exceptions. Lipset, Trow, and Coleman (1956) were explicitly trying to test the universality of Michels's iron law in *Union Democracy*. The coding system for Bales's "interaction process analysis" (1950) was a fairly direct translation of Parsons's ideas about the problems facing all social systems in meeting their functional problems. In addition, Almond and Verba, in developing their measures of the *Civic Culture* (1963), were influenced by Parsons to measure separately the cognitive, affective, and evaluative orientations of their subjects. The existence of exceptions does not, however, invalidate the main point. The great majority of the most important sociological conceptualizations have not led to the development of a persistent and cumulative line of social research. For that, we must look elsewhere.

Cumulative Progress versus Great Advances

DPS were interested in works they could classify as "advances" or "breakthoughs," and they speak of "new operations" and "new discoveries." There is, however, another image of the advance of science that is more concerned with resolutions of the major intellectual challenges of a field through systematic inquiry yielding important *cumulative* knowledge—focused on "progress" rather than "advances." The main sources for evaluating "progress" are the periodic reviews within or across the major subfields of the discipline. I have brought together a sample of these positive evaluations drawn from handbooks, annual reviews, and similar sources.

In examining recent work in the field of social stratification and mobility, for instance, David Featherman (1981) concluded that this subdiscipline "has made greater progress toward cumulative social science than any other branch of sociological research." He asserts "that the last 25 years have been a historical watershed for American sociology as a social science."

Next we hear from James Sweet (1977), reporting on the subfield of demography. As he sees it:

> Much progress has been made in the last decade in understanding the demography of the family. Only a decade ago, the work in the area consisted primarily of summary reports of data from unrepresentative local samples. In the past decades alone, ten major trends in research have emerged and appear to be continuing.

In another subfield, concerned with the effects that the status characteristics of individuals have on their interactions with others, recent reviewers affirm a strong sense of progress over time. The earliest formulations had been "limited to the simplest kinds of social situations in which just two interactants collectively engaged in a single unitary task." The work has now been greatly extended "to diffuse as well as single characteristics; to multiperson as well as to two-person interactions, and to the effects of referents as well as interactants." In addition, progressive reformulations of the theory have made it more precise (Berger, Rosenholtz, and Zelditch 1980).

Moving to social systems of global significance, we find David Singer (1980) expressing optimism that "we are on the way to understanding the causes of war and the conditions of peace" through "systematic research that rests on reproducible evidence." In explaining the relatively low incidence of war compared to nonmilitary conflict and rivalry, Singer finds "a remarkable overlap, if not a convergence" among the models used to explain the phenomena.

The sense of progress also seems very strong in the most glamorous of the new fields, sociobiology. In reviewing the latest developments,

Boorman and Levitt (1980) tell us that the field "is advancing so rapidly that a brief review can orient sociologists and other social scientists to only a few of the field's main results."

Candidates for the Status of Advances

Besides instances of the cumulation of knowledge, we may nominate contributions that might qualify as important advances, along the lines of the DPS article:

Discoveries in the Classical Mode

If there is a competition for scarce openings in a list of fixed size, Durkheim must not be omitted. I would also nominate Michels (1911) for organizational analysis; Simmel (1908) for the study of interpersonal interaction; Sorokin (1937–1941), perhaps along with Kroeber (1944), for the theory of civilizations; and Veblen (1899) for class theory.

From a later period I would also include the "Hawthorne effect" of Dickson and Roethlisberger (1939), in disagreement with DPS, who relegated this work to the category of "more purely political and organizational achievements."

As more recent examples of the discovery of unanticipated regularities, I offer:

- Inkeles and Rossi (1956): The discovery of the relative invariances, cross-nationally, of occupational prestige hierarchies. This was later exhaustively documented by Donald Treiman (1974) in *Occupational Prestige in Comparative Perspective.*
- Goode (1963): Demonstration of worldwide convergence on the conjugal family system.
- Lipset (1959): Explication of the relationship between levels of economic development and the maintenance of a democratic polity.
- Bendix and Lipset (1959): The demonstration (following Lipset and Rogoff 1954) that social mobility rates, especially the rates of entry of sons of manual workers into nonmanual jobs, was broadly similar in all industrial countries.
- The discovery of the pattern of the demographic transition begun by Thompson (1929) and Willcox (1929–1931), and later refined by Notestein (1945) and Davis and Blake (1956), among others.

These examples represent a category of discoveries in which I think sociology is particularly rich. A systematic survey across the various subfields would yield a substantial harvest of this kind, suggesting that there is much more regularity in the structure of large-scale societies than many suppose, and demonstrating that sociological investigation can uncover this.

There is another type of discovery in which no marked empirical regularity is discovered, but descriptive facts are developed that serve to upset received opinion, to startle by their novelty, or to stimulate because they cause us to pay attention to interesting forms of social behavior we had not looked at systematically before. As candidates in this category I suggest:

- The Kinsey reports (1948, 1953) on sexual expression in the U.S. public.
- Berle and Means (1933), demonstration that the American corporation was controlled not by ownership but by self-perpetuating management.
- Sutherland (1949), identification of white-collar crime as a neglected type, and his demonstration of its pervasiveness.

Perhaps only the last of these will be accepted as unquestionably belonging to sociology. My purpose, however, is not to stake claims, but rather to identify a category of research reports that it would be fruitful to augment.

An Alternative Approach

It may also be fruitful to expand the list of advances by identifying those figures whose work seems to fit rather well the DPS criteria, but who were passed over because it had an impact on only one subfield of sociology.

Alfred J. Lotka (Lotka and Sharpe, 1911, 1934) is a good example. In his history of demography, Frank Lorimer (1959) characterizes Lotka's contribution as akin to that of Newton in physics, with his analytical synthesis that set a framework for new empirical investigations. Lorimer credits Lotka with the development of the theory of stable populations, and with "elegant" methods of calculation. Spengler (1968) considers this theory of Lotka's to be "the most powerful of the modern demographer's analytic tools," and quotes Notestein as saying that it is to Lotka that "the field of demography owes virtually its central core of analytical development."

In his review of work on mobility and stratification, David Featherman (1981) assigns a comparably exalted place to the work of O. D. Duncan (1966), especially that done in collaboration with Peter Blau and reported in *The American Occupational Structure* (1967). Featherman sees this book as having had "signal significance," possibly achieving the status of a "Kuhnian paradigm." He credits the work with: (1) developing a conceptual framework "to organize and to focus discussion about questions of inequality and the transmission of differential opportunities from generation to generation"; (2) providing "a focus for discussions of public policy"; (3) being "an exemplar for the design and analysis of national studies of mobility and inequality"; and (4) spreading its influence beyond stratification research "to alter the empirical standards of sociological inquiry."

Marx and Wood (1975) identify a work of comparable general significance in the field of collective behavior, "the theory put forth and elaborated by Neil Smelser in 1962." They say that "his work has probably inspired more research in the last decade than any other single approach." Moreover, they credit him with supplanting a large amount of unsystematic analysis with "a highly systematic and broad, yet parsimonious schema" that generated research generally supporting his propositions.

I could easily supply an additional half dozen examples. What these cases suggest is that contributions of towering importance for a special subfield of a discipline may fail to achieve general recognition even though they seem to be equal in significance to other universally acknowledged advances. Two of these examples may be too recent for us to judge what their standing will be in the long run, but this is not true for Lotka's work. Evidently, it would be revealing to pursue a different investigation for DPS, asking, "What are the circumstances that favor one great advance becoming universally acknowledged while others of equal significance remain known to only a few?"

Innovations in Method

Our statistical procedures, and to a lesser degree our basic methods, are much more widely shared across the social sciences than are our concepts, our data, and our propositions. Consequently, the assignment of particular statistical or methodological advances to particular disciplines may be disputed. A sociologist may object when he finds scaling theory assigned to psychology, particularly when this advance is attributed by DPS to Louis Guttman, a sociologist, and to C. Coombs, who is identified with the social sciences at least as much as with psychology. I might also demur over DPS's placement of Coleman's work on stochastic models under mathematics, and their assignment of attitude and opinion polling to psychology.

Apart from jurisdictional claims, however, we may propose the following as supplements to the DPS list of advances in method, especially from the perspective of sociology:

- The method of participant observation, as exemplified by William Whyte in *Street Corner Society* (1943), and later used by Erving Goffman (1959) in a long series of impressive explorations.
- The use of historical records for statistical investigation of social change, with outstanding examples in the work of Smelser (1962) and Tilly (1964). This work has close analog in the field of social history, as in the studies by Peter Laslett (1972).
- The use of personal documents to illuminate the meaning of socially structured experience, and to increase our understanding of major social movements. The key work was the study of the Polish peasant by Thomas and Znaniecki (1918–1920), followed by a long line of such studies down to the present time.

Turning to more statistical forms of methodological advance, several departments deserve mention:

- The introduction of structural-equation models, especially models for path analysis. These were imported into sociology from economics by Blalock (1969) and above all by Duncan (1966) from genetics. Their use in research on status attainment and mobility was exemplary, however, and their impact on the standards of data analysis in sociology was transformational. Joreskog's (1973) linear structural relations (LISREL) model for dealing with unobserved components or latent variables may prove to be an important extension.
- The log-linear models of Leo Goodman (1978) and his associated development of hierarchical models for analyzing the contingency tables that are so ubiquitously used by sociologists.
- The application of Markov chain models by Harrison White (1970) in the development of network analysis. This entire field, ably summarized by Burt (1980), seems an important methodological frontier with potentially broad application.

Advances: Conditions, Centers, and Problems

There seems to be general agreement about the conditions that make for scientific advance. Obviously, it takes a good supply of talented people; but the potential supply of genius is probably fairly constant, since the underlying gene pool may be assumed to have been relatively continuous. Our emphasis should therefore shift to the conditions of socialization needed for realizing the talent, so that we get the equivalent of a young Mozart or Bach.

This young talent must then be recruited to centers of excellence.

The conditions for advance require an environment that stimulates and sustains creativity. Freedom from excessive burdens and distractions is usually very important. Where the research is expensive, financial support is important; and where technical apparatus looms large, there should be a special structure to keep talent from being drained away on the mechanics of research. A social structure that recognizes and rewards innovation seems crucial, although some innovators persist in the face of indifference or hostility. The milieu should be open to risk taking and tolerant of curiosity-driven behavior, not too preoccupied with practical application or too punitive of high-risk failures. Concentrations of individuals working on the same or related problems can provide significant stimulation, but it is also advantageous to have a diversity of interests in the environment. This condition is reached most effectively in settings that tolerate or encourage interdisciplinary contacts and cooperation through symposia and general forums, or more informally. Good channels of communication and ready means for exchange of experience are facilitative. Finally, it seems to make quite a difference when scholars and scientists feel they are on the edge of new territory, at some frontier ready to be discovered and explored, although it is a moot question whether the important advances create the image of the frontier or the sense of the frontier stimulates the advances.

Sociology has had its centers of general advance that in large part met these conditions. One of the first, gathered around Durkheim and *L'année sociologique* in Paris, included Granet, Halbwachs, and Mauss. Durkheim's own great spurt of creativity, however, began earlier; three of his four greatest works were published from Bordeaux well before he came to Paris in 1902.

I can point to no comparable early development in Germany, although Heidelberg might qualify. Note that Weber was very active in the *Verein für Sozialpolitik*; he worked in close association with Paul Gohre and Adolf Levenstein, and was intimately involved in their field research on agricultural and industrial workers. He was also in contact with other German sociologists through the *Archiv für Sozialwissenschaft und Sozialpolitik*. At a later point the Frankfurt school had characteristics that seemed rather fully to meet the conditions that stimulate and sustain advances. Adorno, Fromm, Horkheimer, Mannheim, and Marcuse, all on the DPS list, can properly be associated with it. [Friedman (1981) argues that Mannheim and Fromm were peripheral to the Frankfurt school, with a shorter association; but this does not weaken the point that Frankfurt was a center of innovation.]

Across the Atlantic, the Chicago school was the dominant influence in the achievements of American sociology. Under the stimulus of Park and Burgess, there were advances on many fronts, associated with Everett Hughes, E. Franklin Frazier, Shaw and McKay, William Ogburn, and others. This school also influenced and was influenced by Robert Redfield and the anthropologists. Samuel Stouffer, from the Chicago school, later became a key element in the heightened sociological activity at Harvard after World War II.

The central figure in the Harvard development was Talcott Parsons; but Edward Shils played an important role, and there were strong interactions with Clyde Kluckhohn in anthropology, Harry Murray in clinical psychology, Gordon Allport in social psychology, and John Whiting in child development. Later, David Riesman and Erik Erikson became part of the galaxy. This was a preeminent center of excellence; of the nine names mentioned here, six were on the DPS list.

During this period, Columbia University proved a serious competitor to Harvard as a center of innovative activity. Columbia had been significant in U.S. sociology from the time of Giddings, and later with Lynd and MacIver. After World War II the main activity was built around the team of Robert Merton and Paul Lazarsfeld, with considerable influence still from Lynd and MacIver and briefly from C. Wright Mills. The products of this period include Peter Blau, James Coleman, Alex Inkeles, S. M. Lipset, Morroe Berger, Alice Rossi, Peter Rossi, Dennis Wrong and many others.

The Universities of Wisconsin and of North Carolina have also contributed surges of notable work in sociology, and these should be included in any study of the conditions for innovative excellence.

One can take some comfort from this record. Yet it is not easy to be sanguine about the current state of sociology as a field of systematic inquiry, or to judge that the immediate future promises many new advances. It would be misleading to suggest that the optimism expressed earlier is the norm, or that progress is perceived everywhere or even in a majority of the subfields. On the contrary, the dominant mood today is one of discouragement—a feeling that researchers go around in circles, that conceptual clarity is lacking, that theory is uninformed by empirical findings, that blind empiricism is rampant, that knowledge fails to cumulate, and that the former consensus about the core of the discipline has largely broken down. [The decrease in consensus is shown by a drop in the number of sociologists named five or more times in leading introductory textbooks, from twenty-four in 1958–1962 and twenty-three in 1963–1967 to half that number in 1968–1972, and 1973–1978, according to Perrucci (1980)].

Here is a small gleaning from a field strewn with such seeds of despair:

Marx and Wood (1975), reviewing recent works on social movements and collective behavior, weigh the various gains but then wonder whether "the increased wisdom [is] commensurate with all the time and energy that have gone into studying them?"

Amos Hawley (1981), assessing the research on human ecology following Burgess's theories of urban space (listed by DPS), concludes glumly that "spatial analysis has encouraged an exhibition of methodological virtuosity with but little or no effect on theoretical imagination." He further notes that for understanding migration, there has been little progress since 1919, when Haddon recognized the joint operation of "push" and "pull" factors.

Short and Meier (1981), surveying recent work on crime and delinquency, find that "theoretical measures remain primitive and suspect," and "too often available data are simply manipulated until an interpretable result is discovered." They anticipate "that future theoretical work will concentrate largely on relatively minor puzzles."

If these seem like jeremiads, they nevertheless are the statements of distinguished sociologists working in the mainstream, who could not reasonably be labeled as cranks or as disgruntled and bitter men. Their evaluations must therefore be taken seriously, and I would argue that the picture they sketch is largely correct.

Basic Limitations of the Social Sciences

We might see all this as merely a manifestation of normal science. In all fields of research, of natural sciences as well as social science, at one time or another, people blunder into blind alleys or sterile lines of work or wasteful instrumentation, or empiricism runs rampant and theory stagnates. Nevertheless, to invoke this as an explanation for the intellectual and scientific state of contemporary sociology is to ignore some distinctive features of sociology that are shared to some degree by the other social sciences. Identifying these features may help in specifying the conditions for advances in these fields.

In sociology, all too often the generation of points of view is substituted for systematic theory; illustration is confused with demonstration or even proof; moral conviction is seriously offered as a test of objective validity; presumed goodness is confused with truth; faddism is mistaken for innovation; and arguments *ad hominem* are confounded with compelling logic. All this is encountered in the other branches of social sciences, but sociology seems peculiarly prone to these afflictions.

Even if we could get around these infirmities, I believe the social sciences would be less productive of advances than the natural sciences, for three reasons. First, the social sciences may not attract individuals as talented or as creative as those drawn to the natural sciences; second, the money invested in social science research is very much smaller. There is a third cause, however, that I consider to be more fundamental—the fact that advances are limited by certain characteristics of the subject matter. Individual natural sciences may also experience their own special limitations, as does geology, for example; but the social sciences operate within limits that, in my view, set greater constraints on their potential.

These limits or obstacles again are three in number. First is the limit on the size and range of the subject matter. Advances in the natural sciences arise as they extend their scope out to ever larger universes or down to ever smaller particles. In recent decades, totally new conceptions both of the whole universe and of the smallest matter have become possible, with discovery and verification heavily dependent on advances in instrumentation.

In the social sciences, however, no progress in instrumentation could offer such advances in knowledge. The scope is limited by the subject matter—that is, the human population inhabiting the earth. Astrophysicists have seen their subject matter expand enormously in recent decades; but there can be no comparable increase in the supply of peoples, cultures, or societies available for study by the social scientist. Indeed, his social universe is not expanding but shrinking, as more and more of the once numerous distinctive tribal societies are incorporated in the standardized forms of the large nation-state.

At the other end of the scale, the limitation for the social scientist in observing smaller and smaller entities has a different character. Logically, the actions and exchanges studied by political scientists, sociologists, and psychologists could be broken into ever smaller units; but there is a severe limit. We quickly reach the point where breaking social action into smaller and smaller units produces data of less and less scientific relevance, because it comes to have less and less meaning. The social scientist cannot refocus all investigation on more and more detailed physical and chemical processes, as the natural scientist can.

A second type of limitation is the extreme conditionality of social phenomena. Physical and chemical reactions also depend on conditions, and the observables have different meaning in different contexts; but most natural events have relatively stable characteristics and may be represented by relatively constant indicators. We can detect the presence of copper, or the intensity of heat, or the direction of movement of an object millions of light years away with the same indicators used for earthly phenomena. Such constancy of meaning over a wide spread of *social* time and space is rare. That is why we are so often puzzled about the meaning, purpose, and associations of the many objects retrieved in archeological digs that we store in a jumble on our museum shelves.

The third obstacle to advancing knowledge in the social sciences follows from the propensity of individuals and public authorities to respond to such work in ideological terms. The natural sciences have enjoyed a long period of relative immunity from this affliction, except for sporadic attacks. The social sciences, however, are persistently debilitated by it. In the Soviet Union sociology was revived only within the last two decades; in the People's Republic of China, training in sociology was resumed only in 1981. Neither country has yet developed anything recognizable to the Western scholar as political science. It is not only governments and the public, however, but even the very members of the profession who war on certain ideas or lines of work purely on ideological grounds, while being intensely committed to other ideologies. In the United States, for example, it is now extremely difficult to get government funding or public approval for studies on the relation of intelligence or skill to racial and ethnic characteristics.

Some will say that these obstacles are beside the point and that it is more productive to concentrate on identifying and fostering the conditions for new advances. We may indeed learn which are the most generative situations by studying the advances made in the past. We must be aware, however, that our very achievements, in our levels of knowledge or technology, may have so transformed this intellectual enterprise that past experience may have only limited relevance to future advances.

References

Almond, Gabriel, and Verba, Sidney. 1963. *The Civic Culture: Political Attitudes and Democracy in Five Nations*. Princeton, N.J.: Princeton University Press.

Bain, Read. 1962. "The Most Important Sociologists?" *American Sociological Review 27* (February): 746–748.

Bales, R. F. 1950. *Interaction Process Analysis: A Method for the Study of Small Groups*. Cambridge, Mass.: Addison-Wesley.

Bendix, Reinhard, and Lipset, Seymour Martin. 1959. *Social Mobility in Industrial Society*. Berkeley: University of California Press.

———. 1968. "Weber, Max." *Encyclopedia of the Social Sciences 16:* 493–502.

Berger, J.; Rosenholtz, Susan; and Zelditch, Morris. 1980. "Status Organizing Processes." Alex Inkeles et al., eds., *Annual Review of Sociology 6:* 479–508.

Berle, Adolf Augustus, and Means, Gardiner C. 1933. *The Modern Corporation and Private Property*. New York: Macmillan.

Blalock, H. M., Jr. 1969. *Theory Construction*. Englewood Cliffs, N.J.: Prentice-Hall.

Blau, Peter, and Duncan, Otis Dudley, with the collaboration of Andrea Tyree. 1967. *The American Occupational Structure*. New York: Wiley.

Boorman, Scott, and Levitt, Paul. 1980. *The Comparative Evolutionary Biology of Social Behavior."* Alex Inkeles et al., ed. *Annual Review of Sociology 6*: 213–234.

Burt, Ronald S. 1980. "Models of Network Structure." *Annual Review of Sociology 6*: 79–141.

Coleman, James. 1954. "An Expository Analysis of Some of Rashevsky's Social Behavior Models." In *Mathematical Thinking in the Social Sciences*. P. F. Lazarsfeld, ed., New York: Free Press of Glencoe.

———. 1964. *Introduction to Mathematical Sociology*. New York: Free Press of Glencoe.

Cooley, Charles H. 1902. *Human Nature and the Social Order*. New York: C. Scribner.

Coombs, Clyde H. 1950. "Psychological Scaling without a Unit of Measurement." *Psychology Review 57*: 145–158.

———. 1953. "The Theory and Methods of Social Measurement." In L. Festinger and D. Katz, eds., *Research Methods in the Behavioral Sciences*. New York: Dryden Press, pp. 471–535.

Davis, Kingsley, and Blake, Judith. 1956. "Social Structure and Fertility: An Analytic Framework." *Economic Development and Cultural Change 4:* 211–235.

Dickson, William J., and Roethlisberger, Fritz Jules, with the assistance and collaboration of Harold A. Wright. 1939. *Management and the Worker: An Account of a Research Program Conducted by the Western Electric Company, Hawthorne Works*. Cambridge, Mass.: Harvard University Press.

Duncan, Otis D. 1966. "Path Analysis: Sociological Examples." *American Journal of Sociology 72*: 1–16.

Duncan, Otis D., and Blau, Peter. 1967. *The American Occupational Structure*. New York: Wiley.

Durkheim, Emile. 1897. *Le suicide: Étude de sociologie*. Paris: F. Alcan.

Erikson, Erik H. 1950. *Childhood and Society*. New York: Norton.

Featherman, David. 1981. "Stratification and Social Mobility: Two Decades of Cumulative Social Science." In James E. Short, Jr., ed., *The State of Sociology: Problems and Prospects*. Beverly Hills: Sage Publications, pp. 79–100.

Friedman, George. 1981. *The Political Philosophy of the Frankfurt School*. Ithaca and London: Cornell University Press.

Goffman, Erving. 1959. *The Presentation of Self in Everyday Life*. Garden City and New York: Doubleday/Anchor.

Goode, William J. 1963. *World Revolution and Family Patterns*. New York: Free Press of Glencoe.

Goodman, Leo. 1978. *Analyzing Qualitative/Categorical Data: Log-Linear Models and Latent-Structure Analysis*. Cambridge, Mass.: Abt Books.

Guttman, Louis. 1944. "A Basis for Scaling Qualitative Data." *American Sociological Review 9*: 139–150.

Hawley, Amos H. 1981. "Human Ecology: Persistence and Change." In James E. Short, Jr., ed., *The State of Sociology: Problems and Prospects*. Beverly Hills: Sage Publications, pp. 119–140.

Inkeles, Alex, and Rossi, Peter H. 1956. "National Comparisons of Occupational Prestige." *American Journal of Sociology 61* (4): 329–339.

Joreskog, K. G. 1973. "A General Method for Estimating a Linear Structural Equation System." In A. S. Goldberger and O. D. Duncan,

eds., *Structural Equation Models in the Social Sciences*. New York: Seminar Press, pp. 85–112.
Kinsey, Alfred Charles; Pomeroy, Wardell B.; Martin, Clyde E. 1948. *Sexual Behavior in the Human Male*. Philadelphia: W. B. Saunders.
———. 1953. *Sexual Behavior in the Human Female*. Philadelphia: W. B. Saunders.
Kroeber, Alfred L. 1944. *Configurations of Culture Growth*. Berkeley: University of California Press.
Laslett, Peter. 1972. *Household and Family in Past Times*. Cambridge: Cambridge University Press.
Likert, R. 1932. "A Technique for the Measurement of Attitudes." *Archives of Psychology*, No. 140, pp. 1–55.
Lipset, Seymour Martin. 1959. *Political Man: The Social Bases of Politics*. Garden City, N.Y.: Doubleday, 1959.
Lipset, Seymour Martin, and N. Rogoff. 1954. "Class and Opportunity in Europe and the U.S.: Some Myths and What the Statistics Show." *Commentary 18*: 562–688.
Lipset, Seymour Martin; Trow, Martin; and Coleman, James C. 1956. *Union Democracy: The Inside Politics of the International Typographical Union*. Glencoe, Ill.: Free Press.
Lorimer, Frank, 1959. "The Development of Demography." In Philip Hauser and Otis D. Duncan, eds., *The Study of Population: An Inventory and Appraisal*. Chicago: University of Chicago Press, pp. 124–179.
Lotka, Alfred and Sharpe, F. R. 1911. "A Problem in Age Distribution." *Philosophical Magazine 21*: 435–438.
———. 1934–1939. *Théorie analytique des associations biologiques, Deuxième partie: Analyse demographique avec application particulière à l'espèce humaine*. Paris: Hermann et Cie.
Marx, Gary T. and Wood, James L. 1975. "Strands of Theory and Research in Collective Behavior." Alex Inkeles et al., eds. *Annual Review of Sociology* Vol. 1: 363–428.
McClelland, David, et al. 1953, *The Achievement Motive*. New York: Appleton-Century-Crofts.
Mead, George Herbert. 1934. *Mind, Self and Society from the Standpoint of a Social Behaviorist*. Charles W. Morris, ed. Chicago: University of Chicago Press.
Merton, Robert K. 1949. *Social Theory and Social Structure: Toward the Codification of Theory and Research*. Glencoe, Ill.: Free Press, 1949.
Michels, Robert. 1911. *Untersuchungen über die Oligarchischen Tendenzen des Gruppenlebens*. Leipzig: W. Klinkhardt.
Mills, C. Wright. 1951. *White Collar*. New York: Oxford University Press.
———. 1956. *The Power Elite*. New York: Oxford University Press.
———. 1959. *The Sociological Imagination*. New York: Oxford University Press.

Murray, Henry. 1938. *Explorations in Personality*. New York: Oxford University Press.

Notestein, Frank Wallace. 1945. "Population: The Long View." In T. W. Schultz, ed., *Food for the World*. Chicago: Chicago University Press.

Ogburn, William Fielding. 1922. *Social Change, with Respect to Culture and Original Nature*. New York: B. W. Huebsch.

Oromaner, Mark Jay. 1968. "The Most Cited Sociologists: An Analysis of Introductory Text Citations." *American Sociologist 3*(2): 124–126.

———. 1969. "The Audience as a Determinant of the Most Important Sociologists." *The American Sociologist 4*(4): 100–102.

Pareto, Vilfredo. 1916. *Trattato di sociologia generale*. Firenze: G. Barbera.

Parsons, Talcott. 1937. *The Structure of Social Action*. New York and London: McGraw-Hill.

Parsons, Talcott, and Shils, Edward. 1937. *Toward a General Theory of Action*. Glencoe, Ill.: Free Press. Second edition, 1951.

Perrucci, Robert. 1980. "Sociology and the Introductory Textbook." *American Sociologist 15* (February): 39–49.

Riesman, David; Glazer, Nathan; and Denny, Ruel. 1950. *The Lonely Crowd*. New Haven: Yale University Press.

Short, James F., Jr., and Meier, Robert. 1981. "Criminology and the Study of Deviance." In James F. Short, Jr., ed., *The State of Sociology: Problems and Prospects*. Beverly Hills: Sage Publications, pp. 182–198.

Simmel, Georg. 1908. *Soziologie: Untersuchungen über die Formen der Vergesellschaftung*. Leipzig: Duncker and Humbolt.

Singer, David. 1980. "Accounting for International War: The State of the Discipline." In Alex Inkeles et al., eds., *Annual Review of Sociology*, Vol. 6, pp. 349–367.

Smelser, Neil J. 1959. *Social Change in the Industrial Revolution*. Chicago: Chicago University Press.

———. 1962. *Theory of Collective Behavior*. New York: Free Press of Glencoe.

Sorokin Pitirim. 1937–1941. *Social and Cultural Dynamics*. 4 vols. New York: American Book Company.

Spengler, Joseph J. 1968. "Lotka, Alfred J." *Encyclopedia of Social Sciences 9:* 475–476.

Sutherland, Edwin. 1949. *White Collar Crime*. New York: Dryden Press.

Sweet, James A. 1977. "Demography and the Family." In Alex Inkeles et al., eds., *Annual Review of Sociology*, Vol. 3, pp. 363–406.

Thomas, William I. 1923. *The Unadjusted Girl*. Boston: Little, Brown.

Thomas, William I., and Znaniecki, Florian. 1918–1920. *The Polish Peasant*, 5 vols. Chicago: University of Chicago Press.

Thompson, Warren S. 1929. "Population." *American Journal of Sociology, 34*, pp. 959–975.

Tilly, Charles. 1964. *The Vendée*. Cambridge, Mass.: Harvard University Press.

Tönnies, Ferdinand. 1887. *Gemeinschaft und Gesellschaft: Abhandlung des Communismus und des Socialismus als Empirischer Culturformen.* Leipzig: Fuess Verlage (R. Reisland).

Treiman, Donald. 1974. *Occupational Prestige in Comparative Perspective.* New York: Academic Press.

Veblen, Thorstein. 1899. *The Theory of the Leisure Class.* New York: Macmillan.

White, Harrison. 1970. *Chains of Opportunity: System Models of Mobility in Organizations.* Cambridge, Mass.: Harvard University Press.

Whyte, William F. 1943. *Street Corner Society: The Social Structure of an Italian Slum.* Chicago: University of Chicago Press.

Willcox, W. F., ed. 1929–1931. *International Migrations.* 2 vols. New York: National Bureau of Economic Research.

Wirth, Louis J. 1938. "Urbanism as a Way of Life." *American Journal of Sociology 44*: 1–24.

Wrong, Dennis. 1961. "The Oversocialized Conception of Man in Modern Sociology." *American Sociological Review 26*: 183–193.

Discussion

(Deutsch, Dror, Bruckman, Miller, Coleman, Bell)

Edited by Andrei S. Markovits

Two Types of Science

Karl Deutsch began by suggesting that there are two types of science. "Science #1" involves additional knowledge concerning the capacity to do certain things—the conception at the center of the DPS paper. "Science #2" involves the understanding of meaning and the refinement of interpretation. This type of science, which does not necessarily add new facts or new powers, is traditionally called *hermeneutic* or *ethnomethodogical* science. Deutsch asked Inkeles whether both these types of science are important in sociology and whether they are mutually contributing something to each other.

Inkeles responded that he liked to think of them, not as two types of science, but as two modes of inquiry or intellectual activity. He felt that a large part of the social sciences and of sociology involved the understanding of meaning, or hermeneutics. The phenomenon has to deal with itself. In addition, there is a great deal of small-scale change that is enormously important to human beings or to the life of a given human actor, but is only an incidental phenomenon—just a little noise—from the point of view of the other kind of science. It is therefore inevitable that within the intellectual enterprise and within sociology, some people will practice the hermeneutic approach, whereas others will practice the other kind, which comes closest to science.

Inkeles felt that the two modes of inquiry would always exist side by side, but that he was not sure what one had to offer the other. The big problem in his view is that sociology is not simply a scientific discipline but also an important social activity. Sociologists would have to learn to live with that fact. Inkeles admitted that although he had chosen to wave constantly the banner of the possibility of creating science out of the study of society, the hermeneutic approach offered a sensitivity to those issues and valuative concerns that were eternal and that helped to find relevance. A scientist should not go to the extreme of becoming a raw empiricist who does meaningless things endlessly simply because every body of data permits endless operations on it.

Yehezkel Dror asked Inkeles to comment on applied sociology in this context. Inkeles said that as a rule he saw no significant difference between applied sociology and sociology. Applied sociology is an activity that someone pays for because of some practical interest. One might start with an interest in personality and social structure, for example, and figure out how this contributes to criminal behavior or a delinquent career. Public authorities concerned with delinquency, however, would usually not pay a sociologist to engage in conceptual clarification; thus applied sociology is not enough. He emphasized that good social research is always potentially applied; but a larger understanding, historical knowledge, and generalizations are needed to run social systems and to build public policy.

Diffusion and Diversity

Gerhard Bruckmann complimented Inkeles on the level of engagement in his paper, but felt that one should not overstate one's case. It might be true, as Inkeles said, that we now have a CocaCola culture from California to Moscow, but there is also increasing local diversification. Where there were once three distinct attribute groups, there are now six. Bruckmann would not recommend studying history so much as investigating contemporary reality.

James Miller intervened to point out the diversification between the two great communist blocks—that CocaCola applied only to China, whereas it was PepsiCola in the Soviet Union.

Inkeles said that Bruckmann was really raising a substantive issue—that we certainly need to examine diffusion and transformation across cultural lines, as he had been doing in his own work. Is diffusion uniform, or uneven? Does nonspecialization increase as a reaction against the spread of specialization, producing dedifferentiation? Bruckmann said that his question was aimed partly at clarification: Is there necessarily an increase in specialization?

Inkeles reaffirmed that this was a substantive matter. However, one needs some kind of theory that specifies types of diffusion or localization, and one must know what techniques would be appropriate for studying the phenomenon. One would also need procedures to determine how the amount of dedifferentiation or redifferentiation was related to the amount of diffusion. Inkeles suggested that this relation could be tested and might yield a sociological law. He claimed to be trying to get people to put such observations in the following form: Obtain an indicator of worldwide diffusion of certain tendencies; get appropriate additional indicators of dedifferentiation; then make the measurements and test how far there is a relationship between them. You could also ask which dimensions would increase diffusion on the socioeconomic level and produce increasing differentiation at the cultural level, and so on. Inkeles noted that this was an area in which Daniel Bell had done a great deal of work.

James Coleman then asked whether what was happening was not so much a decline of variability, as that the variability was now located in different areas. In looking for cases of differences in authority structures, he said: "I didn't go back in history, I ended up looking at communes of the 1960s in the United States, in which there was an enormously wide variation in types of authority structures—even though it is true that people wear jeans and drink CocaCola."

Daniel Bell agreed that the decline in variability might be a misleading notion. He suggested instead Comte's term, *syncretism*, to refer to the extraordinary variety of things that were now borrowed and could be easily disposed of. He believed there had been an increase in fads, fashion, and syncretism so that what was available could be available in any country. We have all become tourists: "Anywhere we go, we buy; we come back from China with some kind of clay horse or porcelain, and put it up on our walls with the Tantric medallions and Nepalese figurines from previous trips." Bell considered this central position of syncretism to be one of the most extraordinary processes in the modern world, not traditionalism but a new spirit of culture.

Approaching Global Limits

Inkeles said he was not sure whether this disagreed with his own position, because syncretism would seem to indicate the loss of the kind of variability that existed in the past. Bell disagreed, saying that syncretism was the recombination of a multitude of different things. Inkeles argued that the number of recombinations was still determined by the number of units, which was becoming smaller; Bell replied that one could add Eskimo music to South American saddles in one's own house.

Inkeles continued to say that the combination was from a decreasing pool, and that in any case there was no basis for any anxiety that we had run out of phenomena to study. There were many things that had not yet been looked at in a certain way. Along Coleman's lines, "One could turn to communes and find a lot of variation in authority structures that should keep a scientist going for quite some time." With Bell's syncretism, there will certainly be plenty of previously unknown combinations to study.

Inkeles argued, however, that there was a limitation now, that sociologists would have to overcome by turning to history. At the level of analysis of complete societies, there would not be many new complete societies emerging, despite the 150 nations in the United Nations—indeed, they were all suffering from syncretism, too. They were sufficiently alike to be profoundly different from historical societies, such as feudal societies or the societies studied in the last generation by the great wave of anthropology. Inkeles argued that this was a good example of the stimulus of new studies to produce new conclusions: "What a tremendous transformation occurred in our thinking as a result of the study of differences in behavior that simply could not have been imagined by most people! Even if they could have been imagined, they would have been thought to be only of novelistic interest, and not taken as concrete objective facts that had to be confronted, about the varieties of human organization, human behavior, and human values." Inkeles claimed that these discoveries had suffused the period in which he grew up and represented a great stimulation and challenge to him, but that it was hard to find comparable models now, so that this study of the nonliterate areas and cultures had just about been exhausted. That was why sociologists needed to turn to history.

A second aspect that to Inkeles made this issue a real problem was the aspect of *content*. There were all sorts of combinations of blue jeans and soft drinks; but these would be relatively unimportant in the long run, and they would be taking place in a larger nonvariable context. Not completely nonvariable, considering the enormous differences between the United States and the Soviet Union in political structures, popular values, and other important matters—yet a far cry, Inkeles maintained, from the contrast between the Trobriand Islanders and the modern nation. We were rapidly losing that kind of esoteric unit and the special contrasts it supported; and we would have to study higher levels of generalization, such as authority structures and their variations—for example, in communes, as Coleman was doing, or in families under different systems, as Eisenstadt had suggested. However, these could not be varied as before, giving us the equivalent of a natural experiment. Social scientists, Inkeles felt, would have certain limits, like some natural scientists, such as astronomers: "You can't make any old arrangement of the stars that you wish, you have to work with those that are there."

CHAPTER 3

Current Theoretical Developments, Research, and Controversies in Sociology

S. N. Eisenstadt

THE PROBLEM OF ADVANCES IN SOCIOLOGY is a more difficult one than it was in the 1950s and 1960s. It is possible to point out important developments in theory, in research, in methodology, and in the combinations between them; yet it is not easy to delineate clearly which of these can be called advances.

The reason for this lies in the state of sociology today. During the last two decades, the controversies and developments in sociology, and perhaps in most social sciences (outside of methodology) have often been connected with ideological and political discussions; and very often it has been the interaction between them that was decisive for the crystallization of sociological work and for what may be called advances in the field. This fact necessitates a closer look at the meaning of *advances* in sociology and perhaps also in the other social sciences.

The Major Theoretical Controversies

The starting point of most of the developments since the 1960s was the predominant functional-structural school, and the great impact of the empirical and comparative research connected with it, especially in the United States. This school had become dominant for several reasons (Eisenstadt and Curelaru 1977): (1) its close relation to the classical problems of sociology; (2) its elaboration of a new systematic conceptual and analytical apparatus for analysis of social relations, behavior, and organization; and (3) its corresponding generation of far-reaching systematic research programs.

From the late 1950s, however, the criticisms of this school and these research programs gathered momentum and gradually occupied the center of sociological science, giving rise to new approaches and new research programs. The criticisms focused on several different themes. First, this model was seen as unable to explain social conflicts and social change because it assumed a basic consensus around central societal values and goals, it emphasized boundary-maintaining mechanisms of social control, and it implicitly minimized the importance of power and coercion as a means of social integration.

Connected with this criticism was the charge that the structural-functional model was necessarily ahistorical. In explaining concrete historical situations, it was said to favor a "static" or "circular" theory, neglecting past processes. It explained social phenomena as functionally adjusted to one another through their contributions to societal needs, and assumed the existence of equilibrating mechanisms that counteract functional maladjustments or inconsistencies.

The most general and principled accusation against this model, however, was that it assumed that the analysis of the mechanisms of social division of labor solved the problem of social order as traditionally formulated. Such an allegation against the structural-functional school in general and Talcott Parsons's work in particular might have been seen to be unjustified, since this group had heavily emphasized the values of social action and the construction of meaning through social interaction. Yet what had seemed to be the great strength of this approach—its analysis of how meaning and trust were institutionalized, and their definition in terms of the needs of social systems—came to be perceived as its major weakness.

This contribution of the structural-functional school was criticized for seeming to conflate the organizational division of labor with the regulation of power and the construction of trust and meaning, so that the classically emphasized tension between these dimensions of social order had disappeared. In fact, this school did analyze all these aspects of the social order in systemic terms—that is, in terms of their contribution to maintaining various system boundaries—seemingly taking their emergence and crystallization for granted. This approach was seen as negating the creative autonomy for individuals or groups in constructing the social order as well as denying its tensions. The structural-functional school in general and Parsons in particular were alleged to have neglected almost entirely the components of power and exploitation in the construction of social order.

Alternatives to Structural-Functionalism

These criticisms became closely connected with the attempts to construct and revive alternative theoretical approaches, whose upholders more and more entered into controversies with the older school. The most important of the new schools have been the following:

1. The "conflict" school or model as developed by Dahrendorf (1964) and more closely related to the structural-functional model by Coser (1956) and Gluckman (1956).
2. The exchange school, as developed by Homans (1961); Blau (1964a, 1964b, 1977); and Coleman (1966, 1970).
3. The "group interest" model, as developed by Bendix (1968) and Collins (1975).
4. The "symbolic interactionist" and ethnomethodology models with their emphasis on the social construction of reality and the development of meaning through interaction.
5. The "symbolic-structuralist" model, as developed by Lévi-Strauss (1963, 1966, 1967, 1969), which initially addressed its criticism to social anthropology (a peculiarly British version of structural-functionalism), but later took up more general problems in sociological analysis.
6. The Marxist model or models that were revived in the late 1960s (Godelier 1972, 1973; Habermas 1979).
7. The "systems approach" or "secondary cybernetic approach" to the analysis of social systems, developed especially by Buckley (1967), Maruyama (1968), and Deutsch (1963).

In Europe and particularly in Germany, these theoretical models have developed in several stages, which were closely related to developments in U.S. sociology and the structural-functional school as well as to developments in empirical research. In the first stage there was what René König later called the controversy between "theory of society and sociological theory." On one side, the Frankfurt school produced a strong critique of "positivistic" sociology but did little original research. On the other side, the major thrust of research, as represented by König, Mayntz, and Scheuch, followed the "positivist" U.S. pattern (Eisenstad & Curelaru, 1976, 1977).

The second stage of this debate was focused in Germany with the development of Habermas's critical sociology in general and the Habermas-Luhmann debate in particular. There were also subsequent attempts to construct new overall paradigms, such as those of Touraine in France and Giddens in England; the latest work of Collins in the United States may also belong here.

However great the differences between these approaches, they have focused on one basic theme—of rejecting the assumptions attributed to the structural-functional school, such as the "natural givenness" of any institutional order in terms of systemic prerequisites. Such particular institutional arrangements might include the formal structure of a factory or a hospital, the division of labor in the family, the official definition of deviant behavior, or the place of a ritual in a given social setting. These, however, were no longer to be taken for granted as given or derivable from their functional place in the social system; the patterns of behavior developed in connection with them were no longer to be examined primarily in terms of their contribution to the working of the institution or to deviance within it. Instead, the very setting up of institutional arrangements was viewed as constituting a problem for analysis.

The various new models differed in their explanations of concrete institutional orders. One approach emphasized that every institutional order develops, is maintained, and is changed through continuous interaction, negotiation, and struggle among the participants. In this framework of the negotiability of the social order, explanation had to emphasize several aspects:

- Developing power relations and coalitions.
- Coercive and conflict elements.
- Manipulation of symbols and attachments to them, and combinations of symbolic and power orientations and their patterns of interaction.
- Different meanings attached to such situations by the participants, perhaps related to their different roles.
- Autonomy of subgroups or subsystems, with goals differing from those of the broader institutional setting.
- The larger "environments" within which institutions and organizations operate, with special importance of the international system for the analysis of "total" societies and macrosocietal orders.

The new approaches varied in the ways in which they explained the emergence and continuity or reproduction of institutional settings. Some emphasized that all institutional arrangements are to be explained as negotiated order, whereas other approaches searched for explanations in terms of hidden or "deep" structure. Within the "negotiation" group, the conflict and exchange schools emphasized the elements of power and bargaining in negotiations, whereas the symbolic interactionists and ethnomethodologists emphasized the construction of meaning by the participants in social situations and social interactions.

Structuralism

The structuralists, following Lévi-Strauss (1963, 1966, 1967, 1969), and the Marxists made a search for some principles of "deep" or "hidden" structures in institutions, akin to those that have been postulated for the development of speech and language by linguists such as Chomsky. The structuralists stressed the symbolic dimensions of human activity, ultimately resting on some inherent rules of the human mind. Lévi-Strauss's emphasis on the autonomous character of the symbolic sphere and its inherent internal structure was to no small degree derived from his dissatisfaction with Durkheim, who tended to explain the symbolic sphere in terms of its contributions to the working of the social system. Instead, Lévi-Strauss presented the symbolic realm as the autonomous and constitutive dimension of human nature, culture, and social order.

Structuralism, as he developed it, goes further, however. The essence of the structuralist claim is as follows:

1. There exists within any society or culture some "hidden structure" that is more real and pervasive than that which appears in overt social organization or behavioral patterns.
2. The rules that govern such structure are not concrete rules of organization, nor are they derived from organizational or institutional needs or problems; instead, they are crystallized and coded as rules of the human mind.
3. These rules are the constitutive element of culture and society, and they provide for deeper ordering principles of the social and cultural realms.
4. The most important of these rules are those of "binary opposition," which are inherent and given in all perceptions of the world by the human mind, together with rules of transformation that govern the ways in which inherent contradictions in the working of human minds are resolved.
5. It is the foregoing principles, and not the concrete social organization or division of labor, that constitute the real models of society—the principles according to which society is in fact structured.

Note that these models need not be identical with their representations—for example, in the minds of social participants, or as symbolized in particular concrete situations or in myths; but through a structural analysis of such representations, the rules can be derived and understood.

The more sophisticated Marxists shared with the structuralists the emphasis on "deep structure," but they differed from them greatly about the nature of the constitutive elements of that structure. They emphasized a combination of power and symbolic dimensions—such as the dialectic between the forces and relations of production, alienation, the class struggle, and class consciousness—as the deep structural elements that explain the institutional features and dynamics of societies.

Moreover, unlike the structuralists, they were fundamentally concerned with the problems of social change and history. They believed that the interaction between these constitutive elements—especially between the forces of production and formative relations such as the crystallization of antagonistic classes—provide the moving forces of social change and of history. Among many Marxists and semi-Marxists, above all on the Continent, the problem of historical development and consciousness and its relation to social activities and structure became central.

Relations between Theory and Research

These theoretical discussions became connected in different degrees to new research perspectives and *problematiques*. The most important new research perspective was the examination of the basic dimensions of the ecological and international environments of societies. Another was the renewed study of social morphology in general and the processes of intra- and intergenerational mobility in particular. There was also widespread use of comparative analysis, especially comparative macrosocietal analysis as focused on problems of modernization and historical-sociological studies.

The study of environments has generated a spate of research on the structure of international systems. This has provided an important corrective to recent studies of modernization and development. Indeed, it has helped to correct the whole self-contained "bias" of classical and contemporary sociology and anthropology, which have usually dealt with "total" societies as though they were almost entirely self-enclosed units (Heintz 1972; Wallerstein 1974).

The new emphasis on the ecological environment of societies began with an environmental-technological evolutionary perspective, best represented in the work of White (1949) and Steward (1955), and followed up later by Lenski (1970). Their neoevolutionary orientation was shared with the structural-functional school, but they viewed such evolution not as an "internal" unfolding of structural differentiation, but rather in terms of the impact of "external" environmental-technological forces on social organization. They attempted to analyze how these forces generate different levels of energy and different patterns of complexity as they develop in human societies.

The social-morphological perspective gave rise to a wide range of research on social stratification and mobility (Duncan and Blau, Hauser and Featherman, Wright, and others) as well as studies in the Simmelian tradition (Blau 1977).

The comparative and macrosociological perspective led to a strong emphasis on comparative historical analysis, studies of modernization, and comparative studies of civilizations, in an almost Weberian perspective. (For a survey, see Eisenstadt 1973; see also Eisenstadt 1963; Eder 1973; Habermas 1979; Schluchter 1981; Bendix 1978; Moore 1969; and others.) This was, of course, very closely related to the work of several historians—first of all the work on civilizations of Toynbee (1972), and second that of McNeill (1963), who has been developing a vision of world history involving the continuous interrelation of different civilizations. There are also related developments in anthropology, such as those emphasizing the importance of trade and movements of population in shaping societies (Adams 1974).

Because of this mix of the internal momentum of research in some areas, together with the principled confrontations among the different models and approaches, far-reaching shifts have occurred in the major areas of sociological research.

The structuralist-symbolic approach has led to the analysis of the autonomous symbolic dimension and to a search for the basic rules of "hidden structure." This had its greatest impact on studies of kinship and of human symbolic creativity, especially creative methodology, folklore, and literature. Later it was also applied to macrosocietal fields, for both primitive societies and more complex societies, as in the work of Dumont (1970) and De Heusch (1966, 1971).

The conflict, exchange, and group-interest approaches, emphasizing the negotiability of the social order, gave rise to a reexamination of the place of power in social systems and of the mechanisms of its regulation. The conflict approach, as represented by Dahrendorf (1964), Coser (1956), and Gluckman (1955), emphasized studies of different political systems and mechanisms of political allocation. The group-interest approach led to the study of boundaries of different parts of societies. The impact of the exchange model was on the study of behavior and interaction in small groups, as well as on processes of stratification, especially of status systems.

The symbolic-interactionist and ethnomethodological approaches contributed to the exploration of "informal" and "subterranean" human interactions that cut across formal arrangements and institutional settings. The focus was on the phenomenology of behavior in such settings; on the structure and rules of interaction as distinct from the formal institutional definition of goals; and on mechanisms such as those by which the hidden code-languages of human interaction are constructed and perceived by participants. This approach is found in the studies of Goffman (1959, 1961a, 1961b) on face-to-face situations and informal daily encounters. It has also been applied to organizational studies, such as the interaction of informal groups in institutional and role construction.

The Marxist approaches have emphasized the relation between the power elements and systemic characteristics of social order, the basic ("hidden") laws through which the structure of the system is regulated, and the conflicts and systemic contradictions in the dynamics of social systems. Their research impact has been on comparative institutional studies of primitive and historical societies, of modernization and development, and of systems of power in modern societies.

Within this context there also developed an emphasis on the international system and the multiple relations of dependency or hegemony among the constituent societies, as shown by the work of Latin American scholars on dependence and by Wallerstein's book *The Modern World System* (1974). Other research areas influenced by the new theoretical developments include studies of modernization and the dynamics of civilizations, and the sociology of knowledge and of science.

Metatheoretical and Ideological Controversies

To evaluate the impact of the theoretical discussions on advances in research, however, we need to move to a third level of discussion, a *metatheoretical* level (Eisenstadt and Curelaru 1976). Originally, such discussion focused on problems of the philosophy and methodology of science or on the history of sociology, and was relatively segregated from central research concerns and even from theoretical sociology. This picture changed radically after the late 1960s, when metatheoretical discussions by such scholars as Gouldner, Friedrichs, and Atkinson, and some aspects of Habermas's work, became transformed into far-reaching criticism of the philosophical and ideological premises of mainstream sociology. There were highly ideological analyses of the sociology of sociology, many of which attempted a delegitimization of the whole sociological endeavor hitherto.

Many of these discussions were tinged by a denial of the possibility of a value-free sociology; with the relativization of all possible approaches, they showed increasing doubts about even the possibility of objective scholarly research in sociology. After the late 1960s, all these controversies became closely connected with extreme ideological and political trends, with the intellectual antinomianism of student protest, with radicalism, and with both the sophisticated and the "crude" Marxism that swept over the United States and Europe in a protest against even the premises of Western culture (Eisenstadt and Curelaru 1976).

Broadening the Framework of Analysis

During this period there has been a continuous growth in most fields of sociological research. There have also been attempts to codify them, as in the various readers published in the 1950s, especially those from the Free Press, covering all the major areas of sociology; and in *Current Sociology; Sociology Today;* and their French, German, and Dutch counterparts. These attempts expanded in the 1970s with an enlargement of *Current Sociology* and the introduction of general *Annual Reviews of Sociology* and special reviews of separate fields. These developments attest to the gathering strength of sociological analysis and the broadening of its framework.

The enrichment of research can be seen in the convergence of research perspectives developed from different theoretical bases. Thus several French scholars have tried to combine structuralist and Marxist orientations (Godelier 1972, 1973). In Germany, Habermas and others have developed an interesting convergence between their semi-Marxist perspective on the evolution of human societies and the view of Parsons in his *Evolution of Societies* (1966), along with a strong Piagetian bent emphasizing the importance of the evolution of consciousness and communications (Habermas 1979). There is also a convergence to a neo-Weberian perspective that combines a stringent conceptual analysis with a differentiated vision of the historical process (Bendix 1978; Eisenstadt 1978). Similarly, Inkeles has combined in his work a world system analysis with comparative studies of modernization.

There is also a contrary trend, however, characterized by growing sectarianism. Some research programs are self-enclosed within theoretical frameworks that in principle do not admit other approaches or schools. In the 1970s such programs could be found in most research areas, giving rise to a growing balkanization of sociological research that minimized many of the potential advances described earlier.

Self-Doubt and Sectarianism

Today sociology is torn between these two tendencies—multiple enrichment of approaches versus sectarianism. This situation has resulted from the impingement of external intellectual and ideological forces on sociological developments (Eisenstadt 1977). The central problems are now often reformulated in terms of their relation to other disciplines, and internal developments in sociology are often confronted with other intellectual traditions that ordinarily are relegated to the periphery of sociological inquiry.

This tendency to combine internal with external discussions shifts the central preoccupations of sociologists. There are temporary fads and fashions that move the discourse into peripheral fields such as social philosophy, the philosophical examination of sociology, or methodology. Instead of serving as catalysts, these preoccupations seize the center of sociological endeavor. Such topics as the hidden dimensions of society; or the existential possibility or impossibility of pursuing sociological research; or the existential, personal, or social bases of the pursuit of such research—these questions, which in normal times accompany and enliven the interpretation of social phenomena, now become the central concern of the profession, replacing instead of aiding substantive research and theoretical analysis. This may lead to a sharp dissociation between philosophical analysis and empirical research. In extreme cases, the proclamation of general "principled" stands on these problems is taken as the main task of the sociologist—especially when the stand so adopted contains a denial on philosophical grounds of the objective validity of empirical research.

These tendencies have their fullest impact when they become interwoven with another trend that tends to develop in such situations—namely, the transformation of sociological schools of thought into ideological sects. Each of these sects has its own metaphysical-political-ideological-analytical paradigms, all of them developing strong symbolic closure and esoteric personal or sectarian discourses. As a result, there has developed among sociologists a continuous oscillation between their perception of sociology as a scientific or scholarly endeavor, and sociology as a substitute for religion or philosophy.

Likewise, there is a growing preoccupation with metascientific problems, such as the philosophical or epistemological foundations of sociological research and method, and the continuing construction of new theories and commentaries on theories and ideological pronouncements, at the expense of substantive inquiries. There are important and promising developments in the field, as described earlier; but the sense of disorientation and disaffection generated by these recent tendencies has not yet been overcome. The more extreme manifestations have abated, but there is still abundant sectarianism and the loss of needed contacts between different approaches to similar problems.

Institutional Conditions

What are the conditions and institutional settings that have shaped these trends? A full-fledged discussion is not possible here, but some suggestions can be made (see also Eisenstadt and Curelaru 1976; and Eisenstadt 1977). The dominance of different trends has depended not only on their intellectual content or their relationship to research, but also on the combination of these aspects with institutional forces and settings.

Thus the ability of the constructive tendencies to find a base for sustained activity has depended on the ability of sociological communities to absorb external pressures, to reformulate them in terms of their own analytic premises, and to shape these influences through their internal momentum. Systematic study of the relationship between these institutional patterns and advances in sociology is still very much needed, but we can attempt to see some of the implications of these patterns for the understanding of crises in sociology. In order to absorb such impacts, sociological communities have needed institutional autonomy and self-assurance so that they can continue to generate sociological analysis and research.

The continuity of such work, and the possibility of internal innovation, have depended in turn on the existence of a mix of several types of research and several types of role orientations of sociologists. The most beneficial arrangement has been a combinaton of technical-professional research, such as field research or comparative or statistical research, with an orientation to broader external philosophical or intellectual trends. All this, however, needs to be unified by a strong core of analysis focused on some aspect of the *Problemstellung*. Sustained sociological work benefits best from a mix of broad intellectual and academic orientations with critical or professional orientations, combined in an institutional base that ensures stable sociological roles, career patterns, and professional identity. Presumably the academic framework should have provided the best such setting. Indeed, in the later stages of development, in more dense sociological communities, the major constructive developments have taken place in universities or their associated research institutes. The mere acceptance of sociology in a university, however, if based on too narrow a conception, does not ensure such an environment. The community and autonomy of sociological analysis do best in a university or institute combining graduate and undergraduate teaching with other contacts such as professional or public agencies, so that there is a combination of sociological approaches—speculative, comparative, institutional, and methodological—and a wide range of role referents for sociologists.

Eisenstadt and Curelaru (1976) showed that it was the institutional settings characterized by these features that facilitated the more constructive trends and advances in the development of sociology. Much more research, however, is needed here.

References

Adams, R. M. 1974. “Anthropological Perspectives on Ancient Trade.” *Current Anthropology 15*:239–249.

Bendix, R. 1968. *State and Society.* Boston: Little, Brown.

———. 1978. *Kings or People*. Berkeley and Los Angeles: University of California Press.

Blau, P. 1964a. "Justice in Social Exchange." *Social Inquiry 34*:193–206.

———. 1964b. *Exchange and Power in Social Life*. New York: Wiley.

———. 1977. *Inequality and Heterogeneity*. New York: Free Press.

Buckley, W. 1967, *Sociology and Modern System Theory*. Englewood Cliffs, N.J.: Prentice-Hall.

Coleman, J. 1966. "Foundations for a Theory of Collective Decision." *American Journal of Sociology 71*:615–627.

———. 1970. "Political Money." *American Political Science Review 64*:1074–1087.

Collins, R. 1975. *Conflict Sociology: Toward an Explanatory Science*. New York: Academic Press.

Coser, L. 1956. *The Functions of Social Conflict*. London: Routledge and Kegan Paul.

Dahrendorf, R. 1964. *Class and Class Conflict in Industrial Society*. London: Routledge and Kegan Paul.

De Heusch. 1966. *Le Rwanda et la civilization interlacustre: Études d'anthropologie, historique et structurale*. Brussels: Université Libre de Bruxelles.

———. 1971. *Pourquoi l'épouser*. Paris: Gallimard.

Deutsch, Karl. 1963. *The Nerves of Government*. New York: Free Press.

Dumont, L. 1970. *Homo Hierarchicus*. London: Weidenfeld & Nicholson.

Eder, K., ed. 1973. *Die Entstehung von Klassengesellschaften*. Frankfurt am Main: Suhrkamp.

Eisenstadt, S. N. 1963. *The Political Systems of Empires*. New York: Free Press.

———. 1973a. *Traditional Patrimonialism and Modern Neopatrimonialism*. Beverly Hills and London: Sage Publications.

———. 1973b. *Tradition, Change and Modernity*. New York: Wiley.

———. 1977. *The Sociology Tradition*. In J. Ben David and T. N. Clark, eds., *Culture and Creators*. Chicago: University of Chicago Press, pp. 43–72.

———. 1978. *Revolution and the Transformation of Societies*. New York: Free Press.

Eisenstadt, S. N., and Curelaru, M. 1976. *The Form of Sociology—Paradigms and Crises*. New York: Wiley.

———. 1977. "Macrosociology: Theory, Analysis and Comparative Studies." *Current Sociology 25*(2).

Gluckman, M. 1955. *Custom and Conflict in Africa*. Oxford: Basil Blackwell.

Godelier, M. 1972. *Rationality and Irrationality in Economics*. New York: Monthly Review Press.

———. 1973. *Horizons, Tarjets Marxistes en Anthropologies*. Paris: Maspero.

Goffman, E. 1959. *The Presentation of Self in Everyday Life*. New York and Garden City: Doubleday, Anchor Books.

———. 1961a. *Asylums*. New York and Garden City: Anchor Books.

———. 1961b. *Encounters*. Indianapolis: Bobbs-Merrill.

Habermas, J. 1979. *Communication and the Evolution of Society*. Boston: Beacon Press.

Heintz, P., ed. 1972. *A Macrosocietal Theory of Societal Systems with Special Reference to the International System*. Bern: Hans Huber.

Homans, G. C. 1961. *Social Behavior: Its Elementary Forms*. New York: Harcourt Brace Jovanovich.

Lenski, G. E. 1970. *Human Societies; A Macrolevel Introduction to Sociology*. New York: McGraw-Hill.

Levi-Strauss, C. 1963. *Structural Anthropology*. New York: Basic Books.

———. 1966. *The Savage Mind*. London: Weidenfeld and Nicholson.

———. 1967. *Totemism*. Boston: Beacon Press.

———. 1969. *The Elementary Structures of Kinship*. Boston: Beacon Press.

McNeill, W. 1963. *The Rise of the West*. Chicago: University of Chicago Press.

Maruyama, M. 1968. "The Second Cybernetics: Deviation-Amplifying Mutual Causal Processes." In W. Buckley, ed., *Modern Systems Research for the Behavioral Scientist*. Chicago: Aldine, pp. 304–313.

Moore, S. F. 1969. *Law, Culture and Society*.

Parsons, T. 1966. *The Evolution of Societies*. Englewood Cliffs, N.J.: Prentice-Hall.

Schluchter, W. 1981. *The Rise of Western Rationalism—Max Weber's Developmental History*. Berkeley and Los Angeles: University of California Press.

Steward, J. 1955. *Theory of Culture Change: The Methodology of Multilinear Evolution:* Urbana: University of Illinois Press.

Toynbee, A. 1972. *A Study of History*. London: Oxford University Press in association with Thames and Hudson.

Wallerstein, I. 1974. *The Modern World System: Capitalist Agriculture and the Origins of the European World Economy in the 16th Century*. New York: Academic Press.

White, L. 1949. *The Science of Culture*. New York: Grove Press.

Discussion

(Bell, Coleman, Inkeles, Dror, Miller, Weingart, Nowotny, Deutsch)

Edited by Andrei S. Markovits

DANIEL BELL started the discussion with a general question. He noted that in 1927 Sorokin wrote *Contemporary Sociological Theories*, and fifty years later Eisenstadt wrote a book on forms of paradigms in sociology. He wondered to what extent Eisenstadt was aware of the earlier Sorokin overview and how he differed in his view of the basic paradigms.

Samuel Eisenstadt stated that he had known Sorokin but did not consider him a model, at least not consciously. His own book in 1977 and his chapter here were written from a theoretical rather than a research point of view. In his book he had tried to show the interplay between the tendency of sociologists to create concepts and paradigms, and the process of groping for a common framework that would also be applicable to research.

He said that Sorokin had made a list of different sociological approaches, but that fifty years later there had come to be a sociological tradition with its own *Problemstellung*. Institutionally and conceptually, it was a very shaky tradition, alternating continually between paradigms and crisis, between sectarianism and openness. This alternation vividly characterized sociology in the 1960s but was less vivid now, although the problem would always be with us. Sociologists should learn from these experiences how to create better conditions for doing good work.

New Methods, New Relations, New Units?

James Coleman wanted to respond to a question that was partly posed and partly answered in Eisenstadt's paper: Why did the theoretical developments in the 1960s and 1970s never become more than debates over concepts; or rather, why were they not expanded more fully? Coleman argued that the reason was that none of these developments was compatible with the new developments in sociological methods. It was true that there had been some research using more traditional methods that was related to these theories, but the theories were not linked in any clear fashion to the new methods. Coleman felt that if any theoretical idea was going to create any new explosion of substance, then it had to lend itself to some existing or newly emerging methods.

Eisenstadt intervened to say that a theory could lend itself to newly emerging methods—or it could call for them. Coleman replied that it would have to call for them in such a way that they could emerge quickly.

Coleman went on to say that he was thinking of two kinds of new methods that would be of potential value for social theory. First, there were qualitative methods with observational studies like those of William F. Whyte. Second, there were quantitative methods directed toward individuals as units of analysis but, in contrast to much current quantitative research in sociology, with propositions that were between individuals rather than intraindividual. He felt that the intraindividual character of current quantitative methods was a major reason that developments in methods had not been linked more explicitly to substantive advances, as Inkeles had pointed out.

Coleman said that he saw only three possible ways in which quantitative methods could be useful in sociology. The first was with the individual as the unit of analysis, with samples drawn in such a way as to be representative of a well-defined population, such as a nation's adult population. Quantitative use of such data in a way that might be valuable for social theory required a number of samples in order to allow comparison of many social units, as in the cross-national work on occupational prestige by Inkeles and Rossi. The second possibility was one in which individuals were the units on which observations were made, but where relations and structure between individuals were not lost, either in sampling or in the kind of data collected.

The third case was that in which individuals were not even the units of measurement. Coleman recalled an example in which a very large number of communes was studied and the commune itself was the unit of analysis. The sociologist Benjamin Zablocki made measurements of the communes and then made propositions, for example, on the conditions under which charismatic movements in the commune would develop or not develop.

Coleman argued that sociological substance and method had not come closer over the past three decades because of the explosion of research methods in an area that had been wholly intraindividual until recently.

Eisenstadt replied that he welcomed new methods or new mathematics that could capture social relations, but he thought this was like the debate over whether a glass was half empty or half full. In his fields, comparative and historical macrosociology, he had not seen any great new methodologies. There had been some very refined users of historical methods, as well as combined historical and ethnographic analyses such as those of the French school, but no great breakthroughs on formalized methods. He felt, however, that there had been considerable progress, even using the old methods. He emphasized that it was important to develop methods that were appropriate to the problems raised, and not to force the problem to fit inappropriate methods or units of analysis. He felt that progress could still be made with more sophisticated use of existing methods.

Need for Testable Propositions

Alex Inkeles followed these comments by saying he was pleased that Eisenstadt had elaborated and illustrated points that he had made only in passing in his own paper. He wanted to explain his own position further, however. He had not meant to give the impression that new "orienting perspectives" contributed nothing; on the contrary, they were indispensable to the advancement of science. The further elaboration of conceptual schemes with regard to these perspectives was also essential. No progress was possible without either the stimulus of such new orienting perspectives on specific concepts, or the obligation to confront and develop them with various types of evidence.

Inkeles pointed out, however, that his own emphasis was on a peculiar characteristic of the sociological tradition. Researchers would develop orienting schemes and corresponding concepts, but did not take the two essential additional steps that Eisenstadt had emphasized. That is, they did not ask what operations would be necessary to give form and content to these concepts, and what operations would make them measurable and specify relationships that would be a test of the adequacy of the overall orienting theory. This was not generally done; conventionally, it had been sufficient simply to elaborate the theory.

Inkeles felt that Eisenstadt had correctly emphasized two things about these schemes. First, they were very often little more than a struggle to get people to accept one's particular view as the correct way to look at the world—what Eisenstadt called "sectarianism." In sociology this was partly disruptive, but it had once been the situation in the physical sciences as well. One should not become discouraged when too much of the field included this kind of activity, he said, "but sometimes we would almost conclude that this is what the field is all about, because there is nothing else going on."

Nevertheless, he pointed out that from time to time appropriate empirical operations were actually made. A good example was the Wallersteinian World System Model. Inkeles said, "Within the framework of the sectarian group a certain number of empirical studies have been done to test the model—because it makes predictions." For example, there was an explicit proposition that peripheral states of a certain type had to remain so, and had to grow more slowly economically than advanced countries. Also, any growth had to rest on trade in primitive products rather than in complex technology. Both of these, Inkeles argued, were testable propositions; and in fact they were being partly tested by people within the school.

The point where the sectarianism became obvious, however, was when some members of the group arrived at the wrong conclusions—and, if they persisted, were asked to leave the movement. Such requests might be expressed directly; but more often the message is communicated through the content of public criticism, the systematic rejection of articles submitted for publication, and exclusion from the lists of those invited to attend the movement's meetings and conferences.

Inkeles said that this kind of situation was still encountered in the social sciences but no longer in the natural sciences—that is, a world view that had to be dealt with as a matter of faith. Inkeles noted that it would be unfortunate to stop at that point and not recognize that the Wallersteinian approach did in fact have implications for research; indeed, research had been done that made possible a revision of their propositions and therefore some kind of true scientific progress.

Inkeles said that he wanted it to be clear that he was all in favor of the generation of new orienting perspectives. One needs to make these perspectives distinct however—as, for example, in the conflict model, where one must ask what are the concrete forms that conflict takes so that they can be specified. If one simply stopped with the model and did not go on to add propositions such as that there would be more conflict between this class and that, or under this set of circumstances rather than that, then no sociology was going to advance.

Finding the Coordinates in Sociology

Chairman Wolf Lepenies decided to take four more questions to which Eisenstadt could respond all at once. First, Yehezkel Dror said that he would like to make a query bridging this discussion with other topics of the conference. He said it was hard to imagine a more interesting laboratory in which one could get new insights into social behavior than Nazi Germany. In doing a preliminary literature search in the work done on Nazi Germany by political scientists writing in English, he had found that there were very few studies involving concepts other than the fascist stereotypes. He asked, "Isn't this an illustration of a missed opportunity for new knowledge—and why has it been neglected?"

James Miller spoke next. He noted that each discipline had its own problems, but that in sociology a major question was what were "the four points of the compass" in the conceptual field. Yet this was not a unique situation, and it might be helpful to talk about comparable problems in other fields and the ways in which they tried to solve such problems. He referred to Inkeles's mention of comparing the chapters of many textbooks, comparing course listings from major universities, getting indexes made by computer programs, getting indexes made by librarians who were not experts in the field, getting indexes and reviews by experts, having overall theoretical and critical summaries like Sorokin's, having integrative theoretical books like Pareto's, and so on. Miller said that Alex Inkeles had been a founding editor of the *Annual Review of Sociology*, whereas he himself had been a founding editor of the *Annual Review of Psychology*. During his five years on that board, however, he had struggled every year to find some dimensions or parameters to describe the content of what was going on in psychology—and found that there was no agreement within the field itself on what the four points of that particular compass were.

Miller had also worked in psychiatry, where there was a series of huge diagnostic manuals, each of which "cost many thousands of dollars a year for the American Psychiatric Association to put out." The most creative type of identification of this field centered around these diagnostic manuals. The problem in psychiatry is that Freudianism has lost its dominance and the discipline has become theoretically eclectic; yet it is important to practice to get agreement among psychiatrists on the diagnosis of individual patients: "Agreements among psychiatrists on the diagnosis of individuals have often been poor—like the study reported earlier: zero correlation. This is extremely embarrassing, particularly if you have to go into court or if you have to give veterans disability awards which may amount to hundreds of dollars a veteran per month—when you have zero correlation." Miller argued that in each different discipline there were very practical reasons for trying to "find the coordinates of the field," and that this was what sociology had to do.

He then quoted Ralph Tyler, who at one time was dean of the social sciences at the University of Chicago, and who once asked the members of his executive committee whether they thought the field of sociology should have been abolished. Miller stated his personal interpretation of Tyler's reason for asking this—that in the intellectual geography of the social sciences, sociology was "landlocked." "It doesn't have any border that is not contiguous with another social science—unlike geography or psychiatry, which can extend in some directly entirely out of the social sciences." He argued that there was nearly complete overlap between almost any course given in sociology and some course given in economics, political science, psychology, geography, history, or anthropology. Such a field would inevitably have internal tensions unless it was unified by a strong theoretical approach that was generally accepted.

Miller claimed that from his position as both a psychologist and a psychiatrist, he believed that psychiatry is now in a healthier theoretical state than psychology because most psychiatrists have an increasingly clear conception of the physical structures underlying the process they study. Psychology, on the other hand, is a process science in which most members of the field are uncertain or uninformed about the physical structures related to the processes they are studying. Miller thought this was also largely true of the disciplines of anthropology and sociology.

Given this state of affairs, Miller felt that one way to integrate theory would be to foster serious efforts within the discipline to connect structures in space with the processes over time on which it focuses. This was the form of orientation that was used by the natural sciences; in the social sciences, however, with the lack of something that they all wished they had—like the Mendeleev Table or the various taxonomies in biology or the grand integrative scheme of Darwin—something else would have to be developed in order for sociology to achieve greater coherence and consensus.

Miller then said that he thought the DPS paper gave no adequate recognition to those who were involved in integrating the fields—perhaps because such work was considered to have low status. It was often looked on as something done by book reviewers, authors of *Annual Review* articles, or writers of diagnostic manuals, instead of being recognized as an essential scientific activity. A really integrated and practical set of diagnostic manuals is not considered a breakthrough. The system of financial and academic rewards, national organizations, and so on did not give any recognition to that kind of integrative activity. He argued, however, that if sociology was as full of ships lost at sea as the previous talks had indicated, perhaps the professional organizations in the field should make a serious integrative effort to try to identify the coordinates.

Miller wondered if a next edition of the DPS paper would give special recognition to such endeavors. He emphazied that he did not want to see sociology eliminated, but he did hope that Inkeles or Coleman could give a list of important breakthrough researchers in the field "in terms of the overall geography of the field. What are the coordinates of these researchers?—so that when their work appears in sociological publications, through key words or some other method, one can be aware of what other studies they relate to." Miller felt that editorial policies should require authors to indicate where they believe their work is located in the vast sea of this discipline that seems to be so highly disorganized, with such uncharted intellectual geography.

Testability, or Politicization and the Quest for Meaning?

Peter Weingart noted that Eisenstadt and Inkeles had agreed on the ideological component in some contemporary sociology but were ambivalent about it. One could not call on institutions to cure the problem, however, because it was something on the conceptual level, so there seemed to be only one way out; yet it was not really a way out because it would involve making concepts so abstract that they became depoliticized. In the natural sciences that was possible, although even there the concepts are becoming increasingly politicized because of their subject matter or their implications for society. In the social sciences, however, as with the IQ-race debate, the problem was obvious. It was not simply an ideological question but a deeply rooted political conflict over what one could take as legitimate subject matter. The same thing was happening on a less dramatic scale with "indicator research" and, in the natural sciences, with the whole DNA debate.

Weingart maintained that this raised the epistemological issue of whether it was possible to escape the constructivist notions that were implicit in sociological theory and concepts. He felt that these notions were no longer viable; the dilemma was one of being either entirely remote and withdrawn from society, or of being political. As Eisenstadt had said, we simply had to live with this problem.

Helga Nowotny commented on the split between the picture that Eisenstadt painted—showing the cunning of sociological reasoning in expressing continuity despite disruption—and the previous discussion of methodological advances. She felt that the split occurred between the substantive component of an advance and the institutional infrastructure. In this infrastructure, some of the advances are becoming more and more tied to apparatus and large-scale technology such as the computer, with the consequence that only certain types of problems are addressed. The service function also presses toward this, as do formal organizational structures and management methods.

Nowotny argued, however, that on the other side there was a kind of cultural infrastructure. Thus Eisenstadt's interplay between conceptual advances and research occurred in a part of the cultural scene that was marginal in the sense that it was between established disciplines. Bourdieu's work in France was a prime example. Other work was antiestablishment in orientation, and still other work occurred at the very margin of academia.

Nowotny felt that this showed a higher differentiation process, where one kind of research, tied to the natural sciences, tended to be institutionalized, but where there was another cultural infrastructure loaded with things like the quest for meaning and explanation as the goals of life. She suggested that this was also a legitimate area of endeavor to be considered along with the former.

Reconciling Both Approaches

Karl Deutsch noted that neither Eisenstadt nor Inkeles had mentioned the recent developments in sociobiology. He wondered whether they believed that this work represented a major contribution now or potentially in the future.

Deutsch also had a second question, on the sociology of sociology. Science Number One, the large science that Nowotny mentioned, was capital-intensive and tied to large organizations involving many people—a sort of industrial production of knowledge. Science Number Two, the quest for meaning of the science or hermeneutic interpretation, was an ideal form of handicraft production, Deutsch claimed. A person could sit down, think about meaning and produce a proposition about meaning, and be in business. On the one hand, the large research projects risked being disconfirmed. For example, if Selig Harrison predicted that the Indian political system would collapse, Eisenstadt could catch him and point out that he was wrong. On the other hand, if Harrison produced a profound interpretation of the meaning of Indian culture, no one would call him wrong: "He would be almost entirely free—or, in economist's terms, he would be in a quasi-monopoly for his line of handicraft."

Deutsch wondered if the increase in calls for "meaning" might not be part of the need of many people to stay in certain fields of social science, while escaping the pressure of hunting up budgets, of disconfirmation, and of having to struggle with computers and program tapes and data bases and innumerable other things. He argued that since these ideas sometimes produce something very useful, it could be a good thing that the industrialization of one type of science also produced an increase in the number of specialized craftsmen to do the other.

Daniel Bell intervened to say that he thought Deutsch's example had been misleading, and had thereby obscured an important distinction. The reason that Selig Harrison could do as he did was because he was a *journalist*, "very attentive to the actual by-play of politics as against the theoreticians who deal with abstract schemas." Bell contended this was not just the case of two different cubbyholes of research. He felt that the "neglect of intelligent journalists, attentive to the diversities of specific situations that social scientists using purely abstract schemas could entirely miss, was a crucial problem for so-called major research."

Eisenstadt responded to his critics in order. With regard to Dror's questions, he said that Nazi Germany was indeed an interesting case to study and a missed opportunity so far. He felt, however, that it was a case of different traditions of cross-national study, rather than the type of sectarianism he had been talking about.

For More Explicit Theory

Eisenstadt agreed that sociology needed to make its theoretical dimensions more explicit and to be more self-conscious about the limits of its conceptual apparatus; but he felt it would be extremely dangerous to devote too much of the discipline's efforts to these questions. There were productive research problems within the basic parameters of the sociological tradition, and he felt that sociologists knew more or less what they were interested in.

He argued, nevertheless, that the cutting edge for advances was in the encounter between the two different understandings. He did not agree with Deutsch about the two entirely different types of social science; the major problem was to bring the two together. Computer research was not the only research. The Louis Dumont book, for example, was not only an interpretation of the meaning of Indian culture, but also generated concrete field research from which many concrete propositions could be drawn. Eisenstadt suggested that this was the best way to get advances—to make progress on various levels while coupling this with efforts to interlink the levels. He argued that above all one wanted to avoid separating these levels any more than was natural.

On the question of sociobiology, Eisenstadt personally felt that it was unconvincing, and he was very dubious about it. He was not dubious about the need to rethink the relationships between the biological system and the social system, but he felt that the way that particular discussion had taken place within sociobiology was very unconvincing.

Eisenstadt then went on to discuss the degree to which advances in the social sciences are "discrete" or cumulative, in the light of recent developments in sociology, anthropology, and political science. (These questions have been raised in a 1981 talk by R. McC. Adams to the American Academy of Arts and Sciences, in which Adams took issue with the implications of the 1971 DPS paper—see pp. 339–41).

Eisenstadt stressed that it is legitimate to talk about advances in improved organization of data, new findings, and testing of hypotheses; but it is wrong to view such advances in a simple positivistic way. Rather, they must be analyzed on two levels: first, in terms of the continuous development of various areas of research; and second, by a *combination* of theory and development of theoretical paradigms, and sometimes metatheoretical discussions, as well as methodological ones. Developments in each of these dimensions have taken place in the social sciences in the last two decades, but the central dynamics has been through the combination between these different levels or frameworks.

Because of such combinations in different areas, concrete research problems develop not only through new data and hypothesis testing, but also by new conceptual reformulations. These may be the crucial elements in breakthroughs, as Ernst Mayr has claimed in his recent *History of Biology*; yet such combinations cannot be evaluated simply as discrete and simple accumulation.

Eisenstadt made a final comment on Boudon's discussion of methodological advances in one area where there was a strong theoretical paradigm, methodological sophistication, and a vigorous research program. He said that in other areas of research there have not been such strong advances, perhaps because, as Coleman pointed out, the methodologies were based on aggregation of individual behavior. Possibly new types of methodology—as opposed to new types of mathematics—may develop that can help in further understanding of collective or structural phenomena.

CHAPTER 4

Milieus for Advances in Political Science

R. Wildenmann

SOME WEEKS AGO in Florence, as I was thinking about this chapter on the conditions for recent breakthroughs in the social sciences, I realized that it was a vast field and that my presentation would have to be very subjective. My mind went back to the conditions under which the Florentines found themselves during the Renaissance. Florence had only a small population—about 50,000—but because of its milieu, its spirit, and its constitution, it contributed in a remarkable way to the arts and sciences, including the science of politics. Considering our present state of national and global politics, perhaps a Renaissance of the Renaissance, a second rebirth, is possible today.

Conditions for Individual Advances

I shall start by concentrating on conditions and the sorting out of models. Another biographical note may help. When I was taken prisoner of war in 1941, I was held in Canada for five years and was able to bury myself in books. I worked constantly and, with the help of an anthropologist, undertook my first empirical research. My study was dedicated to disproving the so-called race theory of creativity. It mapped out the streams of movement in Europe for three thousand years, together with the places of birth of "geniuses." The patterns were almost identical—proving that certain social conditions created by the mass movements of people were the most favorable for the development of talented individuals.

The major criteria for good working conditions for this kind of research seem to be a protected environment, or, in Weber's terminology, *Innerweltliche Askese.* The Canadians treated us very well and left us to do our studies, in a situation where we were cared for, like people in universities receiving various forms of aid today. Our situation only lacked a concrete definition, and we defined it.

Such a protected milieu suits individual research. Obviously, one also needs access to good sources of information, and to institutes that can provide such milieus. It would seem, however, that many important innovations in the list given by Karl Deutsch and his colleagues were completed under similar conditions.

Confrontation of Different Cultures

On the other hand, many other important works in that list were carried out in totally different milieus—for example, the Viennese milieu before and after World War I. That situation has been described in two excellent articles by Rainer M. Lepsius on the development of the social sciences between the wars and on the impact of immigration during the Nazi regime. In Vienna, the capital of the Austrian melting pot, many different types of people converged to create a multiethnic and multinational community, in which an explosion of the social sciences took place. A theoretical approach to explaining what happened could be Simmel's theory of the *Kreuzung sozialer Kreise*—or the overlapping of social layers. The confrontation of different cultures seems to create ideal conditions for the development of new ideas.

Lepsius also notes the impact of immigration on the United States in the 1930s and 1940s, with encounters between hundreds of European immigrants and the indigenous social scientists, which contributed considerably to the development of the social sciences. It was an ideal situation, with favorable material conditions, plus a confrontation of two very different worlds—the European with its diversified paradigms, and the American with its pragmatic philosophical approach.

Role of Institutional Structure

After World War II the social sciences developed in many European countries, but their growth remains marginal compared to that of the natural sciences. In West German universities, for example, out of approximately 100,000 academics, there are only about 3,500 social scientists, including economists, sociologists, social psychologists, political scientists, and so on. There are, however, 2,000 lawyers; 1,200 theologians; 20,000 academics working with hermeneutic methods in fields such as languages and history; and about 60,000 involved in the study of medicine, natural sciences, and technology.

This quantitative difference indicates qualitative differences that do not favor the social sciences. The practice among natural scientists of creating research units with long-term financing for five to ten years, with constant checks on the progress of their work, is not common for social scientists. The norm in such units is to assemble a group of people who are either theory-oriented or practice-oriented and who then work on common problems. The system requires of the scientists a certain research behavior, of a type that natural scientists have been achieving for a long time.

Such a pattern overcomes the so-called "kangaroo financing" of research, whereby one must develop a project and then develop a second project a short time later in order to receive continued sponsorship. To avoid the kangaroo problem, many years ago Professor Wilhelm Krelle created a special research environment so that he could carry on his work. It is imperative that social scientists today form such research units to guarantee long-term financing. In West Germany, however, a number of the social science special-research environments have broken down because many social scientists find teamwork difficult. In addition, large sums are not being spent on the social sciences because of unfavorable value asessments of the work. Society asks, "Social sciences—what for?" People like Stein Rokkan and Seymour Martin Lipset, however, have succeeded in conducting creative teamwork and have made major contributions to contemporary social science.

International Research Teams

Another type of milieu has been created by research organizations such as the International Consortium for Political Research (ICPR) in the United States, which concentrates on empirical research, and the European Consortium for Political Research (ECPR), with a somewhat broader spectrum of paradigms. The ECPR is an organization of 110 research institutes, which holds regular workshop meetings, cooperates in research programs, and aims for a higher degree of professionalism in the social sciences. It has created a good milieu for research, and its goal is to train social scientists to work together. Within the ECPR there is cooperation among people from many different nations (with the unfortunate exception of France, where the social sciences lean toward more traditional practices). The teamwork has involved England, the Scandinavian countries, the Netherlands, and West Germany; and progress is being made in Italy. This international cooperation is a major development of the last twenty years.

To elaborate this point, there was a recent workshop in Turin in honor of the late Paolo Farneti, one of Italy's great political scientists. Farneti was educated in the United States, Germany, and Italy, in the Pareto-Mosca tradition as well as in that of Max Weber and the empirical research tradition of Columbia University. Most of Italy's political scientists attended this workshop, representing a huge body of political thought. They are now moving to incorporate their older type of political philosophy with a body of empirical evidence in order to refine their theories and to develop a truly political science.

On the basis of these examples, we can formulate the following hypothesis: Singular theories, such as mathematical theories, result from work done by individuals; but these individuals need a milieu in which to work. Humans cannot live alone; they are social animals. Comparative study, on the other hand, is often the result of teamwork. There are many ways of doing teamwork and hence a need for many different types of institutions in which to do it. The social sciences are rapidly moving from an individual, armchair-philosopher's science to one in which teamwork is necessary. An individual may develop theories; but for empirically oriented sciences, teams of scientists must be trained to work together, to cooperate, and to learn to understand each other. It is necessary not only to have an institution,but also to establish cooperative behavior.

The Development of Professionalism

To prove (or falsify) this hypothesis, note that in the last twenty years the ICPR, based in Ann Arbor, and later the ECPR have produced a huge amount of empirical comparative research. In the terminology of Popper, we now have substantial material on which to construct reality and to test many assumptions hitherto taken for granted; and we have a body of people who can do such work. In this sense, political science has already become a profession, whereas other disciplines in the social sciences have yet to achieve this. This step has been greatly furthered by such organizations as the ICPR and the ECPR. We have developed not mere behaviorism, but consistent theoretically and empirically oriented research.

I can compare the state of affairs in 1950, when I started my first political science book in Heidelberg, with the situation today. Now we have an infrastructure and a large body of people with whom to identify, who know each other and communicate with each other. There is a common language and common methods, and the macro-theories grow. It is an important scientific development, an established and stable kind of relationship that is becoming independent of the attitudes of the various governments toward political science. The knowledge cannot be forgotten anymore.

There have also been some interesting defeats, however. Between 1970 and 1974 we attempted to create a Max Weber Society, somewhat like the Max Planck Society which has existed for a hundred years and has fostered numerous research institutes in the natural sciences. In this case, however, the Max Weber Society was stopped by the president of the German Research Foundation, who said: "For the social sciences, we need to give a little bit of money to young people, let us say 10,000 DM, to write a book. If they are successful, they may get some new money." He really did not understand the problem involved. Today, however, the Max Planck Society has taken over part of this intended program. The idea is to create an infrastructure—an international organization for the social sciences—that would provide money for institutions, time for research, and education in cooperation with young researchers.

Fortunately, this basic idea has been independently realized in other ways. A number of institutions have been created all over Europe—for example, the Science Center in Berlin, organized for teamwork; the *Wissenschaftskolleg*, a high-level think tank; and the Institute for Advanced Study in the Netherlands (NIAS). In England the universities have this function and are very well provided for, as in the case of Nuffield College. In Italy there is now the European University Institute for social science in the wider sense, including law. In Scandinavia there is comparative or theoretical research in Aarhus, Odense, Stockholm, Copenhagen, Oslo, and Bergen, with many people producing both quantitative work and fine theoretical work—trying to create a body of empirical knowledge tested with proper methods. Social science has created a new reality, so to speak, but it still has to be explained with proper theoretical instruments. We still live with theories conceived before World War II, and we need to resume this theoretical discussion.

Cross-National Studies

In addition to these institutions, there have been many cross-national teams at work. Examples include the activities of Stein Rokkan, those of a number of groups working in England, the work of Peter Flora on the development of the welfare state, and that of his former teacher Wolfgang Zapf with his economic-social model.

A large group of younger people spread over several countries and financed by the Volkswagen Foundation are studying European integration at a level that is thoroughly based theoretically. This group is steered by Karlheinz Reif from Mannheim and Mike Gordon from England; in their work they have interviewed the middle-level elites of about sixty parties all over Europe, and have created an extensive body of data that describes the problems and interrelationships between European development and the various national societies.

Another international group, studying political behavior of several countries in the context of macrosystem theory, has produced a first book—*Political Action* by Sam Barnes and Max Kaase. Ned Muller is working with a group in Germany along similar lines. This is helping us to understand what is going on in societies today, and the alienation of the younger generation.

One international team is studying "interest politics." It is based in Scandinavia, France, and the United States, and is connected with scholars in Berlin, directed by Fritz Scarpf and Philippe Schmitter. Their basic theoretical concept goes back to Helvetius, but they are making new contributions to understanding our societies and political systems. Still other groups are working on comparative studies of party systems and party government, on international relations, and so on.

As a result of this international and institutionalized cooperation since 1960, the European scene, including the United States, has shown a major breakthrough in sound methodological study of political-social reality. This will be a necessary base for further research.

Problems Needing Study

Serious gaps and problems still lie ahead. International relations need much more intensive study. In foreign policy analysis, our writers are still, so to speak, "standing between the big actors of politics" and trying to interpret their dialogues. Such studies tell us more about the writer than about the reality. International studies also need a much better institutional basis and better financing, with groups of scholars cooperating. They cannot be done by a scholar sitting in one of the beautiful abbeys or colleges in Oxford, or a nice place in Odense or Aarhus or Florence, and singing about the world.

Unfavorable conditions for research also result from the diversification of disciplines within the social sciences. This is demonstrated in the history of the German *Verein für Sozialpolitik*, which is now 100 years old. This organization has been the scene of major developments and confrontations in social science, such as the debate between Max Weber and Schmoller on "value problems" in 1908. After World War II, however, the *Verein* came to be dominated by economists; the other social sciences are no longer represented, and there are no confrontations. Such changes may be unavoidable, with increasing division of labor, with mathematicization driving the economists in a different direction, and with the recent feeling that economics is needed more than the other fields are. For ten or fifteen years, however, the other social sciences were much more neglected. As we would say in Berlin, they were sitting "in a little *Schrebergarten*"—that is, in five square meters with a little wooden house, a few flowers, and a little bit of cabbage.

Nowadays we need confrontations. We need intercommunication. Perhaps we can no longer comprehend the knowledge of all the social sciences as Max Weber and others did in their time, because the disciplines are so diversified. In politics, however, we are faced with a huge number of economic questions. Economists face just as many political questions. These special and separate developments have been detrimental to the interests of all the disciplines in the social sciences. We ought to ask our friends in the economic field to enter the field of politics, and vice versa.

Another need is for a new theory of government. Sometimes it seems to me that political science goes astray because it is looking for the trees and not the woods. Political science is, in my understanding, the study of *government*. It is a very difficult study—not as simple as it sometimes seems in discussions of political philosophy. The study of government has to look much more carefully into the interrelationships between governmental institutions, decision-making procedures, elites, and populations.

The field of mass communication is another weak area in our science. We are at the dawn of a new technological revolution. Many people are still contesting it, but such a struggle may be a waste of time. In the Federal Republic of Germany the new communications should be fully implemented in the next few years. There will be a new structure of communication in society—not just television, but also communications in industry, between social groups, and for all sorts of services.

This will create a new area of social communications, with unknown impacts on social structures and politics. Studies of this field will need a thorough new approach. I would not like to have the social sciences again complaining that we have been left behind, as in the case of the student revolution of the 1960s. In that case only a few saw early enough the impact of a value change on politics, and none of the theories of social development predicted such an evolution. The same might happen in the field of mass communications. Instead of waiting for ten years to draw up history, we should use the theories available today to try to affect it.

This new technology is an objective fact, and we should study its coming problems and their effect on "government." It will drastically alter all relationships with respect to behavior, to interest representation, to decision making—to everything. Our systems are changing.

Another major shortcoming today in the political sphere is our neglect of the long-term historical perspective. Instead, we are confronted with numerous historical philosophies. I myself have been a student of one of the historical philosophers, Alfred Weber, who commanded in his mind 5,000 years of history. When I read a new book by Habermas, I think that someone like Alfred Weber was a hundred times better in that approach because he really understood historical philosophy. What Habermas has produced is rather a sort of ideology, a systematic point of view.

We need deep historical perspective to solve some important puzzles. Take just one question (it may be the wrong question, but we have to study whether it is the wróng question). Is there much variety for governments, or is there only a limited number of possibilities? If there is enough variety, what are the conditions for democracy? You cannot deal with those questions using aggregate data of the last twenty-five years; you have to deal with it in a deep historical perspective. There are several such fields where we can identify unsolved problems.

Need for New Theoretical Development

In summary, we have had a major quantitative development—a sort of explosion—of the social and political sciences in Western Europe and the United States after World War II, because the infrastructure was provided for it. The major emphasis of political science for the last twenty-five to thirty years has been quantitative, on empirical work, comparative work, for the construction of "reality." It is now methodologically very sophisticated, and there is a body of people who can carry on such research. In terms of developing a theory or an applied theory of society and politics and especially of government, however, we are still relying on the theories of the nineteenth or early twentieth century. After sixty years, Max Weber is now available in good translations in English, and *Herrschaftsorganisation* is a word one can use as easily as *kindergarten.* This notion originated seventy years ago, however, and we have a deficit in new theoretical conceptions today. I can mention one new notion—Lepsius's important theoretical work on the "three-class concept." I hope he will publish this as a book or will contribute it to his new critical edition of Max Weber's work, because the impact of this concept on political science is considerable.

We are about halfway through the process of creating an infrastructure of political science and of the social sciences. This is a necessary condition for major new work. As the proverb says, *Armut kommt von der Pauperität*—"being poor comes from poverty." Everybody is shocked if you ask for $1.5 million as a political scientist on an important study like our new study of elites in West Germany. If a natural scientist wants another $2 billion, people are apt to say, "Oh, don't you need 2.1 billion?" Social science still needs special legitimation for its research; and now, as a result of current economic problems, with shrinking funds, many of our research institutions in the political and social sciences are in danger.

Comparing the situation of the 1960s, 1970s, or 1980s with that of the 1920s and 1930s, we are theoretically poorer, and are still dependent on earlier developments. Now, however, we have created a body of professional scientists. For the first time we have the humus in which things can grow. I hope that this will permit a thorough reconsideration of our concepts and theories, as the postwar generation emerges.

Discussion

(Miller, Deutsch, Nowotny, Eisenstadt, Dror, Krelle, Bremer, Bell, Klingemann

Edited by Andrei S. Markovits

The Information Revolution

James G. Miller began by discussing the sudden arrival of the revolution in electronic information and mass communications referred to by Rudolf Wildenmann. He said this was a revolutionary phenomenon that had an impact on nearly every sphere of society, including business, government, technology, and even fundamentalist religions. In 1981 the so-called Moral Majority group in the United States sponsored a Christmas-day broadcast that was transmitted to thirteen different countries, including Israel and South Africa.

Miller said that this rapid transmission of information could transform politics. Crane, the historian of Southeast Asia, once said that the ability of emperors and warlords to rule their dominions through Chinese history was directly related to the rate at which information could be transmitted from the capital to the periphery. Today, the instantaneous transmission of information throughout the world certainly changes the discipline of political science. Other disciplines, such as economics, are also affected, because money can likewise be transmitted instantaneously around the world. Miller suggested that this information revolution therefore could not be handled simply on the basis of the individual disciplines, and that it might be a factor in nearly every paper at a conference like this one.

Miller said that a second, more fundamental point concerned the problem of distinguishing the past from the future. Wildenmann had referred to the failure of political scientists to recognize the significance of electronic information-processing, and their surprise when it became so important. Is it the role of participants in this conference to tell people who are going to attend a similar conference ten years from now what issues they should start working on? "Should we list a series of topics—such as electronic information-processing, genetic engineering, and nuclear energy—that are so central to the continuation of society that *all* disciplines must deal with them, if social science is to fulfill its responsibility to society?"

Karl Deutsch responded that if participants wished to emphasize that certain issues were very urgent, that was excellent. Wildenmann commented that the recent book by Daniel Bell, *The Social Sciences since the Second World War,* in discussing the major advances, was oriented toward past achievements and problems. He felt, however, that this conference should have a responsibility for the present as well, including the relevance of electronic information processing.

Preconditions for Developments in Political Science

Helga Nowotny embarked on a different tack, in discussing two preconditions for the developments in political science since World War II, especially in Europe. First, there was a trend toward professionalism, which was, in a way, a process of catching up with the United States. Second, and connected to this, was the service function that political science had to fulfill for governments, including the collection and proper presentation of data.

Nowotny pointed out that not only were there major achievements in political science, but there were also major gaps or dark areas of knowledge. Wildenmann had contended that creativity took place at two kinds of centers. As a sociologist, Nowortny wondered how people got into those institutions—a question as interesting as the institutions themselves, especially if there were two different types of creative thinking going on in such places. This raised the further question of what could be done to ensure a flow of people between the different places. Nowotny claimed that such a flow was necessary because heterogeneity and richness of composition seemed to be major ingredients in environments that were ripe for advances. In this area, we needed to think about how to create opportunity structures conducive to the mobility of people and ideas.

Nowotny said that a second dark area, even more fundamental for our understanding of advances, dealt with the social and political conditions under which new concepts were derived. This is not just a matter of their impact on old-style political thinking or armchair theorizing, but the question of connecting new concepts with reality. Information technology was a good example—a challenge to scholars because they had to come to grips with the concept of information. Nowotny also suggested that it would be worthwhile to look back at historical advances. We knew how the major thinkers of the nineteenth century came up with very powerful concepts, but how much of this was individual effort and how much achieved by a collective endeavor? She commented also that too little was known about what made a concept powerful—what made it work? Nowotny concluded that it would be fruitful for scholars to analyze the social and political preconditions for major cognitive advances.

Wildenmann responded to Nowotny's comment on the service function of political science by noting that the first service monitoring system was created in Germany, but was designed to serve all of Europe. On the question of how people get into research institutes, he said that in the European Consortium, in his experience, great importance was placed on making a creative milieu. Also, a tremendous amount of effort was made to bring scholars together, to increase intercommunication. He cited the annual workshop sessions sponsored by the Consortium for Political Science as an example. Nevertheless, he said, it was difficult to get six or seven nations to define a workshop. Often the milieu simply was not there; also, people were interested in their careers, so that it was hard to run a creative research institution.

As for the social and political preconditions for major advances in political science, Wildenmann suggested that we look again at the method of constellation analysis that was developed, though somewhat crudely, by Max Weber's brother Alfred Weber. Specific situations were defined by general developments in society, including social, economic, and cultural developments as well as the development of knowledge. In this method of analysis, Alfred Weber may have gone much further than his brother Max.

Wildenmann commented on a discussion he had had at the Max Planck Institute in Munich, where they were using a biological approach to study creativity. He contended that this was neglecting the social and economic conditions and the whole milieu in which the creativity takes place.

The Definition of Advances

Shmuel Eisenstadt then began another line of questioning, on the definition of *advances*. He said that Wildenmann had noted several advances, where nevertheless the major theoretical problems had been forgotten.

Lipset and Rokkan, for example, had started with a central theoretical problem of the preconditions of democracy, but the later work acquired such a methodological and specialized momentum that the broader questions were to some degree overlooked.

Eisenstadt went on to a second point, saying that social scientists had always claimed to be making the contemporary world more comprehensible, and had mentioned this goal several times at this conference. Wildenmann, however, had pointed out that no social scientists had predicted the student upheavals of the late 1960s—"a very important event!" There was evidently a problem of social reality that could overtake the thinking of social scientists, even while we had many so-called advances in social science that were irrelevant to theoretical understanding—or to reality itself. Eisenstadt asked, "To what degree are what we call advances only combinations of good methodology and good conceptual thinking, which still do not address the major problems both of the discipline and of reality?"

Eisenstadt went on to a third point, related to Nowotny's remarks: What institutional conditions would be needed to help make the new advances more related to major theoretical problems or real problems? The new concepts in the nineteenth century were invented in social milieus, not by lonely scholars. We should think seriously about recreating institutions in which such meeting points between theory and reality would be encouraged. Social scientists should pay attention to the "possible conditions under which the lacunae pointed to by Wildenmann may to some degree be overcome."

Wildenmann responded by saying that, in his experience, what were seen as advances had actually been posed by social and political developments: "In a sense we are all retrospective historians." What is needed in political science now is better probability theories of social and political development, even though it would be complicated and unlike a physical laboratory situation: "We should attempt to understand the world better" so that we can minimize or reduce our risks.

On the difficulty of improving institutional conditions, Wildenmann gave the example of the "institutionalized altruism" of the Zentrum für Umfragen, Methoden und Analysen (ZUMA) project at Mannheim in Germany. This was an institution that extended support to social scientists doing theoretically oriented research. It now involved thirty people; but it had taken six years to get organized, and it required him, as the organizer, to write thousands of small memos and letters instead of the two books he might have produced in that time.

Science Overtaken by Events

Deutsch then interjected that the problem of being overtaken by events was something that natural scientists were familiar with also. Pasteur worked on rabies, and Koch worked on tuberculosis in the early twentieth century; yet no one foresaw the great influenza epidemic of 1918 that killed over 20 million people. Scientific geology went on for a hundred years after Lyell; yet it took the great earthquake at Messina to stimulate serious work on seismology. Being overtaken by events from time to time is probably inevitable.

Yehezkel Dror then made six points concerning Wildenmann's paper. First, being overtaken by external events could also have positive effects in political science, simply as a stimulus for the development of new concepts. For example, Machiavelli and others were confronted by the events of the Italian Renaissance, which they could not explain in terms of existing mind sets, and were thus stimulated to develop new ones.

Second, Dror suggested that culture shocks could affect political science by creating an upsurge of interest in other systems. Examples included the insights obtained from studying Japan, and New Guinea, which continued to be a strong democracy, though only one generation removed from the Stone Age. Of course, in the sociology of science, the question remained why such upsurges of interest were followed so quickly by declines.

Dror's third comment was that it would be valuable to distinguish between the various kinds of institutes Wildenmann had mentioned. On the one hand, there were institutes of advanced study such as the *Wissenschaftskolleg*, Diaz, the Center at Stanford, and Princeton itself; then there were "think tanks" such as the RAND Corporation, the Hudson Institute, and the like, where the interdisciplinary work was supposed to be relevant to specific contracts or problems.

As his fourth and fifth points, Dror reemphasized the need for more communication between political scientists and historians, and the need for interdisciplinary approaches such as political psychology and political economics, which could be undertaken more successfully than they are now.

Finally, Dror recommended that political scientists study the effects of career patterns on the development of innovations, so that changes might be made to encourage more innovations in the future.

Need for Interdisciplinary Work

Wildenmann agreed on the need to encourage political scientists to do more interdisciplinary work, but reiterated that "Most interdisciplinary institutes just don't work!" Nevertheless, he thought it would be a good thing if political scientists should be required, as they often had been required in the past, to have a background in other disciplines such as history, economics, and the law. On the question of career patterns, he cautioned that a political scientist is not a politician: "He is not a bird, he studies the bird." If Dror was emphasizing the need for interchanges between government activities and science, Wildenmann agreed that one needed experience, but he said that this was very different from cross-disciplinary exchange. The level of experience in government among political scientists was quite varied across countries: in Germany it was low, in France it was very high, in England it was very good, and in the United States there were varying experiences.

Chairman Deutsch then gave the floor to Wilhelm Krelle. Wildenmann had mentioned the Verein für Sozialpolitik in his talk. Krelle felt that since he had been the president of that organization for a number of years, he should say a few words about his experience. The Verein had shifted toward an exclusive emphasis on economic problems, in order to avoid the historical approach of economics and political science, in which very honorable men had tried to solve all problems at once.

It was better, Krelle maintained, to start out with much more modest aims—for instance, to focus on economic problems proper and to leave out anything that could not be solved. What was left out eventually needed to be put in, but this was like the problem of selecting the primary features in discovering the laws of physics. It was not possible to estimate the many laws that governed an apple falling from a tree, so physicists were forced to start with simple physics in space without any gravity. Newton considered only the sun and one planet, disregarding the effects of all the other planets, because the three-body problem had not been solved. One had to correct for that afterward. It would be wise to follow Wittgenstein in trying to explain only what one could explain and leave the rest out at first. That was how science progressed.

Krelle said there were encouraging examples of interdisciplinary attempts to incorporate political science with economics, such as the work of Nordhause, Fry, and Hibbs. It was necessary, however, to develop a well-defined system of concepts and to spell out the logical relations between them first. To bring political science into economics would be valuable for understanding reality, but it would be only part of reality. Simply to claim that there was a connection between economics and politics, or that it was immanent, was not science. One had to isolate and concentrate on special things so that one could really understand one part of reality. "Only after this has been done can we go on to another part of reality and attempt to understand that; or have another parallel science try to understand the other part." Only such a procedure could produce a common understanding. That was the way science progressed, and not by simply saying that there was intuitive commonality between the parts of reality dealt with by the different social sciences. Krelle referred to a remark Goethe once made, in which the author claimed to be able to commit any crime because he was a human being and understood what crime meant. This, however, was intuitive understanding, not scientific understanding. In conclusion, Krelle said that interdisciplinary efforts needed to be more modest, to focus on what was possible to understand, and then to try to expand slowly into relations with other areas.

Division of Labor in the Social Sciences

Wildenmann responded that he had referred to the Verein für Sozialpolitik not to attack it, but to demonstrate the division of labor between the social sciences. If an institution was originally meant to create encounters among the social sciences, it was not helpful to have it identified with only one discipline. It was true that it was no longer possible to conduct social science as it was done in 1905, with the whole body of the social sciences working together in an undifferentiated way on specific problems. Nevertheless, if phenomena today demanded cooperation between the disciplines, then clearly that was something that had to be developed.

Wildenmann said he was reminded of a famous banker who had spoken at the last meeting of the Verein für Sozialpolitik on the subject of "Political Decision Making in Economic Affairs." He had started his talk by saying, "In order to understand what is going on in political decision making in economic affairs, you must be either a cynic or a political scientist." Wildenmann said: "The banker was simply confused. . . . These are the kinds of things that political scientists should be able to explain and that deserve to be studied." Another colleague had said that economic policy was diminishing itself: "They have well-developed understanding of economic decision making." It was true, Wildenmann argued, that one of the great achievements in the social sciences was the development of the division of labor between the disciplines, but what was now lacking was any kind of encounter between them.

Stuart Bremer next introduced what he called some mundane considerations on the conditions favoring advances today in political science. He estimated that there were perhaps 25,000 political scientists in the world, with about 10,000 doing research, although more than 80 percent of their time was probably spent in teaching. That brought the total to a full-time equivalent of approximately 2,000 persons doing political science research; but he estimated that only half of this effort—"1,000 man-years per year of research"—had an orientation like the one Wildenmann was talking about, with empirical, sophisticated methods, contemporary approaches, and the rest. "Thus," he said,

> given the magnitude and the difficulty of the problems that political science has to deal with—all the way from why a small city in the United States decides to fluoridate its water or not, up to the level of what is going to happen in the Falkland Islands war tomorrow or next year—it is incredible that one could expect much to happen in political science, when in fact we devote so few resources to understanding this huge gigantic animal we call politics.

Bremer said that the resources that were invested in political science were minuscule compared to those in physics or chemistry. In political science his own situation, which enabled him to do full-time research, was an anomaly, whereas tens of thousands did full-time research in the natural sciences.

Careers and Support

Bremer explained that in calling these considerations mundane, he meant that one of the conditions that would favor advances in political science would occur when governments decided that the support of objective, empirically based research in this field would be desirable. He said: "But what we are seeing at the present time is, in fact, a contrary trend. Social science in the United States is suffering from disproportionate cuts in its funding, and the trends do not show signs of being reversed." When one talked about progress in any field, it had to come down ultimately to a willingness to invest resources in the development of that field.

Bremer said he did not believe that people who entered political science were less intelligent than those who enter physics, because he did not believe that intelligence was a criterion in such decisions. The real difference was that in political science there were no career advancement patterns. People were considered a little foolish to choose a career in political science because, Bremer said, "the likelihood of a career beyond your Ph.D. is very small." He was not saying this to denigrate all the fine intellectual notions that had been put forward so far; but he felt it was necessary to consider the practical questions as well, especially the question of the resources devoted to the field.

Wildenman took issue with these points. He agreed that the absolute numbers in the field were too small, but he claimed that the fraction of political scientists doing research—which he estimated as 1 in 60—was not unfavorable. The ratio between research and teaching in political science was perhaps not as small as in engineering. He noted that he had given a good deal of consideration to the allocation of funds within the field, both in England and in the European Science Foundation. He found that the ratio of total funds to research funds was approximately 9 to 1, which was in line with the prevailing ratio in the other social sciences.

Wildenmann suggested, however, that the problem of career patterns was a different kind of issue, although it varied between different countries. Nevertheless, he had long been preaching in the European consortium that political scientists had fallen into a *Schrebergarten.* He said that "it takes five years to get research groups together, to get them out of the *Schrebergarten.*" He referred to an interview he had had with Helmut Schmidt several years before. The chancellor, sitting at his desk behind piles of papers, literally threw Wildenmann's proposals on the desk. Schmidt asked: "What should I do with all that? They are filled with problems that are not my problems." Wildenmann said: "Of course they were not his problems, and they should not have been; but my point is that there is a deep gap between the output of political scientists and the political decision making of these people in the real world."

Wildenmann said he was not suggesting that political scientists take up problems like the student rebellions, but that they should at least be concerned with possible theoretical approaches to solving problems in society today. That was very different from studying concrete problems, as well as from basic research or blind research. It had to do with understanding the nature of contemporary political reality. Political science, however, would not find answers to these problems as long as it stayed in the *Schrebergarten*.

The small total number of political scientists was certainly a problem, Wildenmann said, but it was a problem that affected all the social sciences and the humanities: "We represent an analytic tradition in culture, and it is an important part of our culture. Unfortunately we cannot convince Ronald Reagan of that, or Helmut Schmidt, even though in the past he has shown some sympathy to such questions." Wildenmann noted that some German politicians refer to the political sciences as "the discussion sciences," as a form of rebuff. He believed that Bremer's point about the small numbers was not irrelevant for the development of political science, but that it could indicate the irrelevance of much political science to real problems.

Broader Need for Political Science

Daniel Bell intervened at this point to say that there was a risk of distortion in the way the discussion was progressing. The perspective being offered was narrow and almost misleading because its focus was on academic political scientists and their careers. If one thought about the world at large, a huge amount of political research was being conducted. In government, for example, the Central Intelligence Agency had hundreds of people doing research on politics. In Congress there were tremendous numbers of committees and subcommittees turning out studies of various kinds. Bell speculated that there was perhaps a study available on most any subject a scholar would want. Bell explained that he thought of these things just because he himself did very little research—he called himself a kind of piranha, feeding on others—but he said that he often found himself simply overwhelmed by material on almost any question he wanted.

Bell also thought that there were dozens of intelligent political commentators working today as journalists, such persons as Theodore White and David Broder in the United States, or Theo Sommer and Michael Naumann in Germany. To narrow the notion of the field just to academic

Klingemann, the last questioner, said that he was deeply dissatisfied because he had thought the group was supposed to discuss the conditions favoring major advances in social science, but all he saw was random hopping from very general problems to isolated points dealing with political science. He said that if what Bremer said was true, then we could adjourn and go home, because all we really needed was more money and more bright people. "That may indeed be the case," he commented, "but it still leaves us without any kind of model to work with." We had not systematically addressed the question, "What would our dream world look like if we had all the money we needed to work with?"

What We Know Now

Klingemann suggested that if our topic was to be major advances, we should ask straightforwardly: What is known today that people earlier did not know? He felt that there were several such things: an understanding of democracy and its breakdowns, which Eisenstadt had mentioned; or the behavior of mass publics. We knew more about mass psychology than was known, say, in the time of Freud. Methodological breakthroughs like the nationwide sample survey have helped scholars learn more about people's attitudes, and about social processes.

Klingemann felt that the place to focus the discussion was on how the breakthroughs occurred. Wildenmann had mentioned such a case in his talk, in the establishment of the Institute for Social Research and the Center for Political Studies at the University of Michigan. People had gone around to major universities looking for a place to establish a center. Once there was such a center, clever statisticians successfully applied area samplings to the entire United States. This made possible better predictions and attracted the further funds necessary to continue the research.

Klingemann's last point concerned the range of problems that could be handled: "If political science can process only a few problems at a time because of limited resources—and there will never be enough resources—then you have to anticipate problems." This requires a powerful body of theory; an example would be the Parsons, Bales, and Shils theory of the succession of investigative cycles. Given such a grand-scale theory, political scientists could anticipate problems that they thought were going to arise and have an impact on society. Political science and sociology had always tackled the problems occurring at the time, as in the case of Marx and his successors, or in the analyses resulting from the recent student rebellions, but in the future there would be ways to anticipate what was coming, as well.

CHAPTER 5

Advances in Economics: Perspectives and Conditions of Progress

W. Krelle

ECONOMICS AS A SCIENCE

THE CONCEPT *ECONOMICS* in the broader sense comprises the different branches of economics proper (economic theory, policy, public finance, and so on) as well as business administration, operations research, econometrics, and statistics (as far as it is concerned with economics problems or provides the mathematical instruments for economics). In this chapter we are mostly concerned with economics proper, but the basic statements also apply to the other branches of economics in the broader sense.

It is appropriate to start with some methodological remarks. What constitutes a major advance in economics is a matter of subjective judgment. Thus the general perspective of the author from whom these judgments are derived should be of interest to the reader.

The first aim of economics is to observe the facts and explain them. Observation is only the first step. Without explanation, the facts remain blind and do not help much in economic policy. Explanation is more than simple description or intuitive judgment and evaluation of the facts. *Explanation* means knowing and understanding the laws governing the human actions that yield the observed facts. These *basic laws* are general principles that are not explained by themselves but are accepted either because they are intuitively acceptable or (if one has no judgment on these grounds) because the consequences yield exactly or approximately the results that are observed. As an example, take the principle of utility maximization for households or that of profit maximization for firms.

Observations and explanations refer to phenomena that have to be well defined. The logical relations between these definitions must be known. It is not the least achievement of a science to produce a system of definitions that make it possible to observe and measure the corresponding facts in a consistent way and to explain them in the simplest way.

A system of definitions and of behavior relations that is derived from these laws constitutes the general framework for understanding the observed economics facts. This framework is now usually called a *model*. The laws or principles from which models are derived are usually called *economic theories*.

In principle, all models or theories should be tested by comparing them directly or indirectly (via their implications or their consequences) with reality—that is, with the observed facts. This, unfortunately, is not easy and is sometimes almost impossible because of a lack of data or difficulties in measurement. Theories or models that principally cannot be tested by reality (and hence may never be refuted by the facts) are useless and do not belong to science, at least not in economics. They may have a political value as an instrument to promote the coherence of a society, but this lies beyond the scope of economics.

The task of economics, however, is larger than mere description and explanation. Economics should also help to improve the economic performance of a society. In this respect it resembles more the science of engineering than, say, meteorology or astronomy, where one can only observe and perhaps forecast but not influence the events. Thus the optimization of the economic results are part of economics. In this respect, economics is a normative science. It tries to derive optimal rules or optimal decisions in an economic context either for individual households and firms or for society as a whole. Now the problem of a preference ordering of all possible outcomes arises. Does a consistent ordering or even a utility function exist that assigns a numerical value (often called *utility* or *degree of satisfaction*) to each possible state of the society? If this could be answered affirmatively for the individual, does a consistent preference ordering exist for a society as a whole? The answer to the latter question is, in general, no.[1] Thus the social organization decides on what is to be the social preference ordering for the society in question. Moreover, the preferences are not static: They change over time, both individually and socially.

Traditionally, economics has taken the preferences of individuals or of the society as a whole as given, assuming that other sciences (psychology, sociology, political science) should explain the formation of these preferences. In the last decade, however, economics has moved into this field also and has produced some useful results.

Remarks

The general principles (or axioms) of economics are not explained but are basic assumptions (or hypotheses), which may only be accepted or rejected in favor of others. This is where subjective judgments come in. Kuhn, Feyerabend, and others stress this point.[2] Fortunately, there is a broad range of accepted hypotheses in economics, but as always there is a dissenting group, mostly consisting of Marxists. This dissent seems to be more apparent than real, however; economists from Eastern countries use the same concepts and models for economic planning and decisions.

The subjectivity of Kuhn, Feyerabend, and others applies only to the basic general principles, not to the propositions that constitute the body of economic knowledge. These propositions that follow from the theory have to be tested against reality. If the test fails, one has to reject the model and (possibly) the whole theory and all principles from which the model has been derived—at least, if a better theory, which explains reality more satisfactorily, is available. In this respect one should follow Popper, although there is also a subjective element in his criterion of refutation of the theory.[3] The subject of economics is a stochastic system. By definition, there is no theory that could explain the stochastic term. Moreover, there is no measurement without error. Thus one cannot reject theory simply because one finds an observation that contradicts it. Only if there are too many contradictory observations does the theory have to be discarded. What is meant by too many, however? This question remains open.

The Vanguard of the Social Sciences

Compared to other social sciences, economics has the advantage that the basic concepts and the underlying principles of explanation are largely accepted both by the profession and by the public, and that the concepts are to a large extent measurable and currently documented in statistical yearbooks and other publications. This constitutes a large advantage over the other social sciences such as sociology and political science. The basic GNP definitions, such as consumption, investment, exports, imports, production, prices, exchange rates, and so on, as well as the basic economic agents such as households, firms, and public institutions are also broadly accepted—namely, preference orderings (utility functions), production possibility sets (production functions), budget constraints (or liquidity constraints), discounting of future results, and so on. Basically, all the concepts are measurable on the individual level.

This whole conceptual approach is rather similar to the basic approach in theoretical physics. In both sciences there are basic units that in their behavior (or actions) follow basic laws or principles (which may be stochastic). The interactions of these basic units and the results of these interactions are studied. Thus it is not surprising that somewhat similar mathematical systems are used to explain physical and economic facts.

This refers to the individual (or microeconomic) level. In order to be helpful for economic policy, however, one must go on to the macroeconomic level. Instead of individual households and firms, one must consider all households or firms as a group, and similarly for economic flows or stocks such as consumption, investment, or capital. Here the problems of index numbers and of aggregation come in. Up until now the transition from microeconomics to macroeconomics could be analyzed only in very simple and restrictive cases. The situation is similar to that in physics and in engineering science, where the statics of buildings cannot be derived directly from nuclear physics. Thus macroeconomics usually rests on more restrictive assumptions, such as the existence of a representative household or a representative firm, which are only approximately true. Therefore, one must be careful in applying these results to practical economic problems.

This is particularly true because in order to reach even the present situation, economics has had to "exogenize" all the facts that did not quite fit into the theoretical scheme sketched earlier or for which the basic concepts are not measurable. Until the end of the nineteenth century, sociology and political science were much more intimately connected with economics. Great economists such as Adam Smith, John Stuart Mill, Marx, Max Weber, and others, were great sociologists as well. The German historical school tried to preserve this intimate connection with sociology and political science. It essentially failed, however; no real progress in economics proper has come out of this type of universal approach. The Anglo-Saxon and Austrian or Walrasian type of approach to economics has proved much more appropriate and is now more or less universally accepted. This means that the institutional framework, as well as the formation of preferences and the information system, has largely been left outside of the analysis and has been taken as exogenous. In the words of Walter Eucken, it has been delegated to the *Datenkranz*.

Lately, however, there is some change of approach. Economics is moving into the field of organizational theory, especially team theory, and into information theory and other fields that have been left outside for almost a hundred years. The so-called new political economy is an effort in this direction, as in the works of Bruno Frey and Hibbs and Fassbender.[4] Information theory is becoming a new branch of economics. Thus it seems that a bridge to the neighboring social sciences is going to be built from economics.

Recent Advances in Economics

Following the substantial expansion of the GNP and the standard of living in the developed countries, there has been an expansion of the educational system in most of these countries, which in turn has led to an explosion of scientific work as documented in the number of publications.

In Germany, for example, the number of students at universities expanded from 658,000 to 1.044 million between 1972 and 1980; this is an expansion of 85.6 percent in seven years. The number of teachers of the university level expanded between 1972 and 1979 from 72,900 to 94,400 persons—a rate of expansion of 29.5 percent in seven years. In 1972, 14.6 percent of all persons from twenty to twenty-five years of age have been studying at universities. By 1980 the number was 23.2 percent, and it is still rising.[5] It is quite clear that many more publications come out of a larger body of professors and research workers. As a consequence, many new journals have been founded in the last decade: *European Economic Review,* 1969; *Journal of Mathematical Economics,* 1974; *Journal of Economic Theory,* 1968; *Mathematical Social Sciences,* 1981; *Journal of Policy Modelling,* 1979; and *Empirical Economics,* 1977. It becomes more and more difficult to keep informed on what is going on in the field of economics as a whole. Thus review journals have been founded, such as the *Journal of Economic Abstracts* and the *Journal of Economic Literature.* It seems to be urgent to reorganize the system of publications—for example in such a way that substantial progress should (as a rule) be published only in a few leading journals, whereas general, all-purpose articles may find an outlet in the bulk of the other journals. This is difficult to accomplish, of course.

Since many more people are now working in research in the field of economics, there are many small steps forward in different directions. They may be called epsilon steps or advances, where "epsilon" means an infinitesimal advance. Then there are major steps forward, which are delta-level advances. Here substantial progress has been made in an otherwise well-known field; the advance remains in the same field, however. There are very few real breakthroughs that open up new fields. It may even be that any breakthrough cannot be accomplished by one person or one publication alone, but rather requires a group of collaborating scholars. In this case the whole group should be credited for the progress.

Of course, it is sometimes difficult to judge whether some new idea only extends the limits of knowledge a bit or whether it opens up a new field. There are fashions in science as in other areas. Someone may take up an issue with some variation in the assumptions or some apparently new results, and a lot of followers will then rush into this field. After some time, however, it is seen that nothing really new comes out of all these efforts. So the interest in this field fades away, and nothing substantial is left. In what follows, my personal judgment is involved in distinguishing between these types of advances in economics.

Mathematization

An economist of the nineteenth century or of the first quarter of the twentieth, with very few exceptions, would not understand the leading economic journals of the present time. He would think he was reading a journal of mathematics where—just for fun—the mathematical symbols had acquired some economic names. There are still economists today who believe that the whole process of mathematization of economics is wrong-headed, but they are mistaken. Of course, sometimes one does find simple relations that are unnecessarily put into more scientific-looking equations. The editors of good journals, however, would not tolerate such a style. The reason for mathematization of economics is that mathematics, as the most developed part of logic, is able to extract more implications from a given set of assumptions than can the unarmed mind. Our intellect is able to follow chains of causality but not to see through the functioning of a network of interdependent relations. The essence of economics is the analysis of the interdependence of economic agents. Take the simplest example of an interdependent system: a linear system of two equations in two unknowns, such as

$$2x + 3y = 8$$
$$3x + 2y = 7$$

Very few people would guess the solution ($x = 1, y = 2$), and still fewer people would be able to guess what the effect will be of a change in one of the parameters. Suppose that the system changes

$$3x + 3y = 8$$
$$3x + 2y = 7$$

By this change, will x go up and y go down, or the other way around? (The new solution is: $x = 5/3; y = 1$).

Of course, the difficulties for the unaided intellect are much worse in the case of systems of many variables, nonlinear systems, or systems of differential or difference equations. Business cycles or long-term growth cannot be described or understood without the use of difference or differential equations, whether this is realized by the writers or not. Thus the mathematization of economics is an inevitable development, comparable to the mathematization of physics in the eighteenth century. There is no way back to the "old economics." This does not exclude the fact that in many cases the basic idea or the suppositions are nonmathematical and qualitative in nature. After all, mathematics is a tool. It takes intelligence and imagination to put the tool to the right use. Thus there is still room for nonmathematical economists in case they understand the current state of economics and therefore are able to develop new, fruitful ideas. Ideas and guesses, however, are not science. One must test whether they follow from well-established and generally accepted assumptions and whether they are compatible with the observed reality and with other facts that are logically related to them.

At first economics took mathematical instruments developed for physics or other sciences, especially linear algebra, differential equations, measure theory, topology, control theory, statistical test theory, and (nowadays) catastrophe theory. Today, however, mathematics itself has received in turn an important impact from economics. The theory of difference equations, methods of econometrics and of operations research, stochastic control theory, the theory of stochastic systems, and especially game theory are mostly developed by mathematical economists or mathematicians working in the field of economics or business administration. The methods of linear, nonlinear, stochastic, or integer programming have been developed with respect to their economic applications. The same is true for estimation and test procedures in econometrics. However, the outstanding example of the development of a new branch of mathematics is game theory. We shall return to this in the next section.

Looking from this point of view at the other social sciences, especially sociology and political science, one is inclined to think that these sciences, to a large extent, still have to develop a generally accepted framework of basic concepts that are (at least in principle) measurable, as well as a basic set of assumptions (or axioms) from which the relations between these concepts could be derived. There are many starting points in this direction; take, for instance, the theory of teams, the theory of the organization, theories of government behavior based on the expected outcome of elections, theories of voting behavior and of the development of the popularity of the government, and so on. This seems to be the right way to narrow the gap between economics and the other social sciences. After all, there is only one society; economic, social, and political relations are interwoven.

Thus let us hope that the process of mathematization can extend also into sociology and political science. This would greatly facilitate the unification of the social sciences.

Game Theory, a New Approach

Game theory, initiated by von Neumann and Morgenstern,[6] is an absolutely new approach. It takes into account the basic situation in social decision making: A person has to consider the reactions of other persons to his own decision, knowing that the other persons will do the same. The social action is always a decision vis-à-vis an intelligent partner or opponent—not vis-à-vis nature, which follows natural laws irrespective of human actions. Mathematics has largely been developed under the influence of physics. That means that (in the wording of game theory) only "games against nature" are considered.

Control theory and economic theory for fully competitive markets are of this kind. In the case of small numbers of interacting economic agents, however, this is not the right approach. Moreover, the possibility of forming coalitions in order to coordinate the strategies available for the different economic agents (called *players* in this context) has to be taken into account. Coalitions will form only if the distribution of the common profit among the different members of the coalitions is agreed on.

Game theory has developed quite a bit from the initial work of von Neumann and Morgenstern. New solution concepts have been developed, and different coalition structures and different assumptions about compensation payments among the members of a coalition, and about the information structure of the players, have been introduced. There are types of games where the solution concept is now generally accepted, especially in the case of zero-sum two-person games. For the case of noncooperative games (which are considered by von Neumann and Morgenstern only for the case of two-person games) the concept of the Cournot-Nash equilibrium point has been more and more accepted as a reasonable solution concept. Unfortunately, there are many such equilibrium points in general. Some of them may be in mixed strategies that are difficult to interpret in some cases. There is now a theory for selecting the "right" equilibrium point (the "tracing procedure," developed by Harsanyi and Selten).[7] Games with incomplete information have also been analyzed and solution concepts have been suggested.[8]

Von Neumann and Morgenstern also developed a rather convincing axiomatic system that allows the derivative of an optimal behavior under uncertainty. This *utility theory* has been accepted by the large majority of economists, but not by all of them. (Maurice Allais and others have raised some objections.[9])

Game theory has had an important impact on many branches of economics and other sciences. A whole school of ethics, started by Rawls, rests on the minimax principle of game theory.[10] There is also another approach in ethics stemming from another part of game theory, which may be called the *new utilitarianism*.[11]

There have been efforts to reformulate statistics on the basis of game theory, assuming that the problem of the statistician is a sort of a game against nature.[12] This is too pessimistic a view of nature, however; nature does not try to inflict the maximum loss on the statistician. Murphy's law, "What can go wrong will go wrong," is an exaggeration.

There are many applications of game theory in economics proper.

The main applications are oligopoly theory and bargaining theory, team theory, utility theory, and general equilibrium theory. The literature is too large to be quoted here. We will return to general equilibrium theory later on.

Econometrics

The basic idea of econometrics was introduced into economics when the Econometric Society was founded in 1930 by such eminent scholars as Irving Fisher, Divisia, Ragnar Frisch, Amoroso, Bowley, Schumpeter, and others. The basic idea is written in the constitution of the society:

> The Econometric Society is an international society for the advancement of economic theory in its relation to statistics and mathematics. . . . Its main object shall be to promote studies that aim at a unification of the theoretical-quantitative and the empirical-quantitative approach to economic problems and that are penetrated by constructive and rigorous thinking similar to that which has come to dominate in the natural sciences.

The development of econometrics was a success story. To put a theory into the framework of an econometric system is almost the general procedure now, at least in the macroeconomic context. Estimation methods, and tests for the identifiability and significance of the parameters have been developed and are currently applied more or less as a matter of course. The general approach that has been put forward in the famous Cowles Commission Monograph No. 14 is still untouched.[13] Understandably, however, the limitations of this approach are now much better understood than they were at that time. The method is now applied to large econometric systems simulating the functioning of a whole economy. The real tests of these systems are the forecasts they produced. Unfortunately, these forecasts are not very reliable. This shows that the basic approach has some weaknesses. These are mostly due to the assumptions that the theory from which the econometric system is derived is the right theory and that the economic variables can be observed without error.

There are ways out of these difficulties. The most radical would be to forget about all economic theory and to take the economic observations as stochastic time series. This Box-Jenkins-type time-series analysis has again become fashionable. In my opinion, however, this means throwing the baby out with the bathwater. Economic theory gives some guidance as to how the economic observations are related to each other, and to ignore this knowledge cannot be an optimal procedure. The results of the large-scale application of econometrics show that we have to introduce the forgotten variables (especially sociological and political ones)—possibly in the form of latent variables if there are no measurements as yet—and to assume that the parameters do change in time. This, of course, raises important difficulties in the estimations. Kalman filter techniques or other procedures might be more appropriate.

There are several tests of significance of estimations, which are used to test economic hypotheses. Unfortunately, the small sample characteristics of such tests are not known. Thus there are numerous open problems in econometrics. As a whole, however, econometrics is now an indispensable part of economics. It is more or less taken as a matter of course that assertions in economics are conjectures that must be tested against the observations. That is where econometrics comes in.

As already mentioned, the most advanced products of econometrics are econometric forecasting systems. Starting with the famous Klein-Goldberger model, they have developed into large-scale systems of several hundred or thousand equations, which are able to simulate the functioning of a national economy or even of the world economy as a whole. Input-output systems, though independently developed by Leontief and others, may be considered a special case of econometric systems. They are especially useful for short-term analysis of interindustry relations.

A special case are world models of the Forrester-Meadows type. They use system-analysis as an instrument. World models of this type do not belong to econometrics proper, however. They analyze the consequences of preconceived ideas under the restrictions of the systems-analysis philosophy. Their truth content is debatable. I do not think that this approach, as it is used now, could contribute much to economics.

General Equilibrium Theory

We now come to specific fields of economics that have been opened up in the last decades. Without any doubt, general equilibrium theory is one of these fields. It started with the famous Arrow-Debreu article of 1954 and with Debreu's *Theory of Value*.[14] The subject of this research is to make the "invisible hand" of Adam Smith visible. What does it really mean to say that the price system coordinates the independent actions of economic agents? Does a price system exist that simultaneously allows the clearing of all markets (full employment especially) and the maximization of the utility by all households (subject to budget constraints) and the maximization of profits by all firms (subject to technological constraints)? If such an equilibrium exists, does it have some features of optimality? Does the economic system find an equilibrium-point by itself? That is to say: Is the equilibrium, if it exists, stable? Is the equilibrium point unique, or are there many equilibrium points—perhaps infinitely many? Is it possible to find these equilibrium points computationally? Is there an equilibrium point if there are monopolies or oligopolies in the economy, and how are the optimality conditions influenced by these facts? Does an equilibrium exist in the case of uncertainty about the future and the case of different expectations on future prices and income?

These are the main problems that have been considered and partly solved in general equilibrium theory. The principal mathematical tools of analysis are topology, together with different fixed-point theorems. Thus this field requires a fundamental mathematical knowledge and is therefore confined to mathematical economics proper.

Results of this research are presented in the *Handbook of Mathematical Economics* and cannot be elaborated here.[15] There are numerous open problems, especially in relation to stability. That means that the dynamics of a general equilibrium system are largely unknown. The problems of imperfect knowledge and information transfer should also be examined. Thus the field is not at all explored. The remaining problems are very difficult ones. Game theory plays an important role. The cooperative concept of an equilibrium (all coalitions are allowed) depends on the game-theoretic concept of the core.[16]

Growth Theory

Growth theory really means *dynamic theory*. The bulk of economic theory is static. Despite some efforts by eminent scholars (Ricardo, Marx, Schumpeter, Harrod, Domar, and others) to dynamize economic theory, modern growth theory really started with the work of Solow, Meade, Phelps, von Weizsäcker, and others.[17] What came out of the common efforts of many scholars is now called *neoclassical growth theory*. It has branched out into many directions and is now generally accepted as an important contribution to the understanding of the growth process of the industrialized market economy. Technical progress, population growth, money, and foreign trade have been incorporated into the theory. Different sectors of the economy may be considered. Recently, exhaustible resources have been introduced. Growth with exhaustible resources has been one of the main fields of research in the last ten years. A starting point of the research in this area was the symposium on the economics of exhaustible resources.[18] There are many contributions in this field. The "state of the art" may be seen from the book of Dasgupta and Heal and from the conference of the Verein für Socialpolitik on "Erschöpfbare Ressourcen".[19] The main results of this research may be condensed in the proposition that even in the case of exhaustible resources there is a chance for humankind to survive and for the possibility of economic growth if savings (meaning capital accumulation) and the rate of technical progress (research and development) are large enough, and the rate of growth of the population is small enough. This contradicts the popular thesis of Meadows and others that humankind is doomed to extinction in a hundred or two hundred years if economic growth is continued.[20] The concept of growth theory that is used here comprises limits to growth, stagnation, and even decline as a special case. Environmental economics as well as developed economics is part of it.

I consider the fields of game theory, econometrics, general equilibrium theory, and growth theory as the main advances of economics in the last few decades. There are other fields of progress as well. Scholars working in these fields may find that their progress is at least as important as that in the fields mentioned herein. There is an important difference, however; the fields mentioned here have been newly opened up in recent decades and were virtually nonexistent before. That is not true for the following areas of economic research, which have been main fields of research for a long time. I consider the progress that has been made there more as the regular progress to be expected in each field of science if scholarship is continuing.

Monetarism

The new monetarism takes up the old problem of Ricardo ("The High Price of Bullion"), the controversy between the currency and the banking school in the nineteenth century, and the ideas of the quantity theory of money. The main problem is to clarify the transmission mechanism between the monetary system and the real system of the economy. The classical view, as condensed in Say's law, is that money does not matter in the sense that all real variables and all price ratios are determined in the real part of the economy. Only the absolute price level depends on the amount of money in circulation. Thus, in order to keep the price level constant, it is only necessary to control the amount of money. This has, at least in the long run, no influence on the real part of the economy, especially no influence on employment. This contradicts the Keynesian view that money does matter, at least in the short run. Patinkin showed that there is a contradiction in the classical dichotomy between the monetary and the real sector: An expansion of money would have a real effect by changing prices, which in turn change the real value of the monetary balances. According to Patinkin, this real balance effect is the link between the monetary and the real system. The size of this effect has been disputed, however. Besides, there are many other effects—for instance, speculative effects stemming from expectations of future changes of prices. The main promoters of modern monetarism (Milton Friedman, Brunner and Meltzer, and others) had an important influence on monetary policy in the United States, Germany, and other countries. From the point of view of economics, however, this is a further development of the ideas of the currency school, in opposition to Keynesian short-run economics.

Disequilibrium Analysis (Fixed-Price Models)

Starting in the late 1960s and the early 1970s with the works of Leijonhufvud, Barro and Grossman, Malinvaud, and others, there has been a rival of Keynesianism. The basic assumption of Keynes in his

General Theory—at least in the first twenty chapters of the book—is that prices and wages are fixed. The multiplier theory, as well as his recommendations of fiscal and monetary policy in order to cure unemployment, rests on this assumption. The modern disequilibrium theory spells out the implications of these assumptions. For instance, if the wage level is fixed in such a way that there is a surplus supply of labor (or, in the wording of this new disequilibrium theory, if the households are rationed on the labor market), their income will decline—that is, the former equilibrium prices on the commodity markets cannot stay the same. Thus there may be an oversupply of commodities on the goods market (that is, the producers are rationed on the commodity market). There might be different combinations of rationing on the different markets, where some agents may be rationed on one market and other agents may be rationed on other markets. From the outside, it is not easy to determine the real reason for this rationing—which prices are too high and which prices are too low.

The weakness of the theory is that prices are not explained but are taken as given. There is no adjustment process: Prices stay as they are. Thus the theory could be applied only to the very short run. It does not help very much in practice.

The Theory of Allocation

This is one of the oldest areas of economics and may be considered the core of static economics. Nevertheless, some important advances have been made in this field. These are mostly the result of a better understanding of the duality theory. The theory of the firm rests on the existence of a production function (this covers only the simplest case of a one-product firm, but it is not necessary to go into details here). This production function is defined on the *commodity space* (the space of the final product and of the factor inputs). Dual to this production function there is a cost function, defined on the *price space* (price of the final product and of the factor prices). Factor demand systems that are derived from production functions may also be derived from the dual cost functions (Shephard's lemma). Similarly, demand systems for households are derived from utility functions, which are defined on the commodity space. Dual to these utility functions are indirect utility functions, defined on the price space. The commodity demand systems of household demand may be derived either by maximizing utility under a budget constraint or by taking the derivatives of the indirect utility functions (Roy's identity). If the shape of the production function or of the utility function is not known, one may approximate these functions by Taylor expansions. The same may be done with the cost or the indirect utility functions. Thus approximate demand systems may be formulated that approximate the unknown real demand system.

All this refers to a single household or single firm, but in macroeconomics this approach will also be used for aggregates. There has been some progress made in weakening the assumptions necessary to guarantee the aggregation properties. Unfortunately, these conditions are rather restrictive. If one is willing to be content with approximations, however, this approach can be shown to be appropriate.

A very important part of allocation theory is the theory of income and wealth distribution. Substantial progress has been reached in these areas too, especially in the field of personal income distribution. The determinants of this distribution (natural gifts, family background, education, inheritance, etc.) have been analyzed and quantified. New measures of inequality have been developed and tested.

Information Theory and the Theory of Rational Expectations

Von Neumann and Morgenstern's *Game Theory and Economic Behavior* as well as the new approach of general equilibrium theory (Arrow et al.) induced a new interest in the problem of optimal behavior under uncertainty and utility theory. As pointed out earlier, von Neumann and Morgenstern developed an axiomatic system that yields rules of optimal behavior under uncertainty. The new approach in general equilibrium theory allowed dealing with economic decisions conditional on states of nature. Thus future markets conditional on these states are considered.

Information reduces uncertainty about the future. It changes the probability distribution of future states of nature. Information may be costfree but may also be costly. Thus the problem of the value, production, revelation, and spreading of information comes in. Jakob Marschak, Roy Radner, Stiglitz, Rothschild, and Jerry Green opened up the field of information theory dealing with these problems. The main ideas in this field may be sketched as follows.

A "message" changes the probability of a given future state of the economic environment (called *nature*). Usually, Bayes's theorem is used to determine this probability. This theorem asserts that the probability of a future state, given a certain message, equals the conditional probability of the message, given the state, times the unconditional probability of the state divided by the probability of the message. The utility connected with an economic action depends on this action and the probability distribution of the future states, given this message. The value of the message is the difference of the utility of the action that is connected with a new probability distribution and the action that would be realized otherwise. This "value of a message" is an *ex post* measure since it is generally unknown what the message would be before having it. In other words, as a rule, an information service may be available. It comprises a probability distribution of messages or a whole matrix of likelihoods of different messages. From this matrix the value of an information service is derived (Jakob Marschak, Roy Radner, and others). It is defined as the expected utility associated with the value of messages that may be procured by the information service (without taking into account the costs of the information). Some information services may be more informative than others. Some may be available without costs, some with costs.

It can be shown that the market system is efficient only in the case that a full set of complete contingent markets (also for information services) exists. Actually, the markets are incomplete.

Other fields connected with information are the production and the transfer of information (Machlup, von Weizsäcker, and Krelle). The patent system provides incentives for production of information in a market economy. Other research fields are the revelation of information (by advertising or signaling of different kinds, for example, as to the quality of the product); the economics of insurance (Karl Borch); and the problem whether market prices (for example, at the exchange) are able to transfer information on the situation of different firms from insiders who know this information to the uninformed public. Stiglitz and others showed that this is not the case. Hellwig in turn showed that information may be transferred if the price system reacts with a certain delay.

A related field is that of rational expectations (Muth 1961). The problem is whether it is possible to substitute calculations on the basis of current prices for future markets. Current economic decisions are based on the expectations of future prices. The idea of "rational expectations" is that the economic agents expect exactly that price system which will be realized in the future. This is possible if the economic agents know the functioning of the economic system and could therefore forecast the future economic development, contingent on their own actions now. Rational expectations are determined by solving this system for the future assuming that the expectations governing the current decisions are realized by the economic consequences of exactly these decisions. This approach allows us to avoid the problem of finding out how expectations are formed. Is this procedure justified? Errors and miscalculations are a common feature of reality. Thus it may be questioned whether this approach helps much in explaining the actual behavior.

Another related subject is the economics of education. Starting with the human capital approach of Becker and others and with the manpower approach, there has been substantial progress in this field. However, since (because of financial constraints) the expansion of the educational system has come to an end, the work in this field has also declined.

The New Political Economy

These ideas pick up the threads of eighteenth- and nineteenth-century economic thought. Formerly, economics, politics, and sociology formed a more or less coherent body of ideas. On the other hand, they grew out of modern economics, especially experience with econometric forecasting models, and of modern political science. The economists working in the field of applied economic theory, especially forecasting systems, realized that they had to forecast the economic decisions of the government as well in order to come up with reasonable forecasts for the economy as a whole. These decisions, however, depend on political situations that have not been taken into account. On the other hand, political decisions depend on the economic situation of the country. Thus political science was approaching economics from the other side. The "new political economy" as developed by Nordhaus, Bruno Frey, Hibbs, and many others tries to view macroeconomic performance, mass political support, and macroeconomic policy as an interdependent system of dynamic political-economic relationships. The economic-policy instruments of the government and of the central bank influence the economy, which "produces" employment (or unemployment), growth (or stagnation), and stable prices (or inflation). These economic variables influence the mass political support for the government (or for the opposition). The voting system transfers this mass political reaction to the government and enforces the government to react in the field of economics in order to stay in power. Of course, superimposed on this are shocks and systematic influences from the rest of the world; noneconomic considerations; and goals and institutional divisions of power (for example, between the government and the central bank) that make things much more complicated. It was possible to establish reaction functions of the government with respect to the main economic indicators and thus to explain the economic decisions of the government to a large extent.

Although this new approach is still in its infancy, it seems to be a very promising road, which may open up a whole new field and at the end yield a unified theory of politicoeconomic interrelationships.

The fields mentioned in the previous section are those where a sort of delta-progress may be reached. Of course, there are other fields in economics in which there has been progress as well. I should like to mention the portfolio theory (which is used to explain interest rates and capital flows), theories to determine flexible exchange rates, welfare theory, the theory of foreign trade. Thus one may continue. But I consider this the usual pattern of progress in science. There are new efforts under way in the economic theory of institutions and in the theory of competition. They may open up new fields, but it is too early to say so for sure.

Conditions of Progress

What are the reasons for this progress in economics? Where are the centers of this progress, and what should be done to continue this accumulation of knowledge? As far as I can see, the following points are most important.

It is generally true that young people learn faster and, as a rule, have more imaginative power than old ones. Thus it is necessary to bring young people as soon as possible to the frontiers of economic knowledge. The precondition for that is a good school system and a first-class university system. Nations without a good school system do not have much chance to contribute anything to the progress of science, although the natural intelligence of people living in these societies may be the same or even greater than that of other societies with a better school system. Of course, not all schools or universities in a nation need to be of the first quality with respect to education in science. However, there must be a broad base of fairly good schools and a certain number of first-class institutions and a good screening system, which selects the most able pupils at a rather early stage. A formal education at the highest possible level requires discipline and much work from young men and women and exerts some pressure on them. With growing standard of life, a resistance against this type of "elite education" builds up, which impedes further development to a certain extent. Yet it remains true that the contribution of the different nations to science is more or less proportional to the quality of the school and university system of the nation in question.

There is a probability distribution of natural gifts in all nations. Thus a large nation has a greater chance to produce first-class scientists than a smaller nation (given the same school and university system). Thus it is clear that the United States, Europe, and Japan as a whole contribute more to economic science than smaller regions or large nations with a less-developed educational system. There is also a "law of large numbers" in science. It is not fair to compare the outcome of economic research of, for example, Switzerland or Sweden with that of the United States.

Looking at history, it is easy to see that science moves to the center of political and economic power. This has predominantly economic reasons: Scientific research needs time and sometimes very expensive instruments or installations, which could only be procured by wealthy societies. As long as Europe was a center of power in the world, Europe was also a center of research, especially in economics. When power shifted to the United States and (at least economic power) to the Far East, especially to Japan, the centers of research moved to these regions as well. Thus the contributions of the United States to economics became more and more important in this century. Shortly after World War II the United States became *the* international center of economic research. After the rebuilding of Europe and Japan, these regions worked hard to close the gap between them and the U.S. state of the art. This goal has been reached more or less. There have been substantial contributions to economic knowledge from Western Europe and Japan in the last few decades. Eastern Europe and the USSR still lag behind in economics as a science.

There are historical reasons why economic research is centered in some universities and institutions in the United States, Europe, and Japan.

There must be a "critical mass" of scholars of high standing within an institution to attract able collaborators and to form a center of research. Moreover, there must be a compulsion or moral obligation to do research and to withstand competition from other centers. The incentives of an inspiring scientific environment induce economic research that otherwise would have not been accomplished. Connections to other centers, mutual impulses, and criticism are indispensable. As a whole, these centers stay at the same institution for a very long time, but their relative importance changes with the leading members. New institutions have a good chance to emerge if several leading personalities in a special field move in and establish a new center of research.

Some Consequences for Germany

Germany has expanded its high school and university system substantially during the last two decades. Twenty years ago only about 5% of young men and women in a given age bracket went to the university. This corresponded almost exactly to the number of so-called academic positions in the society. Now almost 25 percent of an age class come to the university. Many new universities and so-called *Gesamthochschulen* were founded, and the old universities were substantially expanded. This destroyed the equivalence between the educational and professional system as far as the number of students and academic positions was concerned, but it made it also more difficult to maintain a high standard of learning and research. The policy of the state governments, especially in the states with a social democratic government, was to keep all universities and *Gesamthochschulen* at the same level. This was not possible, however, since there are fewer gifted scholars who are able to do research and teaching at a very high level and fewer students who are interested. Moreover, there is not enough money to finance research at the highest level at each university. Thus the problem of diversification of the university system becomes urgent. The majority of the universities, especially the *Gesamthochschulen*, must concentrate on teaching and research that is related to the future opportunities of the majority of the students. This majority will never reach the academic positions of former times. They have to squeeze into the middle positions in the private economy or in government, which were occupied by less well-educated persons in the past. It is difficult to accomplish this diversification in practice. Which university should have the privilege of getting first-class professors and selecting the best students? All universities are public in Germany, and a democratic government has some difficulty in stating openly that some universities should be put in a better position than others. Nevertheless, this has to be done.

Frontiers of Research

As I see it, the frontiers of research in economics should lie in the following fields.

First, dynamic formulation. The bulk of economic theory is static. Growth theory and business cycle theory have been the main dynamic fields in economics until now, but the dynamic formulation has to be extended to all other fields of economics. Not only the asymptotic equilibrium state but also the transitory states—the time shape of adjustments to changes in the exogenous variables—must be analyzed. This is a difficult task. No one has really seen until now a way to do it. There are some successful examples, however, especially in growth theory, which may serve as a guideline for other fields as well.

Second, the introduction of new economic variables. Substantial progress in economics may be reached if social and political repercussions can be taken into account. Although the social, political, and economic systems of a society form a coherent general system, to model the connections between the social and political side of the society and the economic side means to model mental or personal attitudes and organizational structures. This is very difficult. The introduction of latent variables may help, but this might also be only a transitory state. The basic concepts of sociology and political science must be defined in such a way that they can be measured and connected to the economic system. This seems to be a task for a century of research, but nevertheless one has to start.

Next, the development of a theory of social institutions. There are some attempts at this—for example, in the theory of teams (Jakob Marschak and Roy Radner and others), but this does not seem to be the final word. Connected with a theory of institutions there must be a further development of the theory of information and valuation, because information and valuation are produced and transferred by institutions, and the institutions rest on information and valuation as well as on technology. This is also a very ambitious task. It will keep economists and other scientists busy for the next fifty years or so.

Finally, a new econometrics. In the long run, there is only as much progress in a science as there is measurement. There are many different times series in social sciences, partly of an economic and partly of a social and political nature. To use this information in order to test hypotheses and implement theories, one needs a well-established econometric science. Unfortunately, the small-sample characteristics of distributions are almost unknown, and there are very few and not very well developed methods to deal with variable coefficients and latent variables (the Kalman filter technique and Herman Wold's partial least-squares approach are two of them). Errors in the variables could be treated appropriately until now. The lag structure of the system must be fixed before the economic estimation, and so on. Economics also depends on econometrics in order to filter the information out of time series. The goal is to have the reality explained and influenced by human actions in an optimal way.

It is not always easy to do research on such new ideas or to apply them. In Germany, there is a special problem with the actual application of economics in practice. The ministries and other public institutions are rather critical about any immediate application of economic theory to economic policy. This means that economic research does not get much incentive from the government. It also takes more time than it does in the United States before a new method or a new theory is applied in government. There is a more conservative spirit in the administration than there is in the United States. It is hoped this will change after a while as the better-educated students come into the higher ranks of the hierarchy.

On the world scale, economics has done quite well in the last decades. It was somehow a great time for economics. Now we are at a point where new impulses must come in and new ideas must be put forward, in order to keep the same rate of growth of knowledge in the next few decades as we have had in the past.

References

1. K. J. Arrow, *Social Choice and Individual Values* (New York: John Wiley, 1951).
2. T. S. Kuhn, *The Structure of Scientific Revolutions,* 2nd ed. (Chicago: 1970); P. Feyerabend, *Erkenntnis für freie Menschen* (Frankfurt: 1980).
3. K. Popper, *The Logic of Scientific Discovery* (New York: Basic Books, 1959).
4. B. Frey, *Modern Political Economy* (London: Oxford University Press, 1978); D. A. Hibbs and H. Fassbender, *Contemporary Political Economy* (Amsterdam and New York: Oxford University Press, 1981).
5. Figures calculated from *Statistisches Jahrbuch 1981 für die Bundesrepublik Deutschland,* pp. 59, 341.
6. J. von Neumann and O. Morgenstern, *Theory of Games and Economic Behavior* (Princeton: Princeton University Press, 1944).
7. See, for example, J. C. Harsanyi, *The Tracing Procedure,* Working Paper No. 15, Institute of Mathematical Economics, Universität Bielefeld, May 1974.
8. See, for example, J. C. Harsanyi, "Games with Incomplete Information Played by 'Bayesian' Players," *Management Science,* November 1967, January 1968, March 1968.
9. See W. Krelle, *Präferenz- und Entscheidungstheorie* (Tübingen: 1968),

Ch. 6, pp. 171ff.; and M. Allais, "Fréquence, Probabilité et Hazard," Manuscript, Centre d'Analyse Économique, Centre National de la Recherche Scientifique, Paris, February 1982.

10. J. Rawls, *A Theory of Justice* (Cambridge, Mass.: Harvard University Press, 1971).
11. See, for instance, D. Höffe, *Einführung in die utilitaristische Ethik* (Munich: 1975).
12. A. Wald, *Statistical Decision Functions* (New York: 1950).
13. W. C. Hood and T. C. Koopmans, eds., *Studies in Econometric Method* (New York and London: 1953).
14. K. J. Arrow and G. Debreu, "Existence of Equilibrium for a Competitive Economy," *Econometrica 22*(1954): 265ff; G. Debreu, *Theory of Value* (New York: John Wiley, 1959).
15. K. J. Arrow and M. D. Intriligator, ed., *Handbook of Mathematical Economics* (Amsterdam and New York: Oxford University Press, 1982).
16. See, for example, W. Hildenbrand, *Core and Equilibria of a Large Economy* (Princeton: Princeton University Press, 1974).
17. R. M. Solow, "A Contribution to the Theory of Economic Growth," *Quarterly Journal of Economics 70*(1956); J. E. Meade, *A Neoclassical Theory of Economic Growth* (London: 1961); E. Phelps, "The Golden Rule of Accumulation: A Fable for Growthmen," *American Economic Review 51*(1961); C. C. von Weizsäcker, *Wachstum, Zins ünd optimale Investitionsquote* (Tübingen: 1962).
18. "Symposium on the Economics of Exhaustible Resources," *Review of Economic Studies* (1974).
19. P. S. Dasgupta and G. M. Heal, *Economic Theory of Exhaustible Resources* (Cambridge: 1979); H. Sieberg, ed., *Erschöpfbare Ressourcen, Verhandlungen auf der Arbeitstagung des Vereins für Socialpolitik in Mannheim 1979* (Berlin: 1980).
20. D. Meadows et al., *Limits to Growth* (New York: Universe Books, 1972).

CHAPTER 6

Recent Innovations in Economic Science

Jan Tinbergen

WHAT IS SCIENCE? WHAT IS IMPORTANT?

THIS CHAPTER ATTEMPTS TO IDENTIFY scientific innovations in economics. In order to avoid misunderstandings on the difference between innovations in the economies of the world and in economic science, the essence of scientific activity is briefly summarized. The latter consists of a succession of bits of new theory and empirical checks of such innovative ideas. Checking may reveal falsification (with a margin of tolerance). This induces a change of the theory, which will again be checked. If not falsified, the additional element of theory constitutes a possible new insight. Possible, but not necessary—an alternative theory may exist that is not falsified either. Autonomous criteria may help to select the theory adhered to. (For example, Einstein did not like stochastic theories of physics.) Theories may also have to be changed because of the discovery of new facts (for example, stagflation). Thus there are three sources of scientific innovations: new facts, alternative new theories, and a new criterion for choosing among alternative theories.

Only important innovations in economic theory are to be discussed in this report. So we need another criterion—namely, one telling us what is important. This is even more subjective. This section presents the author's subjective ordering of a number of world problems according to the urgency of their resolution. They are: (1) avoiding a great war; (2) ending starvation in the Third World; (3) stopping the moral degeneration of the First World (violence against innocent people, addiction to drugs, vandalism, etc.); (4) organizing a recovery and reducing inflation; (5) developing safer forms of energy; (6) stopping the deterioration of the environment; (7) controlling the carbon dioxide content of the atmosphere; (8) reducing welfare inequality everywhere. This list is incomplete. The items listed are related to economic science in very different ways. Taking into consideration the degree of relevance of economics to these urgent problems, the following survey of recent developments in economics will go into considerably more detail, to enable the reader to make her or his own choice of important innovations.

Short-Term Economic Modeling

Economic models are the principal though not the only technique of economic science. A large variety of models have been elaborated since World War II. Because of the multiple purposes they try to serve, it is difficult to establish a system of discussing them. In this section the emphasis will be on models for short-term movements (up to about five years). The next section will deal with longer-term models, with an emphasis on quantitative policies. Later sections are devoted to antistagflation policies and to qualitative issues (social order). Some topics have been allocated arbitrarily to one of these sections. Models for Third World development policies are dealt with in the section on longer-term models.

Improvements and Generalizations of Traditional Models

Texts to be recommended as a background are Fox et al. (1966) and Stone (1981).[1] A remarkably successful attempt to establish a consumption function (at constant prices), using permanent income, transient income, and wealth as independent variables, is shown in one of Stone's equations (Number 10.2), with *t*-values from about 10 to 20, $R^2 = 0.999$, and $DW = 1.91$. It is one of the 759 stochastic equations in a model with 2,759 equations and endogenous variables and 794 policy instruments. This equation illustrates the advances made in model building for short-term policy use in developed countries; it is part of the Cambridge (England)

[1](The references given in full are restricted to the tentative list of innovative publications at the end of the chapter.)

multisectoral dynamic model (MDM). The American Brookings model plays a comparable role for the United States, although the number of variables is less ambitious. In a 1975 publication (Fromm and Klein 1975), Waelbroeck gives a survey of thirteen other country models. The most recently published model for the Netherlands is discussed in Driehuis (1972). For the present discussion of the "monetarist counterrevolution"—to quote Tobin (1981)—it is appropriate to cite Klein (1975, p. 28): "It is less important that the effort [of building the MPS Brookings model] be labeled Keynesian, monetarist, neoclassical or anything else than that we get good approximation to explanation of this complete system. . . ." This is also the gist of the discussion on this subject in *The Economic Journal*, Vol. 91 (1981), pp. 1–57. In other words, if the Keynesian revolution is the thesis and the monetarist counterrevolution the antithesis, then the scientific way out must be a synthesis. As for the concept of rational expectations being expectations based on knowledge of the operation of a complete model, H. A. Simon produced a very realistic answer: Most agents can only grasp a finite number of steps in the economic game.

Apart from adding variables in order to improve traditional models, we may speak of generalizations through the addition of new dimensions. Relevant examples are the addition of *spatial* elements (Isard, Bos, Mennes, Waardenburg, Paelinck, Klaassen); of the *informal* sector (Gershuny 1979; Feige 1980) and the related subject of *tax-evasion* estimation (Frank, 1977 and after); of *education* (especially the formal part, *schooling*); of the *military* and *electoral* aspects (Deutsch, Bremer, Cusack, Eberwein, Sonntag, Ward, Widmaier); and of some *social* elements, in particular income distribution. These generalizations are highly relevant, although often they have been neglected for lack of data, a poor excuse. Another common excuse is that they do not belong to the subject of economic science. The inclusion of these elements must be based on their importance and not on the artificial frontiers between traditionally defined sciences. This is all the more realistic as we concomitantly witness the growing interdisciplinary character of research and also an increasing degree of overlapping, owing to the fact that all sciences are expanding their areas of activity for the reasons mentioned. This interdisciplinary integration constitutes one of the major innovations. (It also takes the form of applying economic techniques in political science.)

Further clarification is due to one concept or definition that is often used: the expression *social* is employed in a number of different senses, especially when social *accounts* are being presented as something similar to economic accounting. A social-accounting matrix is sometimes provided to record demographic transitions between age groups; sometimes, to record schooling transitions between student cohorts. A more profound deviation from conventional economic subjects is indicated by the psychologist Barker, who proposes to include in the analysis all activities—called *settings*—including those performed in leisure time. Moreover, the way to measure these settings is by the time spent on them. In essence, this amounts to a *time budget* alongside the economic spending (or *household*) budgets. This is an innovation worth mentioning since all settings now have to satisfy two restrictions and, accordingly, optimum conditions involve two Lagrange multipliers. Gallais-Hammono (1972) provides data on this subject.

Nontraditional Models

Not only equations but also inequalities must be taken into account: Many variables cannot, for instance, be negative. There are also other limits on economic variables. For some time this has been overlooked by economists. Linear programming is the simplest way to take care of this necessary element. After eliminating as many variables as there are equations, we are left with a smaller number of them. In their space, the inequalities define *prohibited regions*. If that space appears to be totally prohibited, no solution to the problem exists. In other cases a *feasible space* (in a two-dimensional space, a *feasible area*) may remain. This makes it possible to apply an objective function and find the optimal solution within the feasible space. This method has been used by Cohen (1978) and by Van Ginneken (1980) to investigate and compare differing power structures. In an economy where power is in the hands of landowners, the objective function may be to maximize their incomes. In an economy where power is in the hands of some groups of employers and employees, their total income may be the objective. Both authors elaborate interesting examples of the consequences.

Another feature not considered by traditional models is the existence of *more than one policymaker* (the government)—for instance, various ministries with different objective functions. In solving a policy problem, an activity called *compromising* (Nijkamp 1980) enters the arena; it is similar to Cournot's theory of duopoly or, more generally, to the theory of games (Morgenstern and Von Neumann). The game strategies used can be chosen out of a variety of strategies and constitute a new area of econometric research. Data on the consecutive steps taken by each of the negotiators are needed for such research. If Morgenstern complains that so little attention has been given to the theory, this is due to the lack of such data.

A last example of a nontraditional modeling feature concerns the question of how to make explicit a policymaker's objective (or social welfare) function. Frisch applied interviews of policymakers; Nijkamp and Spronk (1979) replaced the interview by introducing "interactive decision making," which may be described as a dialogue between policymakers and their consultants. Policymakers are better able to judge alternative (numerical) sets of the variables in their objective function; and so, by iteration, the optimal set can be approached.

Production functions, an important set of relations in any model, will be discussed in a later section.

Developments in Long-Term Modeling

Types of Growth

The model building to be discussed in this section may refer to developed as well as developing economies. In both cases the models aim at providing a general orientation on short-term policies. So far, long-term aims have included some form of growth as an important feature. The debate has gradually been extended to include various types of growth. In a very original way, Kornai (1972) introduces the concept of *rush growth* as opposed to *harmonic*, or *balanced* growth. The latter characterizes a growth path composed of equilibrium situations, in principle for all markets and government interventions. The concept of *unbalanced* growth has also been used by some authors and has caused some confusion. Whereas balanced growth can be defined with the desired degree of precision, unbalanced growth, taken literally, would be all other growth and hence needs restriction in order to be exact. In fact, the authors who used the term saw it as a means rather than an end; it was meant to evoke a response (from the private sector) so as to obtain balanced growth. Recently a *slow-growth* concept has evolved (to be discussed later) as an answer to the "limits to growth" (Meadows et al. 1972; Mesarović and Pestel 1974).

Developed and Developing Economies

In a way, the aim of the development policies of underdeveloped countries is to attain the condition of welfare or well-being of developed countries, or at least some features of that condition—the absence of starvation at a minimum. Ideally, long-term models should reflect the complete process from the most primitive initial situation—seen by many historians as the "natural" way of life (with many cruelties of nature as components)—to a situation of fully unfolded human capabilities. In that sense, long-term modeling constitutes a tremendous challenge to scientists. Only modest parts of it have been met so far.

The primitive living conditions that prevail in many nations are expressed in various shortcomings denoted by experts in development modeling, with Myrdal (1968, 1970) as the most meticulous observer. It is his observation that underdevelopment shows up in a "soft state," one that is technically unable to meet the challenges facing it. Some aspects of the *power structure* in most developing countries have been discussed. The existence of an *informal sector* is most pronounced in these countries.

Gradually, Western model builders have learned to distinguish the groups most in need of assistance. Accordingly, *land reform*, representing the elimination of big land holdings, has been almost unanimously accepted as the most urgent reform by all consultants. Irma Adelman (1978) has given the most constructive shape to this reform. Adelman and Cynthia Taft Morris together (1967, 1973) have also made innovative interdisciplinary contributions toward understanding the problems of developing countries.

One of the principal factors contributing to the development process of both developed and underdeveloped economies is technology, closely connected with capital formation. A common distinction is made between embodied and disembodied technological change. The former is manifest in machines and other equipment of changing shape; the latter stems from a better organization of the production process. Whereas in the 1950s attention was given to the relations between capital, labor, and technology in developing countries (compare, for instance, Verdoorn 1959), during the last two decades interest has shifted to the differences in technology between developed and developing countries. In conjunction with the theory of international trade, to be taken up later, there was much debate over the *appropriate* or *optimal technology* for developing countries, with a good deal of emphasis on the need for more labor-intensive or simpler technologies in developing countries. Considerable empirical work was accomplished by Boon (1964 and later) as an independent scientist and by at least one of the transnational corporations (Philips N.V., Netherlands), which have often, and not without justification, been criticized for introducing overly capital-intensive technologies in developing countries.

The links between developed and developing countries are those of trade and finance. Let us now turn to trade.

International Trade

This issue is one of the important chapters of economic science. Many contributions have been made by Samuelson, who further developed the Heckscher-Ohlin principle that the optimal production and trade pattern of a group of countries is the one that as fully as possible uses the production factors with which each country is endowed. Put simply, this boils down to saying that labor-intensive products should be produced by the Third World and capital-intensive products by the developed countries. Among other things, Samuelson carefully classifies cases of total or only partial specialization, according to the number of factors, of products, and of countries.

Many of the theoretical models, however, do not pay attention to a certain category of products, namely the *nontradables*. These are products that, for physical or other reasons, cannot be transported from one country or even one location to another. Buildings are a clear example, but a large number of services are also nontradables. A crude estimate shows that roughly one-half of the national product consists of nontradables. This has some important consequences for economic policy. In order to eliminate a balance-of-payments deficit, imports must be reduced or exports expanded. The remedy is to reduce the national consumption of tradables, but a reduction in the consumption of nontradables does not make sense. This has been overlooked in some advice to countries suffering from a balance-of-payments deficit. In order to clarify the implications of the existence of nontradables, the so-called *semi-input-output method* has been developed at Rotterdam University (Kuyvenhoven 1978).

For practical purposes, models are needed that include the production of nontradables. This implies that a more realistic picture of international cooperation may be obtained by linking national models. Interesting work in this field has been done by Mosak and a number of authors whose work has been edited by Waelbroeck (1976).

Techniques of Long-Term Planning

Models composed of a large number of variables are not only difficult to construct, but also difficult to understand. Both aspects can be remedied by a technique known as *planning in stages,* which is a method of successive approximations, well known in mathematics. Frequently, three stages are introduced, called the macro, the meso, and the micro stage. They can be applied to economic aspects as well as to geographical or space aspects. *Macroeconomic* aspects deal with variables aggregated over sectors and households, as well as over the surface of the nation. *Mesoeconomic* variables deal with sectors such as industries, and *microeconomic* variables with projects—often units financed by, say, a World Bank loan. *Mesogeographical* variables deal with relatively large areas—in a country like India, maybe the states. *Microgeographic* variables may deal with big cities or with one valley. There are many choices to be made, and as a rule one criterion is some sort of homogeneity of the units at the meso or the micro level. Often it will also be advisable to let the subdivisions coincide with the structures of lower public authorities or private business. The actual planning *procedure* may be organized *in line with the stages.* A first procedural step may be a proposal of the central planning agency to those involved in sectoral or state planning. The latter may propose amendments to the first setup, and negotiations will be organized in order to agree on the sector or state framework. This may be repeated at the micro level. Sometimes ad hoc connections may come into play—if, for instance, some industry has factories in three states only.

An important role is assumed by *projects* and their appraisal. In principle, each project should contribute optimally to the development of the economy. This means that of all available projects, those should be selected that make the largest contribution to future national income per unit of capital invested. An innovation in project appraisal was made by Helmers (1979) in order to include *income distribution appraisal.*

Sector planning may be said to imply choice of the sectors to be developed. It is here that comparative advantages, as defined in the theory of international trade, are the guiding principle. Ideally, the allocation of activities over countries (or countries over activities) should be based on a worldwide exercise. Actual planning may take place at the national level, considering world market prices as if they were not distorted by other nations' policies. Agriculture may be the best example of worldwide sector planning. Not only the Food and Agricultural Organization of the United Nations (FAO) but also the universities have made efforts in this area. The initiative of the Club of Rome has led to the impressive Model of International Relations in Agriculture (MOIRA) by Linnemann et al. (1979).

Education, Human Capital

Schooling, Development, and Human Capital

Parallel to the development of technology and the growing complexity of production processes, the importance of *learning processes* has increased. This implies a growing importance of education in the economy. On the one hand, the full unfolding of the individual personality is a source of demand for schooling ("social demand"), constituting the consumptive aspect of education. On the other hand, because of its impact on ability, productivity, and income, the demand for schooling can be seen as an *investment,* whose relative importance has risen.

This viewpoint prompted the human capital concept introduced by Mincer (1957), Becker (1964), Schultz (1963) and others. The process of investment in education induces a rise in income, and it is possible to calculate the rate of return on such investment. Income need not only be money income but may also be *psychic income*—that is, the satisfaction derived from one's occupation. For society as a whole, investments in physical and in human capital are alternative uses of investible funds. For the individual, the process of investment in human capital will stop at the point where the rate of private return falls below the interest rate on the capital market to which he or she has access.

In the preceding paragraphs, two types of learning processes were included, often called *formal* and *informal.* Formal education takes place in institutions such as schools and, in a number of countries, with the aid of *apprenticeship contracts* between pupils and the organizers of production. Informal education takes place in the family, in the environment where the family lives, and during the process of on-the-job training to the extent that no apprenticeship contracts have been concluded.

Investment in human capital consists of expenditure on education. For the individual, these costs include payments to the school, payment for books and other materials, and the cost of living. The amount of any scholarship must be deducted to arrive at the *private* costs of education. *Social* costs are those of the production factors involved (the teachers and the equipment—schools and books subsumed under the private costs) plus production foregone as a consequence of the learning process. This item consists of the value that the student would have produced if she or he had chosen to work instead of learning. For students below the termination of obligatory schooling, this alternative does not apply; hence there is no production foregone.

Genetic versus Learnable Capabilities

Whereas capabilities can, to a considerable degree, be acquired by schooling and on-the-job training, a certain portion is considered *innate*—that is, determined by *genetic* (inherited) factors. This problem has long been formulated in terms of the question of which part of the variance in IQ is inherited, and the answer given by a number of psychologists was: ca. 0.8. The answer is important since it suggests that the scarcity of some relevant capabilities (IQ and Lydall's factor *D*, for drive or dynamism) can hardly be changed by giving more disadvantaged students access to schooling. As a corollary, income inequality could be affected only within narrow limits. This opinion is not generally shared, however, and Goldberger has shown that the empirical material used is partly the product of scientific fraud.

Empirical Evidence

Industries show considerable differences in capital intensity, as was discussed earlier. This applies not only to physical capital but also to human capital. One may even note a certain parallelism: High physical capital intensity demands more skill on the part of the labor force. Sattinger (1980) sees a *comparative advantage* for highly skilled personnel to operate heavy equipment. It is not certain that automation as it is now developing will continue that trend.

The roles played by genetic factors and schooling have been the subject of extensive research using *path analysis*, a technique very similar to econometric models but applied some twenty years earlier. Well-known examples are the research by Jencks et al. (1972) for the United States, Bulcock et al. (1974) for Sweden, Psacharopoulos (1977) for the United Kingdom, and Dronkers and De Jong (1979) for the Netherlands. Although these and some related investigations have furthered our understanding of econometric models extended into the realm of education, their contribution toward singling out genetic factors is limited: They cannot explain differences between children of the same parents. A more promising approach to this question is research on *monozygotic twins* (Taubman, in Behrman et al. 1980). This form of research considers the abilities and occupations of twins brought up in differing environments, including differing schooling. It appears that schooling differences have less impact on success than previous research had suggested, presumably because schooling is correlated with genetic data. Taubman's results, however, may underestimate what can be achieved through more creative and imaginative schooling processes; the twins considered were presumably educated in schools with less qualitative differences than the extremes in teaching methods and curricula already in existence, not to mention what future inventive educators may introduce.

In recent decades, as will be discussed later, schooling has contributed toward reducing inequalities in income and occupational status. Lately, however, new factors have developed in the United States and Europe that threaten the continuation of this trend. A considerable decline in student motivation and perhaps also in the quality of teachers counteracts the hopes for the future. Sociologists, psychologists, and criminologists are working hard to analyze this new trend, which may well be called a *cultural crisis*.

How to Get Rid of Stagflation?

Aims and Means at the National Level

Most of today's governments strive to eliminate the two joint diseases of *stagnation* and *inflation* by applying a national policy—in contradistinction to an international effort, such as will be discussed later. Some governments give priority to reducing inflation. In addition to the monetarist-oriented Anglo-Saxon countries, the Federal Republic of Germany has opted for this priority, presumably because of the 1922–1923 hyperinflation trauma. Other governments, such as the French and, it seems, the Austrian, give first priority—rightly so, in my opinion—to a recovery of production and employment.

In an attempt to identify the means of an anti-stagflation policy, it is not a necessary precondition to know the causes of the disease. Causes that cannot be altered are not interesting since their elimination is not feasible. Only eliminable causes and other feasible means are relevant to define a policy; the impact of possible "other means" must, of course, be investigated. This confronts us with the Friedman-Keynes controversy, mentioned earlier. The monetarist preference for using only the stock of money M as the instrument for reducing inflation seems oversimplified. An argument sometimes cited in its favor is that M is the main determinant of money income Y, itself equal to yp, where y is real income and p is the price level. It is furthermore suggested that changes in M primarily induce changes in p.

The following comments seem justified: The situation in different sectors or industries is not uniform. Sectors operating at full capacity will be subject to price rises if M is expanded. Here, in fact, mainly p will change. For sectors operating below capacity, increases in y, in the volume of production, and after a while in employment are more likely and, in any case, feasible. These comments imply that a *mixture of monetarist and Keynesian* policies may be warranted. The purely monetarist policy of using solely M and relying on the so-called free forces of the market is too simple and presumably is based on an ideological aversion to government intervention. A policy pursuing more than one aim has to use a corresponding number of instruments. I myself prefer an increase of the flow of money, rather than a change in stock, combined with an *incomes policy*. In a set of polls, as Hibbs (1982) tells us, the general public showed preference for price and income controls (a study by the NBER). One wonders why Lerner's (1980) and Colander's proposal (1980) for a market anti-inflation policy (MAP) has not been supported or at least discussed more intensively by monetarists.

A relevant argument in favor of a permanent incomes policy is the structural change we have experienced during the last decades—namely, the virtually complete "unionization" of the economy. Unions started with worker unions. Today we have unions for all socioeconomic groups: industrialists, farmers, small entrepreneurs, higher-level personnel, and many free professions. This generalization of the pressure-group phenomenon requires an answer, and I see no other instrument to counter this process than an incomes policy, except perhaps MAP.

Empirical Evidence and New Models

There is hardly any empirical evidence available on instruments for ending stagflation, simply because stagflation itself is a novel experience. We can draw on past experience with previous periods of inflation and how they were brought under control. Four of them were the subject of a study by Sargent (NBER 1982). It is correct that their termination partially corroborates the "rational expectations" theory, but in the periods considered (one of them being Germany in 1923–1924), the situation was much simpler than it is today—so different that these past experiences cannot be expected to provide much help in designing optimal policies for today.

Today's model builders are manifestly involved in attempts to adjust their models to present problems. The spirit in which this is being done, as discussed earlier, seems the best guarantee for arriving at a satisfactory answer. In a sense, we are in the process of one of the biggest experiments ever organized—the policy changes in the United States and the United Kingdom. However, the unemployment figures of these two countries are not very convincing evidence in favor of their policies.

Some commentators expect changes for the better from a new wave of technological innovations. Old theories about Kondratiev forty- or fifty-year cycles and Forrester's attempts to model them are attracting increased interest. My only comment as an economist is that innovations need not be technological but may also be social—that is, innovations in policy instruments. An incomes policy combined with a Keynesian impulse may be such an innovation.

Supranational Policies?

Another innovation might be called for—namely, to organize a recovery through a *supranational* policy. Shishido et al. (1980)—a group of six Japanese economists—have shown that a Keynesian impulse applied simultaneously by six countries affects production and employment more favorably than does an impulse applied by a single country. The same point has been made by Siebrand (1981). Of course, simultaneous action also has a more favorable impact on the balances of payments of the countries concerned. Thus what is called for is an EEC policy instead of national policies by single countries. Such an impulse may be financed by borrowing from OPEC countries (as France and Germany have already done on their own). This would be tantamount to executing one of the recommendations made by the Brandt Report (Brandt et al. 1980)—namely, the creation of an additional fund for providing financial assistance to the developing countries—a fund financed by donor countries unwilling to lend to the World Bank. More monetary financing seems permissible.

Limits to Growth, Additional Research

Need for Increased Research

One of the undisputed innovations to economic thinking in the last decade was induced by the Club of Rome and found expression in a number of reports solicited by that club. The first message, formulated by Meadows et al. (1972) and elaborated by Mesarovic and Pestel (1974), was that there are *limits to growth* as a consequence of the scarcity of safe energy and the necessity of protecting the environment. To support their message, both reports used new forms of modeling—Meadows et al. for the world at large, and their successors for a world consisting of regions. Admittedly, the models were crude first attempts; some of the figures used were incorrect, and several have been improved by other authors. Given our present knowledge, the clearest grounds for concern are (1) the need for safer energy, (2) the conservation of the gene reserve for world agriculture, and (3) control of the carbon dioxide content of the atmosphere.

Common to these three problem complexes is our *insufficient knowledge.* We need to know more about how to use solar radiation, which is the only practically unlimited and safe source of energy. We need to know more about the portion of land that must be kept in its natural condition in order that its wealth of plant species may serve as a gene reserve for agricultural production. Finally, we need to know more about how to keep the atmospheric CO_2 content under control: without such control, climatic changes may occur, leading to massive inundation of inhabited land. This lack of knowledge affects a number of other problem groups, including social problems, and demands an expansion of the world's nonmilitary *research effort* to, say, twice its present volume.

The developed countries have the *manpower* needed for that additional research: in the last twenty years, the percentage of labor force with college education has increased substantially. Research is an activity in which the developed countries have comparative advantages, so part of the needed recovery may lie in increased research activity. In the role of consultants, the firms specializing in research might even be financed by such countries as the OPEC countries or by institutions of the United Nations. Part of the funds allocated to the development of the Third World could be made available to finance such consultant activities: The development of technologies to export solar energy would certainly be an attractive project.

It goes without saying that a major *coordination* effort would be needed in order to raise the efficiency of research. Not only consultant firms but also universities and transnational enterprises are involved.

Is Growth Essential?

In discussing the limits to growth, the question arises whether growth is a necessary precondition for an economy and for society. There is a widespread belief that this is so. Elsewhere, I have set forth the reasons that I do not think this is a correct statement (Tinbergen 1982). A theoretical counterargument is that, irrespective of the rate of growth of total production, there are forces at work that maintain productivity. The labor force is composed of vintages or age cohorts. At the age of about 65 years, vintages withdraw; at the lower end, new cohorts have to find occupations. The total labor force is a self-renewing set of cohorts—in French, *un ensemble renouvelé*. All members of the arriving cohort have to compete in the attempt to take over the best occupations of the previous cohort, and this maintains the *maximum productivity* possible with the available equipment.

It is empirically demonstrable that the average productivity of an economy can be explained to a large extent by the physical and human capital per capita, and that the rate of growth of the economy, when added to these independent variables, does *not* contribute significantly to the explanation.

In light of the reports to the Club of Rome for the developed countries and for the world at large, slower growth than that attained in the 1950s and 1960s seems to be called for. However, the low level of well-being characterizing large parts of the world population does require growth for these groups. Thus the distribution of the total product has to be changed, if not for humanitarian reasons, then at least in the interest of greater political stability. In the developed world, production should grow more quickly than consumption so as to increase the transfers to the Third World, especially poor groups, and even to poor groups within the developed world. For those who are now enjoying the privilege of high prosperity, "voluntary simplicity" (Elgin 1981) may be the best suggestion. Let us now take up this distributional aspect in somewhat more detail.

Reduction of Welfare Differences

Measurement of Welfare

Welfare, utility, or "ophelimity" (in Pareto's terminology) is the central concept of economic science. Hence it is paradoxical that the *measurement* of an individual's welfare or satisfaction remains an object of controversy among economists. The majority of today's economists probably suscribe to Samuelson's treatment of the issue. A small group is working on attempts to measure welfare, some using "social indicators." A particularly interesting contribution was published by Levy and Guttman (1975) in the journal *Social Indicators Research*. Its main message is that, among the determinants of welfare, the purely economic ones contribute only a small part to the explanation of the variance in welfare. (This does not exclude the possibility that their contribution to the average level may be more substantial.) Larger parts of the variance are explained by a good family life, pleasant relations with friends, and conditions at work. The method used is basically the same one applied by Van Praag (1968, 1973, and later): it consists of scaling in words and then assigning the appropriate figures, as is done in the scaling system Schook use to appraise students' performance. A similar scale is applied in job evaluation (cf. the Dictionary of Occupational Titles used in the United States by that country's employment service). Van Praag collected a huge amount of information from inquiries among the members of consumer unions in European countries and concentrated on the welfare function of income. He found convincing evidence of a close relation between welfare and income, with a few additional determinants (family size, age (or experience), and type of occupation). The remainder of this section will concentrate on the determinants of income distribution as a contribution to the search for policies aiming at a reduction of income inequality. Since we have already dealt with one determinant, power, we shall now concentrate on an economic treatment.

Supply and Demand of Production Factors (Labor)

In pursuing such an economic treatment, let us investigate the supply of and demand for production factors, in particular labor. In a developed society labor is available in a large number of skills, and for the most part the individuals concerned have completed a formal learning process. The *labour market* may be described as a complex of *compartments,* each of them characterized either by the skills required or by groups of occupations. To each compartment an income (wage, salary, or fee) is attached; and each individual will supply herself or himself in the compartment that *maximizes welfare.* Deviations may exist between the actual skill of an individual and the skill required in the compartment if the wage offered induces the acceptance of such a job. This trade-off expresses itself in the price elasticity of supply.

The supply of capital or natural resources as made available by their owners may also show a certain price elasticity of supply.

Demand for production factors is exerted by the organizers of production and hence determined by production functions. If, for instance, the organizers are competing for factors and hence are price takers, they will extend their demand until the marginal product of a factor equals its price. Production functions have attracted a great number of econometricians, and in recent decades considerable inventiveness has been displayed in this area. The invention of the CES function by Arrow, Chenery, Minhas, and Solow (1961) marked the beginning of this process. Space considerations forbid a detailed presentation here, but some of the methodological issues involved may be briefly mentioned. The four pioneers used the assumption of competition between employers and had to use prices in their regression equations. Others used the duality of cost functions and production functions in order to arrive at a testing relation. The attractiveness of the CES function is also that Cobb-Douglas and Leontief (input-output) functions can be seen as special cases. Another way of generalizing Cobb-Douglas is the translog production function. An innovation can also be seen in the idea of two-level production functions. The same applies to the idea of putty-clay production functions or envelopes of short-term functions. The newest enrichment, also an innovation, concerns the problem of estimating production functions with a large number of factors, especially various types of labor—say six or eight. Here, Gottschalk (1978) introduced the idea of considering production as a *combination of two or more processes*—for example, the technical process and its administration. I mention this in more detail because of the political significance his numerical results may bear. These will be discussed later.

Confrontation of Demand and Supply

The simplest confrontation is embodied in the traditional equilibrium scheme, which yields both prices and quantities transacted (for labor, *employed*). Complications, well known to students of commodity markets, arise as a consequence of lags and the ensuing adaptation processes. Incomes equations (for labor, *earnings equations*) also result here, though in a more complicated form. Two recent publications will be discussed since they seem to represent innovations. Hartog (1981) proposed a *multicapability theory* of earnings, meaning that earnings can be interpreted as the total of the money values of the quantities of the capabilities supplied. In other words, each type of labor constitutes a bunch of quantities (or intensities) of capabilities sold. He also shows that the relative price of manual capability as compared to intellectual capability rose in the United States between 1949 and 1959. Later figures could not be estimated because of data incomparability. A plausible interpretation is that, as a consequence of more schooling, the scarcity of intellectual capabilities had decreased.

Using his method, Gottschalk found that important differences between the *earnings* of eight types of labor and their marginal revenue product existed around 1959 in the United States. In comparison to marginal productivity, sales workers and managers were "overpaid," manual and clerical workers "underpaid," and professional and technical workers paid "adequately." One explanation for the overpayment of sales workers and managers was offered by this author: The macroproductivity of competing salesmen must be relatively low since their task consists of *neutralizing* each other's efforts. Their true contribution to a country's national product is that they are the *carriers of competition*. Under competition, the national product is considerably higher than it is under monopoly (Tinbergen 1982b).

In all probability, managers in the United States were and are still overpaid. Burck (1976) showed that top executives in 1976 were paid the same real income as in 1952, whereas other incomes had increased by more than 30 percent. Reddaway (1981) found that British executives are paid much less than their U.S. (and other) counterparts, without there being evidence of less performance. The research done so far is too limited in scope to allow for clear conclusions, but the provisional results justify an extension so as to arrive at more reliable knowledge of the forces at work in income distribution.

The Optimum Social Order

A major point of dissent among social scientists as well as politicians concerns what social order best serves human happiness. The largest gap in opinion and most serious ideological controversy is between Marxists and adherents of laissez-faire. Both pretend to base their opinions on scientific arguments, the nature of which was briefly indicated earlier. Essentially, the problem is one of social science; given the increasing integration of sciences referred to earlier; and because, among the social sciences, economics is one of the more advanced, it is probably no mistake to proceed from an economic basis. In fact, *welfare economics* is the branch of economics closest to the problem. The appropriate formulation seems to be: How—that is, by what set of institutions—can a community's social welfare function be maximized, taking into account the restrictions imposed on that community? As restrictions, we usually consider the laws of nature, as far as they are known, which determine technology in the broadest sense. We are now also aware of those discovered through the Club of Rome. The restrictions due to human nature are, at least partly, reflected in the individual and (following Bergson and Samuelson) social welfare functions; perhaps they require additional attention. A number of cultural restrictions should also be included.

Optimum Conditions and Institutions

The optimum conditions may be derived from a setup with Lagrange multipliers. Their number is equal to the number of variables appearing in the social welfare function plus the number of restrictions. The optimum conditions may be met by a number of institutions whose code of behavior is described by the same equations as the optimum conditions. Exemplary institutions may be concrete or abstract. A concrete institution might be the Ministry of Justice, including the courts and police "to maintain law and order." It might also be a Ministry of Finance, collecting taxes and paying subsidies; but not all taxes are in conformity with optimum conditions. An abstract institution may be a market. Not all market forms are acceptable; for instance, monopolistic or oligopolistic markets turn out to be nonoptimal.

From the setup described and as a consequence of the assumptions about technologies, the proponents of laissez-faire may derive an optimal order consisting of markets and "law and order." Introducing other assumptions about some of the restrictions, it is possible to derive an optimal order that resembles some form of welfare state. One may even arrive at an optimum order of the central-planning type provided that the central planning bureau's code of conduct is to fix production quantities and prices *as if* free competition were in operation. From these examples, it becomes clear that a very large research program could be formulated with the object of acquiring more precise information on the social welfare function and the related restrictions. In the preceding sections, we have come across a number of examples. For the purposes of this chapter, the main question is whether innovative additions to the subject have been made in the last two decades. We shall try to mention a few tentatively.

Degree of Centralization

In principle, the two superpowers exemplify complete decentralization (laissez-faire) and complete centralization (centrally planned countries); but in reality neither alternative is feasible. Today the trend is largely toward decentralization. Large corporations in Western countries are deliberately moving toward more decentralized decision making and handing over decision making to groups of workers (as in the Volvo experiment). Japanese managers consult much more with their collaborators than Western managers are accustomed to do. Schumacher's *Small Is Beautiful* has had a great impact on public opinion, especially in environmentalist circles. Yugoslav self-management is another, not entirely successful example: Unemployment is much too great, since free entry into an industry is blocked—perhaps for lack of capital or of skills on the part of the unemployed. In the USSR the importance of the farmers' private lots has been understood and has been encouraged.

More important, there is an incipient understanding that different activities require different degrees of centralization. Differences in the optimum size of factories in different industries have existed for a long time. Political decision making, however, must be done at that level where external effects are negligible. As long as external effects continue to exist, the level of decision making is too low. This applies to ten important problem areas that require supranational decision making (Tinbergen et al. 1976). There is an irrational preference for national decision making even in the case of problems (for example, pollution) where it is in the population's interest not to be nationalist. This also applies to the problem of how to get rid of stagnation and inflation.

Both East and West can learn more from comparative studies of communist and noncommunist countries. It is a step forward that we now have more discussions in which evidence on socialism is taken not from theoretical sources but from the really existing communist countries. Bahro (1977) reports on the unproductivity of large hierarchies. His criticism is not only directed at Eastern countries but also applicable to Western societies: for instance, the excessively materialistic life-style of most developed countries. Another source of interesting comparative studies is Gärtner and Kosta (1979). Finally, a useful tool of analysis is Adler Karlsson's (1967) "functional socialism." He contrasts the socialization of industries to the socialization of functions—quality or price control, legal limitation on working hours, social security of many kinds. An interesting example is Krelle's model of the gradual increase in worker investment funds, now being intensively debated in Sweden (Krelle 1981) as a democratic way to socialism.

Innovative Ideas and Authors, A Tentative List

This chapter has attempted to sketch, in its main features only, the development of economic science during the last few decades. I have made a provisional choice as to which new elements I consider innovative. It is hoped that the discussion will comment on this choice so that a more accurate vision may be attained. My list of important innovations is submitted very tentatively, and some of the innovators are designated. For some subjects, other scientists may have been the originators. Sometimes first publications have been mentioned; in other cases, useful surveys were chosen instead. Some authors stand for groups. The composition of these groups may be relevant when it comes to distributing the innovators over nationalities. In this tentative list, the Netherlands is overrepresented because I have access to more complete information on activities in my own neighborhood. Especially in this respect, this provisional version is in need of correction. The large number of U.S. economists mentioned is the joint effect of (1) the level of U.S. performance, (2) the so-called brain drain, (3) the size of the U.S. population, and (4) the position of English as the present international language.

Need for integration of monetarism and Keynesianism: Klein, 1975.
Spatial elements in models: Isard, 1956; Bos, 1964.
Informal sector: Feige, 1980; Gershuny, 1979.
Human capital: Mincer, 1957.
Military and political components: Deutsch and collaborators, 1978.
Improvements in traditional modeling: Stone, 1981.
Time budget: Gallais-Hammono, 1972.
Power structure in models: Cohen, 1978; Van Ginneken, 1980.

Compromising in economic policy: Nijkamp, 1980.
Rush growth: Kornai, 1972.
Soft state: Myrdal, 1968.
Land reform implementation: Adelman, 1978.
Capital and labor in long-term development: Verdoorn, 1959.
Appropriate technology: Boon, 1964 and after.
Forms of international specialization: Samuelson, 1966.
Semi-input-output method: Kuyvenhoven, 1978.
Linked international models: Mosak, 1966; Waelbroeck, 1976.
Appraisal of income distribution effects in projects: Helmers, 1979.
Model of International Relations in Agriculture (MOIRA): Linnemann et al., 1979.
Comparative advantages of individuals and equipment used: Sattinger, 1980.
Twin research to estimate genetical component in ability: Taubman, 1980.
Supranational policy to eliminate stagnation: Shishido et al. 1980.
Limits-to-growth models: Meadows et al., 1972; Mesarovic and Pestel, 1974.
Growth not a precondition for high productivity: Tinbergen, 1982a.
Measurement of welfare: Van Praag, 1973; Levy and Guttman, 1975.
Estimation of production function by identifying subprocesses: Gottschalk, 1978.
Multicapability theory of earnings: Hartog, 1981.
Carriers of competition: Tinbergen, 1982b.
Different degrees of centralization required for different activities: Tinbergen et al., 1976.
Operation of worker investment funds: Krelle, 1981.

References

Adelman, Irma. 1978. "National and International Measures in Support of Equitable Growth in Developing Countries: A Proposal." Working Paper 78-13, University of Maryland, Department of Economics and Bureau of Business and Economic Research.

Boon, G. K. 1964. *Economic Choice of Human and Physical Factors in Production*. Amsterdam: North Holland.

Bos, H. C. 1964. *Spatial Dispersion of Economic Activity*. Rotterdam: University Press.

Chakravarty, S. 1959. *The Logic of Investment Planning*. Amsterdam: North Holland.

Cohen, S. I. 1978. *Agrarian Structures and Agrarian Reform*. Leiden and Boston: Martinus Nijhoff.

Deutsch, K. W. 1978. "Uber Weltmodellarbeiten am Internationalen Institut für Vergleichende Gesellschaftsforschung, Wissenschaftszentrum Berlin." In *Jahrbuch 1978 der Berliner Wissenschaftlichen Gesellschaft, e.V.*

Feige, E. L. 1980. "The Theory and Measurement of the Unobserved Sector in the U.S. Economy: Causes, Consequences and Implications." Paper presented at the Ninety-third Annual Meeting of the American Economic Association, September 6, 1980.

Gallais-Hammono, G. 1972. *Des loisirs.* Paris: Futuribles, SÉ DÉIS.

Gershuny, J. 1979. "Service Employment and Unpaid Work." Paper presented at Conference on Problems and Developments in the Field of Labor Policy, Netherlands Scientific Council for Government Policy, December 12–14, The Hague.

Gottschalk, P. T. 1978. "A Comparison of Marginal Productivity and Earnings by Occupation." *Industrial and Labor Relations Review* 31: 368–378.

Hartog, J. 1981. *Personal Income Distribution:* Boston, The Hague, and London: Martinus Nijhoff.

Helmers, F. L. C. H. 1979. *Project Planning and Income Distribution.* Boston, The Hague, and London: Martinus Nijhoff.

Isard, W. 1956. *Location and the Space Economy.* Cambridge, Mass.: MIT Press.

Klein, L. R. 1975. "Research Contributions of the SSRC-Brookings Econometric Model Project—A Decade in Review." In G. Fromm and L. R. Klein, eds., *The Brookings Model: Perspective and Recent Developments.* New York, Amsterdam, and Oxford: North Holland and American Elsevier.

Kornai, J. 1972. *Rush versus Harmonic Growth.* Amsterdam: North Holland.

Krelle, W. 1981. *Z. f. Nationalökonomie 41*:223–233.

Kuyvenhoven, A. 1978. *Planning with the semi-input-output method.* Leiden, Boston, and London: Martinus Nijhoff.

Levy, S., and Guttman, L. 1975. "On the Multivariate Structure of Wellbeing." *Social Indicators Research 2*: 361–388.

Linnemann, H., et al. 1979. *MOIRA: Model of International Relations in Agriculture.* Amsterdam, New York, and Oxford: North Holland.

Meadows, D. H., et al. 1972. *The Limits to Growth.* New York: Potomac Associates.

Mesarovic, M., and Pestel, E. 1974. *Mankind at the Turning Point.* New York: Dutton.

Mincer, J. 1957. "Investment in Human Capital and Personal Income Distribution." Dissertation, Columbia University.

Mosak, J. L. 1966. Unpublished research for the United Nations Department of Economic Affairs.

Myrdal, G. 1968. *Asian Drama.* New York: Twentieth Century Fund.

Nijkamp, P. 1980. *Environmental Policy Analysis*. Chichester, New York, Brisbane, and Toronto: Wiley.

Samuelson, P. A. 1966. *The Collected Scientific Papers,* Vol. 2, Cambridge Mass.: MIT Press.

Sattinger, M. 1980. *Capital and the Distribution of Labor Earnings*. Amsterdam, New York, and Oxford: North Holland.

Shishido, Sh., et al., 1980. "A Model for the Coordination of Recovery Policies in the OECD Region." *Journal of Policy Modeling 2:* 35–56.

Stone, R. 1981. "Aspects of Economic and Social Modelling." *Conférences Luigi Solari,* Vol. I. Geneva: Librairie Droz.

Taubman, P. 1980. "Socioeconomic Success." In J. R. Behrman et al., *Socioeconomic Success*. Amsterdam and New York: Oxford University Press.

Tinbergen, J., et al. 1976. *Reshaping the International Order*. New York: E. R. Dutton.

Tinbergen, J. 1982a. "La croissance: condition nécessaire pour notre bien-être?" In press.

Tinbergen, J. 1982b. "Deviations between Earnings and Marginal Productivity. Two Studies Compared." In G. R. Feiwel, ed., *Samuelson and Neoclassical Economics*. Boston, The Hague, and London: Kluwer-Nijhoff.

Van Ginneken, W. 1980. *Socio-economic Groups and Income Distribution in Mexico*. London: Croom Helm (for International Labour Organization).

Verdoorn, P. J. 1959. "The Role of Capital in Long-Term Projection Models." *Cahiers économiques de Bruxelles 5*: 49.

Waelbroeck, J. L., ed. 1976. *The Models of the Project LINK*. Amsterdam, New York, and Oxford: North Holland.

CHAPTER 7

Demand-Side and Supply-Side Economics and the Future

Bruno Fritsch
Gebhard Kirchgässner

WHEN DISCUSSING CONDITIONS that favor major advances in the social sciences—for example, in economics—consideration must be given to the process by which scientific knowledge is generated. Scientific knowledge may be treated as an economic good, which, like any other good, is produced and consumed. Hence there is a supply side and a demand side of this particular good—scientific knowledge.

The demand for scientific knowledge originates from societal needs—that is, mainly from outside the scientific community. Economic policy decision makers need to know how their instruments influence the economic process. The central bank, for example, should know the effects of alternative money supply rules on inflation and the rate of growth of real income. This requires a thorough analysis. Major advances are usually induced in two situations: (1) when the traditional policy and/or policy instruments, which had been successful in at least partially solving economic problems, suddenly fail, and (2) when new problems arise for which no policy and/or instruments have yet been developed. As we shall see, both happened in economics during the 1970s.

With respect to the supply of scientific knowledge, two aspects have to be considered: first, the production-factors, which come from outside the scientific community and are made available by the society and/or by other sciences (in the case of economics, by computer sciences, for example); and second, the internal selection process, which guides the scientific research and produces results that are recognized and accepted by a majority of scholars within the scientific community (the mainstream). Since the second aspect is dealt with to a large extent in the literature on philosophy of science, and since with respect to economics the situation has not changed in any significant way within the last fifteen years, we will deal only with the first aspect. Here the increased availability of large, fast, and—compared to the 1950s and early 1960s—relatively cheap computers is certainly the most important change.

We will first look at the demand side and indicate how some of the major advances in economics during the last fifteen years arose from new social and/or economic problems and the attempt to cope with them by further developing and applying economic theory. Then we shall evaluate the impact of supply of knowledge on advances in economics. Finally, we will consider some new directions in which further research in economics may head. In the appendix we present a list of what we consider the major trends in economics during the last fifteen years. Although this list is necessarily incomplete, we hope it captures the main developments in economics during the last decade and a half.

Demand-Side Influences on Recent Economic Theory

With respect to economic development in Western industrialized democracies, the main challenge during the 1970s was the simultaneous occurrence of inflation and unemployment, now called *stagflation*. When major inflation emerged at the end of the 1960s, Keynesian economic policy was confronted with serious difficulties; stagflation has definitely shown the limits of Keynesian economics. Thus the policies and instruments that were thought to be sufficient to cope with the problems of unemployment and inflation were no longer able to cope with these problems. In what is often labeled the *monetarist counterrevolution*, a first generation of monetarist models, mainly connected with M. Friedman and with K. Brunner and A. H. Meltzer, were developed, and the hypothesis of the "natural rate of unemployment" (Friedman 1968) was presented. This hypothesis, in connection with the assumption of "rational expectations," as proposed by Muth (1961) then led to the second generation of monetarist models, the "new classical macroeconomics," developed mainly by Lucas, Sargent, Wallace, and Barro. These models try to explain the structures and processes of the business cycle within the framework of temporary general equilibrium theory. The main conclusion for economic policy drawn from these models is that any anticipated policy of demand management has no real effects. In particular, any systematic monetary policy will affect only the rate of inflation, not the rate of growth of real output or the unemployment rate. Moreover, unsystematic (erratic) economic (monetary and/or fiscal) policy will increase uncertainty in the private sector of the economy and thus will reduce the rate of growth of real output and hence increase the rate of unemployment. The best economic policy can do is to follow a fixed rule of monetary expansion (the famous Friedman rule) and to leave the private sector of the economy alone.

New Classical Macroeconomics

To solve the inflation problem, the new classical macroeconomics offers a clear-cut prescription to economic policymakers (governments and central banks): Whatever happens, follow the Friedman rule; that is, expand the quantity of money by a fixed percentage rate (say, 3 percent) every year. However, the new classical macroeconomic theory does not say what governments should do to reduce unemployment; it only explains why governments cannot solve this problem. Thus the best way for governments to deal with unemployment is to do nothing—not to interfere with the private economy. This policy prescription is based on the assumption (or hope) that in the long run the private economy will return to the so-called natural rate of unemployment.[1] It epitomizes resignation combined with an exculpative argument for why governments cannot do anything meaningful at all against unemployment, contrary to what Keynesian macroeconomics prescribes as an "activist full employment policy."

This development in macroeconomics is paralleled by a similar development in econometrics. The scientific research program, to use the term of Lakatos (1970), of the development and estimation of macroeconometric models as founded by Tinbergen and Frisch in the 1930s had reached its culmination at the end of the 1960s. Large macroeconomic models of several hundred equations have been estimated for nearly all Western democracies and have been applied for policy evaluation purposes. During the early 1970s optimal control methods for linear and nonlinear models were developed to derive optimal paths for the economic development.[2] However, the predictive quality of these models was disappointing. First, in many cases predictions generated with the help of large macroeconometric models often proved not to be superior to predictions derived from small, mostly univariate statistical models.[3] Second, in a situation where many of the leading economists believed that they had provided governments with the tools and instruments to improve economic policy, the two most important macroeconomic indicators, *inflation* and *unemployment* rates, showed worse results than throughout most of the preceding twenty years.

The lack of predictive performance of large macroeconometric models and the comparably good forecasts of small statistical models led in the beginning of the 1970s to increased research in and application of methods of time-series analysis, especially Box-Jenkins analysis and spectral analysis. At the same time, Granger (1969) presented a new concept of causality, Granger causality, which during the 1970s became the starting point for many new procedures for detecting and estimating relationships between economic variables (time series). However, the new models now estimated were very small: In most cases only two variables were considered—for example, money and income. The largest models now known are the models of Sims, with six (1980) and nine (1978) equations. Such models are far too small to serve for policy evaluation purposes. However, if the new classical macroeconomists are right in stating that governments cannot do anything superior to the application of the Friedman rule, then large models would no longer be needed for policy evaluation purposes anyway.[4]

Lucas (1976) presented a further argument against the use of large macroeconometric models and of control theory for policy evaluation purposes: Traditional macroeconometric models are not invariant against changes in the *rules* of the government's economic policy. Thus we have to distinguish between measures of economic policy, on the one hand, and the rules from which these measures are derived, on the other hand. Traditional econometric models are (at most) invariant against different measures of the same rule but not against different rules. However, the application of control methods to derive optimal policy paths requires *rule independence* of the econometric models employed, as for different government objective functions different feedback rules are derived for the same econometric model. If economic agents optimize and thus react with their behavior to changes in the government's rule, then the coefficients of the reduced form, which is used for policy simulation, depending on the government rule, will also change. Therefore, the same econometric model cannot be used to evaluate the effects of two (or more) different government policy rules.[5] Following Lucas's critique, even if the government recognized the theoretical possibility of an active monetary and/or fiscal policy, it would not know how to design it. Traditional econometric models do not provide the rational basis for it. The policy prescription is, again: Follow the Friedman rule.

Today it is generally accepted that one of the main reasons that the monetarists won the battle against the Keynesians at the beginning of the 1970s was the missing microeconomic foundation of traditional Keynesian textbook economics.[6] The existence of a long-run trade-off between unemployment and inflation had been taken as one of the major propositions of Keynesian theory. To claim its nonexistence certainly is one of the major propositions of all versions of monetarism. The existence of such a trade-off had been "proved" by econometric studies even in the long run. This, however, was obtained by macroeconomic measurement without microtheoretic foundation. Therefore, the use of this trade-off for policy purposes failed: Higher inflation rates were, as argued before, not accompanied by a permanent decrease in unemployment. The explanation for this obvious fact lies on the micro level: As Friedman (1968) had already shown, such a long-run trade-off can persist only if there is a permanent money illusion. This, however, contradicts the assumption of rational behavior that is used by microeconomics. If higher rates of inflation persist, people will revise their expectations and change their behavior to accommodate to the new situation. Thus the fictitious long-run trade-off disappears in the long run.[7]

New Macroeconomics

However, new classical macroeconomics is not the only possible reaction to this fact. Models with quantity restrictions, constituting the so-called new macroeconomics, represent an alternative approach. New macroeconomics shares with its classical counterpart the effort for a micro foundation of macroeconomics. The main disagreement is the implicit assumption in new classical macroeconomics that wages and prices are flexible and markets therefore always clear: New macroeconomics accepts rigidity of wages and/or prices at least for the short run and thus operates with quantity restrictions. To state it differently: Markets might be temporarily in disequilibrium; that is, people in the market are willing to carry out transactions at given prices but do not get any opportunity to do so. Thus we might get involuntary unemployment, whereas in new classical macroeconomics we have only voluntary unemployment.[8]

The first steps in the direction of the new macroeconomics are marked by papers by Clower (1963) and Leijonhufvud (1968); today the efforts center around the works of Barro and Grossman, Hahn, and especially Malinvaud. Malinvaud (1977) distinguishes two types of unemployment: type I, "Keynesian unemployment," and type II, "classical unemployment." If there is Keynesian unemployment, traditional demand management policy will work, but not if there is classical unemployment, which results from too high real wage rates. In this case incomes policy may help to solve the unemployment problem. Thus, different types of unemployment require different government policies. As Keynesian unemployment can tend to last even in the long-run, an active government policy may be necessary to prevent the economy from long periods of unemployment. Hence, the policy prescriptions of the new macroeconomics are totally different from the policy prescriptions of the new classical macroeconomics. This holds even if people have rational expectations. The main clue is the assumption of quantity rationing as opposed to the assumption of market clearing: "without the continuous market-clearing assumption, the postulate of rational expectations would not justify the characteristic strong proposition that anticipated policies of demand management have no real effects." [J. Tobin (1980), p. 789].

The Battle over Social Policies

With respect to the microeconomic foundation, there is no fundamental difference between new macroeconomics and new classical macroeconomics. Both have their micro foundation within the general equilibrium theory. The question is only which of the results of general equilibrium theory are considered to be the most important ones. Is it "now entirely practical to view price and quantity paths that follow complicated stochastic processes as equilibrium 'points' in an appropriately specified space," as R. E. Lucas (1980, p. 708) states—since rational expectations are a substitute for the missing markets that provide the same coordination between economic agents as would happen in an Arrow-Debreu world? Or should we stress more what F. Hahn (1981, p. 136) claims: "If there are monopolistic elements in the economy, and, more generally, if the economy is not large enough, there may now be states in which agents are constrained in their transactions and yet prices do not change. Such a state would have strong claims to be regarded as an equilibrium. It is clear that this could be consistent with involuntary unemployment."

The battle between the two positions—the new macroeconomics and the new classical macroeconomics—is still undecided. It is the area that has attracted the greatest intellectual effort of economists during the last years. If we look at the mass unemployment today in Western democracies, it is certainly also the most important social problem of these societies. It has emerged from the breakdown of the previously accepted economic doctrine—the so-called neoclassical synthesis of Keynesian economics, which at the beginning of the 1970s proved no longer able to do its job successfully—that is, to provide governments with policy guidelines that would prevent mass unemployment and perhaps also inflation.

However, such problems did not arise only in industrialized countries. A similar development took place in the theory of development of less developed countries (LDCs). In the 1960s we had the highlights of development planning. Most of these development plans were based on the Harrod–Domar growth model and thus on Keynesian economic theory. It was assumed that there is a possibility of macroeconomic steering of the whole economy along an equilibrium growth path. As far as these plans were based on statistical data, econometric models were used as a quantitative basis for development planning. However, the development planning methods, as used in most of the developing countries, were disappointing in their results.[9]

As was recognized only too late, one of the major shortcomings of the traditional development planning methods was that they did not take into account cultural, organizational, and educational factors.

Similar problems arose for *international economics* from the breakdown of the Bretton-Woods system of fixed exchange rates. Already in the 1960s, as fixed exchange rates caused more and more problems so that adjustments of these rates became necessary ever more frequently (moving peg), most of the leading economists called for a system of flexible exchange rates. At the same time, the monetary theory of foreign trade became more and more important compared to the pure theory of foreign trade. This became particularly important after switching to flexible exchange rates. Some exchange rates did exhibit considerable short-run fluctuations. Thus it became evident that, at least in the short run, purchasing power parity theory cannot explain exchange-rate fluctuations.[10] As a result of this situation, research on the monetary approach to international economics and particularly to exchange rate economics, was induced during the 1970s.

Economics and Environmental Problems

However, not all demands for new development in economic theory came from the realm of economic problems. Problems of the *environment,* of the depletion of *natural resources,* and especially of *energy* came up in the 1970s and confronted economists with new questions. Economists had, at that time, no well-developed theory, no policy devices, and no proposals for instruments to cope with these problems. Therefore, in the 1970s environmental economics, energy economics, and the economics of natural resources began to emerge as nearly separate fields of economic theory.

The starting point for many of these discussions in environmental economics and the economics of natural resources was *The Limits to Growth* by D. H. Meadows et al. (1972), a noneconomist's contribution to the analysis of an apparently pressing problem. For energy economics, especially the first oil crisis in 1973–1974 gave an important impulse to an increase of literature about this topic.

With respect to environmental problems, it soon became clear that from an economic point of view these are problems of the public good and/or external effects. Once this became clear, economists showed that there is a wide range of instruments available to handle these problems.[11] We can use not only moral suasion and direct controls (instruments that seem to be most preferred in the public discussion) but also taxation of environmental damage, refundable deposits against environmental disruption, or pollution licenses. These latter instruments are in many cases much more effective than direct controls. Today environmental pollution seems to be much more a problem of political implementation (or non-implementation) of appropriate measures than a problem of missing policy instruments.

Energy and Resources

With respect to natural resources, the Meadows et al. (1972) hypothesis of definite depletion proved to be untenable. First, as the theory of optimal depletion of (renewable or nonrenewable) natural resources shows, there will never be total depletion of such a resource. This theory, which goes back to Hotelling (1931), maintains that relative scarcity, which is reflected in increased prices, has a double effect on lifetime: On the one hand, it increases the lifetime because less of this particular resource is used; on the other hand, prospecting becomes more rewarding, and more of the particular resource will be found and will become economically exploitable. Second, it became evident that the problem of depletion of a natural resource is not a problem of physical depletion but one of entropy management; that is, it is not the absolute availability of a particular resource that matters but, rather, its concentration and occurrence in a certain location at a certain time. The scarcity of a particular resource can be reduced by energy inputs, restoring certain degrees of concentration that are required for production purposes. Thus, if cheap energy is available, the resource problem can be solved.[12] Both mechanisms ensure that there will never be total depletion of a natural resource.[13] Nevertheless, there might be even dramatically increased scarcity of some natural resources in the future, which will be reflected in dramatic increases of their relative prices.

If we look at energy problems from a theoretical point of view, energy—or, more precisely, energy resources or carriers—are just special types of natural resources. Therefore, no special economic theory would be needed to investigate energy problems. The main emphasis of energy economics thus lies in the empirical area. If we consider energy to be an input in the production process as well as a consumer good, we have to investigate the role of energy in the production process, its substitutability against other production factors like capital and labor, or its complementarity to other production goods. These types of investigations have benefited greatly from the introduction of flexible functional forms in the analysis of production and consumer demand systems as done by Christenson, Jorgenson, and Lau (1973, 1975). These flexible functional forms allow the analysis of systems of consumer demand equations or systems of input demand equations for production, compatible with neoclassical consumer and production theory and without imposing a priori restrictions on the relations between the input factors or the consumer goods. Such statistical descriptions of consumption and production processes can serve as the core of complete energy planning models, as presented for the United States, for example, by Hudson and Jorgenson (1974). Today, work on energy planning models is done at many places, and at least some of these models are used as simulation models for national energy planning.[14]

The State and Taxation

Other challenges influencing and favoring the development of economic theory came from the growing importance of the state. The old theory of government behavior stated that (democratic) governments behave like benevolent dictators and do not consider their own interests. At least since the pioneering work of Downs (1957) on the economic theory of democracy, this view could no longer prevail. During the 1960s and with increased intensity during the 1970s, much theoretical and empirical work about the behavior of governments, voters, bureaucrats, and so on has been done. Today we have not only a formal theory of collective choice, but also an economic theory of constitutions, and—on the empirical side—politicoeconomic models. These politicoeconomic models describe at least the behavior of two agents: voters and government. The corresponding equations are econometrically estimated and, as in Frey and Schneider (1979), implemented in a traditional econometric model. It is shown that the ex post facto predictions of the combined model are superior to the predictions of the pure econometric model.

Parallel to this development in public choice theory in traditional public economics, a huge bulk of literature about *optimal taxation* arose. The modern theory of optimal taxation, starting with articles by Mirrlees (1971) and Fair (1971) but in some respects going back to the fundamental article of Ramsey (1927), addresses the question of how the loss of social welfare related to collecting a certain amount of a tax revenue can be minimized. This is logically the same as if we ask how the amount of tax revenue can be maximized subject to a given loss of social welfare, or, to state it differently, how the possibilities of legal tax evasion can be minimized. It is not casual that such questions were asked in a situation where, because of increasing marginal tax rates, legal tax evasion as well as (estimated) illegal tax avoidance was increasing. Here the assumption of the existence of a social welfare function may lead to the wrong questions and thus to the wrong policy advice: Public choice theory tells us that there is nothing like a social welfare function, but there are only individual welfare functions, and especially government and bureaucrats do not behave so as to maximize social welfare, but so as to maximize their own individual utility. Therefore, the right question to ask might be how to construct a tax system that minimizes the possibilities of government and/or bureaucrats to exploit citizens by using the tax instruments. As the politico-economic theory of optimal taxation of Brennan and Buchanan (1977, 1978) has shown, the answer to this question may lead to totally different policy advice.[15]

Economics of Information

A last major development in economics during the last fifteen years, which should be mentioned here, is the *economics of information.* Starting with the work of Stigler (1961), the economics of uncertainty and information have founded what has been called the new microeconomics. It became clear that the traditional assumption of complete information—that is, the absence of information costs—made in many of the microeconomic literature and especially in many textbooks, often proved to be too restrictive to arrive at empirically valid hypotheses. In comparison to this approach the new microeconomic theory, which takes into account information and transaction costs, was able to derive many interesting hypotheses, especially in the micro theory of employment. Moreover, information or knowledge is an economic good, which, like other goods, has to be produced and distributed. As Machlup (1972) has shown, these processes may be analyzed by economic theory as well as other production and distribution processes. There is still another aspect of information, however. It is related to the theory of dissipative structures and has to do with the relative shift of scarcities, as a result of dissipation and its relation to information and energy. This rather new development has been analyzed by noneconomists such as Tribus and McIrvine (1971), as well as by Porat (1978), an economist.

Though clearly related to problems of today's world, recent progress in the economics of information cannot be so clearly connected to historical events or economic developments as, for example, the new (classical) macroeconomics or energy economics. Nevertheless, we hope to have shown that the major developments in economic theory taking place during the last fifteen years, were induced by the demand for problem-solving capacity of the Western industrialized democracies. Old theories had either ceased to be helpful in devising suitable policies or were not available at all. Thus the need for new theoretical developments became pressing. However, it does not always happen that such new theories come up with policy devices that show how economic policy decision makers can solve the problems. The new classical macroeconomics is a counterexample: It states that governments can do nothing to solve the unemployment problem, or, more bluntly, that the best they can do is to do nothing. Everything else would, at least in the long run, cause more unemployment.

Supply-Side Influences on Recent Economic Theory

Research in the Social Sciences

Supply-side influences have certainly not so strongly influenced the topics of economic research as did the demand-side influences discussed earlier. Nevertheless, there is something to say about the supply side, too. Taking any available measure, like the number of articles published every year, the number of economic journals, the number of PhDs in economics, or any other output measure that can be thought of, the output of the economic research production process has increased very rapidly during the last decade and a half. Whether this is an increase in quality or only a huge amount of useless paper, only the future can tell. Independently of the evaluation of the result reached, this huge increase in output became possible because the amount of money that many leading Western societies made available for economic research (and for research in other social sciences) was increased substantially between 1965 and 1975. Hence more people could be employed in this sector, and more output could be produced.

One could think of this development in terms of growing awareness: In Western democratic societies a general consensus emerged that social problems had become more important. Therefore more problem-solving capacity was thought to be necessary in order to solve these problems by intensified scientific research. Today it seems to be the other way around: The social problems are certainly not smaller than they were ten or fifteen years ago, but governments have considerably less financial means available. Public research grants for economics and other social sciences are cut much more than are research grants for natural or technical sciences. This supports the alternative explanation that research in social sciences is now seen as a luxury that can be indulged in only if governments have enough money to spend. If this view holds, the demand for such luxury goods will fall drastically whenever governments encounter financial problems. If the first view holds—that is, if economics or social science in general is seen to be helpful in solving social problems—better research, especially research that is closely related to such problems, will attract more funds. If the luxury-goods view holds, the only hope economists can have for getting more money for research is a recovery of the economy. However, if economics is considered to be of any use in solving such pressing social problems as unemployment, research that helps to reduce unemployment (and thus improves the financial basis of governments) will indirectly increase the amount of money made available for economic research, even if research in social sciences is seen as a luxury good.

The Revolution in Data Processing

Besides the expansion of research capacity in the social sciences, there were other factors on the supply side of economic research that favored major advances. Certainly, the most important one was the increasing availability of large, fast computers at relatively low costs. This has very much favored quantitative economic research. It is now that the simultaneous estimation of systems of nonlinear equations has become technically possible. To use these facilities for econometric analysis, new methods of estimation were developed.[16] In addition, mathematicians developed new numerical methods that could be used to solve numerical problems in the estimation procedures.

Large, fast computers also made possible the handling of large nonlinear simulation models. This holds not only for econometric models in the narrow sense, which are mostly designed to make short- or medium-term predictions about economic developments, but also for global models, which today cover a wide range of countries and regions and are related to such problems as depletion of resources, population growth, energy availability, food supply, ecological equilibrium, and so on.[17]) Certainly, the purpose of such simulation models is not to provide forecasts, but to do scenario analysis—that is, to look how the system behaves under different assumptions about its relevant parameters or under different behavior of input parameters. What counts here are the differences in the simulation results due to various assumptions, not the absolute values of the output variables.[18] The area where the most models of this type are available and in use for policy evaluation purposes today is probably in energy planning.

In addition, more and more long-term-series as well as cross-section-series data for many countries have become available during the last few years by national and international institutions; and they are, at least partly, based on coherent sets of definitions. These data sets not only serve as an empirical basis for simulation models but, even more important, allow the application of new statistical methods of economic analysis. Time-series methods, especially frequency-domain methods, need large samples for their application. For many countries, continuous data since the 1950s and collected time series of monthly or quarterly data are now available and allow us to apply such methods.

Another development might be equally important: For the United States, yearly input-output tables are now available from 1929. This has made possible for the first time the application of econometric methods to estimate the dependence of the input coefficients on relative prices. Thus the extremely restrictive assumption of linear-limitational production functions used in traditional input-output analysis could be dropped, and substitution between production factors could be taken into consideration. The theoretical instrument used was transcendental-logarithmic production frontiers, introduced by Christensen, Jorgenson, and Lau (1973) and applied in the energy models of Hudson and Jorgenson (1974) mentioned earlier. Large bodies of survey data supported the development of quantitative response models.

Mathematical Tools

Mathematics itself also provided very helpful tools for economic analysis. The most prominent and influential contribution is Pontryagin's maximum principle of 1959[19], which was a very important step in optimal control theory and became widely applied in economics by the 1960s. Modern theory of quantitative economic policy is mainly based on control methods derived from Pontryagin's principle.[20] Another example is the catastrophe theory of Thom (1972) and the related concepts of *resilience* and *phase portraits*.[21] Some applications of catastrophe theory to economics seem to render promising results. Although the operational difficulties of catastrophe theory in its application to social processes are formidable, there seems to be a great potential for this type of approach in future economic research.[22]

Besides the developments mentioned earlier, there are some social phenomena outside economics that have some relationship to economic problems and that might prove fruitful for future economic research. To list only some of them, we think, for example, of the concept of basic needs and the theory of social indicators; the theory of self-organizing systems; the theory of hierarchies (Mesarovic, Macko, and Takahara, 1970), with its relation to innovations in organizations; the relation between economics and biology with respect to ecological phenomena, which includes new concepts of stability; the concept of an evolutionary window, including the factors influencing the width of this window (Rechenberg, 1973); or problems of changes of preference structures as a function of pattern cognition. These and other concepts of social sciences can broaden the way economists think about their classical problems and thus open new perspectives for economic research.

The Future of Research in Economics

Solving Social Problems

The question of the direction in which future research in economics ought to go in order to be more successful in solving social problems implies an assessment of the most pressing social problems to be expected in the near future. Such an assessment is necessarily subjective. Nevertheless, within the framework of our considerations about conditions for major advances in economics, it makes sense to ask such questions too.

The most pressing social problem today in Western industrialized countries is certainly the *high unemployment rate* that emerged within the last few years. Therefore, a high priority must be given to the development of new short- and medium-run macroeconomic theories. New macroeconomics and new classical macroeconomics compete in this area and, as mentioned earlier, the battle is still going on. If one is not willing to accept the resignative policy advice of today's new classical macroeconomics, further research will be necessary in this direction. However, as Feige (1980) points out, it may be that traditional macroeconomics is well suited to explain what goes on in the official economy, but that the disturbing effects of high measured unemployment rates and high inflation are at least partly due to a large increase in the unofficial (shadow) sector of the economy. Today research has provided several methods for estimating size and development of the shadow economy, and for most Western countries estimates of the size are available.[23] However, only first steps toward a theory of the shadow economy have been done, and we seem still to be far from a general integrated microeconomically founded theory of the legal and shadow economies.[24]

Besides the national problems, there are obviously also *international problems* that have to be dealt with by economics. There is, for example, the North–South conflict with all its economic and political dimensions, including the discussions about a "new international economic order." There are other problems, too. One of them is that of international public goods (or externalities) in environmental economics. Traditionally, environmental economics considered externalities that could be internalized within one national economy. Today, however, we see that we have international overlapping effects of externalities, which cause a new threat and a new demand for instruments to solve these problems. Up to now, environmental economics has assumed that there is a powerful agency above the conflicting interests, which is able to enforce the internalization of the externalities. Such a powerful agency does not exist within the context of international relations, however. Thus new conflict resolution processes are necessary.

With respect to the role of the state, the *growing importance* of state intervention into the sphere of the private economy will call for more analysis of the effects, but also of the reasons for these interventions. Thus the public choice and new political-economy research will be of growing importance. This also indicates that there is a need for interdisciplinary cooperation between political science and economics. Hence, politico-economic modeling will go on. However, one of the major problems in this area, which also relates to standard macroeconomics, is the problem of expectation formation and, related to this, the fact that we do not yet have a coherent theory of evidence formation.[25]

Interaction with Other Disciplines

Besides these obvious mutual exchanges between related disciplines, there is certainly a need for wider interdisciplinary orientation and discussion between economics and other sciences as, for example, theory of ecology, particularly mathematical models in ecology, biology in combination with information theories (Platt, 1981), or general systems theory (Boulding 1972). If such interdisciplinary research is related to policy issues and if policy advice is derived from it, it may become more difficult for governments to find advisors who are willing to serve only as a legitimation for their prejudices and subjective views.[26]

Some aspects mentioned earlier will certainly involve the use of large nonlinear models. Other problem-solving procedures may benefit from the theory of hierarchies in relation to self-organizing systems. Some interest will also go into the analysis of resources and dissipative structures as related to energy, which eventually turns out to be a problem of entropy management. Consequently, future economic theories will deal with nonequilibrium, discontinuous, nonlinear systems having self-organizing properties, hierarchical structures, and dissipative processes that in a nonequilibrium situation imply the formation of new organizational structures.[27]

A List of Major Trends and Developments in Economics Since 1965

In summary, the major developments of economics over the last decade and a half are influenced by the inability of traditional theories to deal with social problems such as unemployment and inflation, or by the emergence of new problems like environmental pollution or energy shortage. Such social problems constitute the demand side of the research progress in economics. On the supply side, the major factors are financial support for research in social sciences; the availability of large, fast computers; and some special developments in mathematics. Future economic research may be heading into more complex and more global problems.

A list of the major trends and developments since 1965 is presented below. It is subjective, of course, reflecting the background and interests of the authors. As the time span between 1965 and today is relatively short, we do not know which of these developments will emerge as major developments ten or twenty years from now. Most of the work mentioned could be listed under more than one heading. Nevertheless, we have tried to select (a) major contributions (starting points for subsequent research) and/or (b) recent surveys (mainly from the *Journal of Economic Literature*).

The ordering of the following subjects does not imply any rank ordering related to importance.

General Equilibrium Theory

Microfoundation of Macroeconomics

(b) E. R. Weintraub (1977)

Application of Neoclassical Theory in the Estimation of Utility and Production Functions (Flexible Functional Forms)

(a) L. R. Christensen, D. W. Jorgensen, and L. J. Lau (1973, 1975).

Microeconomics

Uncertainty and Information

(a) G. J. Stigler (1965), F. Machlup (1972), J. Marshak (1974a, b).

(b) J. Hirshleifer and J. G. Riley (1979).

Theory of Efficient Markets

(a) E. F. Fama (1976).

Macroeconomic Theory

Natural Rate Hypothesis

(a) M. Friedman (1968), E. S. Phelps (1970).

(b) A. M. Santomero and J. J. Seater (1978).

Rational Expectations (New Classical Macroeconomics)

(a) J. F. Muth (1961), R. E. Lucas (1972), T. J. Sargent and N. Wallace (1975).

(b) B. Kantor (1979).

Models with Quantity Restrictions (New Macroeconomics)

(a) R. Clower (1963), R. J. Barro and H. I. Grossman (1973), E. Malinvaud (1977).

(b) J. Trevinthick (1978), J. D. Hey (1981)

Theory of Economic Policy

Quantitative Economic Policy

(a) G. C. Chow (1975), R. E. Lucas (1976).

Foreign Trade

Flexible Exchange Rates

(a) R. Dornbusch (1976), J. Niehans (1977).

(b) R. Dornbusch (1980), R. I. McKinnon (1981).

Environmental Economics—Energy Economics

Environmental Economics

(a) W. J. Baumol and W. E. Oates (1975, 1979).

(b) F. M. Peterson and A. C. Fisher (1977)

Natural Resources
(b) A. C. Fisher and F. M. Peterson (1976)
Energy-Economy Modeling
(a) E. A. Hudson and D. W. Jorgenson (1974), N. Georgescu-Roegen (1975), A. Manne (1977).

Public Economics—Public Choice
Theory of Optimal Taxation
(a) J. A. Mirrlees (1971), R. C. Fair (1971), G. Brennan and J. M. Buchanan (1977).
(b) A. B. Atkinson and J. B. Stiglitz (1980).
Collective Choice
(a) K. J. Arrow (1963), A. K. Sen (1970).
(b) A. K. Sen (1976, 1977).
Theory of Constitutions
(a) J. M. Buchanan and G. Tullock (1962), J. Rawls (1971), R. Nozick (1974), J. M. Buchanan (1975).
(b) S. Gordon (1976).
Politicoeconomic Modeling
(a) W. D. Nordhaus (1975), B. S. Frey and F. Schneider (1978).
(b) D. C. Mueller (1976), J. M. Buchanan (1978).

Econometrics
Time-Series Analysis
(a) C. W. J. Granger and M. Hatanaka (1964), G. E. P. Box and G. M. Jenkins (1970).
(b) S. Makridakis (1976).
Granger Causality
(a) C. W. J. Granger (1969), C. A. Sims (1972, 1980).
(b) D. A. Pierce and L. D. Haugh (1979), A. Zellner (1979).
Models with Qualitative Data
(b) T. Amemiya (1981).

Notes

1. One of the sharp critics of the new classical macroeconomics calls it, therefore, "the macroeconomics of Dr. Pangloss," because with this assumption, apart from state intervention, we apparently live in the best of all possible worlds. See Buiter (1980).
2. See the work of G. C. Chow, especially Chow (1975).
3. For a justification for the use of univariate prediction models, see Granger and Newbold (1975).
4. For a critique, see Malinvaud (1981).

5. This argument has been reinforced by Sargent (1976): Reduced forms of Keynesian and classical macroeconometric models can be observationally equivalent. Therefore, on the basis of reduced-form estimates there might be no way to discriminate between these two types of models with the help of econometric methods, as long as we do not have periods with different policy rules.
6. See Weintraub (1977).
7. This is just one example of Lucas's (1976) critique.
8. This disequilibrium is certainly an equilibrium in a wider, non-Walrasian sense (see Hahn 1981, p. 136).
9. See Waterston (1965) and, for a critique, Hirsch (1977).
10. For the short run, a random walk model often seems to have the best explanatory power for exchange rate markets. See, for example, Pool (1967) or Caves and Feige (1980).
11. See, for example, Baumol and Oates (1979), pp. 218ff.
12. See Goeller and Weinberg (1978).
13. This does not necessarily hold if we have a living resource such as seals. There, a total depletion is possible.
14. See, for example, Codoni and Fritsch (1980).
15. For a comparison of the two theories of taxation, see Frey (1982).
16. See, for example, the papers in the *Annals of Economic and Social Measurement*, Vols. 3–4, 1974.
17. This holds especially for long-run simulations with a range of twenty or more years.
18. See Hughes (1980), Meadows, Richardson and Bruckmann (1982), and Bremer (1982).
19. See Pontryagin et al. (1962).
20. See Chow (1975).
21. See, for example, Mesarovic, Macko, and Takahara (1970), and Grümm and Schrattenholzer (1976).
22. See Mensch et al. (1980) and Ursprung (1982).
23. An overview about these methods is given in Frey and Pommerehne (1981).
24. Examples for such steps are: Isachsen and Strøm (1980) and Frey and Weck (1982).
25. There are at least three different kinds of evidence.

    (1) *empirical evidence*, which, may be reproduced at all times which holds universally, and is demonstrated best by the "exact" natural sciences such as physics or chemistry.

    (2) *contextual evidence*, which implies the cognition of certain signs and information inputs such as threats, withdrawals, and preparations for actions. This contextual evidence is important because it may lead to the wrong reading of signals. The Falkland conflict is only one of the more recent examples for such misreading of signals.

    (3) *societal evidence*, which is formed by the beliefs and information filtering of certain groups within the society. The theoretical background for the analysis of these phenomena can be the theory of cognitive dissonance, as presented by Festinger (1957). A better understanding of the processes of evidence formation may lead to a better understanding of expectation formation and thus to improvements in economic theory.

26. See, for example, Deutsch (1978).
27. See, for example, Jantsch (1975) and Platt (1979).

References

Amemiya, T. 1981. "Qualitative Response Models: A Survey." *Journal of Economic Literature 19*: 1483–1536.

Arrow, K. J. 1963. *Social Choice and Individual Values,* rev. ed. New York: Yale University Press.

Atkinson, A. B., and Stiglitz, J. E. 1980. *Lectures on Public Economics*. New York: McGraw-Hill.

Barro, R. J., and Grossman, H. I. 1973. "A General Disequilibrium Model of Income and Employment." *American Economic Review 61:* 82–93.

Baumol, W. J., and Oates, W. E. 1975. *The Theory of Environmental Policy*. Englewood Cliffs, N.J.: Prentice-Hall.

———. 1979. *Economics, Environmental Quality and the Quality of Life*. Englewood Cliffs, N.J.: Prentice-Hall.

Boulding, K. E. 1972. "Economics and General Systems." *International Journal of General Systems 1:* 67–73.

Box, G. E. P., and Jenkins, G. M. 1970. *Time Series Analysis, Forecasting and Control*. San Francisco: Holden Day.

Bremer, S. 1982. *The GLOBUS Model: A Guide to Its Theoretical Structure*. IIVG/DP 82–105. Berlin: Veröffentlichungsreihe des Internationalen Instituts für Vergleichende Gesellschaftsforschung, Wissenschaftszentrum.

Brennan, G., and Buchanan, J. M. 1977. "Towards a Tax Constitution for Leviathan." *Journal of Public Economics 8:* 255–273.

———. 1978. "Tax Instruments as Constraints on the Disposition of Public Revenues." *Journal of Public Economics 9:* 301–318.

Buchanan, J. M. 1975. *The Limits of Liberty: Between Anarchy and Leviathan*. Chicago: University of Chicago Press.

———. 1978. "From Private Preferences to Public Philosophy: The Development of Public Choice." In Institute of Economic Affairs, ed., *The Economics of Politics*. London: Institute of Economic Affairs, pp. 1–20.

Buchanan, J. M., and Tullock, G. 1962. *The Calculus of Consent*. Ann Arbor: University of Michigan Press.

Buiter, W. H. 1980. "The Macroeconomics of Dr. Pangloss: A Critical Survey of the New Classical Macroeconomics." *Economic Journal 90:* 34–50.

Caves, D., and Feige, E. L. 1980. "Foreign Exchange Market Efficiency and the Monetary Approach to Exchange Rates Determination." *American Economic Review 70:* 120–134.

Chow, G. C. 1975. *Analysis and Control of Dynamic Economic Systems*. New York: Wiley.

Christensen, L. R.; Jorgenson, D. W.; and Lau, L. J. 1973. "Transcendental Logarithmic Production Frontiers." *Review of Economics and Statistics 55:* 28–45.

———. 1975. "Transcendental Logarithmic Utility Functions." *American Economic Review 65:* 367–383.

Clower, R. 1963. "The Keynesian Counterrevolution: A Theoretical Appraisal." *Schweizerische Zeitschrift für Volkswirtschaft und Statistik 99:* 8–38.

Codoni, R., and Fritsch, B. 1980. "Capital Requirements of Alternative Energy Strategies: A Techno-Economic Assessment." *Project ZENCAP Collected Working and Conference Papers*. Zürich: Institut für Wirtschaftsforschung der ETHZ.

Deutsch, K. W. 1978. *Major Changes in Political Science 1952–1977*. PV/78-2. International Institute for Comparative Social Research, Berlin Science Center.

Deutsch, K. W.; Platt, J.; and Senghaas, D. 1971. "Conditions Favouring Major Advances in Social Science." In *Science 171* (February): 450–459.

Dornbusch, R. 1976. "Expectations and Exchange Rate Dynamics." *Journal of Political Economy 84:* 1161–1176.

———. 1980. "Exchange Rate Economics: Where Do We Stand?" *Brookings Papers on Economic Activity 1:* 143–205.

Downs, A. 1957. *An Economic Theory of Democracy*. New York: Harper and Brothers.

Fair, R. C. 1971. "The Optimal Distribution of Income." *Quarterly Journal of Economics 85:* 551–579.

Fama, E. F. 1976. *Foundations of Finance*. New York: Basic Books.

Feige, E. L. 1980. "A New Perspective on Macroeconomic Phenomena, The Theory and Measurement of the Unobserved Sector of the United States Economy: Causes, Consequences, and Implications." Mimeo. Netherlands Institute of Advanced Study, Wassenaar, August.

Festinger, L. 1957. *A Theory of Cognitive Dissonance*. Stanford, Calif.: Stanford University Press.

Fisher, A. C., and Peterson, F. M. 1976. "The Environment in Economics: A Survey." *Journal of Economic Literature 14:* 1–33.

Frey, B. S. 1982. *Political Economy Today*. Special Lecture Series, Lausanne/Geneva, May.

Frey, B. S., and Pommerehne, W. W. 1981. "The Hidden Economy: State and Prospects for Measurement." Mimeo. Institut für Empirische Wirtschaftsforschung der Universität Zürich.

Frey, B. S., and Schneider, F. 1978. "An Empirical Study of Politico-

Economic Interaction in the United States." *Review of Economics and Statistics 60:* 174–183.

———. 1979. "An Econometric Model with an Endogenous Government Sector." *Public Choice 34:* 29–43.

Frey, B. S., and Weck, H. 1982. "Bureaucracy and the Shadow Economy: A Macro Approach." In H. Hanusch, ed., *Deficiency of the Government Sector*. Detroit: Wayne State University Press.

Friedman, M. 1968. "The Role of Economic Policy." *American Economic Review 58:* 1–17.

Fritsch, B. 1977. "From Neo-Classical Economics to Global Political Economy." In *Government and Opposition,* Vol. 12, No. 2. pp. 235–243.

Georgescu-Roegen, N. 1975. "Energy and Economic Rights." *Southern Economic Journal 41:* 347–381.

Goeller, H. E., and Weinberg, A. M. 1978. "The Age of Substitutability." *American Economic Review 68*(6): 1–11.

Gordon, S. 1976. "The New Contractarians." *Journal of Political Economy 84:* 573–590.

Granger, C. W. J. and Hatanaka, M. 1964. *Spectral Analysis of Economic Time Series*. Princeton: Princeton University Press.

Granger, C. W. J. 1969. "Investigating Causal Relations by Econometric Models and Cross-Spectral Methods." *Econometrica 37:* 424–438.

Granger, C. W. J., and Newbold, P. 1975. "Economic Forecasting: The Atheist's Viewpoint." In G. A. Renton, ed., *Modeling the Economy*. London: Heinemann, pp. 131–148.

Grümm, H. R., and Schrattenholzer, L. 1976. "Economy Phase Portraits." Research Memorandum RM-76-61. International Institute for Applied Systems Analysis, Laxenburg.

Hahn, F. 1981. "General Equilibrium Theory." In D. Bell and I. Kristol, eds., *The Crisis in Economic Theory*. New York: Basic Books, pp. 123–138.

Hey, J. D. 1981. *Economics in Disequilibrium*. Oxford: Martin Robertson.

Hirsch, F. 1977. *Social Limits to Growth*. London and Hewley: Routledge and Kegan Paul.

Hirshleifer, J., and Riley, J. G. 1979. "The Analytics of Uncertainty and Information, An Expository Survey." *Journal of Economic Literature 17:* 1375–1442.

Hotelling, H. 1931. "The Economics of Exhaustible Resources." *Journal of Political Economy 39:* 137–175.

Hudson, E. A., and Jorgenson, D. W. 1974. "U.S. Energy Policy and Economic Growth 1975–2000. *Bell Journal of Economics and Management Science 5:* 461–514.

Hughes, B. B. 1980. *World Modeling*. Lexington, Mass., and Toronto: Lexington Books.

Isachsen, A. J., and Strøm, S. 1980. "The Hidden Economy: The Labor

Market and Tax Evasion." *Scandinavian Journal of Economics 82:* 304–311.

Jantsch, E. 1975. *Design for Evolution.* New York: George Braziller.

Kantor, B. 1979. "Rational Expectations and Economic Thought." *Journal of Economic Literature 17:* 1422–1441.

Lakatos, I. 1970. "Falsification and the Methodology of Scientific Research Programs." In I. Lakatos and A. E. Musgrave, eds., *Criticism and the Growth of Knowledge.* London: Cambridge University Press, pp. 91–106.

Leijonhufvud. 1968. *On Keynesian Economics and the Economics of Keynes.* New York: Oxford University Press.

Lucas, R. E. 1972. "Expectations and the Neutrality of Money." *Journal of Economic Theory 4:* 103–124.

———. 1976. "Econometric Policy Evaluation: A Critique." In K. Brunner and A. H. Meltzer, eds., *The Phillips Curve and Labour Markets.* Carnegie-Rochester Conference Series on Public Policy, Vol. 1. Amsterdam: North-Holland, pp. 19–64.

———. 1980. "Methods and Problems in Business Cycle Theory." *Journal of Money, Credit, and Banking 12:* 696–715.

Machlup, F. 1972. *The Production and Distribution of Knowledge in the United States.* Princeton: Princeton University Press.

Makridakis, S. 1976. "A Survey of Time Series." *International Statistical Review 44:* 29–70.

Malinvaud, E. 1977. *The Theory of Unemployment Reconsidered.* Oxford: Basic Blackwell.

———. 1981. "Econometrics Faced with the Needs of Macroeconomic Policy." *Econometrica 49:* 1363–1375.

———. 1982. Où en est la théorie macroéconomique? In *Cahiers du Département d'Econométrie,* Cahier 82.01, Université de Genève.

Manne, A. 1977. "ETA-MACRO: A Model of Energy Economy Interactions." Electric Power Research Institute, EA-592, Research Project 1014, Palo Alto, California.

Marshak, J. 1974a. "Information, Decision, and the Scientist." In *Pragmatic Aspects of Human Communication.* Dordrecht: C. Cherry.

———. 1974b. "Entropy, Economics, Physics." Working Paper No. 221. Western Management Science Institute. Presented at Econometric Society Meeting, December.

McKinnon, R. I. 1981. "The Exchange Rate and Macroeconomic Policy: Changing Postwar Perceptions." *Journal of Economic Literature 19:* 531–557.

Meadows, D. H., et al. 1972. *The Limits to Growth.* New York: Universe Books.

Meadows, D.; Richardson, J.; and Bruckmann, G. 1982. *Groping in the Dark.* Chichester: Wiley.

Mensch, G., et al. 1980. "Innovation Trends, and Switching Between Full- and Under-Employment Equilibria 1950–1978." Discussion Paper IIM/dp 80-5, International Institute of Management, Science Center Berlin.

Mesarovic, M. D.; Macko, D.; and Takahara, Y. 1970. *Theory of Hierarchical Multi-Level Systems*. New York: Academic Press.

Mirrlees, J. A. 1971. "An Exploration in the Theory of Optimum Income Taxation." *Journal of Economic Studies 38:* 170–208.

Mueller, D. C. 1976. "Public Choice, A Survey." *Journal of Economic Literature 14:* 395–433.

Muth, J. F. 1961. "Rational Expectations and the Theory of Price Movement." *Econometrica 29:* 315–335.

Niehans, J. 1977. "Exchange Rate Dynamics with Stock/Flow Interaction." *Journal of Political Economy 85:* 1245–1257.

Nordhaus, W. D. 1975. "The Political Business Cycle." *Review of Economic Studies 42:* 169–190.

Nozick, R. 1974. *Anarchy, State, and Utopia*. New York: Basic Books.

Peterson, F. M., and Fisher, A. C. 1977. "The Exploitation of Extractive Resources, A Survey." *Economic Journal 87:* 681–721.

Phelps, E. S. 1970. "Phillips Curves, Expectations of Inflation, and Optimal Unemployment over Time." *Economica 34:* 254–281.

Pierce, D. A., and Haugh, L. D. 1979. "Causality in Temporal Systems, Characterization and a Survey." *Journal of Econometrics 10:* 265–293.

Platt, J. 1970. "Hierarchical Restructuring." *Bulletin of Atomic Scientists 15.*

———. 1979. *Eight Major Evolutionary Jumps Today*. Berlin: International Institute for Comparative Social Research, IIVG/pre 79-8.

———. 1981. "Research and Development Needs for Solving Global Problems." In *Social Implications of the Scientific and Technological Revolution*. Paris: UNESCO.

Pontryagin, L. S., et al. 1962. *The Mathematical Theory of Optimal Processes*. New York: Interscience.

Pool, W. 1967. "Speculative Prices as Random-Walks: An Analysis of Ten Time Series of Flexible Exchange Rates." *Southern Economic Journal 34:* 468–478.

Porat, M. U. 1978. "Emergence of an Information Economy." In *Innovations in Communications*. Washington, D.C.

Ramsey, F. P. 1927. "A Contribution to the Theory of Taxation." *Economic Journal 37:* 47–61.

Rawls, J. 1971. *A Theory of Justice*. Oxford: Oxford University Press.

Rechenberg, I. 1973. *Evolutionsstrategie*. Stuttgart-Bad Cannstatt: Friedrich Fromman Verlag.

Santomero, A. M., and Seater, J. J. 1978. "The Inflation-Unemployment Trade-Off: A Critique of the Literature." *Journal of Economic Literature 16:* 499–544.

Sargent, T. J. 1976. "The Observational Equivalence of Natural and Unnatural Theories of Macroeconomics." *Journal of Political Economy 84:* 631–640.

Sargent, T. J., and Wallace, N. 1975. "Rational Expectations, the Optimal Monetary Instrument, and the Optimal Money Supply Rule." *Journal of Political Economy 83:* 241–254.

Sen, A. K. 1970. *Collective Choice and Social Welfare.* San Francisco: Holden Day.

———. 1976. "Liberty, Unanimity and Rights." *Economica 43:* 217–235.

———. 1977. "Social Choice Theory: A Re-Examination." *Econometrica 45:* 53–89.

Sims, C. A. 1972. "Money, Income, and Causality." *American Economic Review 62:* 540–552.

———. 1978. "Small Econometric Models of the U.S. and West Germany without Prior Restrictions." Discussion Paper No. 78-105. Center for Economic Research, Department of Economics, University of Minnesota.

———. 1980. "Macroeconomics and Reality." *Econometrica 48:* 1–48.

Stigler, G. J. 1961. "The Economics of Information." *Journal of Political Economy 69:* 213–225.

Thom, R. 1972. *Structural Stability and Morphogenesis.* D. H. Fowler, trans. New York: Benjamin, 1972 (French). Translation published 1975.

Tobin, J. 1980. "Are New Classical Models Plausible Enough to Guide Policy?" *Journal of Money, Credit, and Banking 12:* 788–799.

Trevinthick, J. 1978. "Recent Developments in the Theory of Employment." *Scottish Journal of Political Economy 25:* 107 ff.

Tribus, M., and McIrvine, E. C. 1971. "Energy and Information." *Scientific American 225*(3): 179–188.

Ursprung, H. 1982. *Die elementare Katastrophentheorie: Eine Darstellung aus der Sicht der Oekonomie.* Heidelberg and New York: Springer.

Waterston, A. 1965. *Development Planning, Lessons of Experience.* Baltimore.

Weintraub, E. R. 1977. "The Microfoundation of Macroeconomics: A Critical Survey." *Journal of Economic Literature 15:* 1–23.

Zellner, A. 1979. "Statistical Analysis of Econometric Models." *Journal of the American Statistical Association 74:* 628–651.

Discussion

(Bell, Wildenmann, Miller, Krelle, Fritsch)

Edited by Andrei S. Markovits

DANIEL BELL opened the discussion period by saying that neither Krelle's nor Fritsch and Kirchgässner's papers provided any sense of the internal and external intellectual sources for new advances. These papers and that of Tinbergen (which was not given in person) only seemed to provide lists that were almost ad hoc. In terms of Kuhn's notion of paradigms, for example, what explained the way new advances occurred intellectually? Was there some systematic explanation? Bell thought this was particularly important because none of the papers really dealt with the *decay* of theories either, as, for example, in the current feeling that Keynesian theory has become less adequate.

The Role of Measurement and Measurement Concepts

Bell's second question concerned Krelle's emphasis on the importance of measurement. Bell said he felt a bit wounded, since he was a sociologist and could not measure in that way. He felt he had been excluded from the world. He asked, first, whether the fundamental problem actually involved measurement or, rather, simply an adequate choice of the relations between variables—a more complex conceptual problem. Only after such a choice of these relations would it be possible to decide whether or not to measure what one found. He asked if there was any systematic way to identify the relations between variables.

Krelle had spoken of sociology as becoming a science only to the extent that it could deal with measurement. Bell pointed out, however, that sociology differs from economics in that economics has a metric; everything can be translated into some linear scale, whether in marks or dollars or shadow prices. Bell felt it was more difficult to take the concepts of status or power or any of the other elements in sociology and find a metric which could measure how the "units" of each could be exchanged. He thought, therefore, that the problem of measurement was a very different problem when no clear metric of any kind existed.

Rudolf Wildenmann followed next and pointed out an unrecognized problem in the field of economic development—the empirical study of distributions, which is not only a statistical problem, but also a conceptual problem. Economics had become too concerned with model building, he said, but the economic models could not be tested in the real world, as Hans Apel had emphasized some time ago.

Wildenmann suggested that economists could learn from other social sciences that had been forced to develop more basic conceptualizations. Empirical studies, such as social science surveys, for example, were possible only because the researchers had thought a great deal about what measurement concepts to use and what kind of theories to test. This kind of enterprise may be referred to as number–punching, but Wildenmann said he was happy to be a number puncher because it required a great deal of methodological and theoretical preparation to get reliable data. Perhaps the trouble with economic predictions of development was that the data put into the models was full of too much assumption and too little fact.

James G. Miller then asked if money could be regarded as a major form of social information. "If research focused on the flow of specialized kinds of information, like the flow of money through computers or in credit card networks, would that make it possible to use this information as a bridge to connect economics with the other social sciences that look at society as a whole?"

How Do New Ideas Grow and Decay?

William Krelle responded to Bell's comments first, by saying that new ideas enter a discipline by a process of chance. Everyone, he said, has new ideas that other people think are crazy. He did not think he could explain, for example, why John von Neumann got his ideas. Perhaps it was simply because he was von Neumann; perhaps it was chance; or perhaps von Neumann had natural gifts and a good education that enabled him to invent something new. Beyond that, Krelle did not think it was possible to go. Scientifically, the most plausible position to take was that new ideas occurred by chance, within the framework of various probability distributions and pre-conditions, but we could not know when an advance would occur. Suppose von Neumann had never come to Vienna and had simply remained in Budapest? He would not have gone to important seminars or been exposed to new ideas and probably would not have developed game theory.

Daniel Bell asked if Krelle was rejecting Merton's notion of multiple discoverers. Krelle replied that even in this case, the problem of how people came to have ideas was impossible to solve because it was part of a stochastic system.

But Wildenmann then charged that Krelle was already admitting more than simple chance when he referred to probability functions. Was it not possible to change the milieu and improve the chances for a new idea to occur? When Krelle agreed, Wildenmann said that in that case, we could extend the discussion beyond the realm of chance into a discussion of milieu factors, and Krelle admitted that this was a possibility.

Krelle then turned to the question of the decay of theories. He argued that when some knowledge became superseded, it signified that science was progressing. "Progress means that there is also decay."

Measurements, Indicators, and Information

On the question of measurement, Krelle commented that 150 years ago no one would have thought it was possible to measure GNP. Neither would they have thought that there was a general price level in the economy as a whole. However, Bell then pointed out that Sir William Petty believed that it was possible to measure GNP in his book, *Political Arithmetic*, published nearly three hundred years ago; but Krelle countered by saying that Petty's concept was very different. The real conceptual base for thinking about general price levels was not developed until the beginning of the 1920s when different statistical offices tried to estimate the income of social groups, and then finally, later on in the 1930s when Stone and others developed the system of national accounting.

Given this, Krelle felt that there was something to suggest to political scientists and sociologists. He proposed that if things such as preferences were given a scale, and normalized, this would enable a social scientist to ask questions such as, "How do you like the government?", and so on; and to get statistical distributions within some margin of error. One might measure political attitudes within a nation, simply by asking questions in the same way that households were asked to declare their income. No, the world is not one-dimensional, but this is not an insurmountable obstacle to such quantitative studies. Economists did not look at income level in a one-dimensional space; and Krelle suggested that political scientists and sociologists would someday be able to measure in comparable ways.

On Miller's question concerning money and information, Krelle explained that he did not consider money but, rather, prices as transmitters of information. He agreed, however, that information theory could be one of the bridges between political science, sociology, and economics. Preference theory and utility theory also involve the production of information and could be used as bridges. Krelle said that the greatest failing in economics was that it had no well-developed theory of institutions. To be institution-free was sometimes an advantage—for example, in comparing societies with different social and economic systems. Any study of the details of an economy, however, will require some knowledge about the institutions, and that is still lacking in economics.

Bruno Fritsch addressed the question raised by Bell on the issue of measurement. He said that a basic problem remained to be examined, with regard to such economic indicators as GNP. He claimed, for example, that GNP did not say anything, and was never intended to say anything, about the well-being or feelings of people. He said that he always told his students that GNP was really nothing but a speedometer, which told only how many goods and services had been asked for in the marketplace in a given period. It said nothing about the character of the driver or the driver's destination: "It makes no difference whether it is a church or a brothel." All measurement has something to do with social convention and something to do with the transformation of bits into wits. He felt that the meaning of measurement is a very important but unsolved problem.

CHAPTER 8

Social Science and Integration Across Disciplines

James Grier Miller

AS THE ARTICLE ON WHICH THIS CONFERENCE is based made clear [DPS][1], social science is becoming increasingly quantitative. Although phenomena of interest to social scientists are usually characterized by complex relationships among many variables, with the result that they may be difficult or impossible to manipulate experimentally, statistical innovations, increased availability of computers for simulation and data analysis, and use of mathematical models have facilitated empirical research in all the social sciences.

Although important theoretical advances have also occurred, the social sciences still lack a commonly accepted unifying theory. Such theory is essential to a mature science. Indeed, integrative theory is a goal of all science, albeit one that is not clearly and explicitly recognized by all biological and social scientists.

An integrative theory is essential in many ways: It reveals basic principles; it clarifies the relationships among the concepts used by different scientists; it brings order to the mass of accumulated knowledge, and it provides a conceptual structure into which discoveries can be fitted and seen in relation to other work. Such a theory can be the basis for models of actual processes and can indicate where further research is needed to fill gaps and resolve inconsistencies and contradictions. In addition, it can provide common measurement units and terms to relate the special measurements and terms used in various limited researchers. After a new theoretical integration, as the history of natural science has shown repeatedly, basic discovery, experimentation, technological advance, and isolated facts suddenly fit together to make new meaning.

In the absence of such theory, each specialized area of social science stands alone, with its own limited special theories, vocabularies, and measurement units. Social scientists in different disciplines may not understand each others' language and may be unaware of relevant findings in fields other than their own. They are even less aware of related researches in the biological sciences.

Shared belief in the importance and feasibility of integrative theory, and in the value of an interdisciplinary approach to research in the sciences of behavior, was the impetus that led our group of scientists to form the Committee on the Behavioral Sciences, an interdisciplinary group that met over a period of several years at the University of Chicago, beginning about 1950. Members of the committee represented a wide range of disciplines including mathematics and the social, biological, and physical sciences—anthropology, neurophysiology, mathematical biology, political science, psychology, history, economics, sociology, psychiatry, planning, and physics. We were interested in finding general principles that would be applicable in all of our various fields of interest and in discovering how the different disciplines were interrelated in theory and research. An early discussion, for example, dealt with the principles of equilibrium and homeostasis, which we found to be relevant to several different fields.

From the beginning, members agreed that an integrated theory must be applicable to both biological and social sciences, and that it must also be compatible with findings of the sciences that dealt with nonliving aspects of nature.

General living systems theory—a general systems theory concerned with living systems—met these requirements. My book *Living Systems*, is a statement of this theory as it was developed and modified in succeeding years.[2] Work on it began at Chicago and continued after 1955, when several of us who had been members of the Chicago committee moved to the University of Michigan and founded the Mental Health Research Institute. An even greater range of disciplines was represented at Michigan than at Chicago. At Michigan, both the interdisciplinary approach and the theoretical focus on general systems theory continued. As one would expect, considering the creativity and individuality of the people involved, there was always theoretical diversity among members of the group, although all accepted a common set of core principles. The magazine *Behavioral Science* began publication in 1956. It is in its twenty-seventh year as an interdisciplinary publication for the behavioral sciences. In recent years it has concentrated on articles that have a systems orientation.

Since 1950 the number of social and biological scientists who use systems concepts has increased greatly. In addition, it is generally recognized that most of the pressing problems of societies at this time must be addressed jointly by multiple academic disciplines. The International Institute for Applied Systems Analysis (IIASA) in Vienna brings together scientists representing 17 nations for concentrated work on a number of such problems. I arrived there on July 1, 1972, the day it opened, and spent several months there in 1972 and 1974, the first two years of its program, as a fellow working to establish the theoretical and methodological task force. In 1980 eight program areas existed at IIASA: energy systems, food and agriculture, resources and environment, human settlements and services, management and technology, system and decision sciences, and general research and education.[3] Scientists in each of these areas have been concerned with critical issues facing the world today. General research includes work on the state of the art of systems analysis, regional and global models, and computer networks. The latter has led to an international network of more than two hundred host computers in North America and both Eastern and Western Europe. In 1974 some nations now participating were unwilling to cooperate in such a project.

A number of different forms of systems theory have developed over the past several years. My work on general living systems theory, to be discussed next, grew from my experiences in the groups in which I have participated.

General Living Systems Theory

The most basic idea of general systems theory is that the physical universe is made up of a set of *concrete systems* that form a hierarchy beginning with the smallest and least complex systems, which may be atoms, composed of particles; and including molecules, formed from atoms, and larger systems, each including all those below it in the hierarchy up to the ultimate system, the universe.

A *system* is defined as a *nonrandom accumulation of matter and energy in a region in physical space-time organized into interacting, interrelated subsystems and components.*

Living systems, which include the phenomena of interest to both biological and social sciences, are concrete systems in specific loci in space-time with the special characteristics necessary for life. Like other concrete systems, they are composed of chemical molecules, although their most characteristic molecules, nucleic acids and proteins, exhibit a degree of complexity beyond that of any nonliving substance. These very large molecules are not produced in nature outside living systems.

Like nonliving systems, living systems occur in a hierarchy of *levels*. Systems at each level are composed of systems at the level below. I have identified seven levels of living systems, although there may be more. The seven levels are: cells, organs, organisms, groups, organizations, societies, and supranational systems.

Ecological systems are mixed living and nonliving systems. All the living systems on earth interact with the nonliving parts of their environments in ecological systems of various sizes. The planet as a whole is a large ecological system. Ecological systems are coordinated chiefly by flows of matter and energy.

General living systems theory is an evolutionary theory. Each level evolved from the level below and has systems at that level as its major components. This evolution resulted in what I call *shred-out*, illustrated in Figure 8.1. It is as if each strand of a many-stranded rope had unraveled progressively at higher levels into more and more pieces, as more and increasingly complicated units were needed to perform each life process. The living substance in each of these systems is very similar, and each system is organized to carry out comparable life processes. For this reason, it is possible to say that social systems at levels above the organism are "alive" in the same way that cells, organs, and organisms are alive. Each higher level of living systems, however, has developed capacities for behavior that are qualitatively different from those of lower-level systems and has structural characteristics that are not found at lower levels. Such characteristics and capacities are *emergents*. Higher-level systems cannot be described only in terms used for systems below them in the hierarchy without neglecting significant aspects of their structure and process.

Although living systems share many system characteristics with nonliving systems, they differ in several significant ways. They are open systems that maintain steady states by taking in low-entropy substances from their environments, using them in their processes, and returning to the environment materials higher in entropy than their inputs. This allows them to decrease their own entropy and to delay, for varying lengths of time, the entropic dissolution that is the ultimate fate of all forms of matter. Nonliving systems, except for certain man-made machines, do not do this.

Living systems ordinarily process more information than nonliving systems do. They are controlled and coordinated by information flows. A significant number of their critical processes are concerned with the input, processing, and output of information.

Matter-energy (matter and energy) and information processing by living systems are accomplished by a set of distinct subsystem processes, which are necessary either for the life of each individual system or for the continuation of all species or types beyond a single generation. These are processes of specific sets of physical units, the system's components. It is possible for a system to lack structure for a given subsystem process only if another living system with which it is symbiotic or parasitic, or an

FIGURE 8.1 Shred-out

Level	Approximate Number of Years Since Period of Origin	Approximate Median Diameter Size
Cell	3,000,000,000	$\frac{1}{1,000,000}$ meter
Organ	500,000,000 + ?	$\frac{1}{1,000}$ meter
Organism	500,000,000	$\frac{1}{100}$ meter
Group	500,000,000?	$\frac{1}{10}$ meter
Organization	11,000	100 meters
Society	7,000	1,000,000 meters (1,000 kilometers)
Supranational System	4,500	5,000,000 meters (5,000 kilometers)

environmental adjustment of some sort, provides for it. I have identified nineteen processes that appear to be subsystem processes, the critical life processes. They are listed and defined in Table 8.1.

Each subsystem controls a number of *variables,* which it keeps in steady state by adjustment processes among its components. The decider subsystem of the total system employs systemwide adjustment processes to govern and control its subsystem processes and to maintain systemwide

TABLE 8.1
The 19 Critical Subsystems of a Living System

SUBSYSTEMS THAT PROCESS BOTH MATTER-ENERGY AND INFORMATION

1. *Reproducer,* the subsystem which is capable of giving rise to other systems similar to the one it is in.

2. *Boundary,* the subsystem at the perimeter of a system that holds together the components that make up the system, protects them from environmental stresses, and excludes or permits entry to various sorts of matter-energy and information.

SUBSYSTEMS THAT PROCESS MATTER-ENERGY

3. *Ingestor,* the subsystem that brings matter-energy across the system boundary from the environment.

4. *Distributor,* the subsystem that carries inputs from outside the system or outputs from its subsystems around the system to each component.

5. *Converter,* the subsystem that changes certain inputs to the system into forms more useful for the special processes of that particular system.

6. *Producer,* the subsystem that forms stable associations that endure for significant periods among matter-energy inputs to the system or outputs from its converter, the materials synthesized being for growth, damage repair, or replacement of components of the system, or for providing energy for moving or constituting the system's outputs of products or information markers to its suprasystem.

7. *Matter-energy storage,* the subsystem that retains in the system, for different periods of time, deposits of various sorts of matter-energy.

8. *Extruder,* the subsystem that transmits matter-energy out of the system in the forms of products or wastes.

9. *Motor,* the subsystem that moves the system or parts of it in relation to part or all of its environment or moves components of its environment in relation to each other.

10. *Supporter,* the subsystem that maintains the proper spatial relationships among components of the system, so that they can interact without weighting each other down or crowding each other.

SUBSYSTEMS THAT PROCESS INFORMATION

11. *Input transducer,* the sensory subsystem that brings markers bearing information into the system, changing them to other matter-energy forms suitable for transmission within it.

12. *Internal transducer,* the sensory subsystem that receives, from subsystems or components within the system, markers bearing information about significant alterations in those subsystems or components, changing them to other matter-energy forms of a sort which can be transmitted within it.

13. *Channel and net,* the subsystem composed of a single route in physical space, or multiple interconnected routes, by which markers bearing information are transmitted to all parts of the system.

14. *Decoder,* the subsystem that alters the code of information input to it through the input transducer or internal transducer into a "private" code that can be used internally by the system.

15. *Associator,* the subsystem that carries out the first stage of the learning process, forming enduring associations among items of information in the system.

16. *Memory,* the subsystem that carries out the second stage of the learning process, storing various sorts of information in the system for different periods of time.

17. *Decider,* the executive subsystem that receives information inputs from all other subsystems and transmits to them information outputs that control the entire system.

18. *Encoder,* the subsystem that alters the code of information input to it from other information processing subsystems, from a "private" code used internally by the system

TABLE 8–1. (continued)

	into a "public" code which can be interpreted by other systems in its environment.
	19. *Output transducer,* the subsystem that puts out markers bearing information from the system, changing markers within the system into other matter-energy forms which can be transmitted over channels in the system's environment.

steady states as well as steady states with the environment. Many adjustment processes are negative feedbacks. Feedback loops connect all parts of living systems and connect the system with its environment.

The Study of Living Systems

There are three degrees of generality of scientific principles or laws: cross-individual, cross-type or species, and cross-level generalization.

In most scientific specialties, cross-individual generalization occurs first. Differences obviously exist among individual cells, individual organs, individual organizations, and so forth. There are also certain similarities or commonalities among individuals of a given type, which make it possible to generalize across individuals.

Later, in most sciences, cross-type or species generalizations are recognized. These are powerful because they cover a larger set of phenomena, even though they also involve more variance—both among individuals and among types. As science develops, fields such as comparative anatomy, comparative physiology, comparative psychology, and comparative sociology arise, which involve generalizations across types of systems. The relative size of skulls of rats, cats, dogs, dolphins, apes, and human beings, for instance, can be compared with the average measures of intelligence of each species.

The third degree of scientific generalization is cross-level generalization, which is very rare in science. It is possible to study similarities among levels even though simultaneously efforts continue to study their obvious and equally important differences. Relatively few quantitative comparisons of phenomena have been made across levels. The boundary structures or the decision-making processes or the feedback processes of cells can be compared quantitatively with similar aspects of organs, organisms, groups, organizations, societies, and supranational systems. The relative absence of such researches is a consequence of the way science currently is organized. Scientists usually limit the scope of their expertise to specific aspects of systems at a given level because one person cannot be truly informed and expert on a broader range of phenomena. Scientists working at one level of living systems are rarely current with the literature at other levels. This fact is demonstrated by the paucity of references to researches at other levels in the texts and bibliographies of scientific papers.

The traditional cautiousness of scientists, and the separateness and parochialism of their disciplines, makes them skeptical of any generalization from a cell to a system as different from it as an organism or a society is. Such caution means that once a scientist discovers a principle at one level, he or she typically does not think it likely enough to be relevant to another level to take the trouble to find out whether similar principles have been reported in the literature at other levels. Scientists rarely consider searching the literature to find out whether aspects of their findings at one level are quantitatively comparable to findings at another level. They do not ordinarily make such an effort even if they recognize that such a relationship could exist and might provide a significant insight in another scientific field that they do not consider their own area of expertise. Often they fear disapproval by other scientists if they stray outside their own field.

Research in General Living Systems Theory

In the DPS list Contribution 40, general systems analysis was categorized as philosophy.[1] Since 1971 it has to some degree become science. Explicit quantitative findings have been made relevant to general living systems theory.

Systems-oriented research applies scientific methods and systems concepts to study of previously unknown or poorly understood systems or to correction of malfunctioning systems, such as unprofitable organizations, strife-torn family groups, or depressed or sick patients.

In any case it is important to learn about the structure of the particular system being studied—the arrangement of its components in space-time—and to determine how and by what components its subsystem processes are accomplished.

The *variables* of each subsystem are maintained within steady-state ranges when the system is functioning optimally. The matter-energy processing subsystems control such variables as, for example, quantity, quality, and rate of matter-energy input (ingestor); sorts of matter-energy distributed to various parts of the system and changes in distributing over time (distributor); and percentage of matter-energy used in producing, rate of producing, and quality of matter-energy produced (producer).

Variables of the information-processing subsystems include threshold, channel capacity, rate of processing, lag, codes used in transmission, and meaning of information processed.

Cost is a variable in all subsystems. Each adjustment process is carried out at a cost in energy, time, materials, money, or other expendables. Ordinarily a system will choose a less costly process in preference to a more costly one, if both are available and suitable.

Measures or *indicators* are available for several if not all variables of each subsystem at each level of living system. To the extent that it is possible, measures should be only in centimeter-gram-second and information-theory units or derivatives, because these are units ordinarily used by sciences other than the social sciences. Measurement of information—defined in the technical sense of information theory as nonrandomness of signals—is possible using binary digits or bits. For the *meaning* variables of information-processing subsystems, however, no unit of measurement is available. Developing objective measures of meaning in information flows should have high priority in science.

Systemwide processes are also important in systems. The overall rates of matter-energy or information input or output to a system, and the way in which it adjusts its subsystems both under normal conditions and in response to stress, are examples. Certain adjustment processes are characteristic of a type or species as a whole; others are peculiar to an individual system.

Each type of system is subject to *pathological processes* produced by stresses that force some system variables out of their normal steady-state ranges and require more extreme adjustment processes. If a subsystem in which pathology occurs cannot adjust to it, strains requiring adjustments also occur in other parts of the system.

A systems-oriented study of a living system at any level should include the following steps:

1. Identify the conceptual variables of subsystems or the total system to be studied.
2. Determine the dimensions to use in measuring those variables.
3. Select reliable indicators to be used to measure the variables along the chosen dimensions.
4. Hypothesize, from theory, specific relations between two or more variables.
5. Specify the method to be followed to test this hypothesis explicitly enough so that it could be replicated.
6. Measure the selected variables with the appropriate indicators at specific places and times.
7. On the basis of the findings, determine whether the hypothesis is proved or disproved.
8. Ultimately attempt to integrate the special theory on which the hypothesis was based into general theory.

Cross-Level Studies

A major goal of the basic research of various general systems-oriented scientists with whom I have worked at Chicago, Michigan, and (more recently) at the University of Louisville—where a Systems Science Institute was formed—was to test a number of hypotheses at more than one level of living systems. Living Systems lists 173 such hypotheses, some of which have been confirmed by research at one level and have been demonstrated to have parallels at another level.[5] Others seem testable and possibly relevant to multiple levels. Since most scientists are expert at only one level of living system, interdisciplinary group research appears to be the best approach to such research.

The first experiments testing a cross-level hypothesis were carried out by our group in Michigan in the late 1950s. This work studied the channel and net subsystem at five levels: cell, organ, organism, group, and organization. The "information input overload" hypothesis can be stated as follows:

As the information input to a single channel of a living system—measured in bits per second—increases, the information output—measured similarly—increases almost identically at first but gradually falls behind as it approaches a certain output rate, the channel capacity, which cannot be exceeded in the channel. The output then levels off at that rate; and finally, as the information input rate continues to go up, the output decreases gradually toward zero as breakdown or the confusional state occurs under overload.

Experiments at each level were conducted by specialists in relevant fields. Measurements of information input and output rates were made on single fibers from the sciatic nerves of frogs, optic tracts of several white rats (optic nerve to optic cortex), human subjects working alone, human subjects in groups of three, and laboratory "organizations" made up of two two-person groups and a single subject. In the organization experiment, information was processed through a channel consisting of one group of two subjects as input transducer, another group of two as decider, and a single subject as output transducer. This provided, in extremely simple form, the multiple echelon structure that differentiates an organization from a face-to-face group.

Data from the five levels yielded similar information input-output curves, the shape of which confirmed the hypothesis. Measured in bits per second, the average rate of information transmission at each higher level was lower than at the previous level (see Figure 8.2). In addition, a number of adjustment processes to the increasing overload were found to be common to several or all levels. The more complex systems used more adjustment processes, but they also continued to use those that were found at lower levels.

Other tests of cross-level hypotheses have been and are being carried

FIGURE 8.2. Information Input Overload

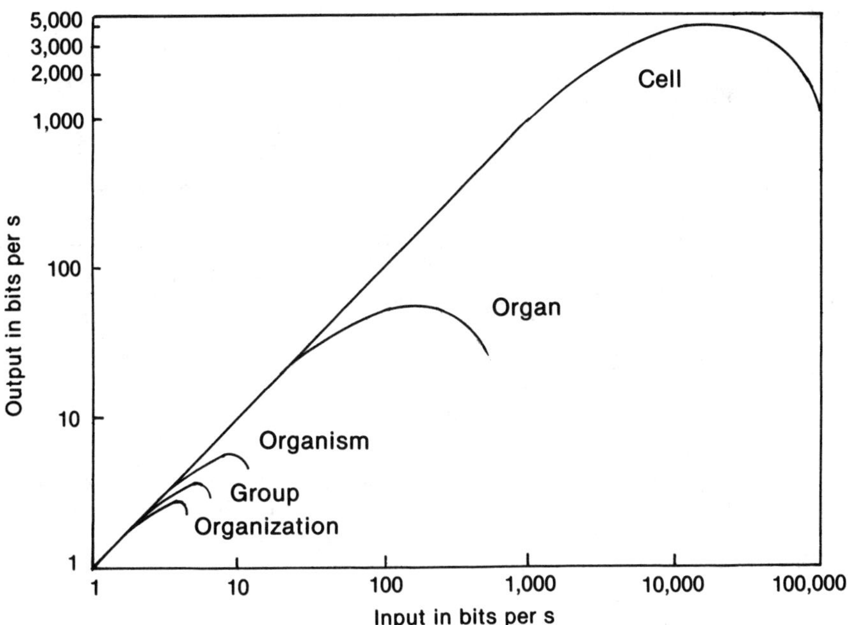

out. These include experiments on comparable components at more than one level or application of the same mathematical model to systems at different levels. Among these are:

1. Research by Lewis on individual human organisms and groups testing another hypothesis from *Living Systems:*[6] The hypothesis, which relates to the decider subsystem, is:

When a system is receiving conflicting command signals from several suprasystems, and is intermittently being a component of all of them, the more different the signals are, the slower is its decision making.

Subjects in these experiments played a game similar to the arcade game "Star Trek," a war game against an extragalactic enemy. A computer presented "commands" from five officers, all of the same rank and all the subjects' superiors. Subjects had to decide which command to follow if conflicting commands were received. Responses were stored by the computer, which also collected and stored data on the independent and dependent variables.

Subjects could "fire," "warp," "scan," "dock," or "wait." Eight patterns of commands with differing amounts of conflict were used, ranging from total agreement on which action to take to total disagreement among the five officers. Subjects were permitted to take actions only if they were ordered by at least one officer.

After each decision, the computer presented its result and a summary of all the results in the game. Subjects were told how many ships they had lost, how many enemy ships they had destroyed, how many sectors of space they had explored, how much energy and time they had left, and so forth.

After forty turns, a final score, based on their success in defending their own ships and destroying the enemy, was determined. The game was scored so that the greater the number of officers that agreed on a command, the more likely it was to be successful. Subjects were paid according to their success.

In the group experiment, three subjects worked together to arrive at a decision. Decision time was longer for groups than for individual persons in all command situations.

Both the individual and the group experiments yielded highly significant results, which supported the hypothesis. Lewis suggests that the work could be extended to the organization level, using at least three groups of three subjects, with one group receiving recommendations from the other two and acting as final decider.

2. The Weber function is a statement of the relationship between the intensity of input and the intensity of output in an input transducer or sense organ of a living system. It has been tested in separate researches at the levels of cell and organism. The Weber function can be stated as a hypothesis as follows:

The intensity output signal of a system varies as a power function of the intensity of its input, the form of the power function being $\Psi = k\,(\Phi - \Phi_0)^n$; *where* Ψ *is the intensity of the output signal;* Φ *is the physical magnitude of the input energies;* Φ_0 *is a constant, the physical magnitude of the minimum detectable or threshold input energies;* k *depends on the choice of measurement units; and the exponent* n *varies with different sensory modalities of the information processed.*

Mountcastle investigated the "touch-spot" input transducer cells in the hairy skin of cats and monkeys.[7] These are minute domelike elevations of the skin from which exquisitely sensitive afferent fibers carry information toward the central nervous system. An apparatus controlled both the amount of indentation applied by mechanical force and the timing of stimulation. Mountcastle recorded the pulses along the nerve fibers that followed mechanical pressure on the sensory cells. Such fibers respond to stimulation by a maintained steady rate of discharge. He found that the input-output relationship of each of these cells was accurately described by a power function.

At the organism level, Stevens found that the Weber function applied to the relationship between the intensity of sensory input and the subjects' reports of the intensity of their sensations.[8] For each sensory modality, the exponent n was different. It ranged from 0.33 for brightness of white light to 1.45 for heaviness of lifted weights, 1.6 for warmth, and 3.5 for electric shock to the finger.

Events at these two levels are clearly not independent. Mountcastle suggests that the characteristics of input transducer components determine the nature of the organism's responses. That is, the internal processing that occurs between input to sensory units and a person's report transmits the information in linear fashion.[9]

3. Staw, Sandelands, and Dutton surveyed the literature about systems at the levels of organism, group, and organization for evidence bearing on their "threat-rigidity" hypothesis, which they state as follows:

"*. . . it is hypothesized that a threat results in changes in both the information and control processes of a system, and because of these changes, a system's behavior is predicted to become less varied or flexible*" (emphasis added).[10]

A threat is defined in this study as an environmental event that has impending negative or harmful consequences for a system. The hypothesis predicts that a threat to the vital interests of an individual, group, or organization can lead to rigid behavior. The authors further propose that such behavior may be maladaptive when the threatening situation includes major environmental changes, since flexibility and diversity of response have survival value in such conditions and prior, well-learned responses are often inappropriate. If no major change is threatened, rigid but previously successful responses may be appropriate.

Organism-Level Effects

At this level, threatening situations have been used to alter states of psychological stress, anxiety, and physiological arousal in human subjects. Although the bodies of research on each of these states are separate, the authors consider it probable that physiological arousal underlies the behavioral effects that are observed in stress and anxiety. They assume that the presence of these conditions indicates that an experimental situation was, in fact, threatening.

Threatening situations in these researches have included such things as the possibility of electric shock; performance-failure feedback on preceding tasks; excess pacing of tasks under time pressure; and formal, unfriendly experimental settings. In addition, standard tests of anxiety, such as the Taylor Manifest Anxiety Scale, can determine the degree of anxiety present in people not being experimentally stressed.

Among relevant findings that tend to support the threat-rigidity hypothesis are those that indicate changes in perception. Subjects under stress in these experiments had reduced ability to identify and discriminate among visual stimuli and were more likely than nonstressed subjects to use previously held "internal hypotheses" about the identity of unfamiliar stimuli. Similar effects were found with anxiety and arousal. Anxious subjects were less able to discriminate visual detail than were those who did not experience anxiety. Under arousal, sensitivity to peripheral cues was decreased, narrowing the range of cues processed.

Problem solving and learning are also affected by stress, anxiety, and arousal. Stressed subjects have been found to adhere to a previously learned solution even when it was not appropriate to the problem at hand and to be less flexible than nonstressed subjects in their choice of solution methods. Stress and training interact in motor performance since stress elicits well-learned, habitual, and dominant responses. In the case of trained subjects, response rigidity of this sort can enhance performance if the learned responses are relevant to the situation. Such subjects, in fact, perform better than nonstressed subjects. Untrained subjects, however, perform less well under stress than do those not being stressed since they lack the appropriate dominant responses.

Natural disasters have provided further insight into threat-rigidity effects. Disasters are extremely threatening situations, which can create feelings of stress and anxiety in a victim. Clinical studies and observations have found narrowing of the perceptual field, limitation of the amount of information input, rigidity of response, and primitive forms of reaction in disaster victims. They may fail to heed warnings or follow directions, or may "freeze up" and be incapable of action.

Group-Level Effects

Investigations of group response to threat have been concerned with the effect of threat on group cohesiveness—that is, on the tendency of group members to remain together, the effect on group leadership and control, and the effect on pressures toward uniformity within the group. In the research surveyed, attainment of group goals was threatened by competition from other groups and by such situations as radical change in rules for a group game that made it impossible for the group to predict what behavior would lead to success.

When a threat was attributed to an external source and the group thought it could be successful in meeting it, group cohesiveness was found to increase. Group members supported their leadership, and there was pressure on members not to deviate from the majority. The search for consensus involved restricting information, ignoring divergent solutions, and centralizing control so that the opinions of dominant members prevailed. These results appear to support the threat-rigidity hypothesis.

When the threat was attributed to internal deficiencies of the group itself and success appeared unlikely, the rigid behavior did not appear. In this experimental condition, cohesiveness is reduced and leadership becomes unstable. New leaders and new consensus forms may arise that promise improved group achievement.

Organization-Level Responses

Threats at this level have been such things as resource scarcity, competition, or reduction in the size of the market. Three sorts of responses have been found:

1. Because of overload of communication channels, reliance on prior knowledge, and reduction in the complexity of communication, the information-processing capacity of an organization may be restricted.
2. Centralization of authority and increased formalization of procedures may lead to a constriction in control.
3. There may be increased efforts to conserve resources within the system through cost-cutting and efforts for greater efficiency.

Depending on the circumstances, these responses may be functional or dysfunctional.

The authors believe that the evidence they have gathered supports the threat-rigidity hypothesis at the levels of the organism, the group, and the organization. They suggest that further research specifically designed to test the hypothesis, discover cross-level implications, and determine the conditions under which rigidity contributes to survival or extinction of organizations should be undertaken.

The relatively consistent findings at the three levels is said by the authors to support a general explanation of reactions of systems to threat that could be stated best in the language of general systems theory rather than in the specialized languages of psychological or sociological theory.

4. The work of Odum on energy flows in systems is compatible in many ways with general living systems theory. He has been particularly concerned with the relationship of power and efficiency in open systems, including living systems. The *maximum power principle,* which he has applied to a variety of open systems, both nonliving and living, was stated in an early article he wrote with Pinkerton:

Natural systems tend to operate at that efficiency which produces a maximum power output. This efficiency is always less than the maximum efficiency.[11]

The processes of open systems of the sort that operate in this way involve an energy transfer in which input and output are coupled in such a way that in one direction there is release of stored energy, decrease in free energy, and creation of entropy; and, in the other, storing of energy, increase of free energy, and decrease of entropy. The second law of thermodynamics is satisfied if the total entropy change for the system and its surroundings is a simple increase. The input and output can be coupled in various ways to produce different rates and efficiencies of processes.

Odum and Pinkerton demonstrated this maximum power principle in a series of thermodynamic equations that embody input and output forces and fluxes, the ratio between the forces, and three constants that describe the particular system to which the equations are applied.[12] The efficiency of these systems, at maximum power, is shown never to exceed 50 percent. The input and output *forces* are *useful* power inputs and outputs to systems.

They apply these equations to a number of physical and biological systems. In the case of one battery charging another, for example, the terms in the equations represent electric current, the voltage of the charging battery, the voltage of the battery being charged, the self-discharge of the batteries during shelf life, and the electrical conductivity of the circuit.

Living systems are more complex because they must include self-replacement to balance wear and remain in steady state. In the case of a pseudoorganism lacking self-repair, the terms represent the rate of glucose utilization, the free energy drop of catabolism, the rate of glucose synthesis, the free energy increase of anabolism, and enzyme rates of reaction.

In a model of food capture by an organism for its maintenance, the terms represent the rate of food use, energy drop in metabolism of captured food units, rate of food capture, energy drop inherent in the capture of a unit of food, basal metabolism spent in self-repair, the effectiveness of the food-concentrating method, and the metabolic equivalent of the food capture process.

They present similar models of photosynthesis, primary production in a self-sustaining climax community, and the growth and maintenance of a civilization.

In continued application and expansion of the maximum power principle, Odum has modeled ecological systems in more detail and investigated some of the ways in which self-organizing systems, which include living systems, maximize power.[13]

The design of systems that have survived by generating more power are hierarchical, with successive transformations of energy. The chains and webs through which matter is cycled in natural systems are of this sort. The food chains and food webs of ecological systems are examples. Larger sources of energy support longer chains leading to larger systems. In any such chain, one unit is the producer, which transforms energy and stores it for use by the next system unit, the consumer. Consumers also have production processes. Models of this sort exist in ecology, economics, chemistry, and geology. Odum suggests that they may apply to all systems.

Many of these producer-consumer hierarchies fit a model with sharp oscillations or pulses. Recurring epidemics are examples. In these, frequency of pulses can be related to energy. Ecosystems often have been found to have long periods of gradual buildup followed by sudden pulsed consumption and recycling. Fire climax ecosystems that alternate growth and fire are examples. Odum shows in a series of models that this alteration maximizes power. The size of systems, frequency of pulsing, and embodied energy are related in such a way that larger systems pulse with longer periods and embody more energy. A general model could represent all systems if the actual time represented were different for each level of system, from molecules to ecosystems.

5. A hypothesis from *Living Systems* is concerned with a mathematical

model that can be applied to the communication networks of living systems at various levels:[14]

The structures of the communication networks of living systems at various levels are so comparable that they can be described by similar mathematical models of nonrandom nets.

Nonrandom nets are those in which flows over some channels are more probable than over others. They are "biased."

Rapoport applied a network model of this sort to neural nets, like those in brains.[15] Biases that affect the probability of one neuron communicating with another include distance; a reciprocity bias, which concerns the probability that if one component contacts another, the other will also contact the first; and a popularity or "field force" bias, the probability that one will be more "attractive" and be contacted more frequently.

A similar model was found to predict with reasonable accuracy some aspects of the sociogram representing the friendship network in organizations (elementary and junior high schools).[16]

Studies of diffusion of information in towns have shown that a similar biased net model would probably be applicable there as well.[17]

Insights and discoveries made at one level of living systems can stimulate comparable research at other levels and result in the discovery of general principles applicable to multiple levels of living systems and, in some cases, to nonliving systems as well. As understanding of systems in general increases, science as a whole becomes more coherent and fragments come together into patterns.

Applications of General Living Systems Theory

All living systems are subject to pathologies of various sorts, which force matter-energy and information-processing variables out of steady-state ranges and may even threaten the continued existence of the system. The living systems strategy for discovering the nature and location of pathology in living systems at all levels is similar to the procedure of a physician in examining a patient.

In such examinations, as almost every patient learns, the physician observes the patient and measures a number of selected variables in one subsystem or organ after another. The examination may begin with the patient's head. The physician checks the mouth, nose, and throat, all of which are components of the ingestor subsystem; and the eyes and ears, which, with the other sense organs, are input-transducer components. He may then make observations and measurements on the heart, arteries, and veins—also components of the distributor subsystem of the organism. Variables such as blood pressure, pulse rate, heart size, and the response of the heart to exercise are all measurable. As the patient's organs are examined in turn, a thermometer, a blood pressure cuff, brain and body scanners, blood tests, X-rays, a reflex hammer, and other tests and instruments may be used as indicators that reveal the variable conditions of each of the matter-energy and information-processing subsystems.

Normal values of a very large number of variables at the level of the organism, established by making measurements on many individuals, are available to physicians. If the "patient" is an unprofitable factory, however, the organization specialist called in to diagnose its problems and prescribe treatment has fewer and less precise normal values for variables available for comparison. His fundamental procedure is similar, however.

The factory ingests raw materials for its processes. These may arrive at a rate that hampers later processing or may sit too long on the loading dock and begin to deteriorate. Trouble on the assembly line—a distributor component—can be reflected in poor quality of product. Worker dissatisfaction and threats of a strike, transmitted to management, are internal transductions that indicate variables out of steady-state ranges. The channel and net subsystem may operate inefficiently so that orders or other important sorts of information do not reach their destinations in timely fashion. The factory may be carrying out, with its own components, operations that could more effectively be performed by some other system. The financial records are, of course, an important class of data for such a study of an organization's pathology.

Normal values of variables are even less well established for societies and supranational systems than they are for organizations. It is not clear, for example, whether a moderate deficit in a national budget is a desirable steady state; how much inflation is compatible with a society's health; how much medical care a society should provide, and to whom; how much decision power should be given to supranational bodies; and so forth—although many people have opinions on all these questions. To the extent that it is possible, these higher-level systems should be studied to determine the normal steady-state ranges of their critical subsystem variables.

After a diagnosis is made of the form of pathology or lessened cost-effectiveness in a system *at any level*, a strategy for correcting it can be devised. This may involve a change in the structure of the system (analogous to surgery); a change in its process (analogous to use of drugs, exercise, or changed diets); or the use of nonliving technological aids (like a contact lens, a wheelchair, or a computer) to improve cost-effectiveness. This strategy is being used by a number of investigators in different programs, studying several types of living systems at the levels of the organism, group, organization, and society.

The Goal of Integrating the Social Sciences

Interdisciplinary environments generate integrative theories and cross-level hypotheses that can test them. The creation of such theories is an important ultimate goal of mature science. Much of my life has been spent in multidisciplinary groups, from the most important educational experience of my life, the Harvard Society of Fellows, to my present environment, the Center for the Study of Democratic Institutions. I have been fortunate. Many scholars find they communicate chiefly with members of their own specialty. Their rewards for achievement—promotions, salary raises, and recognitions—come solely from their discipline. It is hardly proper for university administrators to increase communication across the walls of the specialties by assigning faculty offices alphabetically or at random. Yet surely many institutions of higher learning should create more stable and better supported academic units for sophisticated and informed generalists than exist today. Specialists should support the creation of such units, if the generalists have had sound specialist training as part of their education and are not dilettantes. Departments or institutes of general studies will hasten the urgently needed ultimate goal of integrating the social sciences.

REFERENCES

1. K. W. Deutsch, J. Platt, and D. Senghaas, "Conditions Favoring Major Advances in Social Science," *Science 171* (1971): 450–459.
2. J. G. Miller, *Living Systems* (New York: McGraw-Hill, 1978).
3. International Institute for Applied Systems Analysis. *Annual Report, 1980* (Laxenburg, Austria: IIASA, 1981).
4. Deutsch, Platt, and Senghaas, "Conditions," 453.
5. Miller, *Living Systems,* 89–119.
6. L. F. Lewis II, "Conflicting Commands versus Decision Time: A Cross-Level Experiment," *Behavioral Science 26* (1981): 79–84.
7. V. B. Mountcastle, "The Neural Replication of Sensory Events in the Somatic Afferent System," in J. C. Eccles, ed., *Brain and Conscious Experience* (New York: Springer-Verlag, 1966), pp. 85–115.
8. S. S. Stevens, "The Psychophysics of Sensory Function," in W. A. Rosenblith, ed., *Sensory Communication* (New York: Wiley, 1961), pp. 1–33.
9. Mountcastle, "Neural Replication," pp. 96, 102, 109.
10. B. M. Staw, L. E. Sandelands, and J. E. Dutton, "Threat-Rigidity Effects in Organizational Behavior: A Multilevel Analysis," *Administrative Science Quarterly 26* (1981): 501–524.
11. H. T. Odum and R. C. Pinkerton, "Time's Speed Regulator: The Optimum Efficiency for Maximum Power Output in Physical and Biological Systems," *American Scientist 43* (1955): 331–332.
12. Ibid., pp. 331–343.
13. H. T. Odum, "Pulsing, Power, and Hierarchy." Personal communication.
14. Miller, *Living Systems,* p. 95.

15. A. Rapoport, "Cycle Distribution in Random Nets," *Bulletin of Mathematics and Biophysics 10* (1948): 145–157.
16. C. C. Foster, A. Rapoport, and C. J. Orwant, "A Study of a Large Sociogram: II. Elimination of Free Parameters," *Behavioral Science 8* (1963): 56–65.
17. S. C. Dodd, "The Counteractance Model," *American Journal of Sociology 63* (1957): 273–283.

Discussion

(Platt, Deutsch, Antal, Dror, Inkeles, Cohen)

Edited by Andrei S. Markovits

Advances in Psychology?

John Platt started by noting that Miller had mentioned some, but not all, of a recent list of advances in psychological theory. Miller had spoken of psychopharmacology, split-brain studies, artificial intelligence, biofeedback, and so on. Platt wondered whether he considered "cognitive psychology" to be a comparable advance.

Miller replied that *cognitive psychology* is not a discipline. It is a new term for the kind of studies that were made in psychology even before Watson's behaviorism. It is just becoming an organized movement within psychology, one that is getting a lot of attention of late. In cognitive psychology, as in artificial intelligence, the emphasis is on thinking processes—on similarities between the human being and the computer in terms of information processing. Some experiments—none very distinguished in Miller's estimation—have grown out of what was termed cognitive psychology. Miller felt, however, that some of this was actually no more than a restatement of theses that were accepted in the 1920s and then went out of style in psychology for about forty years.

Platt then asked about "artificial intelligence." Some critics argued that it showed nothing about psychology, only something about the behavior of people who work on computers. Did Miller believe that this area was making a contribution to psychological understanding?

Miller said that it was likely to do so. The workers were first-rate. There was a great deal of excitement about the artificial intelligence research at MIT, Carnegie-Mellon Institute, and Stanford; and *Fortune* magazine had devoted three issues to the work being done there and elsewhere. Industry had confidence in this research, and it was getting strong support from some foundations. Because it is similar to the approach taken in living systems theory, he had a great deal of confidence in it.

Platt said that he had not doubted that work was being done, but he was really asking if Miller considered artificial intelligence work to be a contribution to psychology.

Miller replied that he did consider it so, and that it would be very influential in various sorts of applied psychology and in the development of robots, which would be highly significant. He speculated that in ten years a conference on advances in social science might discuss the impact of robots, and on many levels—not just robots replacing organisms, but robots replacing systems at other levels of organization.

Karl Deutsch followed with a comment from the point of view of the sociology of science. He said that when a radically new technique came into an established field, at first it might be rejected altogether. Then, as the new practices came to be widely used, the old establishment would try to redefine the field and would erect a protective tariff around it so that it would exclude the newcomers.

Thus when the old fields of history and politics were first invaded, so to speak, by the social sciences, the concept of *Geistesgewissenschaften* was invented by Dilthey and others. It was an attempt to understand social actors by imitating their feelings as well as one could by adjusting one's own feelings. But then, Deutsch said, there was an effort to proclaim precisely what *Geistesgewissenschaften* were, and to say that all other ways of doing social inquiry were illegitimate. These thinkers argued that statistical studies, attempts to count and measure, were largely irrelevant. He felt that they had degenerated to arguments of the type, "If you can count it, it's irrelevant," or, "If it is important, you can't count it."

Deutsch suspected that the same thing was happening in psychology today. If artificial intelligence people were beginning to get beyond the stage of being rejected, there would be an effort to redefine psychology. Eventually there might come to be a school of humanistic psychology or something of the sort. Indeed, he speculated that a similar process probably occurred around the time that so-called rat psychology first appeared.

Miller commented that it was only when a robot replaced a single person that one was dealing with classical individual psychology. For larger systems there was group psychology; if a robot replaced a football team or an infantry squad, that would have to be considered group psychology. He went on to say that there had been a two-way flow since the modern development of computers, and that the leading computer pioneers such as Vannevar Bush, John von Neumann, and others applied what they knew of psychology to the design of computers. Conversely, as soon as computers came out, many brain psychologists and others became interested in them as models.

I. B. Cohen pointed out that von Neumann was the first to integrate neuron theory into computer design. His original plan for the first stored program in a computer went into great detail about the analogy with neurological physiology.

Platt noted in this vein that there was a large group, at MIT and elsewhere, who firmly believed in an absolutely literal computer-programming model of the brain. For them, there was no chemistry or any other integrative-network process that could not be described in terms of computers and "bits"—that is, in terms of a network of neurons that could equally well be electric wires. Platt argued that if efforts of that kind were fruitful for psychology in terms of generating testable predictions, and in suggesting experiments, then this work clearly should be considered part of psychology. That was true, regardless of whether such efforts proved to be correct or incorrect in the long run.

Creating Successful Interdisciplinary Research

Ariane Antal of the Science Center Berlin commented that she felt the discussion was jumping back and forth between trying to decide what constituted major advances and trying to decide what conditions favored advances. Part of the problem was due to the different disciplinary approaches. For this reason, she thought there had been a breakthrough in Miller's presentation because he emphasized interdisciplinary research and cross-level research and suggested that that was where future innovations would be found. From her own experience at the Science Center, however, she knew that successful interdisciplinary undertakings were not created simply by placing a bunch of different scholars together in a room and telling them to communicate. She wondered how, in Miller's own experience, he had witnessed or managed to create successful interdisciplinary teams?

Miller said that he, along with Deutsch, Rapoport, and Platt, would simply say that one did it and did it and did it for long periods of time. This group had all talked together for nearly twenty years, two to six hours a week. Each one gradually educated himself in the others' disciplines, they overcame methodological problems, overcame ego problems and group dynamics problems—"if you don't, the group simply dissolves"—and then began to have a profitable dialogue. Their group at Michigan numbered over a hundred people and involved at least twenty different disciplines. Miller quoted what one number of the group said about their interaction:

> He was the historian, and there was a biochemist with whom he talked frequently. At one point the historian said, "I think that 99 percent of all the conversations that go on between biochemists and historians in the entire University of Michigan go on here at our institute—because nowhere else do biochemists ever speak to historians about their research, or vice versa."

Miller stated that in order to have successful interdisciplinary research, it was necessary to create a continuing milieu.

The Stages from General Theory to Tests

Yehezkel Dror wondered how one could determine when innovative approaches coming from a new perspective harden into rigid views: "How does your model move from the stage of reconsideration and integration to that of confirmation, rather than indoctrination?" He did not mean to imply that he was charging the model with inconsistency; but in Miller's example of the students, were they expected simply to apply the models, or was criticism of these new paradigms encouraged?

Miller said that it had taken a long while, with their thinking constantly in flux, before they had come to any definite conclusions. It was a multiperson activity, with discussion and publication of related papers for nearly thirty years before the book appeared. That was a tremendously long time to hold the whole thing open and to keep making adjustments. Wittgenstein was right when he argued that there was a context of discovery and a context of confirmation. In the context of discovery there was brainstorming and flexibility. At some point, however, it was necessary to say arbitrarily: "Well, this is it, we are going to start testing in this format"—and then you have to go to the context of confirmation. Even after that point, one hoped one's students would not slavishly follow it, but would destroy the system if necessary to come up with a better one.

Deutsch then commented on psychology and cybernetics as a similar case. He said that an important stage in the development of a new theory was the moment when a complicated process, which in the past could be seen only as a whole, suddenly became paralleled by a model or structure that could be made, taken apart, and put back together again. Much about the way that a person picked up an object was known to psychologists many years ago, with studies on motor performance, motions, and the like. When there was a cybernetic machine to do the same thing, however—a machine that could be adjusted with a screwdriver and taken apart and put back together—then things would be known that could not have been known before. Later on, of course, it would become clear how different the two processes were: After the discovery of parallelisms, it was important to look for the differences. But the point at which we stop looking at the *Ding an sich*—the thing-in-itself—and move on to looking at the "thing in our own hands that can be changed" was a very fruitful source of further advances.

Platt commented that the development of the camera had been very helpful in illuminating the mechanics and optics of the eye. Deutsch said that that was a good example, but one had to recognize also that the eye could do things the camera could not, such as rapid eye movements.

Alex Inkeles said he felt that important areas of thought needed to have some kind of paradigm. Miller's checklist offered guides that a student of living systems could refer to to be sure to include all the basic elements identified up to that point. He also sympathized with Dror's concern, however. With a framework of that kind, it was possible for the researcher to become embedded in or blinded by his own paradigm; commitment to the paradigm could become a Procrustean bed. In the short term, it could lead to constant efforts to get the paradigm to work—here, there and elsewhere—rather than generating new data and new challenges.

In that connection, Inkeles wondered about the reason it had taken Miller so long to get the cross-level tests of the parts of the system that he cited in his paper. He wondered whether a large part of the intellectual energy had not gone into investigating the appropriateness and applicability of the scheme at different levels, and then working back from those levels to the scheme—and whether that had not held up the empirical applications.

Miller replied that the first framework was conceived of as basic research aimed toward the development of an integral theory, so that they did not begin to test the theory until it was fairly well along. It was now being tested in interesting ways, however. Kjell Samuelson, an electronics engineer and physician working on international communications systems, was writing a book saying that "if you build an electronics communications system without the nineteen subsystems, you are going to feel it is unsatisfactory in some way."

Miller said that Alexander Graham Bell originally had only an input transducer, a wire channel, an energy source, an output transducer, and Mr. Watson on the other side. The next thing they needed was a decider, a network, and a switching system. Next there had to be a memory (first a phone book, and now electronic telephone books). The lesson in this, according to Miller, was that gradually one kept adding subsystems—and the more they grew, the more humanoid the system became. Bell and the telephone companies did not start with a conceptual system, so they had to struggle to develop these things for the telephone system. Now, however, some engineers consulting for developing nations may be designing communications systems from this point of view, and the design and testing of the nineteen subsystems could be done in advance.

Why did it take so long to get the cross-level studies? Miller said that those who were around knew that the difficulty had been just what Inkeles had said. It was extremely hard simply to ask, "How do you go from this concept of levels and subsystems to the design of data collection?" Figuring out how to do that took trial and error, time and money—nearly $500,000 for the first project—but now there were several other people and research groups working on cross-level studies.

Recent Advances in Living Systems Theory

Platt asked how living systems theory should be fitted into advances in social science. It is a kind of holistic approach—should it be regarded as philosophy of science? Second, are the new ideas, since the 1956 entries in the DPS survey, significant enough to be regarded as a new advance? Platt was thinking not only of Miller's further work, but also of Herbert Simon's study "The Architecture of Complexity," which applied these ideas in a useful way to the construction, evolution, and breakdown of systems. Platt also mentioned William Powers's important book *Behavior: The Control of Perception*, which went beyond Ashby's older work on multistability by listing nine levels in a hierarchy of feedback loops between system and environment. Did Miller feel that there had been a new advance in the living systems concept, as a scientific theory and a set of experiments, in the last fifteen or twenty years?

Miller said he thought that there had been. There is now a wide range of applications. There is work on "the family as a system," and he had written an article on this subject that was being used in family therapy and in social work. Other applications included electronic communications systems, army battalions, and hospitals where data were being collected and compared, with studies of information flows and of error, omissions, distortions, and delays. The General Accounting Office (GAO) was also considering this as an approach to studying government agencies generally.

Inkeles said that it was important to sensitize oneself to the dimensions one wants to look at, in examining different types of organizations like battalions and hospitals. Does one assume certain constants running across organizations, or variability, as in the error rates?

Miller said that he did not know but that he guessed that error rates would be comparable, except in unusual or stressful situations, "because of the principle that you have to operate at cruising speed most of the time, and can't go at full speed all the time."

Inkeles said that was precisely what he wanted to hear Miller say. Most sociologists would assume that two such organizations were different enough to have different error rates—like different human personalities, which could be identified in this way. Miller replied that he had a low level of confidence in his guess, but that when he worked with students on doctoral dissertations, he tried to estimate ahead of time what data they would get—and was often wrong.

I. B. Cohen intervened and asked, to general laughter, "If the guess was better than the data, which do you throw out?"

Deutsch said he agreed with Inkeles about this field, that one should distinguish between the sensitizing effect of a new idea or theory, and the actual discovery. *Sensitizing* meant realizing that "X *may* exist"; *discovery* meant that "X *does* exist." This X might exist as an entity; that is, "X is such-and-such and is invariant over a wide variety of circumstances." Alternatively, it might exist as a polarity or an important variable: "For example, *temperature* is not constant everywhere, but it was lucky that somebody thought of it." All the way from medicine to physics and astronomy, the polarity between low and high temperatures was a very significant characteristic.

Deutsch went on to say that in keeping up with "advances," it would be helpful to distinguish between a major advance that revealed something and one that made people sensitive, so that it triggered a lot of research. The cumulative effect of the research would be the revelation that there was indeed something there. He referred back to his example of the electron, which he said had begun as a bookkeeping convenience for physical theory at one stage, until eventually there was enough evidence to conclude that there actually was such a little thing. Then it turned out that various materials had various numbers of electrons, and that there was quite a range between them. Deutsch argued that probably between 1951—when they first thought of living systems theory—and 1982, we had reached the point where we could now say what the "sensitivity operation" was, and that there was some comparability of living systems over a wide range of relevant characteristics.

Miller responded that he wished Daniel Bell could have been present for this discussion. Bell had asked Krallmann earlier how he accounted for cross-cultural differences in the use of business computers. Bell had said, "Do you just plug it in?" and Krallmann said, "Yes, I just plug it in." Miller thought it was as important to look for cultural differences in a systems study of organizations as for similarities. In the totality of scientific effort, however, some people should be studying cross-level relationships while others are doing level-limited studies. Both are needed.

Beyond Numbers to the Tests of Science

Cohen observed that a major use of home computers was in playing computer games, so it was interesting to see that a major use of computer games could be in advancing one aspect of social science. He went on to note that Miller had said that his subject shifted, from using a formal philosophy in his original paper, to using a science. Cohen argued that this was characteristic of the social sciences—to move from something very philosophical and general into something very specific. The whole subject of sociology had changed from a sort of philosophy into something that was not. In Miller's case, did this change really occur because he had introduced numbers?

Miller replied that that was not what he had meant to say. He did not think that systems theory had been scientific in Bertalanffy's time, or in his own earlier work; but numbers were not the only indicators of the change in viewpoint. He argued, however, that whenever one identified specific variables, ranges of variation, and indicators or measuring sticks for them, going through the whole quantification process; and whenever one collected data based on hypotheses of relationships among variables, then one was going through a standard process that other sciences had gone through in the past. This was a change from the earlier papers.

Inkeles interjected that it might be helpful to think of it as a stage of development, rather than as a movement from nonscience to science.

Cohen said that it would make him happier if Miller said it differently—that being able to go to numbers meant that it was *more* of a science than it had been. What troubled Cohen, however, could be seen in the example of his college tutor, G. D. Birkhoff, who had developed a theory of "aesthetic measure" in which he took some general notions of aesthetics and tried to convert them into numbers. "He even did tests," Cohen said; but did this make the theory sound, or make it science?

Miller said that he knew Birkhoff and his book and had often told him precisely the same thing. He thought that Birkhoff knew nothing about aesthetics or about physiology, and had basically admitted as much—but he did have a model. Miller said he agreed with Cohen that the vast mass of what were called general systems theory studies today were clearly nonscientific.

Inkeles asked Miller why he did not consider these studies to be scientific. Miller replied that they did not make statements that were provable or disprovable.

Inkeles said that it was important to make that clear. He had felt that Miller's earlier statements were not provable but were simply a way of looking at a large number of phenomena. They did have a clear implication, however—that "*if* one looked at cross-level studies, like the frequency of responses with overload or conflicting information, the results would be similar across different systems." To Inkeles, it seemed that Miller and his colleagues had then moved into another category of operations, part of a larger scientific enterprise—but in the social sciences things often ended there. Inkeles had once argued in a paper that in sociology it almost always ended there; the interesting ideas stopped just at that point of implication. He said that that was why he was responding here so enthusiastically, because he had not known that such tests were actually being done.

Inkeles claimed that this was precisely the direction that one had to take, to see how far these generalizations were true as one moved across systems. Could some dimensions be identified, where there would be a striking similarity in structure, or frequency, or pattern, or response? He said that there were often instances where this was not found statistically, but such a result allowed one to elaborate the theory further and to specify ways in which cross-level similarities existed and ways in which they did not.

Miller said that he thought they were doing science when they were trying to develop the theory. Rapoport's studies in game theory also had some commonalities; and he and Rapoport both wanted to test some of their laboratory findings by actual experiments in the outside world. From basic research on cross-level studies, practical applications were now possible—for example, on how to make hospitals most cost-effective. Miller believed that these were all parts of science. He did not in any way want to derogate the thirty years of theoretical work, but he felt that it was now pinned down a bit more.

CHAPTER 9

Global Modeling

Gerhart Bruckmann

THROUGHOUT THE HISTORY OF SCIENCE, every period has had its compartmentalization—Aristotle's subdivision into mathematics, physics, and theology; Xenocrates' logic, physics, and ethics; the seven liberal arts of the Romans; the seven additional mechanical arts of medieval times; and on through the disciplines reflected in the agenda of this conference. The field of global modeling, however, stubbornly resists any compartmentalization of this kind. This gives rise to the question of whether it is in fact a science or an art, a craft, or simply a task.

Not much more than ten years ago, not even the name existed, but today the subject is generating numerous studies and debates. In the most recent book on the topic,[1] *global modeling* is defined as

> computer modeling done to investigate social questions or problems of global scale. . . . Global Modeling is distinguishable from other types of modeling of social systems only by the questions it asks. Its methods, strengths and weaknesses are identical to those of all policy-oriented computer models. It draws from the same base of theory, data and technique. Therefore, if there are any distinct properties of global modeling, they follow directly from the characteristics of global problems.[2]

We will come back later to the impact of these characteristics on global modeling, and to why *computer* modeling is needed "to investigate problems of global scale."

The Preconditions for Global Modeling

I consider global modeling to be a major advance in the social sciences. I believe there are three conditions that have favored this advance: (1) environmentalism; (2) systems theory, and in particular the method of system dynamics, as developed by Jay Forrester in the late 1950s; and (3) the advent of the computer. Let us take a brief look at each of these conditions in turn.

After the two decades of unchallenged "growthmania" that followed World War II, the number of warning voices increased. Most of them came from fictional literature, not science, and most of them concentrated on single aspects of the world's problems, such as nuclear overkill, resource depletion, pollution of the environment, and so on. In 1968, however, Aurelio Peccei and several colleagues founded the Club of Rome to stimulate new investigations of the "world problematique" that would be both scientific and comprehensive—in other words, research that would be carried out using scientific methods but that would focus more on the interrelationship of these phenomena than on any single narrow issue. In retrospect, it is difficult to believe that when the Club of Rome was founded, nobody had any practical idea of how such investigations could actually be done.

Parallel to the rise of environmentalism, system dynamics had emerged within systems theory as a new tool, although at that time its very existence was known to only a small number of people. Mathematically, the basic idea underlying system dynamics is an approximation of a set of differential equations by a set of difference equations, the theoretical properties of which had been developed 150 years earlier by Gauss. Forrester's new contribution was in some ways like Einstein's—picking up an existing body of mathematical theory and applying it to a new field. By using the method of difference equations, Forrester made system dynamics a tool requiring only the four basic arithmetic operations,[3] but one that allows us to model the most complex, interlocked, nonlinear relations. In particular, it allows us to model feedback mechanisms and complex loops in an intriguingly transparent and simple (though by no means simplistic) fashion.

The clarity of this approach makes system dynamics a greater invention of Forrester's than his earlier technical invention of the magnetic core, which has been widely used in computers. What made system dynamics really worthwhile, however, was its applicability to complex problems of practical importance whose solution had eluded all other approaches. For example, system dynamics is capable of shedding light on the counterintuitive behavior of social systems.[4] This includes the somewhat surprising situations in which policy efforts to correct a social problem actually succeed in making it worse, as when low-cost housing effectively decreases the living standard of the poor, or food aid eventually increases hunger.

I am convinced that the applicability of system dynamics in the social sciences is only beginning to be explored, and I would urge that it be included in any list of major advances, as a precursor to global modeling.

The third condition needed for the development of global modeling was the advent of the electronic digital computer. Once the set of equations has been established, any system dynamics model can be worked out by simple arithmetic; but calculations by hand soon become tedious if one wishes to investigate a number of alternative runs, so as to analyze the results of various policies. Without the computer, such subjects as econometrics, detailed input-output analysis, and system dynamics would have remained of very limited applicability. Computer modeling is therefore a necessary part of the definition of global modeling; the number of interrelationships to be investigated is so high that, without a computer, the task could not be performed.[5]

"The Limits to Growth" and Its Successor Studies

Given these three roots, the prehistory and the history of global modeling can be quickly related. At two meetings of a small Club of Rome group in June and July 1970, in Bern, Switzerland, and in Cambridge, Massachusetts, Jay Forrester presented a rough sketch of a system dynamics world model (World 1), which he then developed into a more elaborate one (World 2).[6] The presentations were so convincing that the Club, with the initiative of Aurelio Peccei and Eduard Pestel, persuaded the Stiftung Volkswagen to give a contract for 1 million DM to the system dynamics group at the Massachusetts Institute of Technology. The study team there, headed by Dennis Meadows and Donella Meadows, then developed the World 3 model, describing the interaction of several global variables through the next century. A version of this work for the general public was published in early 1972 under the title *The Limits to Growth.*[7] This book has now been translated into twenty-three languages and has sold 3 million copies all over the world.

For this audience, I need not reiterate the shock, confusion, antagonism, and numerous misunderstandings to which *The Limits to Growth* gave rise. Aurelio Peccei was just as overwhelmed by this echo response as were the authors, and he invited all the critics to do better. The consequence has been an outpouring of criticism, competition, and development resulting in what we now know as the global-modeling movement.

The first global model to be developed in response to Peccei's call was the Mesarovic-Pestel model; the public version of this was published as *Mankind at the Turning Point.*[8] This model was much more elaborate and much more highly disaggregated than World 3; yet its major findings did not deviate as much from the findings of *The Limits to Growth* as had been expected.[9] Methodologically, the Mesarovic-Pestel model was no longer based solely on system dynamics.[10] This, like all later global models, proceeded in an eclectic way, applying whatever methodology seemed most appropriate.

The third global model, developed by the Fundacion Bariloche (Argentina), was set up as a direct criticism of both World 3 and the Mesarovic-Pestel model.[11] Both of the earlier models had been accused of being descriptive, of attempting simply to describe what the fate of mankind might be, and of viewing the world through the eyes of the industrialized nations. The Bariloche group instead committed themselves to developing a "normative model" that would be concerned "not with predicting what will occur if the temporary tendencies of mankind continue, but rather with sketching a way of arriving at the final goals of a world liberated from backwardness and misery."[12] As for methodology, the model brought forth several important advances (concerning the goal function, production functions, optimization algorithm, and so on). The world was divided into four regions: Latin America, Africa, Asia, and all developed countries; this fourth region was deliberately kept external. The main result was the conclusion that Latin America "could adequately satisfy the basic needs of the whole population within one generation from the implementation of the proposed policies," whereas the modelers concluded that in Africa, and especially in Asia, problems are more serious.[13]

In this sequence, the fourth model was MOIRA (Model of International Relations in Agriculture), developed by a Dutch team, Linnemann et al.[14] Unlike the three earlier models, MOIRA focused on one sector—food and agriculture—and on one topic—how to reduce hunger in the world. MOIRA, again, brought many methodological advances. Its principal conclusion was that "a program to alleviate world hunger must combine market stabilization with an aid program designed to stimulate demand, and that this policy must be initiated and pursued by the rich nations of the world."[15]

After these four models, global modeling became an activity pursued by a number of teams working in parallel. A scientific forum for this work has been provided by a series of annual conferences held by the International Institute for Applied Systems Analysis (IIASA), which is located at Schloss Laxenburg near Vienna, Austria, and is supported by a consortium of sixteen nations from both East and West. Among the later models are SARUM,[16] FUGI,[17] and about a dozen smaller models that were discussed, in part, at the Ninth IIASA Global Modeling Conference in 1981. The most promising global model presently under construction is GLOBUS, being elaborated by a group at the Wissenschaftszentrum

Berlin. Needless to say, a substantial secondary literature, both on global models and on global modeling, has sprung up.[18]

Meeting the Requirements for a Major Advance

Karl Deutsch, John Platt, and Dieter Senghaas, in their 1971 paper used as a background reference for this conference,[19] asked twelve questions concerning conditions favoring major advances in social science. (See Appendix.) It is worthwhile to run through the answers to these questions in the case of global modeling:

1. Global modeling is indeed a cumulative advance, built on the earlier developments of environmentalism, system dynamics, and computers.
2. It is almost a new field of social science, outside of traditional compartmentalizations.
3. It involves not only theory, but also method, and matters of substance.
4. There have been changes and trends over time, but a discussion of them would exceed the scope of this chapter.
5. In generating these advances, global modeling has required both the impetus given by individuals and the large workload capabilities of teams.
6. The ages of the people involved are an interesting mix. Peccei was sixty when he founded the Club of Rome. Forrester was in his forties and fifties when he developed system dynamics and started the global modeling work. The entire Meadows team was below thirty when *The Limits to Growth* was written.
7. On the quantitative-qualitative axis, as a rule, the quantitative results from global modeling have been toned down later to qualitative statements.
8. As for capital and manpower needs, the first *Limits to Growth* study required ten man-years; and the Mesarovic-Pestel study, fifty man-years; in other words, aside from the large-scale computer facilities, surprisingly few resources were needed, in comparison to the impact produced.
9. The locations and types of institutions and social conditions involved in global modeling were outlined earlier.
10. The ideas and advances in this field have come both from existing disciplines and from interdisciplinary work.
11. The question of the relation of global models to social practice and to practical demands must be answered in a number of different ways. Some models, such as Mesarovic-Pestel, SARUM,

and FUGI, have been applied by government agencies on a national level. The methods developed in global modeling also have had substantial impact on national and regional modeling techniques. More important, however, is the indirect impact of the findings of global modeling. It may safely be stated that many legislative acts in the field of environmental protection might not have occurred if global modeling, and in particular *The Limits to Growth,* had not existed.

12. As for any delay between an advance or breakthrough and its social impact, the stir caused by *The Limits to Growth* had a time delay of zero.

In short, global modeling seems to fit the three principal findings of the Deutsch-Platt-Senghaas study. They concluded:

> (i) There are such things as social science achievements and social inventions, which are almost as clearly defined and as operational as technological achievements and inventions. (ii) These achievements have commonly been the result of conscious and systematic research and development efforts by individuals or teams working on particular problems in a small number of interdisciplinary centers. (iii) These achievements have had widespread acceptance or major social effects in surprisingly short times: median times are in the range of ten to fifteen years, a range comparable with the median times for widespread acceptance of major technological inventions.[19]

I could stop at this point, having shown, in my opinion, that global modeling deserves to be considered a major advance in the social sciences. However, I wish to add a few words about why I consider this advance not only particularly important, but also particularly fascinating.

Uniting Analytic and Synthetic Thinking

In the time of Aristotle, Science itself was One, and Science and Religion were also One. In the Renaissance, Science broke loose from Religion; after the Enlightenment, Science itself fell apart, with Goethe generally being considered the last universalist. Even within each compartmentalized segment of Science, however, analytic thinking increasingly drove out synthetic thinking, so that today a "good" doctoral dissertation is expected to be awfully deep and awfully narrow. I do not believe that I exaggerate if I claim that a substantial part of the mess in which humankind finds itself at the end of the second millennium A.D. is to be attributed to the fact that we have unlearned synthetic thinking.[20] I am by no means alone in deploring this fact. Global modeling constitutes a decisive step to reverse this trend. (As an aside, note that system dynamics can show that both a persistent exponential trend *and* the subsequent trend reversal—as in this case—are caused by the *same* set of underlying relations.) Global modeling cannot help but reunite the sciences; it is the first inclusive paradigm to bring us closer again to the age-old dream, lost since the time of Leonardo and Goethe. What Hermann Hesse tried to establish in *The Glass Bead Game* (*Magister Ludi*), concerning the unity of all the arts—has been approached for the sciences by global modeling.

If this sounds too self-assured, let me go one step further. Global modeling is also teaching the sciences to be *less* self-assured: It teaches us that there is more than one truth, that there is more than one valid answer to many questions. It thereby introduces a kind of Eastern thinking into our Western self-confidence. It teaches us the humility of Socrates ("*scio me nihil scire*") to replace the conceitedness of Faust's companion Wagner ("*Und wie wir's dann zuletzt so herrlich weit gebracht*").

It is with a certain hesitancy that I add my last remark: Global modeling also reflects, in a sense, a reunification of physics and metaphysics, or science and religion. One cannot work on a global model without a deep feeling of commitment—commitment to a goal defined by Aurelio Peccei as human survival in dignity.[20] Today, the construction of the GLOBUS model in this Center—introducing policy variables into a global model—means a great leap forward not only methodologically but also, as I have tried to show, in a metamethodological way.

References

1. D. Meadows, J. Richardson, and G. Bruckmann, *Groping in the Dark: The First Decade of Global Modeling* (New York: Wiley, 1982).
2. Meadows, Richardson, and Bruckmann, *Groping*, pp. 12–13.
3. J. W. Forrester, *Principles of Systems* (Cambridge, Mass.: MIT Press, 1968).
4. J. W. Forrester, *Urban Dynamics* (Cambridge, Mass.: MIT Press, 1969); also, "Counterintuitive Behavior of Social Systems," *Technology Review*, January 1971, pp. 52–62.
5. For a slightly more elaborate assessment of computer modeling in addressing global issues, see Meadows, Richardson, and Bruckmann, *Groping*, pp. 11–12.
6. J. W. Forrester, *World Dynamics* (Cambridge, Mass.: MIT Press, 1971).
7. D. H. Meadows, D. L. Meadows, J. Randers, and W. W. Behrens, *The Limits to Growth* (New York: Universe Books, 1972).
8. M. Mesarovic and E. Pestel, *Mankind at the Turning Point* (New York: E. P. Dutton, 1974).
9. *Limits to Growth:*

   1. If the present growth trends in world population, industrialization, pollution, food production, and resource depletion continue

unchanged, the limits to growth on this planet will be reached sometime within the next one hundred years. The most probable result will be a rather sudden and uncontrollable decline in both population and industrial capacity.

2. It is possible to alter these growth trends and to establish a condition of economic stability that is sustainable far into the future. The state of global equilibrium can be designed so that the basic material needs of each person on earth are satisfied and each person has an equal opportunity to realize his individual human potential.

3. If the world's people decide to strive for this second outcome rather than the first, the sooner they begin working to attain it, the greater their chances of success will be.

Mankind at the Turning Point:

1. Cooperation is better than confrontation, even when one views the world from a narrowly defined and self-interested perspective.

2. Delays in addressing critical global issues can be disastrous, even deadly.

[quoted from Meadows, Richardson, and Bruckmann, *Groping*, pp. 30–31, 40].

10. M. D. Mesarovic and E. Pestel, "Multilevel Computer Model of World Development System," *Proceedings of the IIASA Symposium*, I-VI, CP-74-1/6 (Vienna: IIASA, 1974).
11. G. Bruckmann, ed., "Latin-American World Model," *Proceedings of the Second IIASA Symposium on Global Modeling*, CP-76-8 (Vienna: IIASA, 1976); A. D. Herrera, H. D. Scolnik, et al., *Catastrophe or New Society?—A Latin American World Model* (Ottawa: International Development Research Centre, 1976).
12. Meadows, Richardson, and Bruckmann, *Groping*, p. 45.
13. Ibid., pp. 52–53.
14. G. Bruckmann, ed., "Moira—Food and Agriculture Model," *Proceedings of the Third IIASA Symposium on Global Modeling*, CP-77-1 (Vienna: IIASA, 1977); H. Linnemann et al., *MOIRA—Model of International Relations in Agriculture* (Amsterdam: North Holland, 1979).
15. Meadows, Richardson, and Bruckmann, *Groping*, p. 64.
16. G. Bruckmann, ed., "SARUM and MRI: Description and Comparison of a World Model and a National Model," *IIASA Proceedings Series*, Vol. 2 (London: Pergamon Press, 1979); P. C. Roberts et al., *SARUM 76—Global Modelling Project*, Research Report 19 (London: U.K. Department of Environment and Transport, 1977).
17. G. Bruckmann, ed., "Input-Output Approaches in Global Modeling," *IIASA Proceedings Series*, Vol. 9 (London: Pergamon Press, 1980).
18. H. S. D. Cole, C. Freeman, M. Jahoda, and K. L. R. Pavitt, *Models of Doom—A Critique of the Limits to Growth* (New York: Universe Books, 1973); J. Clark, S. Cole, R. Curnow, and M. Hopkins, *Global Simulation Models* (New York: Wiley, 1975); S. Cole, *Global Models and the International Economic Order* (New York: Pergamon Press, 1977); K. W.

Deutsch and B. Fritsch, *Problems of World Modeling* (New York: Ballinger, 1977); J. Richardson, "Global Modeling—A Survey and Appraisal," *Futures*, 1978; P. C. Roberts, "Modeling Large Systems," *Limits to Growth Revisited*, ORASA Text No. 4 (London: Taylor and Francis, 1978); P. Haas, "Kritik der Weltmodelle," *Minerva*, 1980; K. W. Deutsch, and B. Fritsch, *Zur Theorie der Vereinfachung: Reduktion von Komplexität in der Datenverarbeitung für Weltmodelle* (Königstein: Athenäum-Verlag, 1980); cf. also note 1.

19. K. W. Deutsch, J. Platt, and D. Senghaas, "Conditions Favoring Major Advances in Social Science," *Science 171* (1971): 450–459.
20. A. Peccei, "Foreword," in J. W. Botkin, M. Elmandjra, and M. Malitza, *No Limits to Learning* (Oxford: Pergamon Press, 1979), p. xv.

Discussion

(Platt, Krelle, Kruskal, Deutsch, Bremer, Bell, Wildenmann, Cohen, Miller)

Edited by Andrei S. Markovits

Criticisms by Economists

John Platt opened the discussion by saying that the impact of *The Limits to Growth* was probably due to two factors in addition to the novelty and global implications of the computer results. One was the persuasiveness of the logic and rhetoric of the principal writer of the book, Donella Meadows; the other was the effective publicity and launching of the book in Washington by Potomac Associates.

Eckhart Zwicker then said that he did not agree that global modeling was a major advance. Others before Forrester had used similar methods, such as Kalecki on business cycles, and Tustin on servomechanism theory in the *Mechanism of Economic Systems*. He also criticized the restriction to endogenous variables; the inability to use mixed differential equations, as in econometrics; and the subjective approach, which made validation impossible. Zwicker concluded that "system dynamics is quite a dangerous concept," especially because it is so plausible.

In reply, Gerhart Bruckmann said that such criticisms could be made against any comparable methodology, including econometrics and input-output analysis. He said that Forrester's work was an advance over that of Kalecki and Tustin because Forrester had turned the earlier techniques into an organized and teachable body of knowledge.

Wilhelm Krelle then said that system dynamics was not a theory comparable to econometrics because it did not have well-defined restrictions, and that it had found little use among economists and would possibly turn out to be only a passing fad. Moreover, many global modeling projects did not use system dynamics, including the Link project, input-output analysis as used at the United Nations, the Fairs system, and the system of the Japanese planning office. Krelle said that the Meadows et al. approach had been devastatingly criticized in economic journals because it neglected the essence of economics—the principle of substitution—and neglected the service component of GNP, which *could* go on growing forever. Nevertheless, he felt that, within limits, global modeling was an important achievement, especially as an approach to resource exhaustion and environmental problems. The Ragfron model and the Verein für Sozialpolitik have treated such questions with a good simple model and good economics; but the system dynamics method—Forrester's "mechanical engineering"—was a blind alley.

Bruckmann agreed that we should separate the three things—global modeling, system dynamics methods, and the limits-to-growth idea. Most recent global models have been eclectic, using many other methods along with system dynamics. He felt that the failure of economists to use global modeling was a deplorable situation—perhaps occurring just because Forrester was an outsider who did not have a chair in economics. Bruckmann suggested, however, that the use of several complementary approaches would be valuable in studying a national economy: an econometric model, a mental model, an eclectic model, *and* a system dynamics model.

William Kruskal argued that the general skepticism about all models, including input-output models, could be skepticism either about the data used, or about the functions or relationships assumed in the models. He felt that the sensitivity or robustness of the outcomes to changes in the variables should also be discussed. To contrast global modeling with econometrics might also be misleading, because econometrics was very broad and contained many different approaches. Kruskal thought that comparison with another predictive area, demographic analysis, might be beneficial, especially in attempts to validate the methods by looking at retrospective predictions.

General Analysis of Feedback Loops by System Dynamics

Karl Deutsch then commented: "It was said of Christopher Columbus that when he sailed forth, he did not know where he was going; when he landed, he did not know where he was; and when he returned, he did not know where he had been. . . . No sensible person today would sail across the Atlantic in vehicles like his." Just as with the first global modeling effort, however, Columbus had indeed shown that it was possible to think of the world as a whole—that the effort could be made rational and to some degree retraceable. The World 3 model had indeed been reproduced both in Berlin and in Leningrad (by Skaratov); and it was found that by changing some coefficients, the outcome could be continuing prosperity instead of catastrophe. Deutsch said the important thing was that other models followed and improved on the original ones; what has happened since is as different from the first steps as the settlement of a continent was from the voyage of Columbus.

Stuart Bremer said that he had long been an opponent of system dynamics but had come to appreciate its strengths and to feel that it should indeed be called a great advance. Its applications to problems involving complex feedback loops range from alcohol addiction to the World 3 model. It is not like econometrics but is, rather, a theoretical tool, providing a relatively easy way to construct a theory of complex interactions in order to see what the general implications are. In areas such as continuous-time modeling, there could be a convergence between econometrics estimation techniques and system dynamics. New computer languages, beyond the DYNAMO language, will make it easier to express theories and to elicit their implications. These developments were not "dangerous" in the way that Zwicker and Krelle had argued. To translate ideas into operational theories with clear implications, is not itself dangerous—except insofar as all science may be dangerous when theories become confused with the real world.

Can the Different Realms Be Coupled in a Model?

Daniel Bell then said that he was opposed to Forrester's system dynamics and that there were serious methodological and epistemological objections to be made against the whole approach of global modeling. Unlike Columbus, Forrester *thought* he knew where he was going but, perhaps, should have gone in a different direction. The underlying "global" metaphor seemed to be something like a Calder mobile; you could calculate its different successive configurations if you knew the air currents and had the right differential equations. By contrast, econometrics had the virtue of being very restricted, not trying to become global. Bell claimed that the word *system* could not be applied to the world because many parts of it were incompletely coupled. The realms of culture, polity, economics, technology, resources, and the environment existed in different configurations in different time frames; the notion that they were strongly coupled into a system betrayed a fundamental misconception about the nature of the world. He said he did not think it impossible to make models, but they would have to consist of different incremental segments, small enough that one could define the relationships one wanted to observe.

Rudolf Wildenmann remarked that global modelers had a self-perception that was "semireligious," and that gave him the feeling that he was in church. Agreeing with Bell, he said that there were different developments in the social, political, and cultural spheres, whose composition was quite distinct. It might be possible to construct a model that could comprehend these features of the world in an immanent way, but the models developed to date could not be replicated and therefore were not a useful form of analysis. Nevertheless, simulation methods, when used as analytical and theoretical tools to explore problems, were extremely valuable devices. Global modeling could be considered as a major advance only if its aims were more modest, conceiving of itself as a simulation model for a differentiated approach to the major policy problems of the world.

Defense of Global Modeling

I. Bernard Cohen referred to the comments of Krelle and Bruckmann on the acceptance of new developments, and the severe criticisms of Forrester's work—with some suggesting that he should have 'stuck to mechanical engineering.' But in the history of science, important ideas that come from someone outside a profession are often rejected at first, such as van't Hoff's discovery of the spatial arrangement of atoms, which was rejected by the great German organic chemists because he 'came from a veterinary school.'

Bell interjected that Forrester, on the contrary, also had the advantage of his recognized position: "He had all of MIT behind him," and might not have gotten his attention without this halo effect.

James Miller pointed out that models were built for different levels, from cells or organizations to the global level, but he felt that Forrester selected his variables from different disciplines, such as money, air pollution, and population growth, so that their correlations had no overall connection.

Deutsch then attempted to defend global modeling. The world is radically inexhaustible for human beings of limited capacities, and one has to work on samples and subsystems. But on this small planet—this subsystem—if there are growing problems with carbon dioxide, pollution, and population density, with stress on the food supply and productive capacity, these are legitimate problems to be concerned with. Cybernetics and feedback models of such systems have gone far beyond 'mechanical engineering'! One does not need 'religious' feelings to believe that the investigation of selected world problems, such as war, peace, hunger, and scarce resources, is fair game.

Deutsch suggested various categories of simulation analysis:

1. simulation methods in general, as conceptual rather than mathematical;
2. city and regional models, such as used for municipal budgeting;
3. national economic models, from those of Klein to Krelle's Link project;
4. global models, including Leontief's, Forrester-Meadows, and the GLOBUS project directed by Stuart Bremer.

Deutsch said that of 12 groups that had worked on world modeling, six were still going strong, which is not a bad survival rate for a developing field. There is a large body of work with many different mathematical methods. If we can speak of a world economy, of world politics, and of world population, their mutual interactions can be modeled—even though the total pattern is not as explicitly connected as a Calder mobile.

Bruckmann had two remarks in response to this discussion. First, on robustness, he quoted Donella Meadows: "A good model should show sensitivity where the real world is sensitive, and robustness where the real world is robust." Then, on predictiveness, he said he detested the 'semi-religious' approach when the researcher knew his gloomy or optimistic result ahead of time, and adapted his model to fit. But he quoted the Yugoslav economist Branco Horvath, who said ironically: "If our best tools only allow us to look ahead 15 years, do we then have no obligation to worry about the fate of the next generation?" He approved that kind of religious spirit, and that sense of commitment for our children and for longer-run human survival.

Bruckmann concluded that most global modelers saw it not as a way to predict the future, but as a way to shed light on interrelationships among diverse fields such as ecology, economics, technology, and demography. He hoped that it could be used for early warnings on a global scale, by describing some important interrelationships on this little ball called earth.

CHAPTER 10

Mathematical and Statistical Thinking in the Social Sciences†

Raymond Boudon

THE PROCESS OF CROSS-FERTILIZATION between mathematics and statistics on the one hand, and the social sciences on the other, is a complex one. Genuine novelties are not always easily defined. Advances are seldom indisputable; influence on scientific developments is not only a concept to which a measure can be associated only with difficulty; it is also an ambiguous concept in itself. Advances are real when they lead to a better *understanding* of some social phenomena, but understanding is an unclear and to some extent a subjective notion.

Before identifying some important episodes in this cross-fertilization process after 1965, a few more elaborate remarks on these preliminary points may be useful.

1. Many novelties are elaborations of earlier core ideas. One can take as a familiar example the old Spearmanian idea of making observed variables a function of unobservable variables, and solving the resulting

†Prof. Boudon was unable to give this paper in person, and it was read by James Coleman.

set of equations thanks to assumptions (no correlation between latent variables, or between latent variables and error terms). This basic core idea is present in a set of models which has been continuously expanded from Thurstone's multiple factor analysis to Lazarsfeld's latent structure analysis and to the modern versions of factor analysis.[1]

2. A statistical or mathematical model can gain recognition in the social sciences and be widely used, for a variety of reasons that should be kept in mind. One of these reasons, of course, can be its usefulness—that is, its contribution to the knowledge and the understanding of certain social phenomena. Other reasons can play a role, however. A model or a method that can be mechanically applied to any set of data and easily learned and used is likely to be widely used: factor analysis and path analysis are examples of such models. Data drawn from surveys, for instance, can always be "analyzed" by such instruments in a mechanical way. Thus the fact that a model is widely used is not only a sign that it is useful or that it represents a major advance; it can be also a sign that it meets the demand of many potential users.

3. The contribution of a mathematical theory or model can be *specific* (if it is directly used or applied to data) or *diffuse*. Thus one can easily mention applications of game theory to given sets of data,[2] but there is also a penetration of what can be called the game-theoretical way of thinking in several theoretical or empirical fields of research (for example, political theory or sociology of education).[3]

4. The system of division of labor is probably more segmented in the social sciences than in economics, for instance. An economist, whatever his or her orientation, is likely to have a certain familiarity with mathematical economics. Mathematical sociology or mathematical political science, by contrast, is a matter of interest to mathematical sociologists or mathematical political scientists rather than to the general community of sociologists or political scientists. The influence of a piece of mathematical sociology can be great within the field but negligible within the discipline at large. This circumstance obviously adds to the difficulty of identifying the major advances. One reason for the weak permeability of sociology to mathematical sociology is that the latter includes a very heterogeneous set of models, by contrast, for instance, to mathematical economics. Whereas mathematical economics is tightly connected with the theoretical body of classical and neoclassical economics, mathematical sociology is rather, for some of its parts at least, an addition of pieces without a very narrow connection with sociological theory or current sociological empirical research.

5. It is not evident that the usefulness or influence of a mathematical model or method is correlated with its complexity. Simple ideas or models can be very influential and useful, and complex ones may be less useful. This triviality raises an important problem: To gain recognition, mathematical sociologists have to produce models with a degree of complexity.

Recognition within the subfield of mathematical sociology, however, does not mean influence on the discipline at large. In economics, as theory is impregnated by mathematics, the particularistic norms of those with a mathematical professional training have no dysfunctional effects: Mathematics has to have a minimal sophistication but also must be connected with economic problems, the latter being defined by the scientific community of economists at large. In sociology or political science, as this control of the scientific community is weaker, isolation can reinforce isolation.

6. A consequence of the weak relationship between sociological theory and mathematical sociology, or of political theory and mathematical political science, is that the interaction between mathematics and statistics on the one hand and the social sciences on the other often remains located in the statistical analysis of empirical data. Theory is seldom mathematized in the social sciences. Data are often *explored* or analyzed with the help of statistical models. More rarely they are explained in the light of theoretical mathematized models.

In the following, I will first insist on some *diffuse* effects of mathematics on the sociological and political-science way of thinking, effects that are both important and indirect, since they are mediated in some part by new developments in economics. Then I will briefly describe the interaction between mathematics and empirical theoretical research in the cases of selected fields where this interaction does exist. Then I will consider briefly an important but easy case: the role of mathematics and statistics in the analysis of data. Finally, I will add a few words on the role of new mathematical theories.

The Theory of Action and the Contribution of Mathematical Thinking

The notion of action plays a very important role in the social sciences, both before and after their institutionalization. Social actions or social agents can be considered as the atoms of the social sciences, systems of interaction and of interdependence as the objects these sciences confront. This basic idea is more or less continuously present in the social sciences before their institutionalization: Systems of interaction characterized by the now familiar Prisoner's Dilemma structure of game theory were, for instance, implicitly identified by Thucydides in his *Peloponnesian War*, as well as by Rousseau in his *Social Contract*. Once social science became institutionalized, the theory of action was always considered as essential to the social sciences, from Weber and Pareto to Parsons. However, the connection between the sociological theory of action and the mathematical theories of action (for example, game theory) remained weak.

This situation has changed to some extent in the last two decades, and this may be a major advance, although it is diffuse rather than specific. One of the basic ideas of game theory is that for given orderings of their preferences on a set of situations, the actors can behave "rationally" but, by doing so, create a situation with a low rank in their preference ordering. This idea was applied by Olson in his *Logic of Collective Action.*[4] The production of collective goods is (under specific conditions) subject to a generalized *n*-person Prisoner's Dilemma effect. There is little mathematics in Olson's book (as a matter of fact, game theory is not explicitly used); but the theory is an application to a field where it was not applied before—the field of collective action—of ideas that were formalized and made visible by game theory. This theory was very influential. It can be said that almost all research in the fields of collective action and social movements is now affected more or less directly by Olson's theory. Olson's theory has not only been influential in the sense that it was applied or extended. More profoundly, it affected ways of thinking in the field of collective action. On the whole, sociological theory and research became more efficient in an important substantial field.

The influence of the mathematics of action is not limited to the field of collective action. Political theory was also influenced. Downs's *Economic Theory of Democracy* and Buchanan-Tullock's *Calculus of Consent* are familiar examples in this respect, as is Tullock's *Toward a Mathematics of Politics.*[5] In all these examples, as well as in Coleman's *Mathematics of Collective Action,*[6] a kind of two-step influence process can be detected: A way of thinking familiar to economists is applied with success to problems that are generally considered as belonging to the field of the social sciences; but this way of thinking is impregnated by ideas developed on the soil of the mathematics of action.

Traditionally, the mathematics of action (game theory in particular) had been widely applied to some fields—international relations or conflict situations in small groups.[7] The relevance of game theory in such fields was immediately perceived. Less evident was the fact that it could also be applied to political theory, and still less that it could be applied to social movements. In this respect, applications of the mathematics of action in other fields where such applications cannot be considered as evident or natural can be mentioned. In the field of the sociology of organization, Peaucelle has shown that the findings contained in Crozier's empirical study on "the monopoly" could be predicted by a game-theoretical model.[8] This is an interesting study, in which game theory is used to reproduce a complex body of qualitative data derived from detailed empirical research. In another field in which the application of game theory is also unfamiliar, sociology of education, Boudon has tried to show that game theory could be used to explain the differential attractiveness of various types of institutions of higher education.[9]

To these fields, which to various extents have been affected by a wider diffusion of the core idea of the mathematics of action, another can be added, though parenthetically, since it does not belong to the social sciences paper. Maynard Smith has shown that game theory could be useful in sociobiology.[10] More specifically, phenomena such as restricted aggression, or the distribution of the different types of aggressive behavior in a group (of animals), can be interpreted as equilibrium states of game-theoretical models. The idea is interesting: Natural selection is a process whose connection with game theory is not evident. The outcome of selection, however, can be interpreted *as if* it resulted from a strategic behavior.

On the whole, the mathematics of action have in the last decades penetrated a number of domains in which they were not present before. Whether or not this is an irreversible trend remains to be seen. One point is sure, however: Examples can be shown of a genuine impact of mathematics on traditional fields and ways of thinking in sociology and political science. The traditional views on interest groups proposed by Durkheim or Dahrendorf, for instance, have been profoundly affected by Olson's paradigm.[11] Peaucelle shows in one example that a combination between a game-theoretical approach and formalization and a qualitative refined observation is possible and can be very fruitful. Whether such happy marriages will be generalized in the future cannot be predicted. It should be stressed, however, that the objects of sociology as well as of political science are basically systems of action. For this reason the penetration of the mathematics of action will likely be durable.

Aggregation/Composition Effects

When a number of people act in a given way, they can generate collective effects that are not always intuitive, that may be counterintuitive, and that often can be determined exclusively with the help of mathematical analysis. The cobweb theorem in economics, to take a familiar example, is an illustration of such nonintuitive collective effects: Intuition does not tell that if producers anticipate that the price of a product will be the same the next year as in the present year, the price will oscillate over the years. This oscillation can be called an aggregation or a composition effect.

Such effects have long been familiar to economists, who are more familiar with the mathematical language than are, say, sociologists or political scientists. Also, the principle of methodological individualism, according to which macrophenomena should be considered as the product of the aggregation of individual actions, is much more widely accepted in economics than in sociology or political science. Sociologists and political scientists are often more interested, for instance, in studying relationships between *variables* than in showing that such and such a phenomenon is the product of the aggregation of individual actions.

Obviously, this statement should not be made too general. Mathematical sociology is composed for one part of models where aggregate phenomena are explained as composition effects of individual actions. Coleman's notorious diffusion study is of this type:[12] The diffusion process of a new drug among physicians working in hospitals displays a logistic structure whereas it might take an exponential structure among those working solo. The difference at the level of the aggregates is explained by a difference in the situation of the individuals: The former can easily consult their colleagues, the latter cannot.

Although the analysis of composition effects is a normal product of modeling, a class of pieces of research can be isolated where the counterintuitive character of the aggregation of individual actions is systematically stressed and analyzed. The main reference in this respect may be Schelling's influential article "On the Ecology of Micromotives" and, following this paper, the collection of papers by the same author published under the title *Micromotives and Macrobehavior.*[13] Except in some pages of the book, these works contain (probably in order to gain a wider audience) little explicit or sophisticated modeling, but they include powerful ideas that can easily be turned into models. Also, the final pages of the book present, in the graphical fashion familiarly used in economic theory, a set of models that could be further elaborated and that represent nothing less than a generating device of interaction structures with deficient equilibrium. The classical structures with deficient equilibrium become particular cases of the general framework presented by Schelling. The rest of the book presents numerous examples showing how the aggregation of individual actions can lead to various kinds of unexpected, undesirable, or surprising outcomes. Some of these examples rest on simple mathematical models, other on sequential models that are in some cases analyzed by a simulation method, such as the segregation models. These models are elaborated in an article in the *Journal of Mathematical Sociology.*[14] They show that understandable preferences (not being in a minority in one's environment) can lead, when everybody has the same type of preference to aggregate equilibrium outcomes displaying an overshooting effect: When whites want to be surrounded by a majority of whites and reds by a majority of reds, it will turn out that at equilibrium whites will be surrounded almost exclusively by whites and reds by reds. Moderate preferences generate at equilibrium immoderate collective effects. Schelling's ideas on segregation have been applied to some empirical studies of urban segregation.[15]

My guess is that Schelling's ideas are of great potential usefulness in the social sciences. Moreover, they build a bridge between some familiar ideas of sociological theory (Merton's ideas of the self-fulfilling prophecy and of the unanticipated social consequences of individual actions) and mathematical thinking. As a matter of fact, whereas some of the models developed by Schelling are mathematically simple, as far as both the assumptions and the analysis are concerned, others are simple as far as the assumptions are concerned, but their mathematically analysis turns out to be a very difficult task. That is why Schelling occasionally used simulation. Finally, it should be emphasized that Schelling's contribution to the field of the paradoxical aggregation effects of individual microbehavior can be considered as open. He gives and suggests many examples; many others could be imagined or further elaborated.

Whether Schelling's ideas will actually exert an influence on social research and social theory is still open to question. I mentioned a study on urban segregation inspired by his ideas, but it cannot be said that urban research as a whole has been affected by his way of thinking. His work on segregation can, however, be qualified as a breakthrough: Many studies on segregation have been conducted in the past by sociologists, but none of them seem to have realized the importance and power of the aggregation effects in this area. It could be perceived with difficulty as long as a mathematical theoretical modeling of such effects was not conducted.

Perhaps I shall be forgiven if I mention one of my works along the same line.[16] Empirical research in the field of social mobility had led to a set of surprising findings: One of these is that social mobility does not differ greatly from one country to another and does not vary much over time. This is surprising: Factors such as the development of education and the equality of educational opportunities vary greatly over time and space; on the other hand, the educational level is a powerful determinant of status. Using a simulation model, it can be shown (an example of an aggregation effect) that mobility *can* remain stable as a result of a congestion effect, even though educational opportunities are equalized. Fararo has shown that the first part of the model could be analyzed mathematically, whereas simulation is more convenient in the second part, where a queuing process governed by endogenously moving distributions is created.[17] As functions of the type $\min(x, y, \ldots)$ are introduced and as x, y, . . . are time-indexed, a mathematical statement of the whole model appears to be difficult.

Again, the notion of composition effects is familiar to economists but less so to political scientists and even less so to sociologists. As far as the former are concerned, Hotelling's notable paper on "Stability in Competition" and its application to the political field provides a classical example of a paradoxical composition effect.[18] It has inspired many recent works—for instance, Tullock's work on the mathematics of politics.[19] The idea of composition effects has always, on the other hand, been at least implicitly present in political theory. (See Rousseau's "force men to be free"; in some situations a coercion mechanism is necessary in order to compel rational actors to do what they really want). In sociology the idea had been expressed by Merton, but few mathematical models illustrating the idea have been forged to explain phenomena belonging to the traditional sociological field. One reason for this may be that the mathematical language started penetrating sociology in a conjuncture where what can be called the Weberian paradigm (social facts are nothing but aggregate individual *actions*) was far from dominant in empirical research. For many years, individuals were considered or at least treated as sets of variables rather than as *actors* or *agents*. Schelling's models on segregation and other social phenomena, as well as other models along the same line, may inaugurate a new way of thinking in some parts of sociology.

Economics, Mathematics, and the Social Sciences

This might be the place to introduce a parenthetical comment on the channels of influence. Some of the foregoing examples show that economics often played the role of a mediator between mathematics—more specifically the mathematics of action—on the one hand, and the social sciences on the other. This should not be surprising, because of the long familiarity of economics with the mathematics of action and the more recent trend whereby the economic way of thinking tends to be applied to substantive areas other than those traditionally dealt with by economics. The growing body of literature on the economics of crime, economics of marriage and divorce, and economics of discrimination is a challenge to the traditional sociological or demographic approaches, which have been and to a large extent still remain dominant as far as these substantive areas are concerned.[20] For the time being, a juxtaposition rather than a convergence is observable: The sociology of crime has been little affected by the economics of crime, for instance. Consequently, the mathematical models used by economists have weakly attracted the attention of sociologists. The situation is somewhat different as far as other fields such as the sociology of education are concerned: In this case research is to some extent impregnated by the idea originally proposed by the economists of education that education is *also* an investment implying a cost-benefit approach, though of a generalized type. The influence of economics in this field will likely indirectly generate a more intensive use of mathematical modeling in the future.

The same can perhaps be said of the field of development, where sociologists, political scientists, and economists have to live close to one another. Among the many achievements in the mathematical economics of development, some have a direct interest for the social sciences and may eventually lead to a greater use of the mathematical language and way of thinking in this area. Two examples among others may be mentioned in this respect. Hirschman's "tunnel" model, which was inspired in the creator by the field observation that people may feel released and optimistic when the *others* become wealthier while their own situation is stagnant.[21] The model is an ingenious application to the field of development of ideas contained in the familiar sociological reference group theory. Being an economist, Hirschman built a mathematical version of this well-known theory. The other example will be drawn from a paper by Bhaduri on West Bengal:[22] The problem was to explain why innovations that are apparently favorable to landlords as well as to tenants are sometimes rejected in semifeudal societies—that is, in societies where the tenants are close to the subsistance level, have to borrow money, and cannot borrow it except from their landlord. The classical sociological explanation of such an apparently "irrational" phenomenon rests on the Weberian concept of *traditionelles Handeln,* or on the more modern concept of resistance to change. Using a model including two difference equations, Bhaduri shows that for a large region of the parametric space $a \times b$, where a is the effect of the innovation on productivity and b the marginal propension of the tenant to consume, innovation is threatening to the landlord. In other words, for an extended set of values of the parameters a and b, the landlord can, at equilibrium, draw no benefit and eventually suffer a loss from the innovation. As the landlord cannot anticipate with precision the values of a and b, his resistance to innovation can be simply a reflection of his consciousness of the risk involved by the innovation. Such a model is directly challenging to the sociological theories explaining the hostility toward innovation in so-called traditional societies by the weight of traditions in such societies. One writer, Popkin, went even further, suggesting that the individualistic approach typical of economic thinking can be generally applied to traditional societies.[23] Once this idea is more widely accepted by sociologists, this should make the field of the sociology of development more permeable to mathematical thinking.

I am aware that, by saying so, I am beyond the boundaries of my task in this paper, since I deal with developments that do not yet exist. It is crucial, however, to emphasize that general theoretical orientations can be more or less hospitable to the mathematical way of thinking. Methodological individualism, because it directs the analyst's attention toward aggregation effects and their complexity, is in this respect an orientation that is more favorable to mathematical thinking than are other orientations that are more traditional in sociology. The second point worth being stressed is that the penetration of mathematical thinking in various points of the social sciences is frequently the effect of a penetration of the economic way of thinking.

Mathematical Sociology and Political Science

In my opinion, progress in the institutionalization of mathematical sociology is worth mentioning as an advance. A continuous flow of scholars trained in mathematics and/or statistics devote their time to mathematical modeling in the social sciences. The development of the process has a complicated story. It is due to the pioneering work of men such as Lazarsfeld, Guttman, and some others in the 1950s.[24] It was stimulated by the development of quantitative empirical sociology and political science, which aroused a need for data analysis methods. Also, the pioneers opened paths of methodological research that were followed for a long time. I cannot provide a general survey of the developments of mathematical sociology but will simply describe a few trends.

Leaving aside data analysis for a moment, the activity of mathematical sociologists and political scientists falls into two parts: refinement of mathematical instruments (for example, Markov chains) developed by mathematicians, and refinement of models developed by sociologists or political scientists to solve theoretical or data analysis problems. Obviously, the various fields of the social sciences are more or less hospitable to a mathematical approach. Among the fields where mathematical modeling has been used for a long time in a more or less continuous fashion, the following can be mentioned: social diffusion, social mobility, organization theory, social change, migrations, and social conflicts. I will briefly consider some of these fields.

Modeling of Diffusion and Mobility

The idea of applying mathematical modeling to diffusion processes is already implicitly suggested by Tarde's *Laws of Imitation*, whose core assumption is that most social "facts" are the product of "contagion" processes. Beside the previously mentioned Coleman et al. study,[25] the work of Hägerstrand can be mentioned.[26] As he worked mainly on the diffusion of innovations in a rural context, Hägerstrand had to get rid of the strong assumptions of the classical diffusion models (for example, the homogeneity of the social space in the logistic model): The probability of two peasants meeting and influencing one another is a function of the distance between them; also, other things being equal, the probability of actually being influenced is not the same for all, but depends on age, size of farm, and so on. Hägerstrand had the interesting idea of using simulation rather than mathematical modeling. In a simulation model, complex assumptions, closer to empirical reality, on the distribution of social distances and on distribution of attitudes toward change can be introduced more easily than in a mathematical model. Rapoport's work on diffusion is also concerned with getting rid of the assumptions on the homogeneity of the social space characteristic of the classical models.[27] More recently, Hamblin and others proposed to apply diffusion models (Gompertz) to a field where it had been rarely applied: collective violence.[28]

On the whole, social diffusion is a field where a continuous interaction between mathematical thinking and empirical research can be observed. This interaction was favored by the preexistence of a set of classical models developed by epidemiologists, by the existence of data on diffusion processes (for example, data on agricultural innovations or, more recently, on collective violence). Mathematical modeling became more flexible over time: New models were developed in which rigid assumptions were replaced by more realistic ones.[29] Simulation models were used, beside mathematical models. On the other hand, new fields of empirical research were affected: After the spread of rumors, and the spread of innovations, the spread of collective behavior was analyzed with the help of mathematical models. In the case of diffusion, the progress in the interaction between mathematics and research appears as continuous.

Social mobility is another field where mathematical modeling plays an important role, but the interaction between mathematics and research is less linear in this case.

A number of models have been proposed to solve the measurement problems aroused by the comparison of social mobility tables.[30]

A second problem aroused much interest: the separate concept of "structural" mobility—that is, the mobility mechanically generated by the change over time of the sociooccupational structure. It leads to complex mathematical problems, since the notion of minimal (structural) mobility can be defined only with difficulty in a nonambiguous way as soon as one wants to take care of the social distance covered by a mover.[31] Another difficulty comes from the fact that the set of socioccupational categories cannot always be considered as one-dimensional. Moreover, Duncan, in an influential paper, drew the attention of mobility analysts to the ambiguity of mobility tables (the distribution of a population of individuals as a function of their social origins cannot be considered as giving an accurate picture of the socioccupational distribution at any definite time).[32] Partly as a consequence of this critique, the mathematical reflection on the analysis of social mobility tables was, if not stopped, at least made slower. Following Duncan's critique, mobility tables were considered as ordinary contingency tables and explored with the help of conventional statistical methods.

A third direction of research had been inaugurated by Blumen, Kogan, and McCarthy in the 1950s.[33] It was extended from intra- to intergenerational mobility analysis by Leo Goodman and Harrison White.[34] The problem dealt with by these models is the following: Can an empirical mobility table be made the sum of latent components, some of which are characterized by perfect mobility. The question is interesting. It amounts to asking whether parts of the population can be identified that could be considered as moving freely in the socioccupational structure.

A fourth line of research is characterized by an effort to apply more or less complicated Markov models to social mobility, either intergenerational or intragenerational.[35]

A fifth line of approach conceives mobility as the aggregate outcome of queueing processes wherein individuals develop searching strategies as a function of their resources (for example, educational) and of the available jobs.[36]

The history of the application of mathematical modeling to social mobility is interesting. Progress is much less linear than in the case of diffusion. Promising paths were opened for a while and then closed or half closed, perhaps provisionally. However, the interaction between mathematical thinking and research in this field can be held, if not as leading to a linear progress, at least as permanent.

To save space, I will treat two other fields only in a sketchier fashion.

Organization Theory

Organization theory has always been a field open to mathematical modeling. On the whole, however, although today it is practically impossible to give a course on social mobility or on social diffusion without requiring from the students at least *some* mathematical training, the same does not hold for organization theory. It seems, in other words, that, for complex reasons, this field is less affected by mathematical methods than others are. One reason is that organizations are complex singular systems resistant to the simplifications that have to be introduced in mathematical modeling. Some mathematical models in this field deal with the relationship between organizational size and structure. Thus Doreian worked on Blau's proposition that size determines organizational structure and presented a dynamic model wherein the increase in each of the following variables is made a linear function of the other variables: the number of employees in the production sector and the number of divisions in this sector, the number of supervisory employees, and the mean number of hierarchical levels.[37] Other models deal with the effects of environmental variations on the structure and objectives of organizations.[38] Others analyze the relationship between the requirement for an expected minimal cost of communication and the structure of the organization.[39]

Conflict Theory

Conflict theory and analysis is the last field I will consider explicitly here (although others, such as migration, could also be considered). In this area the picture is somewhat similar to that for social diffusion. In both cases the development of mathematical thinking was originally prompted by the preexistence of an important body of mathematical models. In the case of diffusion, epidemiologists and mathematical statisticians had developed an important collection of diffusion models. In the case of conflicts, game theoreticians had developed an impressive body of models. Rapoport and Boulding in various publications helped bridge the gap between mathematical theory and actual conflicts.[40] Rapoport combined game theory with an experimental or observational approach to groups. Riker applied the concepts of game theory to the problem of the formation of political coalitions.[41] Axelrod and Hirschman, among others, applied concepts of game theory to political life.[42] The study of conflict, however—and, more generally, of the interdependent systems wherein actors have divergent interests—also benefited from the extension of econometric models to new areas, in particular to political phenomena. Many of the relevant contributions in this respect were published in *Public Choice*.[43] With few exceptions (as, for example, Olson's work), however, the impact of "econometric" models applied to political phenomena seems to remain weak. As stated earlier, the economic way of thinking, rather than econometric models proper, had an influence on research in sociology at large or political science at large. That is, research was affected by and made aware of such ideas as methodological individualism, the costs and benefits of action, aggregation paradoxes, suboptimal effects, and the like. As to the actual applications or uses of the specific models developed by econometricians, on the whole they remain scarce.

Even when considering a few fields, one gets a complicated picture of the use and influence of mathematical modeling on the social sciences. As far as social diffusion and social mobility are concerned, the link between research in general and mathematical modeling is narrow, although the development of mathematical models in more linear in the former case. A number of models were produced in the field of organization theory, but the connection is looser between mathematical modeling and organization theory and research than it is in the two other cases. The whole field appears to be less affected by mathematical thinking than is the field of social mobility. For conflict theory, the picture is particularly complicated. Game theory has inspired many works, but the relationship between econometric models and political theory and research is looser. Political *economics* or, rather, the economics of politics has become to some extent a sector of activity of its own with diffuse rather than specific influence on political theory and research.

To conclude this section, I will mention another activity of mathematical sociologists: developing or extending mathematical theories of current use (for example, Markov chains or game theory) in the social sciences without direct regard to specific applications.[44]

Data Analysis

Last but not least, a field of utmost importance has to be mentioned: data analysis. Much of the research activity of mathematicians and statisticians active in the social sciences, as well as of some of the social scientists interested in "methodology," is devoted to developing new methods and techniques for the analysis of data. I placed quote marks around the term *methodology* to recall that the notion of methodology has a much broader meaning. In the practice of the social sciences, however, *methodology* is currently and unfortunately taken as a label for the set of data analysis techniques.

It is understandable why so much energy is devoted to the development of such techniques. In many fields, empirical research produces impressive amounts of data. In most cases these data are collected, not to test a well-defined theory, but rather to explore some area (the "determinants" of social status, job aspirations among students, and so on). In many cases the product of the observation is an $m \times n$ contingency table, where m is the number of observed individuals and n the number of observations. This typical situation arouses a "demand" for methods able to transform this $m \times n$ original information into a more tractable set of parameters.

This transformation operation can be held as an implicit definition of so-called data analysis methods. Basically, these methods have essentially a summarizing function: Exactly as the information contained in a one-variable distribution can be summarized by a small number of parameters (for example, mean and standard deviation), the information contained in a n-variable distribution can be summarized by a set of parameters. I recall this well-known fact because data analysis methods are sometimes considered as having an *explanation* function, whereas their function is essentially a *summarizing* one.

A number of methods have been developed that meet this summarization function with a variable combination of advantages and disadvantages: regression analysis with a single equation or with multiple equations,[15] factor analysis,[16] the now so-called log-linear models,[17] interaction analysis,[18] and so on. Some of these categories themselves include a number of variants: Factor-analytical methods constitute, for instance, a continuously expanding set of methods.

Although these methods are widely used, their exact function is sometimes ambiguous: Once a factor-analytical method has been applied to a collection of data, it can turn out that, say two or three factors explain 60 percent of the variance. In most actual cases, however, the factors will receive a vague interpretation. Very seldom will the structure of the "saturations" be clearly interpretable. In the same fashion, a set of partial correlations between, say, Father's status, Father's education, Son's education, and Son's status is a useful summary of a large body of information. It is nothing more than a summary, however. To explain why these correlations remain stable from one cohort to the next for instance or why they change in some fashion, one has to build other types of models that take account of individual strategies, of the (eventually) changing structure of opportunity, and so on. Obviously, data analysis methods are of crucial importance in empirical research, even though their main function has to be considered as *descriptive* rather than *explanatory*.

Although most data analysis methods are quantitative, some are qualitative or ordinal. Flament in particular is responsible for the systematic development of ordinal methods, the core idea of which can be found in earlier works of Guttman and Coombs.[49]

Finally, it should be emphasized that data analysis is not limited to the treatment of individual informations. Numerous methods have been devised, the purpose of which is to summarize sets of *relational* pieces of information, such as the information contained in sociograms.[50]

The Use of New Mathematical Instruments

Among the older mathematical instruments, *game theory* has been very much used, as we saw, either as a source of application or as a source of inspiration. The more diffuse and not exclusively mathematical body of theory known as *general systems theory* played also the role of a source of inspiration.[51] Easton's work in political theory is one example of this influence.[52] There, however, the influence is conceptual rather than mathematical. In some other cases, as in Forrester's work on world dynamics, impressive systems models have been constructed.[53] As a matter of fact, the influence of general systems theory is both important in the social sciences and extremely diffuse. It helped make social scientists more conscious of the fact that the elements of a system can be mutually interrelated in a more or less tight fashion. Consequently, it contributed to limit the traditional causal or "factorial" way of thinking that is very often used in social theory and research.

Among the new mathematical theories that drew the attention of social scientists, *catastrophe theory* should be mentioned.[54] Whether this theory is likely to have an impact of its own (beyond stimulating the construction of dynamic models) or exert an influence on the social sciences apparently remains to be seen. The same is true of new instruments such as erotetic logic and, generally, of the models used in linguistics, which in some cases rest on new mathematical developments.[55] Sociologists and political scientists are obviously concerned with linguistic problems (a questionnaire, for instance, is a conversation that follows a certain path and obeying certain rules). Nevertheless, the intense mathematical activity that developed in modern linguistics does not seem to have had, up to now, a very important impact on the social sciences.

References

1. J. P. Benzecri, *L'analyse des données* (Paris: Dunod, 1973).
2. For example, G. Snyder, "*Prisoner's Dilemma* and *Chicken* Models in International Politics," *International Studies Quarterly 15* (1971): 66–103.

3. See Notes 7, 9, 40, and 41.
4. M. Olson, *The Logic of Collective Action* (Cambridge, Mass.: Harvard University Press, 1965).
5. A. Downs, *An Economic Theory of Democracy* (New York: Harper, 1957); J. M. Buchanan and G. Tullock, *The Calculus of Consent* (Ann Arbor: University of Michigan Press, 1962); G. Tullock, *Toward a Mathematics of Politics* (Ann Arbor: University of Michigan Press, 1967).
6. J. S. Coleman, *The Mathematics of Collective Action* (London: Heinemann, 1973).
7. T. C. Schelling, *The Strategy of Conflict* (Cambridge, Mass.: Harvard University Press, 1960); *Arms and Influence* (New Haven: Yale University Press, 1966); A. Rapoport and A. M. Chammah, *Prisoner's Dilemma* (Ann Arbor: University of Michigan Press, 1976); A. Rapoport, M. Guyer, and D. Gordon, "Threat Games: A Comparison of Performance of Danish and American Subjects," in H. R. Alker, K. W. Deutsch, and A. Stoetzel, eds., *Mathematical Approaches to Politics* (Amsterdam: Elsevier, 1973).
8. J. L. Peaucelle, "Théorie des jeux et sociologie des organisations," *Sociologie du Travail 11* (1969): 22–43.
9. R. Boudon, "Generating Models as a Research Strategy," in R. K. Merton, J. S. Coleman, and P. Rossi, eds., *Qualitative and Quantitative Social Research* (New York: Free Press, 1979), pp. 51–64.
10. J. Maynard Smith, *Models in Ecology* (Cambridge: Cambridge University Press, 1974).
11. E. Durkheim, *La division du travail*, Preface to the 2nd edition (Paris: Presses Universitaires de France, 1960); R. Dahrendorf, *Class and Class Conflicts in Industrial Society* (Stanford: Stanford University Press, 1959).
12. J. S. Coleman, E. Katz, and H. Menzel, *Medical Innovation: A Diffusion Study* (New York: Bobbs-Merrill, 1966).
13. T. C. Schelling, "On the Ecology of Micromotives," *Public Interest 25* (1971): 61–98; *Micromotives and Macrobehavior* (New York: Norton, 1978).
14. T. C. Schelling, "Dynamic Models of Segregation," *Journal of Mathematical Sociology 1* (1971): 143–186.
15. J. Lautman, *Les Fortunes Immobilières*, forthcoming.
16. R. Boudon, *Education, Opportunity and Social Inequality* (New York: Wiley, 1974).
17. T. S. Fararo and K. Kosaka, "A Mathematical Analysis of Boudon's IEO Model," *Social Science Information 15* (1976): 431–475.
18. H. Hotelling, "Stability in Competition," *Economic Journal 39* (1929): 41–57.
19. See also A. O. Hirschman, *Exit, Voice and Loyalty* (Cambridge, Mass.: Harvard University Press, 1970).
20. See, for instance, G. S. Becker, *The Economics of Discrimination* (Chicago: Chicago University Press, 1957); G. Becker, "Crime and Punishment: An Economic Approach," *Journal of Political Economy 76* (1968): 169–

217; R. B. McKenzie and G. Tullock, *The New World of Economics* (Homewood, Ill.: Irwin, 1975).
21. A. O. Hirschman, "The Changing Tolerance for Income Inequality in the Course of Economic Development," *Quarterly Journal of Economics 87* (1973): 544–556.
22. A. Bhaduri, "A Study of Agricultural Backwardness under Semi-Feudalism," *Economic Journal 83* (1973): 120–137.
23. S. L. Popkin, *The Rational Peasant* (Berkeley: University of California Press, 1979).
24. A single book, P. Lazarsfeld, ed., *Mathematical Thinking in the Social Sciences* (New York: Free Press, 1958), was particularly influential. It opened paths of research in a durable fashion.
25. See Note 12.
26. T. Hägerstrand, "On the Monte-Carlo Simulation of Diffusion," in W. L. Garrison and D. F. Marble, eds., *Quantitative Geography* (Evanston, Ill.: Northwestern University, 1960, pp. 1–32; G. Bahrenberg and W. Taubmann, eds., *Quantitative Modelle in der Geographie und Raumplanung* (Bremen).
27. A. Rapoport, "The Impact of Network Structure on Diffusion Processes," in *Modelle für Ausbreitungsprozesse in sozialen Strukturen* (Duisburg: Verlag der Sozialwissenschaftlichen Kooperative, 1981), pp. 7–36.
28. R. L. Hamblin, R. B. Jakobsen, and J. L. L. Miller, *A Mathematical Theory of Social Change* (New York: Wiley, 1973); B. L. Pitcher, R. L. Hamblin and J. L. L. Miller, "The Diffusion of Collective Violence," *American Sociological Review 43* (1978): 23–35.
29. M. Granovetter, "Threshold Models of Collective Behavior," *American Journal of Sociology 83* (May): 1420–1443; J. D. Hamilton and L. C. Hamilton, "Models of Social Contagion," *Journal of Mathematical Sociology 8* (1981): 133–160.
30. D. J. Bartholomew, *Stochastic Models for Social Processes* (New York: Wiley, 1967); R. Boudon, *Mathematical Structures of Social Mobility* (Amsterdam: Elsevier, 1973).
31. D. Bertaux, "Sur l'analyse des tables de mobilité sociale," *Revue française de sociologie 10* (1971): 448–490.
32. O. D. Duncan, "Methodological Issues in the Analysis of Mobility Tables," in N. Smelser and S. M. Lipset, eds., *Social Structures and Mobility in Economic Development* (Chicago: Aldine, 1966), pp. 51–97.
33. I. Blumen, M. Kogan, and P. J. McCarthy, "The Industrial Mobility of Labor as a Probability Process," *Cornell Studies in International Relations.* (Ithaca: Cornell, 1955).
34. L. Goodman, "On the Statistical Analysis of Mobility Tables," *American Journal of Sociology 70* (1965): 564–585; "Statistical Methods for a Mover-Stayer Model," *Journal of American Statistical Association 56* (1961): 841–868; H. White, "Stayers and Movers," *American Journal of Sociology 76* (1970): 307–324.

35. R. McGinnis, "A Stochastic Model of Social Mobility," *American Sociological Review 33* (1968): 712–722; R. B. Ginsberg, "Semi-Markov Processes and Mobility," *Journal of Mathematical Sociology 1* (1971): 233–262; H. White, *Chains of Opportunity* (Cambridge, Mass.: Harvard University Press, 1970); N. Henry, R. McGinnis, and H. W. Tegmeyer, "A Finite Model of Mobility," *Journal of Mathematical Sociology 1* (1971): 107–118; D. McFarland, "Intragenerational Social Mobility as a Markov Process," *American Sociological Review 35* (1970): 463–474.
36. C. Thelot, *Tel Père, Tel Fils* (Paris: Dunod, 1982).
37. P. Doreian and N. P. Hummon, *Modeling Social Processes* (Amsterdam: Elsevier, 1976); P. Blau, "A Formal Theory of Differentiation in Organization," *American Sociological Review 35* (1970): 201–218.
38. J. H. Freeman and M. T. Hannan, "Growth and Decline in Organizations," *American Sociological Review 40* (1975): 215–228; N. P. Hummon, P. Doreian, and K. Teuter, "A Structural Control Model of Organizational Change," *American Sociological Review 40* (1975): 813–824; H. W. Meyer, ed., *Organizations and Environments* (San Francisco: Jossey-Bass, 1978).
39. J. Marschak and R. Radner, *Economic Theory of Teams* (New Haven: Yale University Press, 1972).
40. A. Rapoport, *Fights, Games and Debates* (Ann Arbor: University of Michigan Press, 1960); K. Boulding, *Conflict and Defense* (New York: Harper, 1962).
41. W. H. Riker, *The Theory of Political Coalitions* (New Haven: Yale University Press, 1962); W. H. Riker and W. J. Zavoina, "Rational Behavior in Politics: Evidence from a Three-Person Game," *American Political Science Review 64* (1970): 48–64.
42. R. Axelrod, *Conflict and Interest: A Theory of Divergent Goals with Applications to Politics* (Chicago: Markham, 1970); A. O. Hirschman, *Journeys toward Progress* (New York: Twentieth Century Fund, 1963).
43. *Public Choice,* The Hague, Boston, and London: Martinus Nijhoff.
44. For instance, H. Hamburger, "Separable Games," *Behavioral Science 14* (1969): 121–132; B. Singer and S. Spilerman, "The Representation of Social Processes by Markov Models," *American Journal of Sociology 82* (1976): 1–54; R. W. Rosenthal, "New Equilibria for Non-Cooperative Two-Person Games," *Journal of Mathematical Sociology 7* (1980): 15–26; J. P. Lehoczky, "Approximation for Interactive Markov Chains in Discrete and Continuous Time," *Journal of Mathematical Sociology 7* (1980): 139–158.
45. A. S. Goldberger and O. D. Duncan, eds., *Structural Equation Models in the Social Sciences* (New York: Seminar Press, 1973); H. M. Blalock, ed., *Measurement in the Social Sciences* (Chicago: Aldine, 1974).
46. See Reference 1.
47. See L. Goodman, "Causal Analysis of Data from Panel Studies and

Other Kinds of Surveys," *American Journal of Sociology 78* (1973): 1135–1191.

48. J. A. Sonquist and J. M. Morgan, *The Detection of Interaction Effects* (Ann Arbor: University of Michigan Press, 1964); B. Schmeikal and R. Reichardt, "Theoretical Considerations and Simulation Models Related to the Method of Sonquist and Morgan," *Quality and Quantity 7* (1973): 171–188.
49. C. Flament, *L'analyse booléenne de questionnaire* (Paris: Mouton, 1976); C. C. Coombs, *A Theory of Data* (New York: Wiley, 1964); A. Degenne, *Techniques ordinales en analyse des données statistiques* (Paris: Hachette, 1972).
50. F. C. Lorrain and H. White, "Structural Equivalence of Individuals in Social Networks," *Journal of Mathematical Sociology 1* (1971): 49–80; F. Lorrain, *Réseaux sociaux et classifications sociales* (Paris: Hermann, 1975); Yee Leung, "A Fuzzy-Set Analysis of Sociometric Structure," *Journal of Mathematical Sociology 7* (1980): 159–180.
51. A. Rapoport, "Some System Approaches to Political Theory," in D. Easton, ed., *Varieties of Political Theory* (Englewood Cliffs, N.J.: Prentice-Hall, 1966), pp. 129–141; F. E. Emery, *Systems Thinking* (London: Penguin Books, 1969); F. Cortes, A. Przeworski, and J. Sprague, *Systems Analysis for Social Scientists* (New York: Wiley, 1974).
52. D. Easton, *Systems Analysis of Political Life* (New York: Wiley, 1965).
53. J. W. Forrester, *World Dynamics* (Cambridge: Wright Allen, 1971).
54. R. Thom, *Stabilité structurelle et morphogénèse* (Reading, MA: Benjamin, 1972); E. C. Zeeman, *Catastrophe Theory* (Reading, MA: Addison-Wesley, 1977); T. Puston and I. Stewart, *Catastrophe Theory and its Applications* (London: Pitman, 1977); N. Schofield, "Catastrophe Theory and Dynamic Games," mimeo.
55. See, for instance, the special issue *Linguistique et Mathématiques* I: *Mathématiques et Sciences Humaines 77*, 1982.

Discussion

(Platt, Coleman, Bell, Nowotny, Rapoport, Kruskal, Eisenstadt, Inkeles, Deutsch, Miller, Dror, Cohen)

Edited by Andrei S. Markovits

JOHN PLATT initiated the discussion by asking if one could derive from Boudon's paper a list of major advances at the same level of importance as those on the Deutsch-Platt-Senghaas (DPS) list. He said Boudon had listed some sixty papers in the last fifteen years, and that it seemed unlikely on statistical grounds that more than two or three of these could be comparable in importance to the eleven major developments in mathematical statistics listed by DPS for the previous sixty-five years, with about one such development every six years. Platt said that the names given by Boudon that were familiar to the outsider were people like Kenneth Boulding, Anthony Downs, Herman Kahn, Mancur Olson, Anatol Rapoport, Thomas Schelling, and Maynard Smith. He wondered if these names would include the two or three most eminent contributions to the field or if the insider would name less familiar ones as leaders.

James Coleman, who had been the reader of Boudon's paper (since Boudon was unable to attend the conference), replied that Hägerstrand's work in geography and Gary Becker's work in applying microeconomic theory to areas of sociology, would also be eminent; and that Anthony Downs's *An Economic Theory of Democracy* was a major contribution to the public choice area.

How Do Ideas Become Important?

Daniel Bell said he had a different kind of issue—that he was disturbed by the conference proceedings so far. He suggested that the participants were acting like a group of scribes waiting for people to come in with a list of names, saying, "Here is a large group: which shall we engrave in stone?" or, "Is it good enough to be engraved in stone?" He said it reminded him of the Oriental Institute at the University of Chicago, where one got lists from old Sumerian tablets with all kinds of names on them, but so old that they were little more than wrinkles on the clay or stone and had little meaning beyond that. He conceded that there was perhaps some value in making such lists, if all the conference participants were well acquainted with all the fields involved, but that many other, more interesting problems were lost sight of in such an approach.

Bell suggested that the relevant question for advances in the social sciences was not merely which ideas were important, but the way in which ideas became important. When he had asked Wilhelm Krelle how one important idea arose, Krelle replied that it was a process of chance—that von Neumann thought for awhile, then suddenly everything clicked, and "game theory" sprang up. Anatol Rapoport had argued, however, that it was not simply a click, but really only one solution among many. Bell continued that what was important was not only how the idea was proposed, but how it came to be accepted. A crude theory of the sociology of knowledge had been developed in this exchange, as illustrated by Rapoport's remark that game theory was accepted because it was compatible with certain interests in U.S. think tanks.

Bell wanted a different approach; he referred to a famous 1931 meeting on the history of science where B. Hessen had presented a paper on the social origins of Newton's ideas. Hessen had created a furor by saying that there was no autonomous development of ideas—that ideas became important because they were a response to a certain element in the social context. The whole dispute in history of science was between those who argued with Koyré that ideas came from within, and those who argued with Horkheimer and Szell that ideas responded to the social context.

Bell noted several advances that seemed to have responded to social determination. Input-output tables emerged because there was a need to find instruments for national planning, so Leontief took the ideas of the physiocrats and refined them with modern mathematical notions. The need for analysis of macroeconomic problems led to national accounting models. But what was the social determination of the double helix? In the search for the structure of DNA by Watson and Crick, everyone knew there was a light at the end of the tunnel, but no one could figure out the exact configuration of the double helix and how the twists worked until the X-ray crystal diffraction data came along. Crick and Watson had beat out Chargaff and Pauling in this, but both of the latter had been working in the same direction.

Bell said he was trying to avoid a situation such as that at the end of Tinbergen's paper, where there were thirty highly disparate items, or in Krelle's paper, where there were many different nominations. He suggested that approaches of that type were like recommendations to the Academie Française, and usually led to the most tedious discussions.

A more interesting problem for the conference was the way in which ideas cross-fertilized one another: To what extent, Bell asked, did certain social contexts lead to a kind of "manic unfolding of themes," as Sorokin had expressed it? Specialists in different areas must have some sense of how significant ideas had come forward, not just saying, "Well, it's accidental," or "It's all a matter of chance." Bell argued for an examination of the context of the ideas, which could help explain how things were able to hang together—rather than sitting around like scribes trying to decide what should be engraved in stone on a wall.

Helga Nowotny added to this that she could remember the euphoria in the early 1970s when mathematical sociology arrived on the scene, and she felt that a number of institutional factors could help to explain this. Now there was the interesting question of what it was in the cognitive structure of sociology that was, or was not, amenable to the mathematical approaches used. Nowotny argued that one could take this a step further than Bell—that the participants in the conference could look more closely at the cognitive structures of their disciplines to see what made them susceptible to change.

Anatol Rapoport, the moderator of the discussion, interjected that the sociology of knowledge did not necessarily have to refer to something as crude as a definite social need. Astronomy did not arise because of the need for navigation. Rapoport felt that the cognitive structure was more subtle but nevertheless played an important part in determining whether something was accepted or rejected.

Bell remarked that he also felt there was another side of the coin: the way in which theories decayed. By *decay*, he did not mean simply that old theories were superseded by new ones, but rather the phenomenon of theories going wrong or turning into blind alleys. The question was, "Why does what was once regarded as an advance become a cul-de-sac?"

Bell admitted that a cul-de-sac could sometimes be fruitful, and Rapoport said that it helped show where not to go in the future.

William Kruskal then emphasized that the conference was on *conditions* favoring major advances; but fundamentally there was no control group. The DPS paper of 1971 did not discuss the characteristics or conditions of *non*major advances. In experimental high-energy physics, for example, virtually all work is undertaken in teams; this would probably be true of all the major advances, also. Should one then conclude that teamwork was especially important for major breakthroughs, if the non-major advances were also the result of teamwork? We were looking at only two cells of what should be a 2 × 2 table. This kind of mistake was dangerous because researchers might be led to describe causes, or at least associations, that were simply wrong.

When Formalization Is Possible

Coleman responded to Nowotny's comments first. He was reflecting on what made some things in sociology more amenable to formalization than others. For example, consider three areas of study that lend themselves to formalization: (1) occupational mobility, (2) diffusion of information, and (3) coalition formation. For all of these there was some record that could be easily tabulated. In occupational mobility, job changes are recorded. In diffusion of information, there were records that showed knowing or not knowing. For coalitions, there were voting records and the structure of the legislature. And many models of voting behavior depended simply on observable votes.

However, Coleman said, there were other areas of sociology equally important and equally formalizable, but without any observable phenomena. He used trust as an example. Trust could be fairly sensibly formalized in terms of behavior under risk on the part of the trusting person, and of strategic action on the part of the trusted person. The question was why this had not been done and why it was not likely to proceed very far. He thought the answer was that it produces no easily observable and recorded behavior in the everyday activities of life.

Indeed, Coleman argued that this is what in general characterized the difference between sociology and economics. Economics had money, which performs a valuable service for economic theory. Apart from money, he suggested that there were good analogies between social exchange in sociology and monetary exchange in economics. Social exchange, however, was an exchange of intangibles, not normally recorded; and Coleman speculated that it would be a long time before any of this work would become fruitfully formalized.

Rapoport responded by saying that it is true that in real situations or in the field it is difficult to record transactions and interactions between people, but that this is not difficult to do in the laboratory. Rapoport had written a paper with Lindemann in which they operationalized four things: benevolence, malevolence, trust, and suspicion. This was done in non-zero-sum games with a 2 × 2 matrix of the four attitudes.

Rapoport said that trust was very clearly defined operationally in such cases. When choosing trust as a strategy, if the other individual did not choose benevolence, then the trusting individual was betrayed. Rapoport said there was a reason for a person to be malevolent or benevolent depending on what payoffs were specified in the matrix. Under these conditions it was easy to get a tremendous amount of data, and the behavior in the laboratory then proved similar to our traditional ideas of malevolence, benevolence, trust, and suspicion.

Coleman agreed that such experiments could be helpful, but he thought they could not yet be taken to the level of macrosociological phenomena; and Rapoport agreed.

Shmuel Eisenstadt next asked why there was so little formalization of macrosociological structural propensities. Was it because the tradition of economics was so strong? He also asked whether there were mathematical ways to show how coalitions were set up and how people behaved in them. He thought there had been few studies on the ground rules for forming coalitions, although he had tried to study this in his sociological and historical inquiries. Eisenstadt said that the writings of Piaget stressed that there could be a mathematics based on social structures rather than individual behavior, and he asked whether this would make any sense and whether this would make it possible to extend the degree of formalization in sociology.

In reply, Rapoport argued that this was already happening in a variety of ways. The mathematics useful for these purposes was not classical mathematics. however; and people with a classical mathematics education still tended to transfer badly the methods of mathematical physics onto the social sciences. He recalled as an example his experience as a student under Nicholas Rashevsky, who tried to make a literal translation from the language of physics into the language of the social sciences. Rapoport suggested, however, that there were other varieties of mathematics that were structural rather than dynamic, as in "network theory," "category theory," and new models of social structure.

Alex Inkeles announced that he would support Coleman on the ease of applying mathematical formulations when there were adequate and systematic recording procedures. Nevertheless he felt that at any given point in time, some forms of mathematical application were more readily available than others, and that this would determine which kinds of data were most suitable. It would be a mistake to assume that Coleman's theses exhausted the picture.

Areas Rich in Data but Not Yet Formalized

Inkeles suggested that there were contextual influences in the environment—either within the discipline or in society at large—that played a very big role. He said that during the discussion he had tried to jot down areas that offered a great deal of data but had not yet been formalized, although they seemed to him to lend themselves to the application of mathematical models. For some reason these areas were not attracting that kind of interest.

His first example was legal *court actions* (which he was studying for the Russell Sage Foundation in a project on "due process"). In this area there was a great deal of precise recording of almost everything that happened, including personal details on the parties involved, the lawyers, and the exact stages through which the actions passed; and it was possible to make fairly sound judgments about the motivations of the people involved.

A second area was that of *medical treatment,* where there were good records on individual behavior and the processing of individuals as they traveled through the system. For example, Inkeles noted that a person has to make an appointment to go to a clinic, then is seen by a doctor; a certain decision is made, the doctor has to write something down, and so on. A good deal could be done in following these patterns.

A third area that Inkeles felt would lend itself to formalized research was that of the *family*. With the rise of divorce, there are records showing the characteristics of the people involved in marriages, the timing and sequence of one or more divorces, and so on. He suggested that there are probably many more areas with records that could be studied and formalized.

Rapoport noted that there was a current study of first offenders involved in shoplifting. As in Inkeles's cases, these are definite events, which are recorded and timed and lend themselves to mathematical analysis. The areas that Inkeles had pointed to were slowly but surely being addressed.

Inkeles agreed but said that the issue was not the listing of particular areas but, rather, whether it was possible to specify realms that met Coleman's conditions yet were not being studied. In such cases the question was why a particular set of data was being neglected, even though the existing methods could be applied. Inkeles felt it had to do with the development of the discipline, or with the mathematics involved, or with the social context.

Karl Deutsch next posed a question in connection with Bell's discussion of why particular problem areas become important. He thought that Hessen's paper and all that followed from it led to a demand-side theory of scientific development. In the Crick-Watson story, however, it was X-ray diffraction data that made possible the breakthrough, and this seemed to lead to a supply-side theory of scientific development. Was there a supply of critical techniques that develop and can be used on problems that have previously been intractable? Deutsch asked. He said that each of these theories was only a partial approach. Tinbergen's paper showed that it was at least thinkable in economics to bring the two approaches together, and this seemed to have parallels in the sociology of science.

Deutsch offered a concrete suggestion, based on the history of the natural sciences. Tycho Brahe had spent a lifetime compiling data about planetary motions—much more than had ever been available before. He was not cocnerned with developing a new law, however, and did not do so. Kepler, on the other hand, did not have to collect a large amount of data, but concentrated on making sense of the data Tycho provided.

Deutsch wondered whether the present situation was not parallel. For example, to get all the data on frequently divorced people was a monumental task, and the people who did it would not have much time or money left to think about the interpretation. Moreover, these different kinds of research might require different personalities. The same was true for court actions and for other areas. Thus at the Institute of Comparative Social Research in Berlin there was an attempt to get large collections of data in certain fields, and to organize them into a tolerably standardized form so that they could be made available for interpretation. In this way one could make it more likely that certain problems would get a mathematical analysis and interpretation.

The catch, Deutsch admitted, was that it was often a theory that told the researcher what data needed to be collected. He maintained, however, that this happened in economics all the time. For example, data had always been collected by customs officers or ministries of finance, not for purposes of theoretical economics but for purposes of government. Nevertheless, these data could be examined by economists who could try to make sense of them; indeed, the origin of econometrics would not have been possible without such large bodies of data.

Rapoport interrupted to point out that in fact the word *statistics* stemmed from the collection of data for states.

Deutsch continued with his argument, stating that he thought a similar situation existed with data collection in sociology. Rapoport had described studies of the level of trust that people exhibited in game situations. Were these measurements available, Deutsch asked, in such a form that other people could get a set of data and data tapes and use them to try out theories with different mathematical models?

Rapoport replied that his particular experiments were done in the laboratory, and the data and results had been published. He said that it would please him more than anything else if similar experiments were done all over the world and a tremendous volume of data of this type was collected.

Opposite Poles: Formalization versus Contextual Influences

Bell spoke next, promising to be less contentious. He did not want to make "formalization" into a villain, but he wanted to introduce some challenges to the idea of formalization, especially in sociology. He did not want to reduce it to an either/or proposition, but there was a problem at the heart of the sociological enterprise concerning whether or not one should go very far toward formalization.

It seemed to Bell that if sociology was going to have any validity in understanding processes, it had to keep itself rooted in "contextual influences," in Inkeles's phrase. The opposing thesis was that of Wilhelm Krelle, who stated at this conference that the success of economics is based on the fact that it has become detached from institutions. These two positions represented two different poles: contextual and noncontextual.

Bell held that the problem with formalization was that it tended to detach itself from institutions and context. This was what gave it its power and transferability, but how far in that direction should one go? Peter Blau, a colleague of Coleman's, had dealt with heterogeneity, homogeneity, and hierarchies, but almost independently of social structure and culture. These concepts became nothing more than abstract variables that could be applied in all sorts of situations. Bell compared them to economic models, which dealt with abstract homogeneity and could be made available in any context, like any other kinds of propositions that received formalizations.

Bell said that the crucial test was the level of abstraction. In the history of the social sciences, particularly sociology, there were always situations where one was caught between history on the one hand and economics on the other. History had variety, diversity, and idiosyncratic elements, whereas economics became a formal model detached from institutions.

The past masters of social science, Bell suggested, were constantly caught in this dilemma. Weber, for instance, tried to create a theory of historical actors using methodological individualism as a kind of fiction. Georg Simmel moved in the same direction that Blau was moving in today. Simmel drew the distinction between form and content and argued that sociology was supposed to be concerned with forms, just as geometry dealt with forms as a general tool independent of specific content. The result, however, Bell argued, was the kind of thing one found in Parsons, where terms became totally abstract and lost their contextual relevance. This was the result whether one dealt with Parsons's "pattern variables"; or the "superordination" or "subordination" of Simmel; or the "homogeneity, heterogeneity, and hierarchy" of Blau. The question was whether the effort to mathematicize—not simply in terms of data, but in the *ordering* of data and its formalization—had not strayed too far from what the sociological enterprise ought to be.

In reply to these various questions, Coleman put aside the issue of how far formalization should go, and addressed himself to Nowotny's discussion of the conditions conducive to formalization—or, more modestly, the conditions for developing "thick description." He felt that his own example of "trust," and Inkeles's three examples, began to offer some ideas on where formalization occurred and where it did not.

Coleman mentioned several other areas that illustrated important points. *Content analysis* was a case for which records had long been in existence of the content of social communication, but where we had only just begun to develop efficient methods for digesting these records so that they would be useful for analysis.

Another example was *marriage models* in demography. (Demography itself was one of the areas where extensive work had been possible because there were abundant records subject to analysis.) Coleman argued that marriage data existed but that the mathematics had not been adequately developed to understand them. For example, marriage by age could be examined, say with males from eighteen to forty and females from sixteen to forty, age of bride and groom both being recorded. There was a certain kind of "market" involving matching processes between age groups, but the quantity was fixed (that is, monogamy implies that one male marries one female), and "price" could not be used in the same way as in economics. There had been a lot of work in demography on this problem, but it had not been solved.

Coleman admitted that he did not know how far formalization should go. When economics was purely village barter, without any medium of exchange or common measure, it would probably not have been useful to formalize the economic aspects of society, at least not in a separate way from other aspects of the culture. In such a case it would probably be better to employ some "thick description" of the networks of relations. He argued that our social life today may be at a similar level of development, complex and nonnumerical like village barter in economics. Joan Robinson once said that one should not take formalization beyond the degree that reality actually exhibited. In some areas of social life our reality may still be in a "primitive condition," at least in terms of our ability to know and measure.

Coleman used his example of "trust" to illustrate his meaning. Perhaps nothing of macrosociological value could be derived from experiments on trust, and macrosociology in this area could be approached only through thick description. Formalization might, of course, profitably be extended beyond the areas already mentioned; but he was not convinced in either direction.

Formalization as More Than a Tool

Shmuel Eisenstadt then said that formalization was a tool for understanding real problems, not an aim in itself. Sometimes the impetus for formalization went too far, so that one lost sight of the problem being addressed.

Eisenstadt went on to discuss the importance of context in social explanation, and he wondered whether it was possible to conceptualize *context.* All the data we observe—income data, social data, and so on—derive their significance from their context. Is it necessary, however, to treat this as a residual category that is highly significant but that cannot be explained or described? He thought social scientists should try to conceptualize context, and try to compare different contextual situations against one another. After that had been done, it would be possible to determine how far this could be formalized.

Helga Nowotny wished to go further. She thought that social science had reached a point where it should use formalization, but not just as a tool. Social scientists should determine the degree of fit between the structure of the problem and the tools applied. If formalization went too far in a given situation, this meant that the fit was not right. This could happen either because we were looking at the wrong data—for example, simply trying to use the data that were available, even though they had been recorded for other purposes—or because the conceptual apparatus had not been developed in a way that was amenable to the tools we possess. She argued that this problem was a far-reaching one. If formalization did not work, we should look into where or why the cognitive structure and the formal tools did not fit together.

Nowotny also wanted to elaborate on Coleman's point that money was a useful medium for progress in economic theory. What could serve a similar function in other aspects of social life? In the history of modern societies, the institution of law was also a generalized medium of exchange, as was technology. In her view, technology had incorporated within it an entire set of rules for the transformation of labor and capital. The substitution effects for the development of new technology could be studied as rules of transformation, and this would provide a handle in trying to formalize the subject. Formalization had a double sense—of developing our conceptual apparatus, and then of looking for the right mathematical tools to make the relations explicit.

Nowotny's last comment dealt with the problem of detachment that Bell had raised. In any kind of scientific inquiry, one must practice a certain amount of detachment from the object being studied. The mistake that commonly arises is for the scientist to misinterpret this necessary methodological distance as a *real* distance from the object. In reality, she argued, the detachment is not there; we are forced to assume that it is only for the purposes of methodology. If we could avoid this confusion, then we could move one step further.

Mathematical Analysis of Organizations

James Miller said that if the discussion was going to focus on the conditions for using mathematics in social science, the existence of the computer could significantly alter the mathematical methods available. He recalled the story of the drunk who had lost his money in the dark alley but kept looking for it out in the street under the lamppost because that was where the light was. Miller said that L. L. Thurstone used to tell this story, and would say that he always felt the drunk was right—that when you have a method, you start using it (Thurstone referring of course to his own development of factor analysis), and perhaps you might find something under the lamppost more valuable than what you had lost.

Miller also felt that the study of organizations would undergo considerable change in the next decade, for several reasons. First, scientists no longer feel that they can simply study one organization and develop general principles from it. Just as you can study a population of 100 individuals and make certain generalizations about them, so you can study a population of 100 organizations; but this concept was not common in social science even a decade ago. The first study that he could recall using a population of the order of 100 organizations was the work done on nearly 100 corporations by a team working under Donald Marquis at MIT on corporations doing contract research for the U.S. government.

Miller suggested that since there are now management information systems operating in government agencies, corporations, hospitals, universities, and other large institutions, it has become feasible to make on-line studies of organizational processes in a way that was not possible before. This may not yet be possible on the macrosocial or international level. He argued, however, that without a doubt new forms of mathematical analysis will arise, particularly appropriate for the new studies. Data could be collected on-line for continuous monitoring and analysis, as well as for directing the operation of these large systems. Miller pointed to a world simulation model of one oil company, which monitors the current flows of oil through all of that corporation's oil wells, pipelines, refineries, tankers, storage tanks, and so on, throughout the world. Data can be collected by sensors that automatically report on relevant variables through a worldwide information network.

Extended Uses of Computers in Social Science

In this connection, Coleman recommended the new nonfiction book by Tracy Kidder, *The Soul of a New Machine.* It was about organizations constructing an organization: the software and the hardware of a new computer.

On the subject of computers, Yehezkel Dror made some comments in one of the other discussions that are most relevant here. He stated that there were seven uses of the modern computer that were potentially useful in the social sciences. One was the internationally connected data bank, with both the Plato and the Delphi data banks now available by satellite.

They provided files on social science and history, as well as a well-developed system for science, technology, and culture, which made it much easier to conduct a complete literature search. Dror said that in the future this system would become much more accessible, and in fact he was a little envious of the next generation for having this luxury available to researchers.

Second, Dror pointed to the interesting new uses of pattern recognition. In defense intelligence, for example, there was an attempt to predict certain international developments by looking for patterns in the international data. Third, Dror said that computers and modern computer languages were beginning to permit stochastic modeling that would go beyond the present global models. He said that social scientists needed to expand beyond smooth curves but that this had been technically impossible before the advent of the new generation of computers.

A fourth use was the simulation of very complex systems. He pointed to the Rand Corporation's new strategic-interaction laboratory, which used a split-level function for this purpose. A fifth example was the use of topological or graphical representations in work done by the U.S. Department of Commerce. Different phenomena could be correlated in space, and diffusion and topological distributions could be visualized.

Sixth, Dror said that the whole idea of using computers to put data in graphic form could stimulate the mind to consider different perspectives.

Finally, there was the interesting possibility of using interactive computer systems to put social science into the hands of top-level decision makers. For example, the international data bank at Yale could easily be introduced into interactive systems. Dror emphasized with these examples that the innovative use of computers for social science research was not an empty set.

Data First, or Theory First?

I. B. Cohen went on to say that he felt Bell's suggestion that social scientists should look into the conditions under which new concepts were formed was very reasonable, but it sounded to him as though there were notable differences between the development of the natural sciences and the social sciences. In Deutsch's example of the approaches of Tycho Brahe and Kepler, Brahe did in fact have a theory and a law guiding his work. The only problem was that it was not a very good one. The data that he collected were data he wanted to use to validate his own theory about the laws of motion and the "system of the world."

Cohen said that the question of the relation between data and the mathematical theories that used them was a vexing one. The notion that one collected data and then had them available for study did not always work out in the history of the sciences. A good example was the field of meteorology. In the nineteenth century, no other field collected so much data or had so little come of it. The first real advance in meteorology came during World War I, when the Norwegians were cut off from the data collected elsewhere. They needed to be able to forecast the weather for their vital fishing industry, so Bjerknes and his group made a great breakthrough with his method of air-mass analysis. This example should give cause for reflection in other areas.

Cohen continued with another field where a tremendous amount of data was collected in the nineteenth century—the field of spectra, with the measurement of the wavelengths of the spectrum lines of many elements and compounds. Nothing came of these tens of thousands of measurements for decade after decade, however, until Balmer and Rydberg began to develop their theories.

The problem of how theory and mathematics get applied to available data needs a great deal more scrutiny from the sciences. Cohen thought that the facile assumption that theory was simply applied to existing data did not really work. Kepler finally, by empirical curve fitting and some mathematics of a very extraordinary kind, arrived at elliptical orbits, but he had no idea what they meant. They did not become part of astronomy from 1609 until after 1687, when Newton showed what their significance was. In the same way, when the Balmer and Rydberg formulas of spectra were discovered, the German spectroscopist Runge is said to have remarked perceptively, "These numerical laws are like Kepler's laws waiting for their Newton." The Newton who came was Niels Bohr. Cohen emphasized that there are these stages that exist in the process of discovery.

Rapoport added to these comments his own favorite story of the man from Mars who came to earth to study the behavior of chess playing. The Martian made tremendous collections of data having to do with the longevity of the different pieces on the chessboard. Since he had tens of thousands of items of data at his disposal, he made extremely smooth curves about how long each of the pieces stayed on the board. He even had a system of differential equations that showed how these curves were related to one another, and he developed a beautiful theory on the basis of this data and presented it back on Mars as the theory of chess. Rapoport said that his point was that of course it was not a theory of chess, because it concerned things to which chess players were totally indifferent. This theory might have some value to you if you were not a chess player but one of the chess pieces, and were very much interested in your longevity on the board—but collectors and interpreters of data always have to beware of missing the point of the game.

CHAPTER 11

Evaluating Social Science Research

William Kruskal

THE WIDELY KNOWN 1971 *SCIENCE* ARTICLE by Deutsch, Platt, and Senghaas (DPS) forms a springboard for this conference. The article's core is its listing of sixty-two unusually significant achievements of social science research, a highly interesting exercise in what might be called retrospective evaluation—that is, ex post facto value judgments about scientific research.

Retrospective evaluation of research has come, at least in the United States, to have an increasing social and political role—perhaps alarmingly so. In this chapter I shall sketch two different aspects of retroactive evaluation—the first at a national level, and the second relatively personal and focused on my own university.

Before beginning those sketches, however, I discuss three methodological aspects of the DPS study: the need for a control group, the desirability of looking at interjudge variability, and the problem of catch-phrase titles.

Methodological Aspects of the Deutsch-Platt-Senghaas Study

The DPS study presents its sixty-two significant achievements in major part to study the circumstances surrounding major social science advances. Did those advances tend to arise in university settings as opposed to industrial or government settings? Were they mainly group or individual accomplishments? To what extent were they quantitative?

A major problem in examining such questions is that there is no *control group* of less significant social science achievements, or of social science nonachievements, or of non-social-science research. Without a control group, I do not see how conclusions can be drawn.

For example, fifty-three of the sixty-two achievements were importantly quantitative (see Table 3 of Deutsch et al. 1971), but our interpretation might be rather different if we could look at a random sample of sixty-two less significant advances, or perhaps at sixty-two attempted but failed research efforts. Consider these two partly hypothetical 2 × 2 tables:

Hypothetical Table A

	Quantitative	*Nonquantitative*	
Significant achievement	53	9	62
Nonsignificant achievement	53	9	62
			124

Hypothetical Table B

	Quantitative	*Nonquantitative*	
Significant achievement	53	9	62
Nonsignificant achievement	9	53	62
			124

In Table A there is no association between degree of achievement and quantification; in Table B there is strong association. Our subsequent analysis about advances in social science, and our searches for ancillary data, might be wholly different in the two cases.

This is, of course, a familiar cautionary note. It goes back at least to the ancient world, when Cicero wrote of a visit to Samothrace by Diagoras the atheist. A friend pointed out to Diagoras the many tablets from those who made vows to the gods during stormy weather at sea and were thus enabled to reach shore safely. Does that not show how the gods are interested in human welfare? Diagoras simply asked where were the tablets of those who perished in shipwrecks. (See Kruskal and Mosteller 1979, p. 117; Robert K. Merton led us to this splendid statistical story.)

To be sure, the foregoing 2 × 2 tables could be expanded in various ways. Suppose, for example, there were a third category of research results: backward steps, or retrogressions. Suppose the data looked like this:

Hypothetical Table C

	Quantitative	*Nonquantitative*	
Significant achievement	*53*	*9*	*62*
Nonsignificant achievement but progress	*9*	*53*	*62*
Retrogression	*31*	*31*	*62*

Where would that lead?

My second methodological note relates to recent interest in variability among judges examining scientific work, an interest shown in a 1981 National Academy of Sciences report on peer review of National Science Foundation proposals (see also Cole, Cole, and Simon 1981). Variability of expert judgment is important in many contexts, including the judicial one of expert evidence in trials and the legislative one of congressional hearings.

The Deutsch et al. study arose from the discussions of three experts on social research as they examined the totality of that research for the period 1900–1965. My understanding is that the three experts did not make initial independent judgments but, rather, discussed the issues among themselves from the start. Thus in this case alone it is difficult to see how an estimate of variability among experts can be obtained. Insofar as the exercise is carried out for other periods of time, for other domains of research, or by other judges, it would be useful to ask the participants for written initial judgments—done separately insofar as possible—before any group discussion. In that way variability could be measured, and indeed the effects of group discussion examined in detail.

A related approach would begin with more than one group of three judges, and would ask the groups to reach their (sub) collective judgments separately. That would give a measure of group variability. For further discussion and references see Bronk (1972) and Kruskal (1978, pp. 165–166).

Third, I call attention to possible bias because of the inevitable influence of catch phrases in the names of pieces of research. The categorization of research results into separate units or groups is necessarily somewhat arbitrary and is bound to be affected by the existence or nonexistence of colorful, catchy titles. Thus in future extensions of the work by Deutsch et al. I suggest thicker descriptions of the advances studied and more detailed statements of the reasons for importance.

For example, consider *factor analysis*, one of the sixty-two significant achievements. Yet factor analysis really includes a great many separate methods and applications under one appealing name. Further, it is by no means clear to me—or to many others—that factor analysis has led to important new understandings.

In the opposite direction, the introduction by R. A. Fisher of the theory and practice of randomization in designing experiments is *not* among the sixty-two achievements; yet it seems to me one of the greatest ideas of the century, almost entirely new, highly useful, and still far from fully understood or exploited. Randomization, however, does not have such an exciting name or so much publicity. Even more striking is the fundamental idea of dealing with entire distributions rather than simply with averages. That is surely a central idea of science, but it has no easily described parents and no evocative name.

Legislative Retrospective Concern About Research

In the United States, and no doubt elsewhere, there is continuing legislative concern about federal money authorized for basic scientific research. We see a constantly shifting tension between scientists who want resources to carry on basic research and legislative (or executive) leaders who do not—by and large—understand basic research and who want to see practical, short-term results: new technology, quick cures for disease, military weapons, and the like. That these practical short-term results spring from a store of capital knowledge hard won by unplannable basic research is a difficult case to make—and make again and again. Presumably, legislative concerns arise from a variety of motives, including the pervasive desire for reelection and the worry whether one's home district is receiving an adequate share of the distribution.

In the United States, the National Science Foundation (NSF) is responsible for a substantial fraction of federal support of basic research. Every year, the U.S. Congress debates levels of funding for the NSF, and often the debate reaches to comparisons among fields of science and even to specific research projects. Senators sometimes gain cheap political points by publicizing a project's title that sounds laughable out of context. In 1981 the NSF debate had a special focus on the social sciences because of the Reagan administration's particular animus against social science.

During congressional hearings in 1979 and 1980 there was pointed interest in a retrospective view of NSF-supported research. "Look back at what you have sponsored," Congress in effect told NSF, "and evaluate it. Tell us in the cold illumination of hindsight how well or poorly you have spent the taxpayer's money." The 1979 Senate Committee on Appropriations directed the NSF "to implement a selected program on a pilot basis of post-research evaluation." Accordingly, NSF selected the field of oceanography and itself carried out a study that was reported in National Science Foundation (1980). Then in 1980 the committee instructed the NSF "to secure an independent third party to develop a methodology for post-performance evaluation of scientific research. . . ." The field of chemistry was selected, and the National Academy of Sciences agreed to carry out the exploratory study, which has recently been published under the title *The Quality of Research in Science* (National Academy of Sciences 1982).

The responsible Academy group was its Committee on Science, Engineering, and Public Policy, whose current chairman is George M. Low, president of the Rensselaer Polytechnic Institute. Among the other members of that committee are Emilio Q. Daddario, former member of Congress; Gardner Lindzey, president of the Center for Advanced Study in the Behavioral Sciences; and Herbert A. Simon of the Carnegie-Mellon University.

The report was prepared by a subcommittee whose chairman was W. Allen Wallis, chancellor of the University of Rochester. Among its other members were Robert F. Boruch, Northwestern University; George E. P. Box, University of Wisconsin; John M. Deutch, Massachusetts Institute of Technology; Charles R. Plott, California Institute of Technology; and Arthur L. Singer, Jr., Alfred P. Sloan Foundation.

NSF Studies: Oceanography and Chemistry

Let us return briefly to the NSF in-house study of oceanography research. It was based on a system of controls: a sample of fifty NSF research projects was compared with a sample of twenty-five non-NSF control projects, selected probabilistically from the 1976 articles in a group of oceanography journals. In fact, there were fifty-one projects but one received no judgments. There were three major kinds of comparisons:

1. Quality of project publications, as judged by members of the oceanography advisory committee (plus three others).
2. Quality of publications, judged in the same way but on the basis of publication *abstracts* only.
3. Counts of publications, citations to publications, and the like.

The primary conclusions included the following. First, NSF projects received appreciably higher judgment ratings than control projects, whether based on publications or abstracts. (The differences tended to be greater for judgments based on abstracts.) Second, citations per publication show little NSF-control difference. An effect in favor of NSF apparently exists for citations to the most highly cited paper. There were, however, a number of drawbacks to the oceanography study, in my opinion, connected with premature or too hasty quantification. First, the selection of the control projects created problems, especially for so heterogeneous a field as oceanography. Second, a number of potential judges declined to participate. Third, and perhaps most important, the judgments could hardly have been blind; in most cases the judges must have known fairly well whether or not a project was an NSF or a control project. Finally, the study was done by a part of NSF itself. In short, I view the oceanography study as heroic, but flawed.

Turn now to the National Academy study of chemistry (1982), a study in fact more generally oriented. This was not an empirical study, as in the oceanography case, although it recommends later empirical study of chemistry projects. The NAS report is well organized and statesmanlike. It begins by reviewing kinds of evaluation research, classified into peer judgments (by far the most used); bibliometric analysis, especially of citations; case studies; retrospective analysis, in the sense of tracing back the roots of current triumphs; and prospective analysis and experiments. In each case there is a finer subclassification, and the arguments pro and con are marshaled.

Among the major findings are the following:

1. Postperformance evaluation is already widely used by NSF, especially in the consideration of grant renewals and extensions. Congress, however, is not adequately informed of the use of such postperformance examinations.
2. More retrospective studies should be carried out to determine the effects of NSF research on particular fields of research.
3. Peer review is the best way of choosing among individual research prospects. No additional use of postperformance evaluation will improve the selection process.
4. NSF should nonetheless continue its small-scale experiments with management improvement and should consider more deeply problems of communicating the results of research to various groups.
5. NSF should explore methods of retrospective evaluation of aggregate programs by outside experts.

The report contains much more—in particular, its Appendix C is an excellent bibliography with brief descriptions of studies about evaluation of research—but the foregoing conclusions and recommendations are perhaps most relevant to present concerns.

On Retrospective Methods

I now present a few reactions to this excellent report.

First, it seems to me that standards of accountability to which some would hold basic scientific research are far tighter than corresponding standards for other government activities: military procurement, police protection, welfare, the courts. Along with this, I suggest that scientists often react too defensively or too literally to demands for accountability. Rhetoric in the political arena is wholly different from rhetoric in science.

I wonder too whether a retrospective method widely used in other circumstances might be emphasized more for basic research: well-written examples or case studies. One might criticize this approach as merely anecdotal, but I think that it can be more. First, it gives a lower bound for accomplishment. Second, it provides increased understanding of what basic research is all about. I know that NSF has put out excellent expository materials of the kind I have in mind, yet perhaps not on an adequate scale or sufficiently widely distributed. It is important that this kind of material *not* be limited to technological or other so-called practical applications. NSF has distributed at least two collections of brief descriptions of basic research activities that have—sometimes serendipitously—resulted in important practical applications. Those are important, but even more important is explaining the fascination of understanding new coherences. That is not easy, but there are writers who can do it—for example, Martin Gardner, Isaac Asimov, and Lewis Thomas. Encouraging Gardner, Asimov, or Thomas to explain basic research further would certainly contribute to national education.

What *is* the comparison population for a reviewer of a proposal to NSF? That always seems to me a difficult question of conscience when I serve as reviewer myself, and I am unaware of any study of it. Presumably what is in a reviewer's mind when he checks "excellent," "very good," or whatever, hinges on some complex amalgam of the form-instructions to reviewers, the prior proposals read or written by the reviewer, absolute standards in the reviewer's mind, and so on. Perhaps NSF should sponsor some research toward empirical analysis of reviewing standards and comparisons.

That problem of comparisons—to what do I compare this piece of research that I am judging?—is difficult and germane. The oceanography study tried to approach it by use of control groups, but apparently a number of readers were not satisfied with the way the controls were formed and treated. I despair of finding satisfactory ways to form control groups in this domain, just as I despair about the possibility of blind evaluation. (As remarked earlier, most experts who are competent to judge the value of accomplished research will know fairly well which projects had NSF support).

An irony of the retrospective problem is our apparently greater difficulty in evaluating accomplished research ex post facto, over evaluating prospective research beforehand. After all, with the research completed, should one not be able to judge it far better than before it existed? Yet we seem to have an extraordinarily difficult time with normative retrospection.

Perhaps one reason is that retrospection looks necessarily at only one realization of what beforehand was a *distribution* of possibilities. The best decision conceivable in the face of random providence may in fact lead to actual disaster, and a poor decision may possibly lead to great success. A quarterback may throw his pass to the ideal spot, but the receiver stumbles and the pass is intercepted. Conversely, the quarterback may misread the other team's plan and aim at a covered position; yet the ball may slip as it leaves his hand and, by chance, go straight to a good receiver.

This phenomenon of chance intervention can slow learning and make for tragic self-criticism. Only when a decision or evaluation is replicated many times does the law of large numbers have a chance to even out the vagaries of chance. Thus the ratings of athletic decisions like those of the quarterback presumably make sense. Whether the support decisions of NSF form real replications, or whether each is individual and sui generis, is debatable.

Still more fundamentally, a problem is that there typically is no bottom line—that is, no single, one-dimensional, accurately measurable criterion of success. Instead, there are many criteria, each one fuzzy and none well measurable. If only time is considered, that itself is a limitation. The results of research may not be visible in ten years, or perhaps even in twenty. Where to stop?

Might that even be analogous to similar questions in circumstances where one supposes there *is* a bottom line: investment by firms or individuals for profit? The question is iconoclastic in some circles, where it is said that you need only arrange for accountants to measure profit or loss, and you will know exactly what happened. Yet is that not often simplistic? First, if success is characterized by the discounted flow of income over cost, one has to stop sometime, future flows are always guesses, and discount rates are inevitably arbitrary. Second, operational definitions of *income*, *cost*, and so on, typically have a great deal of looseness. Third, one cannot—even in principle—know all the alternative modes of investment for retrospective comparison.

In retrospective evaluations of complex behavior—for example, buying a house; instituting a government program (designing a new war plane, starting a new public medical aid program); choosing among graduate schools to attend, and so on—retrospection not only is difficult, but also holds its own metacosts of calculation, emotion, and time.

In short, cost-benefit analysis at even a moderately deep level is difficult and perhaps ultimately impossible. So postperformance evaluation of basic research is like nearly everything else in that regard, but with its own special nuances. Yet decisions have to be made; universities, individuals, and governments have to plan ahead; and some degree of retrospection seems inevitable. These strike me as extremely difficult epistemological waters.

I have two added remarks to close this part of my commentary. First, among the many ironies or paradoxes in this general topic, I call your attention to the following: These political figures who are loud in demanding detailed accountability for research tend to be those who oppose spending government money to do careful research about research. For example, there are at least two research grant segments at NSF that fund research on the research process itself. Those are (1) the economics program, which supports quantitative research on the returns to R&D, as the jargon goes; and (2) a unit that supports research on the sociology of science, *Wissenssoziologie*. It is from studies in such domains that long-range answers about evaluation and comparison of science may someday arise.

Second, my comments have been almost entirely about the United States, but the problems—political, social, and intellectual—of evaluating research know no boundaries. Recent travels to such different nations as Australia and the People's Republic of China make it clear that similar tensions and questions exist everywhere. I have no doubt that in all industrialized countries, even in less developed countries, there is constant debate between practical organizers and rulers who want to see fast, useful results, and thoughtful research scientists who know that the indirect approach of basic study is essential. It seems to me that international comparisons would be exceedingly useful—and, indeed, in the spirit of basic research. Who knows but that a bright young civil servant in Brasilia, or an elderly, shy sociologist in Helsinki, may have fresh good ideas about research evaluation that will allow us to make new starts.

University of Chicago Experiences

I turn from the international and U.S. national scene to an institutionally limited, almost autobiographical, report about the Division of the Social Sciences at the University of Chicago, a division that I have had the honor of serving as dean for seven recent years.

A major function of a divisional dean is evaluation of recommendations from departments about promotions and new appointments; those evaluations centrally include judgments about quality of research. From the over 100 such evaluations for which I have been responsible, I took a (systematic clustered) sample of 39 and reexamined them in the spirit of Deutsch et al. Thus I report here on a study in microcosm something like the far broader study of Deutsch et al. Of course the populations of study were entirely different—not to mention the process—so that a direct comparison would be untenable. Nonetheless, as we shall see, the results hold some considerable similarities.

Any dean, as he or she evaluates the research of others, has the difficulty of usually working outside the limits of his or her own discipline. In my case this was not usually but uniformly true. Edward Levi (president of the University of Chicago before he became Attorney-General) thought it a grand idea to appoint deans, when possible, from outside the division they were to administer. Thus I was persuaded to leave the cozy harbor of the Department of Statistics (part of the Division of the Physical Sciences) for the rougher and more heterogeneous waters of the social sciences, in none of which I could pretend to special expertise.

The problem reminds me of Walter Lippman's famous book *The Phantom Public*, in which he describes the difficulties of a good citizen in a democratic country who wishes to vote with a thorough understanding of issues and candidates, but who cannot possibly find the time or resources to study a single issue or candidate thoroughly. Thus a dean must depend largely on indirect evidence. Of course, one typically has a dossier prepared by the department: summaries of the candidate's accomplishments and promise, letters from eminent scholars within and outside the university, statements from students, and copies of publications. A conscientious dean will study much of this material, and may even add to it—for example, by making independent inquiries of further relevant persons.

Sometimes, of course, direct judgments may be made. If I see a candidate's paper that commits an egregious statistical howler, I must take account of that. The account should be tolerant, however, for I am not judging a candidate for the Department of Statistics, and I know that statistical standards in some fields of social science—not the reader's, of course—are perhaps a little fuzzy.

Indirect judgments are inevitable. If a colleague I know to be both eminent and wise speaks well or poorly of a candidate, I give that great weight, but always with some reserve for lurking sources of distortion. If, on the other hand, an evaluation letter says that so-and-so gives wonderful parties, I might discount the rest of the letter, because inclusion of such a nonacademic characteristic shows lack of intelligent sensitivity.

I turn to my sample of thirty-nine research evaluations, and I give first in Table 11.1 the distribution over disciplines. The two columns on the left show counts, and the righthand two columns percentage distributions over disciplines. For the latter, I look only at disciplines covered by both studies. Thus my sampling did not truly cover statistics (the University of Chicago's Department of Statistics is in the Division of the *Physical* Sciences), and my sample included history and geography.

Despite the small numbers and the great differences in context, the

TABLE 11.1
Social Science Advances by Discipline

	Counts for all Fields		Percentages for Fields in Both Studies	
	Deutsch et al.	Chicago	Deutsch et al.	Chicago
Psychology	13	8	28	24
Economics	12	6	26	18
Politics	11	10	24	30
Math. Statistics	11			
Sociology	7	5	15	15
Philosophy	5			
Anthropology	3	4	7	12
Geography		1		
History		5		
Total	39	39	100	100

percentages look rather similar. The largest discrepancy is in economics; one might speculate that advances in economics tend to get high grades in Deutsch et al. because (1) advances in economics are likely to have wide social influence, and (2) they are relatively more easily described in isolation as units waiting for various awards.

Deutsch et al. asked of each result whether it was nonquantitative (15%), relevant to quantitative problems (34%), or quantitative (52%). The percentages in parentheses are the marginal ones and add up to 100 percent except for rounding. I found myself unable to distinguish between the last two categories, but in the Chicago sample 72 percent of the research units were fairly clearly quantitative; that 72 percent should be compared with 86 percent given previously (34 +52), but I expect that I might have classified some in the middle group as nonquantitative. Thus I see no great difference.

Another approach of Deutsch et al. was to ask of each major contribution whether it focused on theory (76%), method (82%), or results (85%). But this is not a trichotomy; a given contribution might focus on two or even three approaches. Thus the three marginal percentages add up to much more than 100 percent.

I found it more illuminating to work with three dichotomies. Of each of the thirty-nine contributions in my sample I asked whether or not it was primarily empirical (79%), quantitative (72%), or theoretical (in the sense of philosophical) (51%). The percentages are the marginal ones, and Table 11.2 gives the full 8 cell distribution by counts.

TABLE 11.2
2 × 2 × 2 Distribution of Chicago Contributions (Counts)

	Theoretical	*Nontheoretical*	
Quantitative	8	14	22
Nonqualitative	5	4	9
	13	18	31
Nonempirical			
Quantitative	5	1	6
Nonquantitative	2	0	2
	7	1	8
Totals over empirical dichotomy			
Quantitative	13	15	28
Nonquantitative	7	4	11
	20	19	39

Table 11.2 exhibits the unsurprising result that there were no contributions that were neither empirical, quantitative, nor theoretical. The modal cell was that for quantitative and empirical contributions without major direct theoretical bearing—for example, some econometric studies or some experimental work in biopsychology. Anthropological studies tended to be empirical and nonquantitative; they might or might not have major theoretical bearing.

Of course, I present Table 11.2 with modesty. The numbers are small, and everything turns on my own fallible classifications. Unfortunately—and in another sense fortunately, too—those classifications can hardly be replicated because of natural confidentiality.

I repeat the cautionary note that comparisons between my little sample and the Deutsch et al. study must be highly tentative because the circumstances and populations are so different, and I see no feasible way of adjusting for these differences. I regard my sample as primarily a pilot one to persuade myself that characterizations can be made with some personal sense of firmness. If I were to continue along this line, a next important step would be to try to find documentation that could be examined by several judges in an attempt to measure the important degree of reliability.

References

Bronk, D.W. 1972. *The Science Committee.* Washington, D.C.: National Academy of Sciences.

Cole, S.; Cole, J. R.; and Simon, G. A. 1981. "Chance and Consensus in Peer Review," *Science 214*: 881–886.

Deutsch, Karl W.; Platt, John; and Senghaas, Dieter. 1971. "Conditions Favoring Major Advances in Social Science," *Science 171*: 450–459.

Elkana, Yehuda; Lederberg, Joshua; Merton, Robert K.; Thackray, Arnold; and Zukerman, Harriet. 1978. *Toward a Metric of Science*, New York: Wiley.

Kruskal, William. 1978. "Taking Datá Seriously," In Y. Elkana et al., *Toward a Metric of Science*, pp. 139–169.

Kruskal, William, and Mosteller, Frederick. 1979. "Representative Sampling II: Scientific Literature, Excluding Statistics," *International Statistical Review 47*: 111–127.

National Academy of Sciences. 1981. *Peer Review in the National Science Foundation: Phase II of a Study.* Washington, D.C.: Committee on Science and Public Policy, NAS.

———. 1982. *The Quality of Research in Science/Methods for Postperformance Evaluation in the National Science Foundation*, Washington, D.C.: Committee on Science, Engineering, and Public Policy, NAS.

National Science Foundation. 1980. *Evaluation Study of NSF's Oceanography Program.* Washington, D.C.: NSF.

Discussion

(Inkeles, Coleman, Deutsch, Bell)

Edited by Andrei S. Markovits

Normalizing the Statistics

ALEX INKELES opened the discussion by asking William Kruskal about the design of his study at the University of Chicago. Since the recommendations for promotions had come to the dean from the academic departments, there must have been some screening, and the distribution had to reflect the distribution in departments. If the numbers were not standardized to take account of this, however, there was a possibility of error. One would get more promotions in the economics department than in sociology simply because it, the former, was a bigger department.

James Coleman added that it was not just a question of the size of departments, but of the rate of turnover as well. If there were more turnover in the Department of Political Science than in Economics, as was true at Chicago, it was likely that it would have more proposals and more people promoted.

Kruskal countered that the same sorts of objections could be raised regarding the DPS study; but Inkeles disagreed with this. He thought that the size of the fields had nothing to do with their selection by DPS. If there were 10,000 sociologists, it could have been very possible that none of them made an advance. But Inkeles said that in Kruskal's study of the university, such a thing could not happen, because there was a regular procedure of promotion. Kruskal denied this, because there was no guarantee that a department would get an appointment.

Inkeles went on to say, however, that the study would be alright if the size-difference and turnover-difference were taken as a base, or else if you took the following view:

"I have different pools of proposals and I am not going to be interested in the relative numbers because that is the result of the size difference. But I will not decide, within each pool, how many of the proposals were creative and how many were not; or how many were creative in a quantitative way and how many in a theoretical way."

Inkeles felt that if the study reflected that point of view, he could accept it. Kruskal agreed that for this reason and for other reasons, his numbers would not bear much analysis. But what surprised him was that the disciplinary distribution, except for economics, came reasonably close to the DPS distribution, despite these defects.

Inkeles countered by asking if the number of members of each Department at the University of Chicago—and at Harvard and Stanford—did not have the same distribution. He said he was not arguing that it was impossible to learn something from Kruskal's procedure—simply that it had a different meaning from what Kruskal was suggesting.

Gerhart Bruckmann concluded, "Wouldn't that mean that the probability of a major advance is directly proportional to the number of scientists in the field?"

Kruskal commented further that the actual screening for promotions was complicated, but that the informal discussions [by senior members] might kill a proposal before it came to the Dean's office. And he felt that this process was analogous to the criteria delineating major advances in the DPS paper.

Inkeles could not accept this argument because, he said, in order to go that way,

"We would have to reconstitute ourselves as a group of sociologists, then as political scientists, then as economists—with Deutsch and his friends playing Kruskal's role as the Dean—and then each group would promote whoever it felt was a fair candidate."

Inkeles believed that under these conditions, there would be pressure in each group to increase the number of candidates so that the chances for "survival" would be increased. Also "such groups would not have the same kind of interests as Departments, nor the same sense of a fixed historical size." In a given school, this limited the number of promotions which it was sensible to propose from year to year—just so that the Dean would not call on the phone and say, "Stop this nonsense . . . I can't make any more appointments in sociology for three years." A real genius might be advanced on an irregular basis, but otherwise it was not done.

Residual Factors—Such as Chance

Bell announced that he wanted to bring up a question about the way that statistics seemed to operate—in particular the "catch-basin" problem that Shmuel Eisenstadt had raised earlier. Eisenstadt had been talking about the pitfalls of modernization theory, saying that when theorists could not explain something, they suddenly called it "traditional", or they would introduce a "residual". Bell called that the "catch-basin". So when economics could not explain technology in advance, as part of the measure of productivity—the Solow problem—that became a "residual". And when Christopher Jencks, in his study of mobility and equality, found that 35 percent of the variance could not be accounted for, he attributed that to "luck".

Bell claimed that this was an overlooked category that statisticians could use in accounting for advances. The question was, "Are there genuine residuals or not?" He felt this was a serious and important question:

"How does one know when something is a residual? Is it simply because it cannot be explained by the statistical techniques or the variables which are being used? If so, does this point to a way in which statistics can lead to reconceptualizations?"

Kruskal noted that the term *residual* was current in data analysis: It was whatever was left over after a particular model became specific. He was unsure, however, whether the ultimate importance of residuals was even meaningful epistemologically. Deutsch said that in sociobiology a residual existed when heredity could not explain why someone was doing well; the residual became that person's "gifts."

Bell said that his questions concerned a different point. Going back to the statistical problem, when, if ever, did the amount of the residuals become so overwhelming as to overturn the explanations?

Inkeles suggested that this happened when it was difficult to explain very much with the answers one got. Kruskal asked Bell if he was trying to find out whether there was some magic "50 percent point" beyond which residuals dominated?

Bell replied that he simply wanted to know, in the Jencks example, what kind of procedure was exemplified when Jencks claimed that 35 percent of his variance was "luck." Inkeles answered that, as a general rule of thumb, the best that could be done in the highest-level, most sophisticated, best-measured social science investigations was to explain between 30 percent and 50 percent of the variance. He said there was generally 50 percent left over which was unexplained.

Bruckmann interjected that it was possible to come much closer in econometrics. Coleman rebutted that it was not possible to come closer than 30 percent to 50 percent in sociology as long as it dealt with individuals.

Bell accepted that answer, but then claimed it was only half of the problem. The other half, as in the case of the Solow problem, was where the residual was challenged as a failure in the conceptual scheme. He said he was thinking of the residual as a kind of systematic technique which could be used to check for gaps in a conceptual scheme—could the "catch-basin" be used to catch something?

A Game Where The Theorist Cannot Lose

Coleman commented that there could be conflicting explanations, as exhibited by the Jencks study and the Dudley Duncan study in which there were residual so-called unexplained differences in income. In Jenck's case, these were residual differences between persons whose education was the same. In Duncan's case, these were residual differences between blacks and whites whose measured backgrounds were alike. Jencks attributed the residual differences to luck; Duncan attributed them to racial discrimination. Coleman felt that although either could be true, this procedure of attributing a residual difference to some single positive phenomenon was unjustified.

Inkeles agreed, saying that in this case, there was no way of knowing the accuracy of what was claimed. One could not tell whether their inability to explain more of the variance was purely a matter of statistical error, or the nature of the samples, or anything else. This procedure was therefore totally arbitrary. It was a game which they could not lose, because there is always a lot of variance left over which is unexplained. Consequently, he argued, so long as one keeps one's preferred variables out of the measurement, one may then claim that whatever is left must be accounted for by the variable one favors. Inkeles commented facetiously that he could explain 50 percent of any social phenomenon by simply pulling out his variable from a measurement set, and then claiming that it is the factor accounting for all the remaining unexplained variance.

CHAPTER 12

Interactions Between the Natural Sciences and the Social and Behavioral Sciences (Resumé)†

I. Bernard Cohen

TRANSFORMATIONS OF IDEAS

PROFESSOR COHEN SAID that he was working on a critical, analytical, and historical study of the ways in which the natural and exact sciences (which he called "the sciences") have influenced the social and behavioral sciences, by providing methods, concepts, laws, principles, theories, standards, and values. He discussed how scientists use each others' ideas. Cohen said, "I do not believe it is either true or useful that ideas have a life of their own," but said that instead there was always

†*Professor Cohen presented this complete paper first at the Berlin Conference, but wished to use it as the leading article in a book on the relations between the sciences in the eighteenth and nineteenth centuries (Cohen 1985). The following resumé of his paper has therefore been prepared by John Platt to cover his key points, especially those involved in the discussion afterward.*

"the interaction of a thinking mind with the ideas of another mind." This interaction could lead to transformation and to radical innovation.

The great syntheses are examples of transformation, as in Newton's case, when he "did carefully select and use significant ideas from other scientists," transforming them in the process. Cohen discussed in detail Newton's alterations of the fundamental tenets of Copernicus, Kepler, Galileo, and others.

Cohen's research had focused on "revolutions in science," which scientists have been aware of since the time of Newton and which had been called to our attention by Thomas Kuhn's analysis. Cohen had been concerned, not with the gross changes, but with the microhistory of such revolutions, and he discussed the development of Darwin's thought from this point of view.

Scientific Revolutions and Social Thought

Cohen distinguished three stages of scientific revolution: (1) the intellectual revolution involving a new idea; (2) the "revolution on paper," when the idea is communicated to colleagues; and (3) the "revolution in science," when the new idea begins to be used. A revolution may eventually have two aspects—an influence on scientific thought and practice, and an influence on social and political thought, from social science or philosophy all the way to everyday ideas.

This second, ideological component has been largely missing in some of the great scientific revolutions—for example, in Maxwell's field theory, the quantum theory, and the recent revolution in molecular biology. The Newtonian, Darwinian, Freudian, and Einsteinian revolutions, however, had strong effects on social and political thought. Cohen gave examples of the effects of Copernican and Newtonian concepts on political ideas and language, and of the relation of the Constitution of the United States to the "natural philosophy" of the time.

Franklin, Adams, and Jefferson couched their arguments about checks and balances and political equilibrium in terms of Newton's laws of motion. Edmund Burke invoked biological analogies. Woodrow Wilson went on to write that "government is not a machine, but a living thing. . . . It is accountable to Darwin, not to Newton," and he discussed the interaction of its "parts or organs."

Cohen said that many economists of the late eighteenth century, such as Turgot, Adam Smith, Malthus, and Ricardo, saw themselves as both scientists and social scientists. Marx analyzed them in these terms, praising Ricardo's "scientific honesty" but saying that Malthus "falsifies his scientific conclusions"—and he claimed that Darwin had confuted Malthus.

Opposing Strategies for a Science of Society

Cohen presented the thesis that Comte and Quetelet set forth two very different strategies for the development of a science of society. Comte argued for a classification of the sciences in which the chronological development of the separate branches formed a logical sequence. The first sciences to be developed were the most abstract—mathematics and astronomy—and the last to emerge would be the most complex, biology or the science of individual organisms followed by sociology or the science of man and his organizations. He reasoned that astronomy depends upon mathematics, which it therefore follows, and this leads to physics. The physics of gross bodies leads to their interactions and compositions, so that chemistry follows physics; similarly, biology (the emergent science of his day) requires a knowledge of the chemistry of living beings. Only after biology had come into maturity, could there be a science of sociology, since a science of the behavior of groups of individuals seemed to him to necessarily depend on a prior science of single individuals. (In his hierarchical chronology, there was no special place for psychology, which he considered part of physiology and therefore to be developed along with biology.)

Whereas Comte reasoned that there would be a logical, chronological, and natural progression from the science of single biological entities to the science of groups, Quetelet advocated a diametrically opposite point of view: that a science of group behavior could be produced even without knowledge of the laws of behavior of single individuals. Having discovered statistical regularities in regard to crime, health, and other aspects of social behavior, he proclaimed that social laws are statistical, based upon group regularities that are predictable (with some fluctuations produced by variations of such parameters as season of the year or economic conditions). Thus he saw no way of telling in advance which citizen would be murdered or who would commit the murder, but there could be no doubt that the number of murders would be constant, and even their variety (by strangling, shooting, stabbing, and so on).

Cohen stressed the fact that Comte thought of sociological phenomena in terms of the model of classical Galilean-Newtonian physics, or a system of one-to-one cause and effect. Quetelet bypassed the problem of individual cause and effect, and found regularities which he proclaimed were the laws of a "social physics," setting forth a new statistical model that became significant not only for the study of society and the development of all the social sciences, but even for the biological and physical sciences.

Cohen pointed out that both Comte and Quetelet had strong backgrounds in mathematics. Comte, a graduate of the famous Ecole Polytechnique, taught mathematics and was the founder of the school of "positive philosophy," one of the most original philosophical inventions of the 19th century. He invented the name "sociology." Quetelet was a professional astronomer and statistician; he is—according to Cohen—"the true founder of the modern quantitative analysis of society and its laws." Cohen observed that whereas Comte is considered at length in all historical accounts of sociology, Quetelet's name barely appears—if it appears at all—in standard historical works on the history of sociology.

Cohen concluded this section by referring to statistics as an example of the transfer of concepts between the natural sciences and the social sciences. He noted the problems that arose when the concept of "probable error" acquiring a new meaning, when it was no longer applied to the scatter of gunshots with respect to a target and was used in discussions of the variations among biological individuals.

Darwin

Cohen went on to say that "no revolution in science can approach the Darwinian revolution" in creating relations between the natural sciences and the social sciences. The concept of "evolution" proliferated; and "population thinking" was also important, emphasizing "that every individual (in a population) . . . is uniquely different from all others." Also, evolution by natural selection represented a major departure in science, because "Darwinian evolution, although causal, is non-predictive." On the other hand, much of the writing on evolution, including much of Social Darwinism stems not from Darwin at all, but from Herbert Spencer—who, in fact, invented the concept of "the survival of the fittest."

Marx

In studying the relations between the natural and the social sciences in the nineteenth century, Cohen said, "I confess to having been very disappointed in my studies of the writings of Karl Marx." He said that "Marx didn't really know any science," but had a humanistic education, and the actual references to hard science in his works are very few. Marx used popular writings on the life processes to draw analogies for social processes, and he "praised Darwin's *Origin of Species*, on the ground that it ' . . . dealt the death-blow . . . to "teleology" in the natural sciences'."

Cohen commented, however, that "Engels was convinced that Marx's achievement was scientific." At one stage, Engels compared Marx and Darwin; later he said that "what Marx had achieved in political economy was very similar to the revolution Lavoisier had achieved in chemistry."

Social Sciences in the Twentieth Century

In our own century, Cohen believed, "The greatest revolution in the [natural] sciences which has affected the social sciences . . . has been the Freudian revolution." "Freud himself used ideas and analogies from the physical and biological sciences in developing his own . . . system"; and he saw Copernicus, Darwin, and himself as giving "three blows . . . to man's naive self-image."

More recently there has been much discussion of science and of scientific method by psychologists and others, who felt, for example, "the need to make psychology both *be* a science and *appear to be* a science." (Emphasis his.) Sociology was also concerned with scientific method, following Pareto. Cohen went on to compare the articles on science and social science in the *Encyclopedia of the Social Sciences* of the 1930s with those in the *International Encyclopedia of the Social Sciences* of the late 1960s. He felt that the later work, in articles such as one on sociology by Eisenstadt, "shows the growth of a considerable independence from the matrix of thought in the natural and exact sciences . . . a kind of measure of the maturity of thought and analysis in the social science, and . . . an . . . elementary sign of independence and coming of age." He believed, however, that social scientists would still feel "the pressure of advances in the natural and exact sciences," just like everyone else.

References

Cohen, I. B., ed., 1985. *The Sciences and the Social Sciences*, New York: Norton, Norton and Co.

Discussion

(Bell, Fritsch, Nowotny, Eisenstadt, Platt, Zwicker, Inkeles)

Edited by Andrei S. Markovits

The Fringes of Science

DANIEL BELL began the discussion by "supplementing Professor Cohen's paper with four points or questions." First, he said, in conferences of this kind there was usually an emphasis on the history of intellectual achievements, but not on the "pseudosciences." Bell related, for example, that Marx believed in phrenology. Wilhelm Liebknecht, who lived in Marx's home and was one of the founders of the Social Democratic party, wrote in his memoirs, "I was examined by the Party Phrenologist, and he danced his fingers around my skull." Bell noted, incidentally, that this particular passage had been cut out of the official Communist editions of Liebknecht's memoirs.

Bell explained that in those days phrenology was a "science." Even Hegel was attracted to it. Bell suggested that this problem, of why important thinkers of an era were attracted to such notions, should be of great interest to the historians of ideas.

Bell's second point concerned a peculiarity in the history of sociology—namely, that it had never developed a language of its own, but its terms were borrowed. There was something peculiar in the history of a science or a discipline that never had its own language. He emphasized that sociology was almost alone in this respect:

"Key terms such as "power," "force," or "energy," came out of the physical sciences and mechanistic theory; "structure," "function," "growth" and "decay" were organismic metaphors from biology; "variables" and "parameters" came from mathematics; "roles" came from dramaturgy; and "status" came from law—all are borrowed terms."

Bell wondered why sociology was unable to build its own vocabulary for describing social reality.

As a footnote to this, he discussed the problem of the way terms changed. We are all aware of this, but rarely note the exact points of transition. Referring to Cohen's discussion of Marx's view of science, Bell argued that Marx's view had two different phases, the first one involving the Hegelian notion of necessity, which Hegel contrasted to contingency. In his later years, however, Marx began to adopt more of the "scientistic" language of physics—of exact functional relationships as the essence of science. Bell felt that one could find a similar change in the notion of *nature* in economics, in going from Smith through Walras, Marshall, and Keynes: "The concept has different tonalities and different functions in the theories of each thinker."

Bell's third point was on those aspects of science that had immediate repercussions both in the social sciences and in social life. The theories of Copernicus, Newton, and Darwin had a real echo in society; and a wide variety of persons, such as Lavoisier, John Adams, Saint Simon, and Herbert Spencer, adopted them. In the twentieth century there was a new kind of transposition, a carryover of natural-science findings or methods to the social sciences. There was what could be called a halo effect of the achievements of science, making the social sciences try to be more exact and precise. The substantive theories, however, except perhaps for quantum physics, have had less of an echo effect.

Finally, Bell wanted to note that within the social sciences there was also a tradition of *rejecting* the natural sciences. This had its roots in history, as represented by Vico, Dilthey, or Collingwood, and, today, by the interpretive sociologists, Schutz, Geertz, and others. Bell said that Geertz was not exactly rejecting natural science; rather, he was marking off as crucial a different realm— one that dealt with matters of symbolism and meaning, rather than causal and functional relationships.

Bruno Fritsch, the next questioner, noted that in Cohen's three scientific revolutions, Copernicus claimed that the earth was no longer the center of the universe; Darwin claimed that man had developed through evolution and not by unique creation; and Freud claimed that man did not even have control over his own ego. Fritsch said that this all raised the question: "Is it possible to argue that overcoming anthropocentric views is a major condition favoring advances in science?"

Metaphors of Science in marx and Engels

Fritsch went on to say that he was surprised by Cohen's statement that he had been disappointed with Karl Marx in his study of the relationship between the sciences and the social sciences in the nineteenth century. Fritsch mentioned that early in his life he had been greatly enamored of Marx. [Bell interjected, "That's O.K.—we all had a misspent youth!"] Fritsch thought that one example would be sufficient to show Marx's power as a scientist. In the second volume of *Das Kapital*, Marx gave an example of *Reproduktion auf erweiterter Stufenleiter*. Fritsch claimed this was actually the first growth model—a two-sector, two-class, two-goods model—in which Marx offered a numerical solution for a specific case; and the general mathematical solution had now been given 100 years later. Fritsch said there were many similar examples in Marx's work.

I. Bernard Cohen replied that what he had said in his paper was that Marx was not concerned with the development of the sciences, or with science as a truly dynamic force in social and industrial development. Cohen said that before he examined the matter in detail, he had always assumed that in Marx's work, much more would be made of the metaphor of the sciences and of the discussion of the sciences. He assumed this simply on the basis of the great discussion by Marxists of the Marxian analysis of science, as well as the later development by Engels of scientific socialism versus utopian socialism, which continued in the Russian writings of the twentieth century. Cohen said that it had disappointed him simply because he thought there would have been more on this subject, in the light of all the Marxian writings. He noted, however, that Engels's work, on the other hand, was loaded with references to and discussions of science. It ran throughout all his work; the "scientific versus utopian socialism," the *Anti-Dühring*, and the *Dialectics of Nature* were "just full of it." Marx may have had a good sense for mathematics, as Fritsch said, but Cohen was more concerned with the natural and exact sciences.

Cohen recalled that one of his earliest teachers was a man called Gaetano Salvemini, who said, "Karlo Marx, eet is a wonderful theing. Eet wakes you up." Salvemini then added, however, "The only thing is, if you read him too long, eet puts you back to sleep again!"

Helga Nowotny had several comments—first, that the distinction between the terms *science* and *social science* was in fact a historically correct usage. Throughout their history the social sciences had deferred to science as the standard model. Nowotny wondered whether this was still an appropriate distinction at the present time. She said that "by choosing terms, we also fashion reality," and we ought to reflect more on why we choose certain terms and what we intend to accomplish with them.

The Dominant Imagery in Successive Periods

Nowotny went on to a macrosociological issue. In Cohen's discussion, he pointed to major idea systems, or to systems that assumed certain need functions. In the nineteenth century, previous science served a central need-function, whatever one happened to be doing, whether in political life or in the social sciences that were just beginning. Going back one step further in history, Nowotny referred to Francis Yates's writings on the hermeneutic tradition, where it was clear that the previous system of ideas was dominated by the tradition of magic. In the court of Louis XIII, for instance, the tradition of magic infused political life. We had lost that tradition and therefore could not see it any more, but contemporaries felt it very strongly.

Nowotny argued that today the supporting thread of scientific imagery that existed in the nineteenth century was being dissipated. She suspected that we were moving in the direction of what she referred to as *techno-magic*—ideas infused with technology but also having magical properties. Her point was that there were long-term changes in our use of imagery, in the images and concepts that we considered to be powerful, and in the reasons for our choices.

In Cohen's examples, Nowotny suggested that a clearer distinction was needed between the *metaphorical* use of concepts and the *rhetorical* purposes of science. Rhetoric and the politics of rhetoric were real and accepted parts of science. It was a legitimate device that science had adopted to defend its autonomy, and to get support from society in ideological and financial ways.

She made another point about people who assumed the function of "mediators." Nowotny said she preferred this term to the more common one of "popularizers." She noted that some had worked in pairs—for example, Marx and Engels, where Engels played an important role in interpreting and disseminating Marx's ideas. Darwin and Spencer were another case, but with a different sort of relationship. The historical record could yield new insights, if looked at from this point of view.

Finally, Nowotny praised Cohen for being the first participant at this conference who had explicitly mentioned women as being an important part of the scientific enterprise.

Shmuel Eisenstadt emphasized that science was not an isolated system within the culture of society. In the eighteenth and nineteenth centuries, science had become the paradigm of the world of knowledge in Western culture; but that did not mean it was the only one, or that it always had been so or always would remain so. What, then, was the degree of diffusion of ideas from different branches of science into the world, and from the broader world into science? The phases of modern science showed the changes that had occurred in the organization of the world of knowledge.

John Platt commented on the metaphors created by recent research, which had been taken up in social and political and cultural writing in the last forty years. One example was the theory of cybernetics. Norbert Wiener himself had taken ideas of feedback and control from gun-director systems and applied them to psychological behavior. Then the Macy Conferences through the 1940's had brought together psychologists, psychiatrists, and anthropologists to inform themselves about cybernetics and to take the terminology of goal-directed behavior over into their own fields.

The theory of games was now having a similar impact. Indeed Platt felt that the word *games* would not continue much longer to represent children's games, because it had been taken over into so many other ironic and hostile contexts—Prisoner's Dilemma games, "games people play," "war games," and so on. Still another case was information theory, and then the language of computers, with inputs, outputs, data processing, programming, and many other terms. "Over and over again, in newspapers and popular writing, one sees these languages moving out into other fields." Platt thought that the exchange and extension to other fields was more and more deliberate. These ideas were no longer used merely as metaphors but increasingly as models, being applied to social and political relations in concrete applications—cross-level applications—of a general systems approach.

Eckhart Zwicker returned to Marx's thinking on science. He argued that in the field of medicine there was a straight line running from Harvey to Quesnay to Marx. Harvey discovered the circulation of the blood. A hundred years later Quesnay, who was the physician of Louis XV and Madame de Pompadour, introduced the concept of circulation into economics and devised the *tableau economique* which formalized the concept. Later, Marx used the concept of circulation in his schema. Zwicker noted that this concept continued to be important in present-day economic thinking, and nearly every dynamic system can be interpreted in a similar way. He agreed with Fritsch that the Marxian scheme had now been reconstructed with the use of differential equations in describing a system of flows between elements.

Is Stochastic Prediction Possible?

Zwicker then spoke against Cohen's argument that science was unable to predict the future course of evolution. He said that Cohen had formulated a proposition of impossibility, but that in principle it would be possible to make some forecasts of an evolutionary system in a stochastic way. Zwicker gave three examples. First, Ingo Rechenberg of the Technische Universität Berlin had developed a search procedure called *evolution strategy* to reconstruct the mutations of DNA sequences. Zwicker said that he and his colleagues used this to optimize search techniques with mathematical models. A second example was a stochastic simulation of enzyme mutation and of the folding of protein structures in small peptide molecules. In principle it was possible to use simulation to get probability distributions of the shapes of various molecules, within certain limits.

Finally Zwicker thought that there was an important analogy between heuristic hypothesis-finding in the natural sciences and in economics. In physics, some laws could be formulated in alternative ways. For example, Snell's law of refraction of light at surfaces could be described either (1) by a differential formulation, step by step along the path, or (2) by extremizing a total goal function for the whole sequence (a path-integral minimum principle). Zwicker felt that the similar procedure of extremizing was widely used in marginalist economics (to go to step-by-step predictions). He said: "You formulate a goal that the individual should maximize. From this identity, the utility goal, it is possible to deduce social behavioral equations which are the consequence of the extremizing operation."

Zwicker argued that all of marginalism from 1880 to 1982 had developed a heuristic procedure for finding hypotheses, by using this approach through the extremizing principle, which stemmed originally from the natural sciences.

Advances Independent of the Milieu

Alex Inkeles wanted to touch on the relationship of science to its milieu, and the extent to which ideas in science had lives of their own. This had something to do with the nature of scientific advances. "Can there be an advance if no one recognizes it?" Inkeles said that there were many instances in the history of science where major ideas seemed to disappear for a time and became recognized as important only much later on. Probably there were other ideas that never became important later on, which indicated that their impact was dependent on social forces and conditions.

From his own point of view, however, Inkeles felt that the normal mode of scientific advance was highly independent of social context. There were inner logics that led one thing to another in a compelling way, and the scientific enterprise had its own inner life in that sense. He suggested that that was true even for Marx and his relation to Darwin—that Marx could have been able to come to his ideas in any case. The broad analogies that suggest some connection between Darwin and Marx, such as the idea of the struggle between classes or the inevitable replacement of one system by another, were not the most important ideas in Marx's work. Instead, Inkeles argued, the most important ideas were those that developed in the library at the British Museum when Marx was trying to understand the emergence of economic and political systems.

Likewise for other main concepts that Marx worked with—for example, his idea that the working class must become progressively impoverished, or that capitalism could not run without a reserve army of the unemployed, or that there had to be a declining rate in the return on capital. This entire series of ideas did not derive from any general scheme; they were the product of Marx's own interaction with bodies of data—even though they were obviously within the framework of a system of thought. Inkeles felt that if this argument were true for Marx, then it was certainly true in other cases he knew where advances in the social sciences were not the result of an interaction with the broader society.

Inkeles wanted to distinguish this from the so-called branching phenomenon, where scientists went along making choices at various points about which way to go. Those decisions could be influenced by externals: by personality, or by a sense of what was important in a given era, or by general intellectual currents. Once one was on a particular branch, whether one made progress or not depended on inner scientific factors—the level of existing knowledge, the techniques available, the power of a particular theory, sensitivity to unusual findings, or good luck in stumbling on things that had not been observed before. These elements were relatively independent of what was happening in the larger social system.

False Revolutions and False Parallels

Cohen now had to respond to his critics. He said that phrenology, like mesmerism, was an example of what he called "revolutions on paper." Many of these temporarily looked like revolutions in science and were very widely adopted, but then they collapsed.

He also commented that the ideological component of major scientific ideas often was not transferred undistorted, and therefore had to be studied with great care. For example, there was a celebrated book by an American author that dealt with Social Darwinism. Cohen had on occasion asked his students to construct lists of the essential points of Darwin's own thought, and then to turn to this book to see how many of them could be identified there. He said that generally not a single one could be identified, and that Darwin's writing as summarized by the American also never mentioned these essential points. Cohen argued therefore that this Social

Darwinism would be difficult to distinguish from, say, Social Lamarckianism, or from general evolutionism—which was not what Darwin was arguing at all. Thus the ideological use of a work had to be looked at with considerable caution.

He noted a similar effect when people spoke of the influence of Einstein in relativity—a development that created an enormous explosion in the world. Many people who talked about it, however, did not adequately understand relativity; all they got from it was a kind of relativism.

Turning to Fritsch's example of Marx's numerical solution to a problem, Cohen said that was one example among many. However, he was not concerned with the degree to which Marx was acting from a scientific point of view, so much as with the fact that in developing his ideas, the people that Marx called on as his authorities and models tended to be those whom we would call economists and social scientists. Cohen felt that Zwicker's example about the influence of Harvey and Quesnay on Marx was another of the same kind. That is, Marx was *using* Quesnay, but he was not himself *being* a Quesnay. He was not taking great new scientific ideas and applying them to his analysis of society. Cohen carefully added that he did not mean to intend this to be a criticism of Marx, so much as a fact that he had observed in the record.

Cohen then turned again to the question of the use of the terms *science* and *social science* as distinct categories. He said that much of the discussion of the philosophy and sociology of science referred only to that line of science that was like physics. The Darwinian part of science, which was quite different, was seldom brought in as a model. In the past it was seldom clear which model of science one was actually looking at. Cohen felt that it was significant that Engels could not make up his mind whether Marx was more like Lavoisier or more like Darwin: "These were two very different kinds of models to pick from, standing for extremely different elements in the sciences."

Communicating One Central Idea

As for Nowotny's comment on the different metaphors in different eras, and thinkers who tried to attract kudos that came from the prevailing science, Cohen maintained that all this varied with what the science world of the period considered to be of great importance. He felt that the remarks about Jay Forrester (during the world-modeling discussion that followed Bruckman's paper) were apt in this context. The fact that Forrester was at MIT was undeniably important for the impact of his studies—and the fact that his work used the *computer* gave it all the aura of magic and the incomprehensible. He commented that Nowotny's metaphor of technomagic today was a good one.

Cohen argued that the way in which some sciences carried over to other fields often involved the question of whether there was one central unifying idea that could be communicated. The dramatic thing about Copernicus was that he shifted the earth from its unique place. This was not original with Copernicus, of course, but it was his central thought. If one looked at what Copernican *astronomy* was, however,—that is, Copernican science, as opposed to that single major idea—one would discover that it had very little influence at all. (The influence on astronomy was produced by the modified Keplerian revolution later on.) Cohen emphasized, however, that the central idea of Copernicus was one that could be easily grasped and therefore easily transferred, like some of the Newtonian notions of balances and forces, the mechanical notions, and the general evolutionary idea. Perhaps one of the difficulties with the field theory of Maxwell (for cultural absorption) was that there was no simple thought that could be easily transferred at large.

From this Cohen moved on to Zwicker's comment about theorems of impossibility; he agreed that there was nothing more fascinating. Cohen explained that what he had been implying in his paper was not the impossibility of making stochastic models for prediction. Rather, he had claimed that the traditional Darwinian theory did not imply the old kind of one-to-one Newtonian predictability—which had been possible because all the individual characteristics of a given phenomenon were ignored, in that simpler day, in favor of the construction of ideal types. To describe the motion of a falling body, one could ignore its color, internal composition, and so on, factors of a sort that could not be ignored in Darwinian theory.

Relation of Science to Its Milieu

In conclusion, Cohen wanted to say something about "the relation of science to its milieu." He had devoted his whole life to arguing that a considerable part of the development of science, and surely of the social sciences, came from following an internal logic. On the other hand, it was equally true—given a certain state of knowledge and a certain armory of tools—that the solutions that were derived, depended on the individual. On the one hand, as Robert Merton had emphasized, there was simultaneous discovery. Einstein once said that if Newton or Leibnitz had never lived, someone would still have invented the infinitesimal calculus; he added that if *he* had never lived, someone would surely have invented the special theory of relativity. Then, however, Einstein went on to say that if Beethoven had never lived, we would never have had the Eroica Symphony.

Cohen argued that Einstein was wrong on both counts. A symphony consisted of a finite number of notes arranged in a certain order, and it seemed plausible to compute the number of possible ways that these could be arranged (*pace* the famous case of the monkeys and the *Encyclopedia Britannica*). Einstein himself, having propounded the dictum mentioned above, felt that it was true of special relativity but not of his theory of general relativity (a much more idiosyncratic creation); Cohen commented that in his view this was certainly correct.

More seriously, Cohen said that although he had not looked at all of the cases of independent simultaneous discovery that Merton cited, he had looked at a number of them and had found that the solutions were *not* identical. They were apt to be different, because more than a "inner logic" of science was involved in the way that an individual thinking mind, after reaching different branch points, decided where to go. It seemed to Cohen that if one wanted to understand this process, one could not simply look at the ideas in the abstract, but had to look at the individual cases in detail.

The answer to the next step—to what extent the creative individual represented in that creative process the outside forces of the society—was something Cohen felt he could not provide, but he tended to think it was less than some of his colleagues did. There was no doubt that the goals of society, its financial support, and so on determined what areas would receive much attention. Nevertheless, how much the notions of the generally received philosophy of a society actually affected the thinking of individual researchers was an unresolved question. Cohen said that the degree of influence could vary between individuals. Thus Darwin lived in relative isolation for a large part of his life, but in his earlier years he was certainly aware of and influenced by notions of society and economics that he then carried over to his thinking about biology. Cohen felt that the way to learn more about the interplay here was to look at individual cases.

CHAPTER 13

T. S. Kuhn: Revolutionary or Agent Provocateur?

Peter Weingart

A Methodological Foreword

ONE WHO IDENTIFIES major advances in a field as Deutsch et al. have done is invariably in danger of being attacked as acting in a more or less sophisticated way to promote one's own interests, biases, and friends, much the same way as in other accounts of the state of the art or a history of the field. In order not to fall under that verdict, instead of quarreling with their choices, I choose a different strategy. My first claim is that since the publication of the paper by Deutsch et al. in 1971, no major advances have taken place in the philosophy of the social sciences or in their history other than those listed by these authors. This claim can be substantiated, by a look at the books that have appeared during the last decade on the philosophy of the social sciences, and that have had some impact. It can be said with some certainty that none of them has broken new ground.

My second claim is that the work of T. S. Kuhn represents the last major advance in both the history and the philosophy of the social sciences, as Deutsch et al. have identified correctly, but that this is true for reasons that differ from those listed ("cognitive dynamics of science") and that were partly unknown at the time. I will try to indicate these reasons for this one entry in the list of sixty-two advances, as they have emerged in the decade since the list was made, 1970–1980. I select Kuhn rather than J. Conant, J. B. Cohen, or Derek Price because he has made his impact on both the history and the philosophy of the social sciences, which is unique and economical at the same time. Twenty years after Kuhn, I will limit any explanation and references to his work to mere allegations, assuming that the scriptures have been studied thoroughly; but to explain his parallel impact two aspects must be distinguished. Kuhn, read as a historian of science, has had an influence on the historiography of the social sciences in ways, as I will show later, that he himself did not intend or even necessarily support. This influence could be labeled the *sociologization* of the history of (social) science. Kuhn, read as a philosopher of science (which is possible and necessary because of the mutuality of implications of historical and philosophical accounts of scientific development) has had an impact on the philosophies of the social sciences—to the degree that his ideas are now being taken as a normative frame of reference for judging the scientificness of disciplines. I will elaborate on these two aspects, trying to deal with them separately although they are inherently intertwined, for it is not only since Kuhn that the history of science has served philosophical purposes and that the philosophy of science has advanced models of the (historical) development of science.

A word about methodology: As is appropriate in dealing with the metasocial sciences, I used a metamethodology to approach the problem. As a first step I looked at the *Social Science Citation Index* for the ten years in question to get an impression of Kuhn's impact, as customarily measured by the number of his citations. The sheer number of citations of his work shows that we are on the right track: roughly 1260 for 1971–1975; 1,160 for 1976; 540 each for 1977 and 1978; 700 each for 1979 and 1980. Although 1976 must have been the height of the debate, his impact has not weakened. Another feature is the overriding impact of the "Structure of Scientific Revolutions" as compared to Kuhn's other works. Without having counted the numbers precisely, about 90–95 percent of his citations seem to have been made to that book; and it would be even more if one included the references to the immediately connected works in which he responds to criticisms. Thus the inescapable conclusion is that it is not so much Kuhn as an excellent historian of science who is receiving such unusual recognition, but that his one book is what stands out. That says something about the intellectual (and perhaps the social) context in which the reception takes place, but although I leave speculation on that aside, it also legitimates the next step. Since it is the "Structure of Scientific Revolutions" that has this enormous impact, it may be assumed that this is due to the principal claims of the book and the controversies surrounding them. To facilitate the search I therefore looked in the *Permuterm Index* for entries under *social science(s))*, *paradigm*, *scientific community*, *history*, and *phi-*

losophy. (Search for *social structure* and *cognitive structure* proved fruitless.) The emerging titles were then screened by judgment if they promised contents of interest for either of the two aspects mentioned earlier.

What one gets this way is clearly much less than actually exists (it is a minute fraction of all the works actually citing Kuhn, but then one can also surmise that a large share of them use the term *paradigm*—and cite Kuhn—in inconsequential fashion); but one cannot get more than there is, and one cannot get something that does not fit. Thus I refrain from quantifying and return to qualitative evaluation. Although it may be that I missed some important debates, the conviction is justified that a fairly good segment of Kuhn's impact on the social sciences has been identified. I will use this mainly in an exemplary fashion; but in a very few instances I have given up the self-limitation of this method and ventured, for example, into the well-cultivated garden of Kuhnian and post-Kuhnian history of sociology—just because it happens to be there.

Kuhn's Impact on the Philosophy of the Social Sciences

There are two ways in which the reception of Kuhn takes place in the history and philosophy of the social sciences: First, Kuhn the internalist is "applied" in an instrumental fashion, with philosophical intentions and legitimating motives. In these cases history of science becomes philosophy of science; or, rather, the history of the discipline becomes its philosophy: Second, Kuhn the inadvertent externalist sociologist is used as a witness to legitimate histories of disciplines. History of science becomes sociology of science, and sociology of science turns historical.

Works that fall into the first category reveal that the application of Kuhn the internalist is neither revolutionary nor a progressive research program. In fact, the notions of paradigms and paradigmatic revolutions often seem to be taken up only in order to be rejected. The beneficiary of this exercise in several cases is Lakatos, mostly because he appears as a type of moderate Kuhn. Blaug explicitly compares Kuhnian paradigms and Lakatosian research programs in their applicability to the history of economics and significantly enough speaks of the (Kuhnian and Lakatosian) "methodology applied to economics," when he means the application of the concepts to "history of economic thought."[1]

Focusing on the Keynesian revolution, Blaug concludes that he can think of no"unambiguous examples" of instances that corroborate the externalist theses in the history of economics and that, therefore, Lakatos's "rational reconstruction" would suffice to explain virtually all past successes and failures of economic research programmes."[2] In strikingly similar fashion, D. P. O'Brien compares the "*philosophies* of the history of science" of Popper, Kuhn, and Lakatos in understanding the "progress of Smith's influence during the development of economics."[3] Like Blaug, O'Brien concludes after a diligent application of Kuhn's and Lakatos's key concepts that Lakatos's philosophy of the history of science "seems the most successful in explaining the history of Smith's unparalleled achievement."[4]

There are also other authors in the history of economics, who have not discarded Kuhn so readily but, rather, have identified the Keynesian and the so called marginal revolution of the 1870s as Kuhnian revolutions.[5]

The most interesting feature of the application of Kuhn to the history of economics common to believers and skeptics is that it is apparently motivated by a philosophical interest in claiming (contrary to Kuhn) the status of a science for economics. This is, of course, possible either by proving its paradigmatic status and thus its propensity to revolutions or by denouncing the relativistic implications of Kuhn and swimming to the safe shores of Lakatos's internalist rational reconstruction. This same mix of historical analysis and philosophical demarcation exercises can be found in many other disciplines, including such unlikely cases as education.[6] Another particularly good example is linguistics. Keith Percival examines "the applicability to the history of linguistics of Thomas Kuhn's conception of the history of science" and concludes that although the notion of *revolution* can be applied to the history, the notion of *paradigm* "cannot be applied either to the history *or the present state* of linguistics."[7] Percival is expressly worried that practicing linguistics "began to look upon all theoretical disagreements within their profession as conflicts between rival paradigms" that could result in a "lowering, rather than a raising, of scientific standards within linguistics."[8]

Another outstanding example of applying Kuhn to linguistics in order to put the field on a solid philosophical basis is Finke's "Konstruktiver Funktionalismus—Die wissenschaftstheoretische Basis einer empirischen Theorie der Literatur,"[9] although he does not apply Kuhn crudely but Kuhn's ideas as elaborated by Sneed. However, the attempt to turn reconstructive concepts into constructive ones is more explicit than anywhere else I know. With this example I have already crossed the line into the category of philosophical efforts that are characterized by a philosophical use of Kuhn without recourse to the history of the field. Here the rationale of using Kuhn is directly the legitimation of the field as similar to or, in essence, identical with the natural sciences—or, from the opposite viewpoint, to denounce any such claims.

Use for Adaptation and Legitimation

A paper by Overington in which he concludes on the basis of a discussion of Kuhn's theory of scientific revolutions that scientific knowledge is not different from political ideology or magicians' lore has triggered a small debate, which reveals this pattern nicely. Overington suggested that we should "extend the same analytical tolerance to the varieties of sociological rationality as we do to the diversity of human groups, whose beliefs and rationality we treat with even-handed analytic appreciation."[10] Storer called this the "I'm okay—you're okay" sociology, denounced the battles for legitimacy and supremacy, and insisted on the possibility of empirically based standards of validity within paradigms.[11] Naroll applies Kuhn in a translated set of "tests to the behavioral sciences of today" and concludes that "clearly none of these is a mature science."[12] Percival, finally, reflects on the sociologists' and psychologists' enthusiasm for Kuhn's theory, which he finds ironic because Kuhn regarded fields such as sociology "as beyond the scientific pale." Kuhn, according to Percival, replaced the older view of science as characterized by gradual cumulative progress with an alternative view, "which postulated that the essence of science consists in community-wide commitment to one single all-embracing Weltanschauung," which, of course, leaves the social sciences in the cold. Although they like to agree with him that a distinction between scientific and nonscientific disciplines can be drawn, they claim to have "gained admittance to the scientific fraternity. It is this attitude which explains why sociologists or psychologists, on making acquaintance with Kuhn's theory of scientific revolutions, have straightway hastened to apply it to their own fields. Not surprisingly, Kuhn himself finds this reaction puzzling."[13]

The ambivalence toward Kuhn and at the same time his inescapable fascination is apparent in what could be called adaptation by compromise. Bryant refrains from endorsing "a particular kind of sociology by referring to Kuhn" but wants to "take up certain aspects of Kuhn's account of scientific paradigms in order to characterize the present state of sociology and its future prospects." He, then, recommends "a qualified response to Kuhn": "examples in sociology are few and far between and pluralist in. . .that sociology is multi-paradigmatic and likely to remain so, given that agreement on concepts is as elusive as ever."[14]

Political science has not been exempt from these debates. Stephens differeniates the uses of "the Kuhnian paradigm" into three fairly distinct types. The first is exemplified by Truman's application of a very loose concept of paradigm to the history of political science, as well as Almond's. Truman regrets the loss of paradigmatic orientation since the 1930s; Almond sees a new one emerging—systems theory. Holt and Richardson represent a second type of use. They identify four elements of a paradigm, which are, according to Stephens, only a relabeling of what is usually called a theory, and conclude that comparative politics is in the preparadigmatic stage. Finally, Landau, Wolin, Thorson, and Euben all use Kuhn's original formulation of the paradigm concept and identify it with their respective views of political science. They do so without questioning Kuhn's concept of science, says Stephens; therefore, "the debate by political scientists about *adequate* criteria for assessing political science formulations has yet to come: what we have had thus far are merely polemics that assert that we should adopt a given philosopher's, or group of philosophers', standards for assessing political science formulations."[15]

As a final example in this category I cite a case where Kuhn's notion of paradigm shift is used to legitimate one's own model or theory as the latest revolutionary achievement, to which the other members of the community should adhere. Unfortunately, there are always some who do not rally 'round the flag. Harré and Secord have put forth a model of the understanding of human and individual behavior that they claim represents a paradigm shift. In contrast to the mechanistic explanatory model of human behavior, they propose an explanation in terms of reasons with reference to rules and roles; they reject the dependence on observable causal relations and suggest instead the notion of self-monitored behavior; finally, they criticize the adoption of the methodological program of logical positivism and operationism. They juxtapose an old paradigm and their new one, a mechanistic versus an anthropomorphic one.[16] Be that as it may, Tibbetts has taken issue with this claim to destroy it by going back to Kuhn and questioning whether "there could in principle be a paradigm shift in contemporary social scientific theorizing."[17] His conclusion is interesting because it is itself normative. He rejects the Harré/Secord model "as representing a significant paradigm shift in contemporary psychological theorizing. . . ." According to Kuhn, a science in its preparadigmatic state frequently draws on the concepts of traditional metaphysics. The psychology envisioned by Harré and Secord, with its doctrine of "powers," among other concepts, would invariably lock psychology into such a preparadigmatic state.[17]

These are only a few examples of the reception of Kuhn in the philosophy and methodology of the social sciences. Many more could be added. They all have the common feature that Kuhn's ideas and concepts are being used to legitimate or deligitimate particular positions, achievements, and theoretical development—or the scientific status of a discipline as a whole. As Perceival has pointed out, the irony of these debates is that they are carried out in those disciplines where Kuhn himself would have deemed them futile in the first place. One could wonder if this says something about Kuhn's theory and/or about the conditions favoring his achievement. One final remark may be added in this connection: A glance at the textbooks, monographs, and anthologies of the last decade explicitly dealing with the philosophy of the social sciences reveals little or no impact of Kuhn.[18] One speculative explanation comes readily to mind: The "professional" philosophers and methodologists of the social sciences do not "use" Kuhn in the way that the disciplinary foot soldiers do. Kuhn is a fad with the privates, not with the officers in the general staff.

Kuhn's Impact on the History of the Social Sciences

The second category of the uses of Kuhn is what I have called the history of disciplines turned sociological. In contrast to the first category, Kuhn's impact here has been substantial but, again, far beyond what Kuhn himself had in mind and sometimes even in contradiction to it. As the developments that were initiated by *The Structure of Scientific Revolutions*, particularly in sociology and the sociological history of science, are too voluminous to be traced here, I must oversimplify. In essence, the sociologization of the history of scientific disciplines is due to one element of Kuhn's book: the postulated connection between the activities of scientific (or, more specifically, disciplinary or specialty) communities and the institutionalization of new paradigms, as well as the resistance to that. Aside from the many misinterpretations and Kuhn's own disbelief in the conclusions drawn from it by sociologists, the impact was first and foremost in the sociology of science. It opened a way to overcome the sterile division of labor, according to which (functionalist) sociology had to deal with the social-structural prerequisites of pure science while the history and philosophy of science legitimately dealt with contents. In this constellation, it is significant that the latter two could lay claim to the aura and prestige of the natural sciences, whereas sociology, having nothing to do with and no knowledge of their contents, remained the dog barking at the moon.

That situation has turned upside down now. Because the internalist, continuous Whig history was delegitimized, knowledge about social structures and process has become essential for at least the partial explanation of the development of contents. The sociology of knowledge was reinstated, albeit in the different guise of ethnomethodology; but that was already the most far-reaching consequence of Kuhn's thesis and the cognitive dynamics of sociology proper. Also, what had been the "science of science" before Kuhn—but had remained a dried-up flower ever since the Ossowskis coined the term—was renamed the "social studies of science" and developed into a sizable weed resistant enough to trigger the anger of the establishment historians of science.

If one leaves these wider implications aside and focuses on the history of the social sciences proper, the history of sociology is interesting in its own right. While Kuhnian (as opposed to the preceding Mertonian) sociology of science jumped on the newly discovered prey and concentrated on the study of the natural sciences, the social sciences were virtually ignored as objects of study, particularly sociology, a fact noted by Robert Merton.[19] The explanation that this was due to the unquestioned rule of structural functionalism in the 1950s and that the self-thematization set in only as a reflection of growing dissensus in the discipline, can only be half the story. I claim that the revulsion against structural functionalism in sociology and the impact of Kuhn's ideas must be attributed to same evolution of thought, which of course was not limited to sociology. The first ones in the field to take note of that were the sociologists of science, whose traditional object of study was the natural sciences. As their role within sociology is marginal, it is the more central sociologists who took up the job of self-thematization in a way unique to sociology—namely, as the sociology of sociology, for which, again, Kuhn's analysis of the natural sciences and his ideas on paradigm choice are the frame of reference.[20] Thus the time lag and the surprise.

The new history of sociology, psychology, linguistics, political science, and so on therefore follows paths previously paved by the Kuhnian history of the natural sciences. The shift away from Whig history and "presentism" becomes apparent in the change of metaphors. The description of the growth of knowledge is replaced by the vocabulary of political conflict. The absolutism or *ancien régime* of established theoretical traditions is attacked for injustice and incompetence, which can be rectified only by revolution or *putsch*.[21]

One example of this shift in statu nascendi is Hymes's anthology on the history of linguistics. In his introduction Hymes struggles with the paradigm concept or, rather, the problem if the development of linguistics shows paradigmatic revolutions or successions. In the concluding section we find Wolff's and Thorn's "Notes on the Sociology of Knowledge and Linguistics" and Stocking's "Comments on History as a Moral Discipline: Transcending 'Textbook' Chronicles and Apologetics." Stocking aptly evaluates the relation of this section to the rest of the book: There is "a certain narrowness of focus" in the contributions on the history of linguistics which he suggests should be replaced by "another kind of micro-history. . .: the study of the interaction patterns of the men who form the community of linguistics in any given period or place. And at a somewhat broader level, there is the whole question of placing these interactions, the technical history of linguistics, and the broader issues of linguistic theory, all within the most meaningful framework of social, cultural, and intellectual context."[22]

The "History of Sociology" Essays

"For these reason Lepenies" four-volume collection of essays appearing under the title *History of Sociology* diverges radically from previous histories of a discipline in just that way. Rather than being a history of the intellectual development of the field, it is a kaleidoscope of probes into the political, social, and intellectual contexts of sociology; into the interactions of sociological (and philosophical) traditions; into the role of national traditions and their mutual influences; and, of course, into the role of "theory-groups," schools, and processes of institutionalization, to which an entire volume is devoted.

If we take a superficial look at that volume alone, Kuhn's impact may be demonstrated beyond what has been said already, by the many explicit references to Kuhn. Thus Tiryakian says that his essay begins where Kuhn stopped, meaning the elaboration of the community concept and the plea for comparative studies of communities in his postscript of 1970.[23] Mullins places his formation of a model for the development of sociological traditions in the sequence of Kuhn's thesis on the change of scientific thought ("revolutions") and Price's conception of a theoretical-social structure, the "invisible college."[24] His chapter on ethnomethodology has no explicit allusion to Kuhn but is, of course, an elaboration of the program—that is, the study of a specialty on the cognitive and social level in the process of its institutionalization.[25]

Robert Geiger begins by also referring to Kuhn's paradigm concept and its inapplicability to sociology. He contests that thesis and goes on to study the institutionalization of paradigms in early French sociology.[26]

The chapter by Clark also has no explicit reference to Kuhn. As it is a chapter from his book *Prophets and Patrons, the French University and the Emergence of the Social Sciences*, however, it must be kept in mind that his approach is Kuhnian nonetheless. The same applies to Victor Karady's *Statégies de réussité et modes de faire—valoir de la sociologie chez les durkheimiens*, in which he links the strategies of a disciplinary school to the legitimation it needs to obtain to become fully institutionalized. Karady starts off with the "self-evident" claim that Durkheimian sociology, like every important epistemological innovation, owes its success or failure to the "peculiar combination of the more or less favorable social conditions of receptivity and the more or less conscious effort to further one's own cause."[27]

In the following four articles in Lepenies's volume (the fifth is a collection of letters), we find no explicit references to Kuhn, either because they are specialized histories of institutions as contexts of sociology and/or because references are no longer needed, as their underlying approach is a development of Kuhn's ideas that has long since left him behind. Without him, however, no historian would have found much use in the study of the "social structures of a research organization."[28]

The number of examples could be quadrupled; their representativeness could be improved beyond the frame of reference of Lepenies's *History of Sociology*; and they could be extended to other fields, notably psychology, and linguistics; but the point has been made.

Not only have the metaphors changed, but the objects of study as well. The emergence of ideas and their chronology is just one unit of analysis. Others are the groups that are the producers, the proponents, and the sales managers of these ideas; the institutional frameworks in which these groups operate but which they also use to advance their causes; the wider social and political contexts that are believed to set the stage for processes of paradigm formation and revolutions. All these units of analysis do not traditionally belong to the realm of concerns of pre-

Kuhnian history of science; if they did appear at all (as in the writings of Fleck, Bernal, Butterfield, and some others), they never assumed the status of legitimate concerns. The reason is obvious: pre-Kuhnian history of science adhered to the philosophical principle of the separation of genesis and validity of knowledge. External circumstances, social processes, and group activities could all be relegated to the footnotes of the history of science. Despite his own ambiguity, Kuhn's thesis and especially its sociological elaborations challenged that principle—a challenge that also had repercussions in the philosophy of science proper. The least that can be said is that with Kuhn's *Structure of Scientific Revolutions* the hitherto happy marriage of the history and the philosophy of science came to an end. The affair with sociology of science left the history of science with a bad case of schizophrenia: It has led the two lives of *before* and *after* ever since.

One could say, then, that Kuhn's theory has turned out to be an unintended advance in the philosophy and history of the social sciences, or, perhaps more aptly, a catalyst for a development that is much more comprehensive and fundamental at the same time. The impact of the sociologization of the history of science on the philosophy of science is fundamental insofar as the underlying epistemological tenets of the subject/object dichotomy and the discovery of a "world out there" are undermined by a sort of second-order reflexivity. Kantian a priorism in epistemology has become untenable; and, as Luhmann once put it, the chair of the "discovery subject" is vacant. It has not been filled again because of the deep-seated fear of the circularity of knowledge or, as it is termed now, of *self-referentiality*. However, conceptions of self-reference emerge in several disciplines—neurophysiology, biology, theory of evolution, logic, and systems theory—aside from the sociology of knowledge.[29] A theory of self-referentiality of knowledge, then, though still being far from a conclusive formulation, appears as a light at the end of the tunnel, promising to liberate present-day sociologized history and philosophy of (social) science from what is considered their insurmountable obstacle: how to determine the truth of the sociological explanation of knowledge that claims to be true.[29] Such a theory would obviously also be much more comprehensive than the history and philosophy of the social sciences, and no doubt would be a major advance. Kuhn, who has inadvertently brought the underlying problems into focus, has nothing to do with that advance as it now emerges.

Conclusions About the Conditions Favoring Kuhn's Impact

By now it is clear that the question of what conditions favored Kuhn's achievement has to be rephrased: What conditions favored his reception in the social sciences? On this, one can only speculate. One reason offered in support of the allegation that it was favored by the external political conditions—a general feeling of crisis, which also extended to the sciences and technology—is the fact that Fleck's work of 1935 was ignored completely. The influence of the Vienna Circle was still unchallenged. Another reason pointing in the same direction is the pattern of his reception: He is influential mostly for a single thesis in a single book, much as a presidential candidate is for a programmatic catchword in his campaign platform. As soon as it is subjected to closer scrutiny, it turns out to be an oversimplification; once he manages to come to power, he begins to qualify it, taking back most of its original thrust. This is by no means to say that catch words do not make things change in history. On the contrary, they are, as I said earlier, the catalysts of change. But that itself says something about Kuhn's or any other scientist's achievements, as well as about the notion of major advances in the (social) sciences. They are as much determined by the intellectual and political setting (both within science and in society), which is receptive to some ideas and not to others, as they are due to the ingenuity of those who produce and propagate these ideas. This rather commonsensical insight Kuhn has given a particular formation, while his critics among the philosophers and historians of science continue to believe in Santa Claus.

References

1. M. Blaug, "Kuhn versus Lakatos, or Paradigms versus Research Programs in the History of Economics," *Hope 7* no. 4,(1975): 399–400
2. Ibid., p. 431.
3. D. P. O'Brien, "The Longevity of Adam Smith's Vision: Paradigms, Research Programmes and Falsifiability in the History of Economic Thought," *Scottish Journal of Political Economy 23* no. 2, (1976): 133 (emphasis added).
4. Ibid., p.150.
5. Cf. A. W. Coats, "Is There a 'Structure of Scientific Revolutions' in Economics?" *Kyklos 22*, (1969). R. D. C. Black, A. W. Coats, and C. D. W. Goodwin, eds. *The Marginal Revolution in Economics: Interpretation and Evaluation*, (Durham, N.C., 1973); B. Ward, *What's Wrong with Economics (New York, 1972);* M. Bronfenbrenner, "The 'Structure of Scientific Revolutions'" in *Economic Thought, History of Political Economy*, Vol. 3, Spring 1971.
6. Cf. H. W. Hodysh, "The Kuhnian Paradigm and Its Implications for the Historiography of Curriculum Change", *Paedagogica Historica 17* (1), 1977, pp. 75–87.
7. W. K. Percival, "The Applicability of Kuhn's Paradigms to the History of Linguistics", *Language 52* (2), 1976, p. 285, (emphasis added).

8. Ibid., p. 292.
9. Finke, "Konstructiver Functionalismus...", Habilitation, Universität Bielefeld, 1979.
10. M. A. Overington, "Doing What Comes Rationally: Some Developments in Metatheory", *American Sociologist 14* (1), 1979, p. 10.
11. N. Storer, "I'm Okay—You're Okay," *Sociology, American Sociologist 14* (1), 1979, p. 31.
12. Raoul Naroll, "Doing What Comes Scientifically," ibid., p. 28.
13. W. Keith Percival, "The Applicability of Kuhn's Paradigms to the Social Sciences," ibid., p. 29.
14. C. G. A. Bryant, "Kuhn, Paradigms and Sociology", *British Journal of Sociology 26* (3), 1975, pp. 354, 358.
15. J. Stephens, "The Kuhnian Paradigm and Political Inquiry: An Appraisal", *American Journal of Political Science 17* (3), pp. 467-–488, (emphasis added).
16. R. Harré and P. Secord, *The Explanation of Social Behavior* (New Jersey, 1972).
17. P. Tibbetts, "On a Proposed Paradigm Shift in the Social Sciences," *Philosophy of the Social Sciences 5* (1975): 289, 296.
18. Cf., for example, the very often reviewed B. Hindess, *Philosophy and Methodology in the Social Sciences* (Hassocks, 1977); D. Thomas, *Naturalism and Social Science: A Post-Empiricist Philosophy of Social Science* (New York, 1971); S. J. Benn and G. W. Mortimore, eds., *Rationality and the Social Sciences: Contributions to the Philosophy and Methodology of the Social Sciences* (London, 1976); Chr. Hookway and O. Pettit, eds., *Action and Interpretation, Studies in the Philosophy of the Social Science* (Cambridge, 1978); v. Prutt, *The Philosophy of the Social Sciences* (London, 1978).
19. As representatives of the new history of science, he names such odd bedfellows as Charles Gillispie, Rupert Hall, Thomas Kuhn, Everett Mendelsohn, and Derek Price; cf. R. Merton, *On the History and Systematics of Sociological Theory,* cited from the German edition: *Zur Geschichte und Systematik der soziologischen Theorie,* in W. Lepenies, ed., *Geschichte der Soziologie,* 4 vols. (Frankfurt, 1981), p. 18, and fn. 3.
20. Cf. R. W. Friedrichs, *A Sociology of Sociology* (New York, 1970).
21. Cf. W. Lepenies, *Einleitung, Studien zur kognitiven, sozialen und historischen Identität der Soziologie,* in Lepenies, op. cit., VI.
22. In: D. Hymes, ed., *Studies in the History of Linguistics,* (Bloomington, Ind., 1974), p. 510.
23. E. A. Tiryakian, "The Significance of Schools in the Development of Sociology," German version in Lepenies, op. cit., Vol. 2, 32.
24. N. C. Mullins, in: Lepenies, *Geschichte,* Vol. 2, p. 69.
25. Ibid., pp. 97–136.
26. R. L. Geiger, *The Institutionalization of Sociological Paradigms: Three Examples from Early French Sociology,* German in Lepenies, *Geschichte,* Vol. 2, p. 137.

27. V. Karady, in Lepenies, *Einleitung*, in *Geschichte*, p. 206.
28. H. Dubiel, "Soziale Strukturen der Forschungsorganisation der frühen kritischen Theorie," in Lepenies, *Geschichte*, Vol. 2, p. 430.
29. Cf. N. Luhmann, *Die Ausdifferenzierung von Erkenntnisgewinn: Zur Genese von Wissenschaft, Kölner Zeitschrift für Soziologie und Sozialpsychologie,* Sonderheft 22, 1980: 102 and Footnotes 1–5.

Discussion

(Bell, Deutsch, Lepenies, Zwicker, Bruckmann, Kruskal, Cohen)

Edited by Andrei S. Markovits

DANIEL BELL began by saying that he assumed, listening to the discussion, that there was evidently a new mode of science, aside from the prevailing "internalist" and "externalist" notions. The new mode could be called "Thomas Kuhn as the coming of reason."

Karl Deutsch mentioned that Kuhn had been invited to attend the conference. He had sent a very polite rejection letter, as follows: "Dear Karl, I like the project about which you and John Platt recently solicited my advice, but I cannot help you. I know a great deal less than I should, and in any case virtually nothing at all, about the social sciences and I will not create confusion by bluffing it."

The Combinatorics of Discoveries

Deutsch went on to make several points about Weingart's paper. First, he fully agreed that unintended consequences were as significant for advances in knowledge as intended ones. Columbus intended to find a way to India and the spice islands. His unintended effect was to discover a new continent. Moreover, the long-range effect of his discovery did not increase, but rather thoroughly diminished, the power of those who had "funded his research"—the Spanish Crown and the Holy Inquisition. So the notion that there was a simple determinism between the results of the scientists and the intentions of those who pay for their work was distinctly a fallacy.

Deutsch said he would also agree with Weingart's point that, no matter what the ostensible reasons for proposing a new scientific result, either a technique or a discovery or a paradigm, one was really asking, "Do we know more than before?" This was what was in the notion of advances—existential statements that answer such questions as: "Do we know more about the things there are? or do we know more about the things we can do? Or even about the things there could be?"

He went on to say that discoveries are not only made by individuals or even by social milieus. He would underline what Cohen said about the autonomous element in discovery. In fact there were combinatorial probabilities implicit in any set of elements and any set of rules connecting them. Piaget, in his approach to structuralism, had argued that a structure had to include its transformation rules. So Deutsch said, "As soon as one has a square, there is the possibility of getting a rhombus, because if you push the top of the square sideways, it becomes a rhombus."

He said it would be no use to legalize only squares and threaten to shoot everyone who thought of a rhombus, because the discovery would happen; any time a child played with a square made of four sticks of wood, it would become a rhombus right away.

Deutsch said it would be worthwhile to go on to study the people who behaved in a non-Kuhnian way. These were the "cats that walked by themselves," those who were not very good at working in communities, who did not play the game of influence, who were not polite—such as Thorstein Veblen in economics or Oliver Heaviside in early radio research.

Likewise, it would be valuable to look at research groups that made a point of not talking to each other. There were many documents that showed that Weber actually read Durkheim but never cited him, and vice versa. Science was not so much of an "I'm O.K., you're O.K." game as people sometimes thought.

Ideas of Change: From Tradition to Discontinuity

Deutsch sketched the Kuhnian model as having itself developed from the intellectual history of the last 170 years or so. During that time, there had been a change, not so much in leading ideas as in polarities. At first, between 1815 and 1890, there was a struggle between the basic notion of continuity—"tradition," "conservation," "things are as they are and as they always have been"—and the notion of gradual change. One such battle was represented by the English Reform Bill of 1852, with a victory of liberals over conservatives. It was true that a traditionalist like Edmund Burke admitted that even traditional structures would change, but he felt this change would occur "infinitely slowly." Darwin, however, went on to the idea of gradual change in species.

Deutsch suggested that the conflict between these older approaches continued until the 1890s. People like Mendel, however, who had developed conceptions of discontinuous change, were not yet accepted—nor was Marx quickly accepted. Before 1890 thinkers who developed such notions were at the margin of intellectual life; but after the1890s this also changed. This was also the time when the great chain reactions of political revolutions began—Cuba in 1895, Crete in 1897, and eventually the Russian Revolution of 1917.

All this pointed to a change in the climate of the world. It was the time when Planck thought of the quantum theory. It was the time when de Vries thought of mutations. A move toward the acceptance of discontinuous change began to develop. Even so, Planck said that his ideas would be accepted only after all holders of chairs in physics in Germany had either retired or died, and their assistants—who understood his ideas—had succeeded them.

The following period, between about 1890 and 1960, Deutsch said, was a period of polarity between those who thought about gradual change and those who thought about discontinuous change. But the debate was then conducted largely in terms of the "central tendencies" of statistical distributions. One spoke of "average per capita income" or the "consensus of American opinion." "One assumed that things were fairly normally distributed, and that one was looking for a particular central tendency in everything."

But Deutsch suggested that after the 1960s a new climate emerged: People argued whether change would be fast or slow, but one was much more aware of the variance in the statistics. One now asked: "What is the nature of the distribution? Could it be bimodal, for example?"

Deutsch said, "We now talk about 'distribution,' which means that we also talk about inequality of income, [not just] average per capita gains."

He said that likewise researchers were beginning to ask about the "outliers," the minorities, the people who did not fit in. And we all knew it was useless to ask about the "average sex" of the German people.

"We don't have a common sex! There are many *women*—and we are indeed beginning to discover that there are many women!—and also that they have been treated badly and unfairly!"

So it was after the 1960s, Deutsch suggested, that "all of our skeletons came out of the closet," and the question of distribution was put in a much more radical way than it had been before. He thought that these dynamics were partly due to social pressures, with minorities and women demonstrating in the streets, but that they were also due to the intrinsic dynamics of the fields of knowledge. He wished we understood more about the latter.

Historiography versus Historical Research

Wolf Lepenies pointed out that the participants were no longer talking about disciplines, but about the history and philosophy of sociology. He did not think that "advances" in sociology, however they were defined, were the same as "advances" in the history of sociology. Again, the history of sociology itself could mean two different things, historical research or historiography—that is, the principles of doing the history. He said that his own feeling was that Kuhn had at least been a success in the historiography of sociology, having over 1,000 entries in the *Social Science Citation Index*. This work was widely celebrated and quoted, but he was not sure that these citations necessarily meant that it had been an advance.

Even if it were, however, Lepenies felt that Kuhn's work was not really an advance in historical research proper. In the history of sociology, he did not know a single good piece of research of which one could say that it was necessary to have Kuhn's book in order to do the research, or that someone had used his theory or his model "and found something new and astonishing." Kuhn had been a catalyst—not in the sense that he had given us a new vocabulary, but in the sense that he had allowed us to use an old vocabulary again: "He drew our attention to certain aspects we had not looked at before."

No Structural Criteria for Advances

Eckhart Zwicker then commented on Kuhn's concepts and the notion of advance in social science. He maintained that Kuhn's themes were of large importance. The question is whether they can provide reliable criteria for determining what progress is in both the sciences and the social sciences. If so, one could check all the advances listed in this conference, in the light of those criteria. Zwicker thought that precisely such criteria were needed for the purposes of the conference, but that in Kuhn's approach, the critical point was exactly the lack of any such criteria, or any adequate notion of the scientific process. This was true not only for Kuhn's "revolutions," but also for his "mini-revolutions," mentioned in the Appendix to the second edition of *The Structure of Scientific Revolutions*.

Zwicker felt, however, that an answer to the question "What is an advance?" might be given by the "structural" concept based on Kuhn's research, which was developed by Schmied and Stegmuller. This has been employed successfully to describe advances in quantum theory and in mathematical physics. Schmied had developed the concept of "reduction," which in principle could be used to follow the progress of a theory, and had given a successful interpretation of Newtonian laws. To use this approach for sociological and economic relations, however, it presupposed that there were theoretical terms to be measured in a theoretically reliable way.

Zwicker noted that two conferences were held in Munich that tried to apply such a structural interpretation in economics, as in developing measures of advance for mathematical equilibrium theory. The result was disappointing, however. Many scholars felt the presuppositions of the structuralist approach did not exist in economics, so that we did not have the good fortune to be able to use Kuhn. He could not offer any criteria for deciding in a systematic way what an advance in economics was.

A Scale for Advances, from Alpha to Epsilon?

Gerhart Bruckmann followed with a comment in the same vein. He said that Kuhn's major emphasis was on large paradigm changes, like those from the geocentric system in astronomy to the heliocentric theory, or from the phlogiston theory to the movement of molecules. Bruckmann said: "If we called these largest changes 'alpha' changes, as opposed to what Krelle was referring to as 'delta' and 'epsilon' changes, then isn't the problem in the social sciences that all sixty-two of the advances listed in the DPS paper, plus the twenty or so discussed here, fall only in the category of 'gamma,' or at most 'beta,' changes of the Kuhnian type?"

Bruckmann felt this was indeed the case and therefore doubted that Kuhn's theory was actually applicable to the *problematique* of the conference.

William Kruskal then turned to a different comment on the notion of "probable error." He argued that there was still a great deal of confusion between the inherent or natural variability of phenomena in whatever units were used, and the uncertainties or variability of the measurements themselves. The confusion was compounded by the fact that in most situations both types of variation occurred simultaneously. This caused difficulties in setting up stochastic models; indeed, in stochastics, the term *error* was generalized to the term *deviation.*

Kruskal remarked that astronomers and physicists like Gauss were well aware of intrinsic variability, such as the frequencies of double stars in the heavens, the variability of cometary paths, and so on. Because of these two sources of "deviations," however, he thought the situation was more complicated than Weingart's analysis showed.

"Science" and Social Science

Kruskal followed this by a remark on terminology. He very much hoped Professor Cohen would change his language and not use the word *science* just to refer specifically to the natural sciences. This usage had played an extremely important political role in the life of the National Science Foundation (NSF) in the United States, right from its inception. The question was: "Should we, or do we, include the social sciences?"

The orginal argument had been that the foundation was concerned with "science," not "social science," and that the two were distinct enterprises. Later the social sciences were included to a significant degree, but Kruskal said they were once again under attack by those on the National Science Board and even by some members of Congress. He felt the terminology itself had played a considerable role in the difficulties.

Cohen responded that he fully agreed and was well aware of the political situation Kruskal mentioned. Cohen felt it was genuinely unfortunate. He remembered talking to one of the associate directors of the NSF, who said he had just discovered that in addition to the hard sciences, there were "all these 'soft sciences'." Cohen had responded, "Do you mean biology?," and the man said, "Oh no!"

Cohen said he had tried to push this official on what he meant by "hard" and "soft," asking him, "Are you talking about the accuracy of earthquake predictions versus the prediction of economic cycles?" The gentleman, however, knew enough not to answer.

More seriously, Cohen related that in the original title of his paper at this conference, he had wanted to talk about the "natural and exact" sciences, but there was a problem in using the word *exact* because it seemed to imply that *inexact* had a negative value. On the other hand, the words *natural sciences* in many people's minds included natural history and the life sciences but did not include mathematics; so when he got into this dilemma, he simply shortened the word he used to *sciences*. He agreed that he had sinned and that the criticism was entirely warranted; yet he thought it was difficult to find an exact and simple alternative. However, one should certainly not say that there were some sciences "of purity and high worth," and then there were those other things described by an adjective with bad connotations.

Bell intervened as the chairman, with an autobiographical note concerning language. His first job, when he was still a graduate student, was as educational director for a local of the International Ladies Garment Worker's Union. The manager of the local was a recent immigrant who was very proud of his new-found command of English as a way of expressing himself. He had told the members of the union: "You know, the other officers of the union, they don't respect you. They talk to you in generalities—but I, I'm going to talk to you at *random*!"

This story suggested to Bell that the conference participants should not talk about the "exact sciences" but should talk about the "stochastic sciences"—and scare everyone!

KUHN AND THE SOCIOLOGY OF KNOWLEDGE

Weingart responded that he would address the questions before him at *random*, and then go on to something very general. Lepenies had remarked that for historical research, Kuhn was unnecessary and offered nothing new. Weingart wondered whether such a radical claim could be so. He felt Kuhn had given legitimacy to questions and subjects that had not previously been considered legitimate concerns. This went back to the question Cohen has asked at the end of his paper: "What were the conditions of reception in other disciplines, and in society at large, which then brought about the [Kuhnian] sorts of developments?"

A related question had been raised by Bernward Joerges: Was not the reappearance of the "sociology of knowledge" a consequence of Kuhn? Or, as Weingart would put it, "Is Kuhn a condition [for this development]?—and if so, why?" One could have a detailed discussion of this; but briefly, what Kuhn did was to give a vague idea that the social structures within science had something to do with the scientific ideas that were produced. Weingart said that Mannheim himself had stayed away from science as much as he could; but the sociologists who had been thinking in Mannheimian terms all along, but under cover, suddenly thought, "This is it!" when Kuhn published his book. They felt, "In science we can do it—Kuhn has shown it!"

Weingart commented that the sociology of knowledge that then reappeared was much stronger than the Mannheimian sociology of knowledge; it was actually sociology of science in a new form. The new questions that guided the theorists were couched in a framework of methodology; and Kuhn had paved the way. Mannheimian sociology had run into a dead end, however, and this was significant in the development of structural functionalism. The new Kuhnian analysis was directed against the structural-functionalism sociology of science. He stated that if one interpreted this whole history as one of different groups having strategic arguments with one another—in other words, doing a Kuhnian analysis of that very history—one would come up with some nice insights.

Weingart then turned to the problem raised by Zwicker and Bruckmann, of whether Kuhn could be used to provide criteria for judging "advances." He said he had been misunderstood—because in his paper this point was explicitly avoided. He claimed he was not passing any judgment on Kuhn [laughter]—or rather he had judged Kuhn on a "meta level."

Zwicker interrupted in his own defense, saying that he asked the question of Weingart because it pertained to the theme of the conference. Weingart replied, "Well then, I should add your comments to my paper—under the heading, 'Uses of Kuhn'!"

Deutsch then asked whether Weingart would delete Kuhn from the list of major advances, or let him stay on the list because of the unintended consequences of his work. Weingart replied that he would leave that to Deutsch since the latter was one of the makers of the list.

Inkeles addressed this point by saying he had gone through the papers at the conference and had discovered that Eisenstadt had not cited Kuhn in his report on sociology; that Bell had not cited Kuhn either, although he had mentioned him; and that Inkeles himself had not mentioned Kuhn.

Bruckmann joined the fray, claiming that the problem was that Kuhn's advance was a meta advance—an advance in the way we see things. Inkeles said he wondered what that statement meant; he tried to "see things" in sociology, but had no need for Kuhn.

Bell then commented that in Kafka's parable, the door was always open until one got there—when when one was ready to enter, the gatekeeper closed it.

Regaining the floor, Weingart said he thought that in the philosophy of science, the whole attempt to find a criterion to demarcate science from nonscience ended in circularity. He had referred to theories of self-referentiality—which were exactly what he considered as a major advance in the making, which would erase all previous exercises. Indeed he argued that the Kuhn-Lakatos-Popper debate would then be dead.

Weingart therefore suggested to Deutsch that he either wait a while to complete this list of advances, or suffer all the faults to which such lists were prone. His general point was that the extreme difficulty of describing such a thing as a major advance, say in the history and philosophy of science, was actually the result of the shift in the directions of analysis, of the sort Kuhn had pointed out—namely, that one had to deal with continually changing frames of reference in the analysis.

Weingart maintained that one was therefore faced with relativism as an inherent property of any such analysis. Any epistemological perspectives on "advances," or intellectual exercises of the sort that said, "*This* is a criterion of such-and-such," or "This is a more rapid change than something else"—this entire debate over what conclusions one settled for, was actually and necessarily shifted to the metalevel.

Indeed, Weingart remarked, one could simply requote the sentence that said: "The hard sciences are just dealing with the soft problems, and the soft sciences are dealing with the hard problems." He held that this was self-exemplification, but it was also the conclusion of his paper.

CHAPTER 14

Examining the Concept of Advances, Especially in Psychology

Anatol Rapoport

The Idea of Progress

IT HAS BEEN SAID that the idea of progress is of quite recent origin, that it sprang up during the rapid development of technology concomitant to the Industrial Revolution and was projected onto other aspects of human activity. Hegel depicted history as the unfolding of an idea, manifested in progressive human emancipation. The idea of biological evolution, as conceived and enshrined by the enlightened Europeans of the nineteenth century, was also embodied in the idea of progress, as were the theories of social evolution of Morgan and Marx. Sheldon Amos (1880) had this to say about the future of war:

> . . .the modes of conducting Wars between civilized states have been steadily undergoing changes in one continuous direction, the object of these changes being the diminution of miseries inherent in warfare, the limitations of its area, and the alleviation of the evils incidentally occasioned by it to the neutral States.

> . . .even if there are those who regard all hopes for a time of permanent Peace as utopian, it is not denied in any quarter that there are general causes which produce both Peace and War, and that these causes can, to some extent, be controlled so as to foster the one and not the other.

The traumas of both world wars, especially World War II, with its outbursts of genocide and indiscriminate massacre of civilians, have made the idea of continued and inevitable progress, as it was conceived in nineteenth-century Europe, untenable. For some time, the idea was dissolved in what I call "absolute relativism"—a refusal to consider *any* generally valid criteria of value. From this point of view, the idea of a forward motion independent of some particular frame of reference was dismissed as naive, just as the idea of an absolute up or down appears naive to anyone familiar with rudiments of physics.

Indeed, it is difficult to argue against the relativity of esthetic values. For instance, no serious art historian will present the naturalism of Hellenistic sculpture as an "improvement" over the stylized Egyptian and Assyrian plastic art, or the sensuousness of post-Renaissance painting as superior to the asceticism of the Gothic, or the music of Wagner or Richard Strauss as greater than that of Bach and Mozart.

With respect to ethical or moral matters—that is, to concepts of what is good (as opposed to what is beautiful)—some still try to discern a line of progress, citing the virtual disappearance of chattel slavery, the spread of democratic ideals, and a growing concern for the dignity and autonomy of the individual as harbingers of continual moral improvement. It goes without saying, however, that dramatic counterexamples can be cited. In sum, this is a disputed area.

The situation in science—defined as the area of human experience where concern with "objective truth" is central—is very different. If the concept of truth is defined in terms of the usual scientific criteria (validity of logical deduction and the primacy of empirical verification), then progress in this area cannot be denied. It is, indeed, even more firmly entrenched in this area than in technology, which is usually regarded as the most conspicuous area of progress. Even in technology, one may note retrograde movements, for example, when certain skills or techniques are forgotten or impoverished as they are replaced by others, not necessarily superior ones from some particular point of view.

In science, on the other hand, one can speak of progress without embarrassment in the sense that all truths (in the scientific sense) known formerly remain known today and are constantly supplemented by empirical extensions and theoretical generalizations. There is no mystery about this, because the notion of scientific progress is embodied in the criteria of scientific truth themselves.

Progress and *advances* are, of course, value-laden terms. So it is not sufficient to demonstrate cumulative change as evidence of advance. To be sure, we speak also of advanced phases of a disease; but I am sure that the concept of advance in science or in the social sciences in particular, which I have been asked to discuss, has a connotation almost the opposite to that carried by the term *advanced disease*. Thus, although we may be forgiven a degree of ambivalence toward advances in some specific areas of applied science—for instance, in military technology or even in some nonmilitary areas of technology—I believe we are expected to welcome advances in science, at least in harmony with the spirit of this conference.

I can fully justify this expectation. For me, "advance in science"—in the sense of a more justifiable, more general, and more refined notions about what is *true*—is an unqualified positive value. I will therefore identify "advances in the social sciences" with a progressive firming of the social sciences (and psychology in particular) on scientific footings.

Having said this, I see a trap that I wish by all means to avoid: the facile spelling out of the process depicted in textbooks as "the scientific method" with its eternal spiral of observation, generalization, hypothesis formulation, prediction, empirical test, reformulation of hypothesis, new observations, and so on. Aside from the fact that flesh-and-blood scientists hardly ever do research this way, this paradigm, if taken literally, can produce an impoverished social science, especially an impoverished psychology. Unmentioned in this cycle is the role of imaginative insight as the guiding light of significant scientific progress—certainly not least in psychology, which began with intense introspection rather than with controlled experiment.

This is not to deny that major advances in psychology during the past century have been associated with the development of experimental techniques, designed around objectivized psychological concepts. *Objectivization* and *quantification* are closely related, since agreement among individual obsevers is easiest to achieve with regard to quantitative comparisons. Accordingly, we find early experimental psychology concerned with directly quantifiable data, generally regarded as manifestations of events in the central nervous system—for example, reaction times, short-term memory spans, and the like. Very soon the interest of experimental psychologists turned toward nonhuman subjects, especially following the discovery of the conditioned response. The earliest truly cumulative advances in experimental psychology were probably those in the area of rote learning. The rat became the symbol of behaviorism, and the stimulus-response paradigm became dominant in psychological research based on "hard" data.

As Kenneth Boulding once remarked, "Nothing fails like success." The fruitful vein lures the investigator to produce unending variations on a theme. Each answered question spawns many others, insuring a steady stream of publishable results, attraction of graduate students, support of research proposals, and everything that spells success and security in institutionalized science. All this triggers, eventually, an inevitable reaction.

Holistic versus Analytic Approaches in Psychology

Reaction against behaviorist psychology came from two sources, based, respectively, on epistemological and on ethical grounds. The critique from epistemological positions came in the form of *gestaltism*, a challenge to the stimulus-response paradigm. In fact, the main thrust of the critique was implicitly directed against the neglect of cognitive components by the behaviorists, who refused, by and large, to deal with concepts that could not be related to immediately and directly observable external referents.

This conflict between adherents of the *analytic* and the *holistic* approach to knowledge goes back to the disputes between the nominalists and the realists in the Middle Ages and continues in our day as the controversy between exponents of hard-headed positivism and adherents of various organismic approaches. "The whole is greater than the sum of its parts" is the slogan inscribed on the banners of the latter, although just what this means is not easy to ascertain, and to evaluate the truth or falsehood of this propostion is still more difficult.

The ethical challenge to behaviorism and generally to the "hard" scientific approach to social science raises the persistent question of relevance. Shall not psychology shed more light on the human psyche, on motivations and values, on hopes and fears, inclinations and beliefs—in short on human inner life? If so, can anything be learned about this inner life by observing rats running mazes or, for that matter, the capacity of people to memorize nonsense syllables or the rate at which they cross out the letter *t* from words in a text? Similar questions are raised with regard to positivistic social science. Should not social science be directed toward improving society? Does statistical processing of mountainous volumes of data or the progressive refinement of statistical techniques serve that purpose? Does not this emphasis on trivia and on quantification rather serve to make social science "value-free" and thus to detract it from humane goals?

The ethical overtones of these concerns about the relevance of positivistic social science to the improvement of society and, in particular, of experimental psychology to the understanding of the human psyche are apparent. "Self-knowledge" has been traditionally related to affects involved in human relations, and "emancipation from ideologies that rationalize existing dominance relations" is the avowed goal of so-called critical social science inspired by Marxist philosophy. It is admittedly difficult to do justice to these goals within the cognitive framework of "positivist" science, because the requirements of "hard science"—for example, operational definitions of concepts, sufficient empirical support of theoretical formulations, and so on—are difficult to satisfy within the ideational climate generated by searching social criticism and humanistic psychology.

The Meaningfulness of Questions About the Inner Life

The "hard" scientist applying his sharp criteria of meaningfulness, logical validity, and substantive objective truth to all discourse purporting to deal with people's inner or social life may feel extremely uneasy in that climate. Still, a summary dismissal as meaningless of questions that fail to satisfy scientific criteria of meaningfulness, or of assertions as unsupported when empirical evidence is extremely difficult to come by, seems somehow not quite fair.

Consider the following questions. Did Othello come to a bad end because he had a paranoid streak in him, that made him pathologically suspicious of his wife—and, if so, did his being black have anything to do with this? Or was Othello, on the contrary, childlike in his trust, which led him to believe everything Iago suggested to him? Did Ivan Karamazov hate his half brother Smerdiakov, because he (Ivan) was a snob and resented a blood relationship with a lackey; or did he hate him because Smerdiakov mirrored Ivan's innermost vile nature underneath the intellectual polish? Was the age-old longing of the Germans for the warmth of the Mediterranean world with its classical aesthetic ideals really endemic, or did Goethe merely give expression to his own climatic and esthetic preferences in the second part of *Faust*?

One does not know where to begin in a serious attempt to define a concrete—that is, operational—meaning of such questions, let alone to find scientifically defensible answers. Nevertheless, I submit that these questions are not nonsensical. They are imbued with solid meaning for most of us, at least those at home in Western culture. Moreover, I submit they are certainly psychological questions. The fact that they deal with fictional characters created by Shakespeare or Dostoyevsky, or with "national character" suggested by Goethe (a most elusive concept), does not make them less meaningful, if the introspective understanding of meaningfulness is not deliberately shut out of consciousness. The feeling of unease on the part of one dedicated to the traditional ideals of science stems from failing to see how these meanings can be translated into the language of scientific discourse.

Adherents of the other camp offer no help. On the contrary, they often deliberately distance themselves from attempts to integrate their concepts and procedures into the main stream of science. When opportunities for building bridges do appear, they are seldom followed up. I recall a dramatic experiment related to me by a psychoanalytically oriented psychologist. The subjects were two girls unacquainted with each other, both suffering from enuresis. One of them was put under hypnosis and told that she would be dreaming and that toward the end of the dream she would wet herself. Then she was commanded to describe the dream, while it was going on, and the description was tape recorded. Indeed, toward the end of the dream, the girl wet herself. (This episode was not tape recorded.) Then the other girl was put under hypnosis and told that she would experience the dream that she heard related. The tape was then played to her, and she, too, wet herself at the end.

I was deeply impressed with this experiment. It seemed to open up magnificent opportunities of investigating the symbolism of dreams experimentally. The result of the experiment seemed to me to be comparable to that of transmitting yellow fever from one person to another hundreds of miles away by means of a mosquito, thus providing definitive evidence for carrier-transmitted infections.

However, when I questioned my informant further about replications of the experiment, about obvious controls, such as using tape recordings of dreams without suggesting bed-wetting, and so on, I drew only blanks. Evidently the psychologist had no idea of the difference between an experiment and a demonstration, was not interested in firming the result by attempting to falsify the hypothesis, cared nothing about establishing the range of validity of one of the most intriguing facets of psychoanalysis—the symbolism of dreams—in fact, did not know the difference between a conjecture and a theory.

What Is "Understanding"?

I assume that differences of temperament and, on occasion, mutual suspicion notwithstanding, a dialogue can nevertheless be established between the positivist and the intuitionist approaches to social science and psychology. In order to do so, a central issue must be identified. I believe such a central issue has been stated by Max Weber, who declared that in contrast to the goals of natural science, which are to be able to predict events and perhaps even to be able to control them, the goal of the social sciences ought to be that of *understanding* social events and processes ("das Verstehen").

For the natural scientist "to understand" is practically synonymous with "to be able to predict." The physicist supports the claim to "understand" the solar system by citing successful predictions of the positions of planets, even the prediction of the discovery of a new planet, on a basis of formal mathematical deductions. What, then, could Weber have meant by contrasting *prediction* and *understanding*?

At the other, subjective, extreme of criteria of understanding, one concludes that one has understood something if one experiences an internal relief of tension—the so-called "Aha!" phenomenon.

Intermediate between the criterion of predictability and the subjective feeling of "understanding" is the identification of understanding with the reduction of an apparently exceptional, hence unexpected, event to a usual, hence expected one. One does not ordinarily ask why a bank clerk who had been a model of honesty for thirty years does *not* abscond with the cash, or why a model husband and father does *not* murder his family. One searches for reasons only when the unexpected happens.

The unexpected and the enigmatic become intelligible when circumstances are discovered that in similar situations produced similar events. For example, in the general population, few people commit suicide; but in the subpopulation of persons suffering humiliating frustrations or complete social isolation, suicides are most common. Thus an event unusual in one context appears as more usual in another. It is then "explained." Predictions of specific suicides are not involved in testing the validity of the explanation. Yet to some extent the principle of predictability is involved if, for example, predictions of suicides of arbitrarily selected persons are realized with larger probability in a particular subpopulation than in the population at large. Nevertheless, the important component of understanding is not so much a specifiable increase of predictability as the possibility of tying in different events or processes—seeing a relationship not seen before.

Even in the natural sciences, the degree of understanding conferred by a theory need not be directly related to predictions. For instance, the degree of understanding of the history of life on this planet conferred by the theory of biological evolution is very great, although the further course of evolution is hardly predictable. The explanatory appeal of the theory stems from the opportunity it offers of tying in geological and fossil data, providing a general principle of taxonomic schemes, and—by no means least—rendering ad hoc and teleological explanations of adaptation of organisms to their environments unnecessary.

Note that in these types of explanation a principle is involved that plays only a secondary role (and a diminishing one at that) in the physical sciences—the principle of recognition.

The ideal of the analytically oriented sciences is *reductionism*. The concepts developed in early chemistry were eventually reduced to the concepts of physics. The latter were completely quantified, so that observations could all be in principle reduced to readings of pointers on measuring instruments. These readings require only the most elementary act of recognition—namely, that of a position of a pointer between two markings on a dial.

As we pass from physical to biological science, recognition becomes more important. Already the taxonomy of plants and animals depends on consensual recognition of types. Even if species are described in terms of sequential decisions, (for example, presence or absence of specific features), the features themselves (limbs, organs, and so on) must still be recognized as "wholes."

Recognition is a *holistic* act. Here, then, is the port of entry of intuitive cognition into science, subjectively determined acts of recognition, which may or may not be possible to break up into more elementary cognitive events.

I can now formulate my conception of advances in the social sciences and in psychology in particular. One point of departure is the realization that the strictly analytic paradigm of the physical sciences (admittedly the most "advanced") is insufficient as the governing epistemological principle underlying the methodology of social science and of psychology. Another point of departure is the realization that the ideal of value-free science is not attainable in the realms of social science and psychology to the extent that it may be approached in the realm of the natural, especially of the physical, sciences.

Once "organismic," "holistic," or "introspective" aspects of cognition and frankly value-oriented approaches are legitimized in the scientific enterprise, the problem arises of integrating these approaches with analytic cognition and with ideals of objectivity predominant in the natural sciences. I identify advances in the social sciences and in psychology with steps toward the solution of this problem.

Psychology: Quantifying the Observable Indicators

Let us look at psychology first. Before being enriched by experimental techniques, psychology was more closely related to philosophy than to natural science. Accumulation of experimental results made attempts at quantification inevitable, in fact in two different contexts. One was via introduction of statistical evaluation of the plausibility of results (tests of significance); the other via the introduction of mathematical models of psychological phenomena and processes—learning, memory span, and so on. Quantification involves measurements. Here the chasm between psychology and the exact (that is, physical) sciences becomes apparent. The question *what to measure* presents no difficulty in the investigation of physical events. The entire edifice of theoretical physics rests on a few fundamental fully quantified concepts: time intervals, space intervals, masses, and numerous quantities derived from these by algebraic operations of the fundamental ones, such as forces, accelerations, and so on. Additional concepts, reflecting physical phenomena—electric charge, temperature, entropy, and so on—also manifest themselves in terms of combinations of fundamental quantities.

No such fundamental quantities—reflecting, presumably, the very essence of "objective reality"—are available for constructing psychological theory. Only rarely can psychological events be directly related to fundamental physical quantities. Reaction times are one example. There are not many others.

The most important acts of quantification associated with experimental psychology are those of counting. This procedure permits the statistician and the mathematical model builder to bypass the problems of measurement and of scaling relating to the processing of raw data. (Measurement and scaling of *inferred* quantities assumed to underlie these data are a separate problem, which I will mention later.)

The counting of events, the most frequently used "measurement" procedure in experimental psychology, has coaxed psychology out of the introspective and speculative mode into the realm of empirical science. At the same time, this procedure provides opportunities to form links between the analytic and the holistic approach.

To begin with the simplest example, the experiments with bar-pressing and maze-running rats represent a link of this sort. Quantification of data amounts to counting bar-pressings, correct and wrong turns, and the like. These are "objective"data. The bar-presses and turns right or left must be recognized as such, however. Usually these acts of recognition present no problems, but the fact that recognition is involved focuses attention on situations where problems do arise. To recognize an "act of aggression," for example, or some other manifestation of affect, whether in an animal or a human being, is not as simple as to recognize a predefined "right" or "wrong" response to stimuli. Furthermore, questions arise whether what the experimenter regards as an instance of particular stimulus is what the subject (especially a nonhuman one) also regards as a similar "unit event."

The natural solution of problems associated with quantification in psychology—namely, via counting events—opened the way for the construction of mathematical models (usually stochastic ones) of behavioral phenomena, thus providing links to the methodology of the exact science with its emphasis on the hypotheticodeductive method. On the other hand—because, in order to be counted, events have to be recognized and consistently classified by independent observers—psychology still remained anchored in holistic acts of cognition. In fact, the necessity of establishing consensus about classification of events raised problems peculiar to psychological investigations and preserved the focal points of that discipline.

This amounts to an operationalization of intuited psychological concepts. All psychological tests, where the measures are essentially obtained by counting coded items (problems solved on I.Q. tests, questions answered one way or another on personality tests, and so on) essentially reflect operationalizations of this sort. Of course, questions are constantly raised whether the tests actually measure what they purport to measure. Such questions can be answered only by indicating what one expects from an "appropriate" measurement, and therein lies the difficulty. If one knew, one would not need to invent indicators for imponderable aspects of the psyche.

This, then, is one area of psychology where advances (in the scientific sense) are possible: finding observable indicators of the unobservable but strongly intuited aspects of the inner life of humans and other animals. To what extent advances in this area have actually been realized, only time will tell. There is an understandable tendency to hail new, fresh approaches as "breakthroughs," especially if they provide opportunities for a plethora of studies, each suggesting the next. One must keep in mind that science—once a calling pursued only by dedicated and, for the most part, creative eccentrics—has now been institutionalized as a profession with well-defined routines and outlooks for promotion, where production of publishable papers is often a decisive factor. Competence is generally required of the professional scientist, but hardly more. This transformation of the scientist from a creator to a producer has released a torrent of publications, growing exponentially.

This development is not necessarily deplorable. To begin with, it probably does much less harm than many other types of mass production I can think of. And it does happen that someone somewhere comes upon a fruitful vein and initiates a genuine advance. On the negative side is the difficulty of discerning these nuggets in the avalanche of pedestrian research.

A case in point is the vast proliferation of papers in experimental social psychology. In the early 1950s a series of ingenious experiments by Asch (1956) povided a dramatic demonstration of social conformity. Subjects expressed judgments about comparative lengths of lines that could not possibly have been in accord with what they saw, presumably only because others had given incorrect answers. The fruitfulness of this line of investigation immediately became apparent, since the degrees of conformity could easily be quantified and related to a variety of experimental conditions. Unfortunately, this experimental technique involves the use of deception —namely, the participation of confederates in the experiment masquerading as fellow subjects. In this instance, deception was unavoidable. Regrettably, however, the use of deception became firmly incorporated in the standard procedure of experimental social psychology. The technique is, in fact, seductive. It makes it appear that it is easy to probe into the deepest crevices of motivations and prejudices of human beings by the simple expedient of making them believe they are in one situation when they are really in another.

Experiments Free of Deception: 2 × 2 Games

Unavoidably, serious ethical questions arose in connection with the practice of deception. Presumably, they were resolved by the requirement that the subjects be debriefed following an experiment. This practice may allay pangs of conscience but has the unfortunate side effect that the subject pool (consisting overwhelmingly of college students, and psychology students at that) is becoming progressively more suspicious, tending to take for granted that there is something phony about *any* psychological experiment. Not only does this give psychology a bad name, but it also introduces an attitudinal factor that may distort results. A correction of this condition—that is, an invention of a technique for social-psychological experiments free of deception—would, in my opinion, constitute a methodological advance in the sector of scientific psychology concerned with the problem of bringing empirical investigations to bear on concepts and conjectures of genuine psychological interest.

The use of experimental games represents, I believe, a modest step in this direction. Admittedly, this may reflect a personal bias, since for the past twenty years I have been concerned with experiments of this sort, using the simplest conceivable games, the so-called 2 × 2 games, in which each of two players must choose independently between two alternatives, the outcome being determined by the pair of choices and associated with a pair of payoffs, one to each player. It has been shown (Rapoport and Guyer 1966) that if the four possible payoffs to each subject, given on an ordinal scale, are all distinct, there are seventy-eight distinct types of games of this sort. If indifference with regard to some outcomes is permitted, there are 732 types (Guyer and Hamburger, 1968). Collection of data on such games, therefore, could employ an army of investigators for years. The results appear to be of psychological interest, inasmuch as the choice of one or the other strategy cannot be justified on grounds of "rationality" alone (except in a very few types of games). In most games, the subject is under conflicting pressures to choose one alternative or the other. These pressures are generated not only by assumptions of how the other player may choose, but also by attitudes toward the other, by the relative weight assigned to individual or collective interests, by the degree of realization that in some cases the giving of higher priority to collective interest actually results in a greater advantage to the individual than acting in accordance with clear individual interest, and so on. Attitudes of trust and suspicion, benevolence and malevolence, prudence and rashness, as well as assumptions about these predilections in the co-player, have been operationalized and incorporated in the structures of 2 × 2 games.

This experimental technique has two distinct virtues. First, a datum—that is, a choice of an alternative—is obtained in a matter of seconds. Thus very large volumes of data can be collected quickly and cheaply; and, because of its sheer volume, this mass of data can be expected to be statistically stable and thus to warrant some general conclusions about how patterns of behavior—reflecting attitudes, assumptions, motivations, and so on—depend on whatever independent variables one chooses to single out for attention. Second, the choices occur so rapidly that the subject can be expected to act more or less impulsively and thus to reveal an actual inclination without giving any thought to the process. Thus deception in the sense of misrepresenting the situation can be avoided.

The use of massed data produced by masses of subjects in effect focuses attention on the composite subject rather than on individuals. This is unavoidable since statistical stability is an indispensable requirement when results are produced by rapid decisions, necessarily subjected to chance fluctuations. There is no reason, however, that this composite subject cannot become an object of investigation in its own right. The nature of this subject can be varied easily indeed in a controlled manner, by varying its composition—that is, by tapping pools differing in sex, age, cultural background, predilections determined by other tests, and so on. The experimental results could then establish connections between three groups of variables: the profile of the composite subject (which can be deliberately constructed); experimental conditions (structure of games, magnitudes of payoffs); and a multitude of dependent variables—namely, the statistical properties of the patterns of choices, to be interpreted in terms of inclinations as described earlier.

In this way, the method of experimental psychology is carried far beyond its origins in psychophysics, rote learning, simple memory tasks, and so on, without losing its anchorage in disciplined scientific procedure. A bridge is being built, so to speak, from scientific psychology to interesting psychology.

The Gap Between Experiment and Introspection

When we look at the gap between rigorously empirical and introspective-intuitive conceptions of psychological inquiry, from the other end, as it were, the prospects are not nearly as bright. One would like to list the achievements of Freud as the greatest advances ever achieved in psychology. One dares not, however, for lack of a guarantee that the whole edifice may not one day come crashing down. Psychoanalytic investigation and others conducted in the same spirit are more reminiscent of a system of paranoid delusions than of building blocks of a scientific theory, in the sense that the construction of a holistic picture of a personality or of a case typically involves compulsive selection of details confirming favored conjectures. Where does one draw the line between paranoid delusion and exquisite sensitivity to apparently trivial but in fact highly significant signals? Did Mendeleyev exhibit a paranoid fixation when he riveted his attention on the periodicity in the properties of elements arranged in the order of their atomic weights?

To take another example, I recall Edmund Wilson's review of Pasternak's novel *Doctor Zhivago*, in which he discovered allusions to the martyred dragon-slayer Saint George. Zhivago's given name was Yuri, the Russian form of George. At one time, it seems, there was a belief that St. George was martyred after arguing with Emperor Diocletian (to which the polemic between Zhivago and Strelnikov was, according to Wilson, an allusion). The dragon is alluded to in a vague awareness of a monster in the cellar of the house where Zhivago and Lara have taken refuge. Finally, one of the poems ascribed by Pasternak to Zhivago is explicitly about St. George.

How much credence can be given to a conjecture based on such skimpy evidence? On the other hand, if Wilson's guess was correct, how can we dismiss such remarkable perceptiveness as irrelevant to "reliable knowledge" on the grounds that it violates all the tenets of "scientific method"?

The final example concerns Samuel Clemens' works built around the theme of mistaken identity or twinning. *The Prince and the Pauper* is the best-known example. There are several others: the mixed-up babies in *Pudd'nhead Wilson*; the twins involved in a murder mystery in *Tom Sawyer, Detective*; *The Interview*, in which the humorist tells the bewildered reporter that as a baby he got mixed up with his twin brother in a bathtub and drowned, so that he is not he but his twin brother; the Italian twins in *Pudd'nhead Wilson*, who in another unpublished story appear as a two-headed monster. The clinching evidence of Clemens's split personality is his choice of pen-name: Twain.

A skeptic might point out that mistaken identity was a hackneyed theme exploited ad nauseam in American popular literature, so that Clemens's choice of pseudonym may well have been a coincidence. Perhaps. But what if these symptoms do add up to a key to Mark Twain's ambivalent personality, an amalgam of misanthropy and compassion? Can we afford to neglect the introspective-intuitive mode of cognition when we pursue psychological investigations that are supposed to shed light on humanity's inner life?

Mendeleyev's insight was vindicated in the best scientific tradition when the gaps in his table were filled by newly discovered elements with the expected properties. But how can insight be separated from delusion in areas explored by depth psychology?

I have mentioned the fascinating experiment with the enuretic girls. It could, of course, have been followed up. If the results had been established as credible (that is, if coincidence could have been safely ruled out), the way might have been opened to putting the conjectures of depth psychology on a firm scientific footing. That is, a bridge from the other side—from introspective-intuitive psychology to positivistic psychology—would have been started.

Mathematical Psychology: From Speculation to Scaling

Here, then, is the other potentially promising direction of advances in psychology: the development of methods of putting under jaundiced-eyed scrutiny the fascinating speculations about the unconscious as a determinant of personality and behavior; about dreams as symbolic representations of repressed desires; about vestiges of instincts, submerged under the veneer of culture or sublimated into an infinitely rich variety of activities, strivings, skills, and beliefs.

Surely more than enough has been written about these matters, but so far these speculations cannot be distinguished from the freewheeling prescientific fantasies about the universe, the origin of humanity, or the human fate. This is unfortunate. People's inner life is too important and too interesting to be left to the admittedly rich but largely irresponsible improvisations of speculative psychologists or to be declared as beyond the reach of scientific psychology. Neither the tabula rasa dogma nor the primacy of biological determinants of human behavior is based on solid evidence. There is no reason to suppose that in becoming human, man has completely divested himself from the rich repertoire of instincts demonstrable in all other animals with nervous systems. On the other hand, to seek genetic determinants of culture in spite of the conspicuous plasticity of human behavior and convincing evidence of nongenetic inheritance of culture seems to be in pursuit of phantoms. It is high time to examine these questions soberly and to construct theories based on solid evidence.

One area of psychology where genuine and steady advances can be pointed out is mathematical psychology. The concern of mathematical psychologists is only partly with the construction of testable mathematical models of psychological phenomena. Most emphasis is put on problems of measurement and scaling.

We said at the outset that problems of measurement were bypassed in quantitative psychology by resorting to counting events, in particular units of behavior—for example, bar-presses, choices among available alternatives, answers on filled-out questionnaires. Implicitly, however, these numbers are thought to represent some *underlying* quantities—habit strengths, intensities of preference, prominence of certain personality traits, and so on.

Consider, for example, the relative frequency of answering "Stimulus x is larger than stimulus s" when a subject is asked to compare the stimuli. If the objective (that is, physical) magnitudes of the two stimuli are sufficiently disparate, the subject will answer one way or the other with certainty. If the difference is small, however, he may answer "x is larger" with a probability that increases monotonically as x becomes even larger compared with s.

Probabilistic fluctuations reveal errors or inconsistencies on the part of the subject. Whereas in the exact sciences, errors of measurement are a nuisance, in mathematical psychology they are a boon, since they suggest ways to construct a subjective scale of magnitude corresponding to the objective scale associated with the physical magnitude of objects. This subjective scale reflects the subject's actual perception of the objective magnitudes (intensity, brightness, loudness, weight). His errors or inconsistencies result from random fluctuations superimposed on the subjective perceptions.

Determination of subjective scales is not limited to stimuli that have obvious objective magnitudes, such as light, sound, or pressure. The method can be used to obtain subjective scales for series of stimuli that have no corresponding objective magnitudes—for example, a scale of aesthetic preference for a series of paintings or a subjective scale for the relative seriousness of crimes or degrees of agreement with a series of statements.

A direct way of establishing such scales would be to ask the subject to arrange the stimuli, objects, statements, or crimes, in an appropriate rank order. This procedure, however, may be inadequate because of inconsistencies in the ordering—for example, intransitivity of the supposed ordering relation or varying judgments on different occasions. Another weakness of the procedure is that it reveals at best only a rank ordering of the objects, not a stronger measure. For example, a person may declare that he considers murder a more serious crime than robbery and robbery more serious than embezzlement. From this information, however, one cannot learn whether the subject regards the difference in seriousness between murder and robbery as larger or small than the difference between robbery and embezzlement. Techniques based on the theory of measurement and scaling sometimes provide answers to such questions.

In consequence, what is being revealed is the structure of perceptive space. Fechner, who could be justifiably called the father of mathematical psychology, regarded his major work (Fechner 1860) as a contribution to the solution of the mind-body problem. In retrospect, I would certainly regard this work as an advance in psychology: the building of a bridge between the subjective and the objective, between awareness and reality.

Recent ramifications of measurement and scaling techniques include multidimensional scaling, a procedure related to factor analysis and serving a similar goal: making manifest a multidimensional structure, be it of intelligence, of an attitudinal field, of perception, or of value. Multidimensional scaling can be applied more generally than factor analysis because, unlike the latter, it does not depend on normality of underlying random variables.

Advances in Mathematical Modeling

The so-called classical mathematical models associated with physical theory are for the most part dynamic. Typically they are constructed on the basis of differential equations, where time is the independent variable. A model of this sort is usually predictive: Given an initial state of some system, its trajectory, that is, the course of its future states is deduced as a solution of a differential equation or a system of such equations. The model is tested by comparing the deduced predictions with observations.

As mathematical methods were extended to the behavioral sciences, attention shifted to static models, aimed at structural descriptions rather than at predictions. Factor analysis, introduced by L. L. Thurstone (1935) and multidimensional scaling, introduced by R. N. Sheppard, generate models of this sort. The so-called unfolding models, developed by Coombs (1964) and his collaborators are other examples. The basic problem addressed by these *structural* models is the following: Given a set of elements and relations among them, what is a space of the smallest number of dimensions required to embed these elements as points, so that the given relations among them are preserved? In factor analysis, the elements are variables characterizing members of a population, and the relations are correlations among these variables across the population. When the elements are embedded in a space, the correlations correspond to cosines of angles between vectors representing the variables. In multidimensional scaling, the relations are distances between pairs of elements. After embedding, the rank order of the distances is expected to be preserved. In unfolding models, some elements may be subjects, some objects. The relations are the subjects' preferences for the objects. After embedding, the distances from the subjects to the objects are supposed to reflect their preferences, the most preferred object being closest.

The power of a mathematical model is in its "portability." It can be transferred from any content to a structurally similar one. Structural similarity entails an isomorphism or a homomorphism between the corressponding sets of elements and relations. For example, the unfolding model, originally developed in psychological contexts, was recently applied by Levine (1972) in a structural analysis of the industrial-financial world. Fourteen large U.S. banks were cast in the role of "subjects" and seventy large industrial concerns as "objects." The distance from a subject to an object was defined in terms of the number of persons who served on the boards of both enterprises ("interlocking directorates"), distance being inversely related to the number of common directors. It turned out that this large system with 980 "distances" could be embedded in a three-dimensional space, where the banks were 14 points on the inner of two concentric spheres, and the 70 industrial concerns points on the outer sphere. Cones projected from the common center of the two spheres to include a bank and a set of industrials in its interior became a geometric representation of the "spheres of influence" of the fourteen banks.

Conceivably the model could be tested by comparing the "spheres of influence" so determined with some behavioral criteria of influence, such as policy decisions. However, the main thrust of models of this sort is not prediction but "understanding," which in the light of these models can be gained independently of predictive power. Surely the "geometrization" of the relations between banks and industrials, which displays the totality of these relations in a compact picture, contributes to "understanding" in the same way as a geographic map contributes to the understanding of important characteristics of a region. For instance, the picture distilled from the given situation could be compared with other pictures of this sort. Or a series of such pictures could be "taken" in a historical period to serve as frames in a film, whereby the history of a portion of the industrial-financial world would become "visible." Botanists employ a similar technique by producing films of growing plants in which months or years are condensed into seconds to reveal the process in its totality. Conceivably the same could be done with spatial models of personality.

An attempt of this sort was made in the 1950s. The instrument was the so called semantic differential, introduced by Osgood and his collaborators (Osgood, Suci, and Tannenbaum 1957), essentially an application of factor analysis to affective connotations of words. It turned out that three factors account for most of the variance of these connotations. The factors define a good-bad axis, a strong-weak axis, and a quick-slow axis. A subject's connotative space is constructed from the subject's evoked connotative associations by assigning a position to each of twenty affect-laden words—*self, love*, *sex*, *death*, and so on—in the space spanned by the three axes.

As has been said, the value of these constructions is the opportunity they offer for comparisons. The semantic-differential model was used to construct connotation spaces for each of the three personality manifestations of the central figure in a much publicized split-personality case, described in a study entitled *The Three Faces of Eve* (Thigpen and Cleckley 1954). Descriptions of the three personae, composed by examining the three-dimensional connotation spaces, agreed closely with independent descriptions made on the basis of clinical findings.

Subsequent evidence threw some doubt on the genuineness of this case. It has been pointed out that the "three faces of Eve" may have been induced by hypnotic suggestions on the part of the therapist. Indeed, psychoanalytic insights have also been suspected of having been induced by a sort of mutual hypnosis involving both the patient and the therapist.

We have already pointed out some disturbing similarities between the methods of depth psychology and paranoid delusions. However, it is just such delusions that rigorous structural analysis is designed to forestall.

Combining Imagination and Rigor: General Systems Theory

To reiterate my conception of advance in the social sciences and in psychology in particular, it centers on the integration of creative imagination, indispensable for understanding events involving human behavior, with analytic rigor in the construction of theories; and the primacy of empirical cognition in evaluating substantive theories, indispensable in all science.

Such an integration is aimed at in attempts to construct a general theory of systems. The general systems approach depends heavily on the theoretical exploitation of analogies—for example, between living systems on various levels of organization, such as cells, organisms, institutions, and societies, or between evolutionary processes of widely different content, such as biological evolution, evolution of languages, and evolution of artifacts. Now conceptualizations based on analogies are often justifiably dismissed as naive. However, all theories are in the last analysis based on analogies, since all of them involve some form of generalization. So taking a critical stance with regard to the use of analogies really amounts to distinguishing between true and false analogies or between fruitful and sterile analogies. The most convincing analogies are those based on mathematical isomorphisms—for instance, between a harmonic oscillator and an electrical system with impedance, resistance, and capacitance; or between the disintegrations of the atoms of a radioactive element and fatalities due to kicks of horses in Prussian cavalry regiments. At the other extreme are irresponsible speculations such as the parallel drawn between war and sex on the grounds that both have to do with penetration, or on the play on words connecting the "dirty" H-bomb and "dirty jokes." Between these two extremes lies a spectrum. I see advances in social sciences as bringing more analogies under the aegis of substantiated structural analysis.

In particular, the generalization of the concept of *organism* proposed in general system theory seems to me a fruitful idea. In light of this generalization we can, perhaps, see the reason for the dismal failure of Sheldon Amos's prognoses regarding the future of war. It appears that Amos was guided by a false analogy, assuming that increased reliance on rational problem-solving conspicuous in the nineteenth century would spread also to coping with problems arising from dysfunctional adaptations to the social and semantic environment.

On the other hand, the analogy between institutions and organisms suggests that institutions in the process of their evolution tend to become autonomous—that is, to acquire a life of their own that may be quite unrelated to their original function.

The War Machine as a Parasitic System

Military establishments are institutions of this sort. In fact, because of strong positive feedbacks among supposedly rival military establishments, it makes sense to conceive of the entire global war machine as a single organic system, or else as a number of organisms in symbiotic relationship with each other, since the existence of each is continually justified by the existence of others. This superorganism has a clearly discernible relationship to the system in which it is embedded (that is, humanity)—namely, the relationship of a parasite to its host. Perhaps a malignant growth would be a more apt designation, since a host's defensive mechanisms (for example, antibodies) can usually be mobilized against an invading parasite but not against malignant cells, whose proteins are recognized as one's own.

How far can the analogy be pursued? Does this organism, feeding on resources that might otherwise be available to nourish its host, have a "psychology"? The answer depends, of course, on how we choose to define *psychology*. We can be sure, however, that if the global war machine does have a psychology, it is not the sum total of the psychologies of its components—that is, the vast infrastructure of people and institutions that serve it. To paraphrase the holists' slogan, "the whole cannot be inferred from the nature of its parts." Least of all does it resemble normal human psychology, in which one usually finds an admixture of love, hate, reverence, compassion, humor, humility. These categories are completely foreign to the psychological makeup of the global war machine. By *psychological makeup* I mean the processes that preserve the continued identity of a *self* and determine reactions to stimuli.

There is ample evidence of energetic resistance on the part of the war machine to all attempts to curb its growth, of its insatiable appetite, and above all of its total maniacal preoccupation with efficiency of destruction. Aside from power-crazed psychopaths like Stalin or Hilter, there are hardly any human beings with a psychological makeup as hostile to what one normally regards as humane traits. Yet the machine continues to function—that is, to prepare for the final suicidal cataclysm—because human beings who constitute its key components act in accordance with its needs and goals. Increased understanding of how this comes about and how to cope with phenomena of this sort would, in my opinion, constitute a major advance in social science and in psychology.

Not Social Inventions but Social Awareness

It will, perhaps, have been noticed that in listing some advances and projecting possible future ones, I did not mention social inventions or problem-solving techniques, made available in the developing social sciences and in psychology. The reason is that although some such social inventions and techniques can be identified, I consider them of comparatively minor importance because their range of application does not extend to the overwhelming problems that confront humanity at present. The main reason for this limitation, it seems to me, is the tenacious viability of obsolete and dysfunctional institutions, of which I have cited war and its attendant technology and infrastructure as the most conspicuous example. Instead, I have subsumed under advances in social science those developments that serve to enlighten rather than to empower. In other words, I take the ancient admonition "Know thyself" quite seriously and extend it to the social domain—the development of an awareness of social structures and social dynamics, which may yet liberate people from self-destructive compulsions. One effect of this awareness might be the withdrawal of legitimacy from ossified dysfunctional institutions.

There is, of course, nothing new in this conceptualization of progress, except perhaps for one element: the role accorded to the rigorously scientific mode of cognition, extended far beyond its original habitat at the interface between humans and their physical environment. Related to this tenet is the conviction that it is not sufficient simply to transfer the paradigm of the natural sciences to the social sciences, as is sometimes urged by enthusiasts of a unified "scientific method." What is needed is an amalgam of imagination and scepticism, engagement and detachment, freedom and discipline in pursuit of knowledge.

References

Amos, S. *Political and Legal Remedies for War*. New York: Harper Bros, 1880.

Asch, S. E. "Studies of Independence and Conformity. I. A Minority of One Against a Unanimous Majority." *Psychological Monographs 70* No. 416(1956): 1–70.

Coombs, C. *A Theory of Data*. New York: Wiley, 1964.

Fechner, G. T. *Elemente der Psychophysik*. Leipzig: Breitkopf und Haertel, 1860.

Guyer, M., and Hamburger, H. An Enumeration of All 2 × 2 Games. *General Systems 13* (1968):205–208.

Levine, J. H. The Sphere of Influence. *American Sociological Review 37* (1972):14–27.

Osgood, C. E.; Suci, G. J.; and Tannenbaum, P. H. *The Measurement of Meaning*. Urbana: University of Illinois Press, 1957.

Rapoport, A., and Guyer, H. A Taxonomy of 2 × 2 Games. *General Systems 11* (1966):203–214.

Thigpen, C. H., and Cleckley, H. A Case of Multiple Personality. *Journal of Abnormal and Social Psychology 49* (1954):135–151.

Thurstone, L. L. *Vectors of the Mind: Multiple-Factor Analysis for the Isolation of Primary Traits*. Chicago: University of Chicago Press, 1935.

Discussion

(Cohen, Eisenstadt, Inkeles)

Edited by Andrei S. Markovits

Is Science Prediction? or Rigorous Understanding?

I.B. COHEN began the formal questioning by going back to an earlier remark that the ability to *predict* is what makes an undertaking scientific. Prediction was a necessary part of understanding. Plato, Kant, Comte, and many others saw in this aspect of the physical sciences the highest ideal of science. One could make all knowledge increasingly mathematical, increasingly similar to physics, and more capable of making predictions. This point of view went back a long way in philosophical and scientific thinking.

On the other hand, Cohen said that the great revolution in biology in the nineteenth century—Darwin's theory, to which Rapoport referred—was not only not predictive in the foregoing sense, but was also based on a concept that made it impossible to be predictive in one important area. This was the area of "population thinking," which Ernst Mayr has called the most radical part of Darwin's thinking. (Cohen explained that in this area one looked at the process of variation and the departure from ideal types, giving a mathematical distribution of individual characteristics reproducible in the sexual process.)

Regardless of whether evolutionary theory might change or be replaced, Cohen claimed that this raises an important issue—namely, that since Darwin, evidently "there is a part of the sciences which follows the traditional physical model, and another part in evolutionary biology which does not." Yet he sensed that there was a general feeling in the social sciences, which Rapoport seemed to share, that accepted the physical model as the highest level of science and as the model that ought to be followed by all true social scientists. This could well be true, but Cohen wondered on what basis Rapoport would make such a statement.

Rapoport replied that he thought he had made it clear in his presentation that he did not believe in such a conception of science. Cohen asked why, then Rapoport had made a statement that it was prediction that made science "scientific"?

Rapoport explained that he made that remark as a description of science in the classical sense, but that he had also referred to elements of understanding that had little to do with prediction. He had specifically mentioned evolutionary theory, but he could also name others.

For example, he pointed to the Arrow "impossibility theorem." "What does it predict?" Absolutely nothing, because it is not based on data. Rather, it was a rigorous analysis that led to the following conclusion: "If one demands from a process of collective decision that it will have four specific characteristics, the only such process. . . is a dictatorship. If one adds another demand, namely that the decision not be dictatorial, then the axioms will turn out to be incompatible with each other." Although this theorem had nothing to do with prediction, however, Rapoport argued that it yielded a profound understanding of what we can mean by democratic processes, and that it was a critique of much irresponsible talk.

Another example was Jeremy Bentham's goal of "the greatest good for the greatest number." If one analyzed a statement like that, one would find that it meant nothing—or, perhaps, a great many things. Did it mean the greatest good per capita, or did it mean minimizing the variance of the distribution? To know exactly what it meant, it was necessary to go into it more deeply. For that kind of rigorous logical analysis, the highest expression and most brilliant techniques had been developed in mathematics.

Rapoport emphasized that mathematics was not predictive but analytic. Geometry predicted nothing unless it was translated into physical geometry. If one had a geometry of five-dimensional space and there were no physics accompanying it, it would nevertheless still be valid—and still give one an understanding of things.

Rapoport said his entire point was to try to legitimate the holistic approach, especially in psychology and in other social sciences—but in a form that was cleansed of mysticism, irresponsibility, and facile babble. He argued he was trying to make psychology scientifically respectable, as defined in the following way:

"Scientific respectability does not necessarily mean dealing with data and predicting on the basis of data—that is only one part of science. There is another part of science, of which mathematics is the highest expression, and that is complete logical rigor and clarity."

So psychological terms should mean exactly what they say and nothing else, and this was what characterized advances in psychology and the social sciences. The kind of descriptions that were given in metric analysis, in category theory, in Campbell's theory of myths, and so on, Rapoport said, predicted nothing; but they provided pictures of social events and social phenomena that assisted understanding. This did not mean they did not have to be tested, but it meant they gave a toehold in understanding that was not available from mountains of data that actually said nothing.

Criteria for Advances in Psychology

Shmuel Eisenstadt asked whether Rapoport considered this kind of mathematical development combined with analysis of certain data to be the only type, or the major type, of advance in psychology. He said that, as an outsider, he was interested in changes in perspective, or what he called *Problemstellungen.* He mentioned a recent paper by Jerome Bruner with data on the way small children developed skills at social interaction—creating what he called a great revolution in psychology; would this be considered an advance? Bruner said there was a revolutionary movement in psychology beginning about 1970, which moved from an emphasis on context. Eisenstadt wanted to know Rapoport's attitude toward this kind of work: What would be his criteria for the kind of work Bruner was doing?

Rapoport replied that he would certainly include that kind of work among the major advances in psychology, along with the insights of Jean Piaget, which seemed to be of the same order. These advances conferred understanding, which in many cases could be translated into equations and experimentation.

Eisenstadt said he still could not get from Rapoport's argument a clear picture of exactly what constituted advances in psychology. Rapoport responded that time limitations had prevented him from going deeply into the content of psychological problems, but that he considered Bruner's work an advance because it was in tune with a number of similar reformulations. The deemphasis of "traits" and emphasis on "context" was analogous to the emphasis on properties and relations in Rapoport's own work. Similarity, in political science, we were witnessing a deemphasis on national traits and an emphasis on social relations.

Eisenstadt said that if that were so, then a crucial aspect of advances had to be conceptual rethinking, not just methodology. Only when methodology served the purpose of merging conceptual rethinking with some data did it become an advance. He felt, however, that it was precisely on this matter of the importance of conceptual thinking that Rapoport's arguments were silent.

Rapoport replied that in psychology, mathematical psychology had provided a definite case of conceptual rethinking. It involved a change in emphasis from the classical type of mathematical model formulation, experimentation, and prediction, to the problem of what it meant to measure a psychological variable. This was a fundamental narrowing down of the problem. Fechner had thought that this was the solution to the mind/body problem. Rapoport said that that was perhaps exaggerated, but that it was fundamental to find relationships between objective magnitudes and subjective evaluations of them. The ability to quantify the subjective, in a hard manner and not simply through speculation, was a fundamental advance, despite the fact that it was largely a methodological advance.

Are New Perspectives Enough?

Alex Inkeles said he was not sure whose side he was on in this debate. He felt, however, that if one said that we need both a correct perspective and a commensurate methodology to test it and reevaluate it, this seemed obvious and not really open to argument. Yet the separation of the two parts in no way insured an advance—particularly with regard to sociology. Often people thought they had achieved an advance merely because they had changed their perspective. For example, people worked for years with the "organismic" view, and then one found that it no longer appeared in the textbooks; they contained "conflict theory" instead. Inkeles argued that if this perceived change were stripped away, it would be difficult to claim there was very much more known in the latter view than in the former.

He said the real issue was whether or not the changed perspectives were productive, which of course raised the question of what could be considered productive. In sociology, *productive* was often taken to mean further eleboration of an original concept that was then broken down into more and more special and complex forms. Whether there was actually any increase in substantive knowledge—either in the cumulative way, or in the sense that there was a problem that could now be solved that could not have been solved before—was a highly doubtful proposition.

Inkeles suggested that this raised an interesting empirical question: "If you had to do without them, what would be the value of a fifth, sixth, or seventh model or perspective—as against a fifth, sixth, or seventh way of measuring something in the social system which we previously could not measure?" He said it was clear to him, at least in sociology, which side one ought to take. He argued that what sociologists should develop was the new way of measurement, because even though it was often said that sociologists were rich in fact and poor in theory, it seemed to Inkeles actually to be the other way around. Most sociologists spent their time elaborating concepts that never got systematically evaluated in empirical reality, while the world went on completely independent of what sociologists thought or did.

Rapoport concluded the discussion by saying that he felt like the old rabbi to whom two parties came for a decision. He said: "One of them stated his case, and the rabbi said, 'You're absolutely right.' But then the second stepped forth and stated his case, upon which the rabbi said, 'You're absolutely right.' Then the rabbi's wife intervened and said, 'Look, how can you do that? You say 'You're absolutely right' to the one, and then to the other, yet each of them said entirely opposite things!'

"The rabbi turned to his wife and said, 'You know, you're absolutely right!' "

CHAPTER 15

The Limits of the Social Sciences: A Critique of the Conference

Daniel Bell

GIVEN KARL DEUTSCH'S DISTINCTION between large-scale research production and handicrafts, I sometimes feel as if I am the last artisan around. I've never had a research assistant in my life. I wouldn't know how to use one. I try to read and think, and I don't trust anybody to read and think for me. So I do not understand collective research.

From my standpoint, I find myself highly resistant to what is going on at this conference. In the last half hour I have been totally dismayed at the rapid rush, in which "advances" are being paraded as if this were a Paris fashion show and we were asked to select, so to speak, the best lines for display. I know that is a rather harsh statement, but let me put it in the following context.

We seem to be becoming subject again to what might be called the Derek Price phenomenon, where everything is placed along an exponential curve to see if it will take off. We are once more at the point where people say that "90 percent of all scientists who ever lived are alive today"—as if to imply also that 90 percent of all scientific advances have been made in our lifetime. Or where they say that in the last fifty years ten thousand new scientific journals have been published—although we rarely hear how many have survived.

The scientists and the kind of science produced now are not necessarily much better in quality than in previous times. Many of the scientists are little more than semiskilled technologists deep in the bowels of research organizations, and many of the journal articles are little more than emendations or elaborations of minor research. So we can rule out numbers of scientists as a criterion, and not be impressed by "breakthroughs" that have simply mobilized numbers.

Do the "Advances" Survive?

To avoid being overly querulous, however, let me use a slightly different perspective, talking not about major advances, but about major survivals. What are the conditions for something surviving? If I look over the "supplementary list" that has been handed out, it is simply a potpourri of new fields that people have gotten interested in, such as "peace research," or new gadgets such as "zero-base budgeting"; and it is all of a kind, with little sense of discrimination. I understand this must be the first round, but that is not the way to go about it.

Let me be more specific. If I think of the social sciences in the last twenty years, it seems to me the major task should be an assessment of failures, or of shortfalls, or or promises not realized. Take the list of Krelle in economics, for example. It overlaps the list I used for some other purposes in my monograph, on *Social Sciences since the Second World War*—game theory, econometrics, general equilibrium theory, micromotive theory, monetarism, Keynesian disequilibrium, business cycle theory, theory of allocation, theory of rational expectations—but most of these are contradictory to each other, crucially so. Many of them, such as game theory, represent promises unfulfilled. Moreover, many of them eclipse some of the others—as the theory of rational expectations, for example, eclipses some expectations aspects of Keynesian theory.

I think we also ought to raise the question: Why is it that if one looks back twenty or thirty years, there were a whole series of extravagant claims that have not been fulfilled? Cybernetics was once the vogue at Josiah Macy Foundation meetings, and people thought that with its discovery of feedback loops, it would be the key to understanding the nature of cognitive processes and social processes. Then there was "culture and personality theory,"whereby anthropologists and psychologists were going to match the modes of culture and personality structures that embodied them, Freudian ego theory, and "structural functionalism," and so on.

The most fascinating question, therefore, is not the question of advances, but of why these various synoptic, holistic, or synthetic theories that seemed to many people to be advances have become desiccated after so much promise and hoopla. That is the kind of question I would like to see raised in this book—not simply a multiplication of lists with different degrees of significance. How do we assess, and what are the criteria of assessment? These theories that people thought would become part of the bright book of life—why have so many of them gone lifeless? Why did they go wrong, why were they oversold—and will some of the things that are now being nominated in this way fail for the same reasons?

Holism? or Multiplicity?

There is one clue, perhaps, in the distinction that Bernard Cohen drew in Chapter 12 between what he called the two traditions—that of Comte and that of Quetelet. One tradition looks for overarching syntheses, and the other looks for distributional effects within populations and the way behavior is distributed in a given period of time. I think the conclusion is this: that most efforts at what might be called holistic theory tend to fail, for a variety of reasons. The phenomena may be recalcitrant by nature to that kind of effort, or the effort may be premature. More important, the changing structure of society limits the range of generalization, and it is difficult to define the "laws" of change.

As against Alex Inkeles's notion of the decrease of variability in cultural phenomena today—which is perhaps true on some micro levels—what is striking to me, especially on the political level, is the degree of unraveling of societies. This unraveling may be due to the fact that the old integrative structures, such as nation-states, have less coherence or less ability to meet new problems; or, more abstractly, there may be more emerging levels of complexity that are still unorganized.

I would argue along these lines that what we see increasingly is a mismatch of scales. With the changes that are taking place, there are larger and larger mismatches that make any single theory or any policy formula very difficult to put forward. On the largest level, for example, today we have an interdependent international economy, tied together in real time, so that there are capital flows, and currency flows, and now demographic flows that older boundaries cannot contain. At the same time we have national political structures that are locked into old units of sovereignty or administration and that no longer match the new economic scales or the new political demands.

As I said a few years ago in a somewhat facile remark, the nation-state has become too small for the big problems of life and too big for the small problems of life. It no longer matches the scale of important activities—neither the diversity of local needs and wants when people become more involved in society, nor the need to deal with larger macro actions.

Beyond this, it seems obvious to me that we have a widening of the *arena* of action as more and more people become actors in this world. The very multiplication of the number of actors who have a certain degree of consciousness, purpose, or interest introduces different levels of complexity and cross-cutting interactions. Any effort at making single, holistic theories may fail because such theories cannot grasp this multiplicity, this widening of the arena, and this mismatch of scales resulting from the maladaptation of different sectors.

Epistemological Issues

This may seem to be a rough, freehand, and even purple description of the social analytical problem. Behind it, however, is a set of epistemological issues. Let me take one such issue. All statements, or propositions, or explanations, or schemas are either historical or theoretical, using these terms in the sense of Popper's formulation. Historical statements are open-ended because one does not know where they may lead next. Statements are theoretical when one can close the system, either logically or empirically. Theory becomes effective only when we can close a system. This has been one of the strengths of neoclassical economics or general equilibrium theory. In closing a system, we have a sense of the complete range of the phenomena and of the parameters that are operative, so that we can have covering laws in the way that Hempel or Nagel has stipulated. Once we have a covering law and the initial conditions, we can derive predictions of phenomena.

I think it is becoming increasingly difficult to have closed systems in the social world—and this seems to me to be of epistemological significance. The best example may be that of neoclassical economics. This has been the prototype of a closed system in its ability to specify a powerful set of finite variables and the equations for their interaction. Its predictive power has become increasingly limited, however, by variables exogenous to that system, so that the economic model becomes less and less effective in dealing with the real-world problems it is supposed to be modeling.

I started out here with a judgment about the unravelings of society because of sociological changes in world social structures, but there is evidently an epistemological route to that judgment. Beyond that, there is a whole series of "crises" that have never come up in these discussions. Epistemology is at the source of our formulations because we have to justify the way in which we make theory, but there has been no discussion here of recent issues in the philosophy of science—such as the challenge by Toulmin and others, the issues of historicism, and the way in which the older sureties of the philosophy of science have been undermined. The only writer who was taken up was Kuhn, but Kuhn is part of a more general challenge to the traditional philosophy of science.

When I was a graduate student, Hempel and Nagel provided a "sure guide" to the distinctions between the natural and the social sciences. The argument they made was: Yes, the subject matters are different, but there has to be a common logic of explanation if the theories are to be science. Yet if the canons of the logic of explanation are themselves historically embedded—which is the kind or argument Toulmin makes—then one is thrown back into a relativism, a perspectivism, a historicism, or some argument that explanations are within—and are limited to—different cultural frames. If there are substantially different processes of explanation in the social sciences from those in the natural sciences, in what ways does this make the processes of discovery or the processes of constructing theory different?

I declare my interest. I do believe there are radical differences between modes of inquiry in the sciences, though not necessarily in the older forms of Dilthey or Rickert, although these are starting points. The differences are not just in subject matter, despite the fact that there *are* radical differences there. They are, rather, in the nature of judgments about phenomena (either constitutive or constructed, to use a modified neo-Kantian language), or about what one is searching for—either for invariance or for interpretation. Any elaboration of these terms, however, would take me far afield, and I would like to restrict myself to the agenda that has been given us.

Four Difficulties

The Medical Model

Take four questions that have come out of the discussions presented in this book to illustrate my point about the difficulties of making propositions in the social as against the natural sciences.

The first difficulty is that every time a problem is raised, we get what I would call—based on the approaches of Karl Deutsch and James Miller—the "medical model." That is, the problem is treated like that of a person who is ill, who has a particular ailment that is difficult to diagnose. Any single person is obviously different physiologically from any other person; yet there are general rules of diagnosis. The doctor tries a whole series of assessments, taking measurements of a particular kind, and finally makes a diagnosis based on the best knowledge he has. Similarly, then, the social analyst looking at the world takes samples, makes readings, and makes a diagnosis of the condition of the group or the institution, and so on.

When we were discussing science, Helga Novotny said, "But science is also a cultural system." Alex Inkeles said that no science can stand outside the history of the culture. If that is the case, then social science is even more a cultural system, for it is constructed, not constituted. The doctor is not an abstract, disembodied entity standing, so to speak, at a point of space outside looking in; he is within the process, and so the very terms he uses are part of a cultural history. In other words, one goes back to the challenge of historicism or perspectivism. This is not a question of relativism, because there are rules we can follow—if we know the standpoint.

The medical model and simplistic positivism are heirs to a naive nineteenth-century scientism that either assumed a "copy theory" of knowledge or assumed that there were fixed points "in space" from which an "outside" observer could make his findings, if he had the correct focusing power. There are no fixed coordinates in space, however, and no single vantage point. The observers are within the frame, and we have the problem of matching observations from different vantage points. Perspectivism therefore raises the question of equivalences, or what in physics are called transformation rules, and of how to translate observations from one vantage point into observations from other points.

In a simple geographical analogy, Europe from the viewpoint of Boston has a different configuration from Europe as seen from North Africa. This doesn't mean that it is all relativist, but just that at some point you have to make a set of equivalences. In physics the transformation rules take phenomena that are covariant within one inertial frame and make them invariant in all frames. Can we have transformation rules like this in the social world? Some people have tried to create them. Lévi-Strauss tried transformation rules in anthropology, which are at least metaphorically equivalent to the Lorentz transformations in relativity theory; by and large, however, this kind of theory tends to be eschewed in the social sciences.

Our nineteenth-century scientistic notion of the scientist or the analyst outside the system is very much like the viewpoint in the nineteenth-century novel, where there is an omniscient narrator who tells us what is going on. The later novelists decry that mode; it is too old-fashioned. It was not wrong, but it was a different perspective. A modern novel breaks up time and moves back and forth in time, be it from the viewpoint of the narrator or from the viewpoint of a character who is being observed. In social science we are still using an odd notion of inquiry, which seems to me quite inadequate in terms of leaving out more complicated and more sophisticated ways of understanding a social milieu.

Physics as the Model

The first difficulty, then, for propositions in the social sciences, is the difficulty of this medical model or naive scientism. The second difficulty is the similarly misleading idea of physics being the model. Here there are two subissues. One is the way physics derives its laws. Modern physics begins with the Galilean revolution. What Galileo did was to eliminate qualitative types and to look at the world as a unified field with a continuum of quantitative measurements. He then moved from the analysis of concrete phenomena to the abstract properties of bodies—mass, velocity, acceleration, and the like—and the equations among these. The phenomena were treated as homogeneous entities, which is why one could invent the calculus and manipulate these entities in a linear way. Modern economics, of the noninstitutional sort, operates in exactly the same way. It finds it difficult to deal with heterogeneity, either of markets or of qualities such as the skills of laborers; but it looks to uniform prices as a metric and to homogeneous entities as the units of exchange. Even Marx, in constructing his model of the capitalist economy in *Capital*—following also a Newtonian or Galilean mode—treated labor and capital as abstract homogeneous entities; and he based his equations, derived from the organic composition of capital (his version of what would later be called a production function), on such homogeneities. But can we, in seeking to understand the varieties and complexities of the "real world," be content with such an idea of homogeneity? Economists now are beginning to wrestle with a "simple" question such as the heterogeneity of markets.

The second subissue is the point, raised by Ernst Mayr, that the model of physics distorts the nature of generalization and theory construction in biology. Evolutionary biology proceeds essentially by statistical population distributions of individual items, or clusters of the types of individuals; but the old notion of *ideal type* or the *ideal form* or *essence* of a species (*essentialism*) is opposed by this "population thinking." In a recent article in *Science*, Mayr has attacked on these grounds the way that physicists understood biology. We can raise the question of whether the social sciences are not guilty of the same mistake when they emphasize modes of thinking that are powerful only because they have made their generalizations in terms of abstract homogeneous units or ideal types. Much depends on the *level* of generalization, but this is a question I will return to later.

Are Social Relationships Even Stable?

A third issue in the social sciences is one we all understand but that some of us compartmentalize or ignore: the question of how *stable* are the relationships we are observing. Earlier, Inkeles was talking about laws in the social sciences; and laws involve some notion of stable relationships. Then, however, as we were discussing the Middle East, Yehezkel Dror was saying that the situations were unstable, so how can we predict? It seems to me that the duration of stability one observes in the social world is highly shortened today, for a wide variety of reasons. One reason is the one I mentioned earlier—the widening of the arena where actions are taking place, with a multiplication of the number of actors and the velocity of interactions. Just at the combinatorial level, we are getting many more different kinds of situations.

If one looks again at the most powerful model in the social sciences—economics—almost all economic theories are built on some notion of stable relationships; increasingly, however, we find that these stable relationships are no longer operative. Economists say, Well, but these are not *economic* difficulties, they are political problems, which are exogenous to the system; yet even that is not true any longer. The whole point of "rational expectations" in economics is to assume we will constantly have unstable relationships. What Robert Lucas is trying to do about this is to build stochastic processes inside of his econometric models, so that he will not have to rely on the lagged data from previous fluctuations in predicting future values. But these are formal probabilities he uses, not empirical fluctuations. So this sharpens up the question of how stable the relationships are, when we talk first of laws and then of things being unstable. It seems to me there are different levels of stability, over different time periods and different kinds of social processes. One would have to go into field after field to deal with this Herculean labor of cleaning out one stable, so to speak, and then the others.

Models, or Maps?

The fourth question or difficulty, though similar to the others, is qualitatively distinct. It is this: that people talk of *modeling*—the word has been used often in this book—but it is never clear whether these are in fact models or maps. It seems to me there is a very real distinction between a model and a map. When a model tries to be a map, it tries to follow close to the contours of the phenomena being described. The closer it comes, the more we can claim accuracy in prediction. An econometric model today is really trying to be a map—"modeling" the economy by trying to get the *exact* relationships of inventory to investment to consumption, or to all the other interacting variables.

There are other kinds of models, however, that we know are not maps. There are mathematical models, for example, abstract models or conceptual models, often far removed and highly simplified compared to detailed mapping problems. They gain their strength through simplifications.

As I go through the lists we have been given, I find a constant reference back and forth, yet no effort to distinguish maps from models. It may well be that they are not completely distinct, but it seems to me there are problems. If relationships in the social world are less and less stable—a proposition that will have to be tested—then the idea of trying to model these relationships may become less useful, or we may have to think of modeling in a different way. In an essay I wrote in a book I edited on *The Crisis of Economic Theory*, I tried to argue that the strength of neoclassical economics comes from the logical working out of its postulates, which are optimization, equilibrium, markets, and rationality. With these four postulates, this is a very powerful model of logical or rational action, as long as we take it as a *fiction*, and not as a *map*—in other words, if we use it as a *model* in the older classical sense of the word, to mean a *standard* (like being a model person) rather than as a description.

With such an approach, rather than trying to map empirically the activities of a society, one could use the postulates of social science as a utopia, as a fiction, as an *als ob*, against which one measures the actual relationship. In other words, should we not retreat to the older notion of models as fictions or utopias? In the end perhaps one could even learn more about how changes do take place.

The Three Levels of Language

I would claim that many of our problems arise from the fact that we do not distinguish between the different *levels* of language and of analysis. This is an issue that is going to become more and more acute in social analysis in the next twenty or thirty years, for the major domain is going to become comparative analysis, and the question will be what "language" we have available for comparisons.

In the political arena, we now have 150 states with different configurations because of the different mix of peoples within each country, the different political and administrative forms, and the varying modes of economic organization. Thus we have a huge "laboratory" for seeing how particular policies operate under varying conditions. More and more, as we move into a genuine international economy, these questions of comparison of different national responses will become a focal point of inquiry. If the future belongs to a systematic, comparative analysis, then the question of language will become central.

I would say, arbitrarily for the moment, that there are three different kinds of language. The first language is the obvious one that historians or journalists use, the descriptive and denotative language. We look at situations in the terms that are *given* by the particular society in that particular time and place. So we talk about the United States and about a Congress and a president as features of the political system. In England, we talk about a prime minister and a Parliament. Clearly, however, if we want to compare the British and U.S. political systems, we cannot use these denotative terms. So we go to another level of abstraction—to what I call a sociographic language—and speak of executive and legislative functions, in order to find a framework for comparability when the specific forms are different.

In physics and in economics, we move to a third level of language, which I call formal-analytic, of the kind involved in Krelle's recent comment about the need to detach statements from institutions. In economics, for example, on a descriptive level we talk of tin, steel, rubber, the things that people make and produce; on a sociographic level, we talk about manufacturing, service, or agrarian activities. On a formal-analytic level, however, we talk about production functions—where capital and labor are abstract homogeneous entities, and where by specifying the coefficients of these functions and their magnitudes, we can determine what proportions of these abstract entities we employ as a mix in our investment or other use.

The problem for sociology—because there is no easy metric, or, as James Coleman put it, there is no "numeraire" like money—is that the effort to proceed to a formal analytical level becomes pure taxonomy. This was the case with the "pattern variable" constructed by Parsons, which was an effort to provide a language for what he thought was theory. Theory, for Parsons as for many sociologists, was an effort to close the system. This meant the specification of the least number of pair terms that would allow one to derive the widest range of possible types of social actions. So if you have four paired terms—*universalistic* and *particularistic*, *achieved* and *ascribed*, *neutral* and *affective*, *specific* and *diffuse*—you have a set that in cross-combination will allow you to include *any* kind of action; therefore you have a morphology of *all* kinds of actions.

In principle, this is no different from what Pareto tried to do with his combinations of residues (although Pareto went through only two of his seven stages), and what Simmel tried to do in a more metaphorical way, and what Peter Blau has tried to do in a narrower form, as I indicated earlier. It is essentially the effort to detach oneself from a sociographic level.

General Theories? or A Disjunctive World?

The curious thing is that sociology had won its place over the years precisely by concentrating on the sociographic level. For example, the introduction of the term *bureaucracy* is sociographic because it has an empirical referent and yet it is sufficiently abstract to allow one to look at a variety of contextual situations. What sociographic analysis cannot do, however, is to provide a *general* theory of society, or of social action. This is what social theorists, following the model of economics, or of classical physics, are constantly driven to try. But can they suceed?

The difficulty with the formal analytical notions—at least in sociology and, I am prepared to argue, in economics—is that by ignoring the contextual situations, there are few guides or decision rules for going back into social reality and dealing with it. Yet there seems to be some kind of compulsion, maybe a Comtean compulsion, to seek these large formal-analytical models or holistic theories, which in the end, I think, become more misleading than not.

I have to end by presenting my own personal mode of thinking about society, to show why I have become so vehement about holistic theories. I mean the theories of functionalism; or in Marxism the theories of totality that go back to Hegel—the notion that there are organized periods of time or cultures that have a kind of *Innerzusammenhangen*, an inner principle that holds them together.

As I think about the nature of the social world, I see it as radically disjunctive. It is so disjunctive that is it difficult to have a unity in any chronological period, even though that is what we too often tend to concentrate on. For example, Shmuel Eisenstadt was talking about the 1960s and the 1970s as if somehow these were integrated periods of time, rather than modalities in which we look at what is on the surface. Although we tend to think in chronological units, it seems to me that there is no *Innerzusammenhangen*, no unity, that defines periods—whether it is the sixteenth, the seventeenth, or the nineteenth centuries, or, in stylistic terms, the Baroque or Mannerist periods—and no unity that can relate them, as Spengler and Sorokin tried to do, to similar economic modes.

My reasoning is this: I think most social processes proceed on a double level, an insitutional level and a cultural level, and that in what goes on, there is often not a good match between the two. In technology, for example, there is a clear principle of change, the principle of substitution, when something is cheaper or better or more effective, so that we tend to use the new thing. In culture, however, there is no clear principle of change. Boulez does not replace Bach. We simply widen the imagination of mankind and both coexist; culture has never been lost, so to speak, and it does not become lost. It is subject to choice with different kinds of combinations, the mingling of tastes in a kind of syncretism. If this is so, there can be no "unity" of period, either in the crude Marxist sense of substructure and superstructure, or in the Durkheimian and Parsonian sense that particular values, such as the "achievement mode," integrate action at all levels of society.

I could take something much more fundamental, such as religion—which is the longest-lived of all the human systems we know, with the great religions, Confucianism, Buddhism, Hinduism, Judaism, Christianity, Islam, going back over millennial periods. Here the crucial point is that the processes of institutional change in religion are radically different from the processes of cultural or symbolic change. Almost every thinker of the Enlightenment, from Voltaire to Marx, from the middle of the eighteenth to the middle of the nineteenth century, assumed that religion would disappear in the twentieth century. They assumed it because of the spread of enlightenment, rationalism, or secularization; or, as contemporary sociologists thought, because the *demagification* of the world, in Weber's phrase, would lead to the end of religion.

This turns out not to be the case. We have had certain kinds of institutional decay of religions; yet we also have had cult revivals and serious efforts to find new kinds of religious belief or renewal. And this has been recurrent, whether it be in the Oxford Movement of Newman in England, or the personalism of Marcel and Mounier in France, or back in Germany the attack of Schleiermacher on the Enlightenment. All of these indicate, it seems to me, that there is an aspect of culture that draws its meanings and problems very differently from the institutional arrangements of society. This does not mean that each of these aspects is disembodied from the others. In the language of systems theory, however, the relationships are not strongly coupled, and I do not even think that coupling is the best way to think of it.

What I have been trying to argue here goes against the grain of the conference, and against the thrust of these various sessions. I trust I have not been churlish in saying these things at the very end, but this is the contribution I felt I could make.

Discussion

(Kruskal, Deutsch, Miller, Inkeles, Klingemann)

Edited by Andrei S. Markovits

WILLIAM KRUSKAL opened the discussion by saying he was curious about an apparent omission from Bell's list of distinctions between the natural and the social sciences. He said that in the social sciences there was also the important "Hawthorne effect"—the fact that human beings are capable of recognizing that they are being observed and of reacting to that situation.

Daniel Bell replied that he had taken that into account in referring to the "medical model" in the social sciences—the view that the researcher is assumed to be outside the whole operation, simply watching the action in a detached manner. Kruskal said he thought that referred to the observer—the person watching—not the person being watched. Bell said he was referring to both parties. Both were within the system together, and therefore there was nobody purely outside it.

Constitutive versus Constructive Phenomena

Karl Deutsch then wanted to enlarge the discussion. He said that certainly a very wise medicine man from Central Africa could say to a medical doctor in Berlin: "You are treating your patients within your cultural framework just as I treat my patients in mine, but you are both hopelessly tangled up in your West European medical culture—you and the patient—while I am not."

Deutsch said that the German doctor could have two answers to this. He could say: "But you are just another kind of doctor; you are tangled up in your African culture." Or else he could say: "How many of your patients survive? And how many of mine do?"

Deutsch suggested that most patients would be more interested in the answer to the second type of question. He said that they do not go to a doctor because they are fascinated by his cultural peculiarities, even though he may win them with a persuasive bedside manner—whether Western or African. In the end, however, what the patient wishes is to be better.

Deutsch wanted to emphasize that sometimes the healing could be purely organic, as with a broken bone that could be set; at other times there could be psychosomatic illness, involving parts of a person's mind and culture. Deutsch thought that Bell's observation of a biasing element in culture would depend on the respective proportions of these two kinds of illness.

In certain fields for certain problems, the cultural element could be overwhelming, whereas the nuts-and-bolts element would be negligible. Deutsch maintained, however, that when one asked, "How many babies were born?" or "How much food is going to be produced for the needs of these babies when they grow up?" or "What are their life expectancies?"—then the amount of information involved that was cross-cultural was very large. Deutsch thought that if Bell wanted more collaboration between the hermeneutic approach and the nuts-and-bolts approach, the proportions of these components in a given type of problem had to be more closely defined, so that the problem could be understood in all its cultural proportions.

Deutsch claimed that over the years many values had been found to be common among various cultures. In most cultures, mothers have a prejudice against their children dying; hungry people want to be fed; and most people have a deep-seated aversion against seeing their homes bombed to pieces. He said there are a vast number of common problems facing humankind that people of different cultures share "even if they do have a hell of a time coming to understand each other."

Bell said he wanted to reply because there seemed to be both a confrontation and a misunderstanding emerging. He had always been afraid of the medical model and had used it in his presentation only because it had surfaced several times during the conference. He did not think the problem concerned "proportions" in the least. Rather, there were two different kinds of phenomena at stake. To go back to the Kantian language, certain kinds of phenomena had a *constitutive* structure, which was there intrinsically in the order of things. It might be difficult to uncover that structure, but it was there, as a given—as in the case of a broken bone.

Other kinds of phenomena, however, were *constructive* notions that derived from meanings or from different perspectives but did not have a given order. They were created by human design. *This* was the relevant distinction, not the one between cultural and noncultural questions.

In Deutsch's example, Bell admitted, there was a universal test of how to set a broken bone, whereas if certain types of psychic illness were purely cultural, then the appropriate treatment would have to be derived from a particular culture. The difference in this case was between phenomena that were constitutive and those that were constructive.

Universal Existential Predicaments

Bell argued that there was a different question that needed to be addressed in a different way. He noted that there was a bedrock to his notion of culture: He did not believe in cultural relativism, and he did believe in cultural universals, like those Deutsch mentioned.

Bell said he had first learned about universals when he was teaching at the University of Chicago in 1947 with Robert Redfield. Redfield thought Ruth Benedict was a dreadful anthropologist because Benedict was the first to develop the notion of cultural relativism in its acute form. Bell said that at the time Redfield said something to him that he had never since forgotten: "Every culture that we know has recognized the idea of courage. It may vary in definition, but all cultures recognize the idea."

Bell believed that there were cultural universals, not because of some pan-human nature, but because the same existential predicaments confronted every human being in every culture. These predicaments contained certain modalities. Thus every culture had to come to some reckoning with the way it confronted death. Every culture had some conception of tragedy, of obligation, of love.

Bell commented that the answers varied, and that was of course integral to the history of human culture. The modal questions existed in all cultures, however. One could try to come to terms with this phenomenon by finding some common ways in which the answers were translatable to one another. This was like the essay by Walter Benjamin where he talked about a storyteller and the different languages, attempting to find some common foci that way. It seemed to Bell that this problem was not one of proportions; it involved, on the one hand, the distinction between the *constitutive* and the *constructive*, and on the other hand the question of cultural universalism.

With regard to the question of hermeneutic versus quantitative distinctions, Bell had a story he felt was apropos. He said it came to him when Shmuel Eisenstadt was making the distinction between a glass of water being half empty and half full. The story involved a caliph who asked a soothsayer to tell him his fate. The soothsayer looked at the crystal ball and said: "Sire, great news! All your relatives will die before you." The caliph shuddered and said, "You've gone mad!" Then he called another soothsayer and said to him: "Tell me my fortune. If you tell me well, I will reward you. But I warn you, I have already had one fortune told, and if yours is at variance with it, you may be wrong."

This soothsayer looked in the crystal ball and said, "Sire, great news! You will outlive all your relatives!" The caliph said, "Reward that man."

Bell pointed out that in this story, the outcomes in both predictions were the same, yet their psychic meanings were radically different. It seemed to Bell that it was precisely this dimension that revealed the power of hermeneutics—one could have the same outcome, but the different ways people interpreted this outcome led to very different consequences.

Society as a System

James G. Miller next commented that many of the problems Bell had described could be adjusted. Whether one was treating an organism, an organization, or a society, there was the old issue of adjustment, which was common to all the sciences. At the organism level, it may be necessary to intrude with a biopsy—say, to diagnose potential cancer. This may be a drastic method, but such adjustments have been dealt with in the medical model, and by physicians in treating individual patients, for a very long time—despite cultural differences in the recording of pain and in the use of terminology. If this was true at the level of the organism, it could be true at other levels. Miller claimed that the problems might be extremely complicated, but did not require the overthrow of the whole (medical) approach.

Bell replied that he would radically deny Miller's argument because he did not believe society was an organism. He believed Miller's examples involved only constitutive structures and did not address the question of highly variable meanings. There was a detailed epistemological problem on the floor, which Miller's argument simply did not confront.

Kruskal interjected that he thought Miller's example of the recording of pain did apply to the discussion at hand.

Bell answered again that Miller's example posed some objective correlate in a particular way; that is, there was obviously a source of pain. But the source of irrational passions in the Middle East, for example, seemed to Bell to involve a highly different notion.

Miller replied that he thought Bell was right, in the sense that society was not an organism. But he did think that they both were "systems," That, he claimed, was a crucial distinction.

Bell said he would not consider society a system in the strict sense of the term. He said he was not a scientist but an artisan.

Working Models of the System

Alex Inkeles suggested it was possible to be an artisan and also to be scientific. In a recent piece, he had described his own activities as "cottage industry." He was not working with a big body of assistants, nor engaged in large calculations. He admitted he was using a computer but claimed he could easily do the calculations by hand. He said none of these things prevented him from trying to discover systematic features of the world society. There were only 150 societies to worry about, so simple accounting schemes and statistics could take one very far.

Inkeles wanted to make further comments to clarify something about models, and to describe one increasingly important kind of model which Bell's scheme had left out. The closed-system mathematical model was not the only model available, and was increasingly going out of use. People had used it partly because it was available in the form of mathematics—which represented a great temptation. A different sort of model, however, which Inkeles said was more appropriately called a "working model," had not been available, so that people had to resort to the purely abstract nonworking models.

Inkeles emphasized that people were now striving to develop models, which were in fact meeting Bell's criterion about the second level of information; that is, they had built into them facts, and sociographic formulations, which were then used as the basis for measurement. They were not closed systems in Bell's sense, and would not be destroyed by adding exogenous variables. Inkeles admitted that they were still of a partial character and did not work perfectly, but nevertheless they were efforts to develop a working picture of a system that Bell claimed did not exist.

Inkeles noted that one group was trying to project what would have to be done in order to meet certain worldwide needs twenty or thirty years ahead. They started out by first taking a ten-year period, making a model, and then testing it out on the next ten-year period, which was historically an already-observed period. After this test, they made adjustments on the model, and then on the third ten-year period they came extraordinarily close to predicting what actually happened in that decade, at least in the main dimensions they were looking at. Inkeles argued that this was exactly what was meant by a working model. He anticipated Bell's reactions by admitting that the observed relationships might not hold up for the following decade—and to a certain extent this would always be true of any model. He was also sure, however, that such working models would come close to succeeding in a meaningful and useful way.

Coupling between Social Structure and Culture

Inkeles argued that such an example was a strong challenge to Bell's questions about (1) whether or not there was such a thing as a system—because the whole model rested on the idea that there was a system being described; and (2) whether there existed a degree of coupling between the elements of that system. Inkeles said that in this case the elements were working exclusively within the framework of an economic model. Any changes in politics were treated as necessary adjustments that had to be made to the model, so that this was not a real challenge to Bell's most interesting statements concerning the forms of coupling between cultural and other systems.

Inkeles commented that if Bell claimed that those systems were loosely coupled, then there was simply no argument. The question, however, was how loosely coupled they really were: "On a scale of 0 to 100, are they down around 2 or 3, or are they around 50 to 60 in terms of the closeness of the coupling?" What Inkeles wanted to convey with this question was that, although Bell's own position was very clear and highlighted the challenge in a very dramatic way, yet this position did not constitute a proof. An illustration was not a proof, precisely because one was dealing with a multidimensional, multiaspect phenomenon. One might point to some aspects of culture that maintained a certain degree of independence, but that did not mean that a systematic test—say, with 100 elements of culture and 100 elements of social structure—would show a random relation between them. The Yale survey showed that such relationships were not random; perhaps there were no strong correlations either, although some seemed to exist.

Inkeles said his own research also demonstrated that quite unambiguously. He had worked in very different societies, on both the macro- and microcultural levels, and found that exposing people to certain institutional frameworks, regardless of the rest of their culture, caused people to adapt their personal values. Their sense of what was a good wife or a proper son changed markedly in a direction suggested by the structures in which they were engaged. Inkeles said that if attitudes and values of daily life were not part of the culture, then Bell was right. If they were part of the culture, however, then these results were certainly a challenge to what Bell was saying.

Inkeles claimed that even at the level of the great religions, one might say that of course Christianity persisted; but he then said: "But what does it mean that 'Christianity persisted' for two thousand years? What about the enormous transformations within Christianity, and the enormous flowering of sects? You might say that that's 'entirely independent' of the social structure in which they occur. You certainly can say that; but I don't think the historical evidence will support you."

Inkeles argued that within the social framework it was possible to show marked tendencies, and very reliable ones, in the ways in which God was conceived and reconceived, nominally within the same cultural system, over a period of time. Yes, there were rigidities and constraints on this. One could not simply make Catholicism anything one wished, but it was possible to have a great deal of variation within it. He said: "You can also do it within Protestantism. There you've got all sorts of possibilities about how you approach God, related to the kind of orientation you have in daily life and the kind of occupation you have."

Inkeles claimed that these relations became progressively easier to see and the correlation became progressively stronger in recent times, as people came to the remarkable position of being able to choose their religion just as they could choose their occupation. He said that this example put a very substantial challenge to social science, a challenge at the highest level of intellectual interest. What in fact are the relations between cultural systems and social structures over the long haul, and what is the degree of independence of the two?

Bell responded with two points. First, he did not want to give the impression that he believed social science was completely impossible. Given the context of the discussions at the conference, however, he was necessarily emphasizing variant approaches—namely, the historical and hermeneutic approaches. He said that everyone knew that by temperament and by political sympathies he was a Menshevik, and therefore it should be clear that what he argued depended on the context in which he was making his argument. When he was with his historicist and hermeneutical friends he became very much a positivist, although he did suggest that his views were not entirely a matter of temperament.

In a more serious vein, he said he would come down to a final position. Clearly, there was a whole area of life that was full of constraints. Bell recalled Deutsch's emphasis throughout the conference, on such essentials as population, food, and natural resources. With these, there were certain specifiable limits, and in many problems it was possible to use what have been traditionally been referred to as positivist approaches. Bell explained that it was because these approaches could in certain cases be very useful that he had never liked the antipositivism of the Frankfurt school and similar theoretical viewpoints.

Bell said, however, that the real question was "What kind of approach is appropriate in what situations?" There had been too much emphasis on either/or propositions. That was why he felt it inappropriate to look at problems as if they were completely unified systems, since certain things could be looked at in systemic terms, whereas others simply could not. The crucial question was: "Is there some principle that tells us, in some way, where one can or cannot apply a systems approach?"

The Variability of Culture

He maintained that as one reached questions of culture, in principle the constraints became less, and the problems became more variable in certain respects. Technical constraints diminished because there were areas of imagination that came to embody life-styles, or the artifacts that human beings created in literature, music,and the arts. These were variable because they were not like the areas of food, population, or other concrete essentials that were constrained by physical, biological, and social mechanisms. Bell said it was not a matter of either/or. Rather, it concerned the more difficult question of what kinds of problems are most amenable to these different approaches. This was not a matter of eclecticism but of choices. It went back to a kind of Collingwood-like argument of "What question is one asking?" So it was not a logical proposition but, rather, a logical question to be answered. The way one proceeded, and the way advances in knowledge occurred, came from linking up the questions with answers that were highly variable depending on the questions asked.

Bell then went on to his second point. He did not mean to assume that because the relationships within models were not stable, it was therefore impossible to do social science. It was clear that a model would work for a certain period of time, and then it would break down, necessitating the creation of a new model. What he was saying led to a rather different epistemological problem. Just because it was possible to get successive different kinds of stability, in order to make them invariant for analytical purposes one would have to develop more general formal categories. He argued that this had been the history of almost every science. As one moved away from concrete elements and tried to make comparability possible, there was a tendency to retreat to more formal elements.

Bell claimed that this was the same kind of problem that we got when Marx said that human nature changes over time, and human history is the history of these changes: Then how did one understand the Greeks? We have to have some invariant category higher than the level of content within which to make that kind of comparison. This of course raised an issue that went back to his earlier problem regarding the Parsonian and other systems in sociology: "If you retreat into formal categories, you often lack a way to go back."

This succession of levels was like a labyrinth, Bell suggested, without the benefit of Ariadne's thread to take one back into the life of the outside world. One could be almost forced into an analytical category in order to comprehend the variety of different stable situations that might be stable only for short periods of time, so that it was not possible to compare them at the content-to-content level. If the category were only a formal one, however, Bell argued, then it became very arid, which was precisely what happened in Talcott Parsons's system—and that was the risk sociology was always having to run.

The Transfer of Culture in Living Systems

Miller spoke again to say that the kind of systems that one observed as organisms, organizations, or societies were entirely different from the kinds that were considered cultural systems. The cultural system was stored in each generation in the memory of the concrete system, by the process of acculturation. It began under the direction of parents, but it was a lifelong process. What was stored included a whole set of modes of behavior, a whole set of values, and a whole set of patterns or designs for artifacts. Miller felt this was parallel to the storage in a comparable system, the lingustic system, which had vocabulary and grammatical structure and accents—and all these things changed from one generation to another. All the cultural things changed in the same way.

Miller contended that as each generation came along in the concrete system, there was a readout process from one generation to the next, and in that process change occurred. What was read out from one generation to the next in the so-called cultural system or the linguistic system went into the memory of the second generation and was significantly different from that of the first. This readout was an entirely different process from the perpetuation of concrete systems, because it was a different kind of system. The process of perpetuation of systems was called reproduction when an organism was reproduced by the sexual process, or a corporation was reproduced by charters that were comparable to corporation charters in the past, or national governmental structures were reproduced by constitutions that were comparable to constitutions in the past. But there were two different meanings of *system* being used that were not interchangeable: "We just needed to distinguish these in order to clarify the discussion."

Bell replied that he would accept Miller's point but did not know how to begin to apply it or how to focus the discussion more meaningfully. He remarked that he simply found it difficult to think of culture as a system. He defined a *system* as something having reciprocal parts in which changes in one element lead to changes in another. It seemed to Bell that the way culture was organized, one could at best speak of homologies of culture, but he found it hard to think about a "system" of culture.

Inkeles said that the transfer of culture was an important empirical issue on which anthropologists had worked quite extensively—and one where they came down on both sides. There was no scheme that suggested any iron laws about what elements of culture were transferred.

Bell interjected that he personally was thinking about modern culture. This exemplified the problem of the nature of consciousness and change. For example, if he started with a book that had been very important to him at an earlier stage in his thinking—namely, John Dewey's *Art as Experience*—then it seemed to him that the very nature of modern thinking rested in the prefix, *re-*. Today we would *re*-design, *re*-allocate, *re*-do—because we were not confronted with the kinds of constraints we had before. It was not simply a matter of cybernetics, but a matter of choice—or, to be precise, the timing of the widening of one's choice. One thing human beings attempted to do in a moral sense was to widen the choices they had. It therefore seemed to Bell that the nature of contemporary culture was to increase the degree of variability, and this made it less and less of a system.

Miller said he thought his main point was that the products of a so-called cultural or linguistic system—a cultural artifact or a song, for example—did not change by themselves. They changed only when they went through the living system into the next generation. The change of culture was not something that went on by itself, but, rather, a sort of readout of the change process in the living system. Miller noted that this was often forgotten. In many books on linguistics, for example, the authors said that over the centuries vowels had changed, or consonants had softened in such and such a way. He argued, however, that the vowels and consonants had not simply become softer by sitting there in a book but, rather, had undergone changes because people were actively using them as living languages. Miller thought that social science often acted as if its systems had a life of their own, when actually they did not: They were mere artifacts.

Hans Klingemann wanted to add that it was possible to have very different degrees of constraint for different cultural systems. If one took a political ideology like Marxism, for example, there were overarching principles from which other statements could be deduced. Such a system had very explicit system properties. On the other hand, it was possible to have a looser type of cultural system, which existed only by some kind of social diffusion—one in which "people know what goes together but don't know why." In this case there would be more flexibility and more instability. Klingemann argued that there could be a whole range of different cultural systems that varied in terms of the degree of constraint they exhibited.

Inkeles suggested that Klingemann could draw the distinction more sharply if he used the term subsystem—that he did not mean complete cultural systems, but smaller systems within a larger one. Each subsystem could have its own laws of development and transformation, and those that determined change in language could be different from those that determined political change, for example. Inkeles felt that not enough was known about the laws of invariance or transformation that characterized these different subsystems.

With this, the discussion ended.

CHAPTER 16

Is Everything Equal, or Can There Be Scales of Importance?

John Platt

DANIEL BELL HAS said that he would not like to see a conference volume that is an indiscriminate "multiplication of lists with different degrees of significance," with no effort to justify or explain the advances. After the recent advances in the social sciences have been looked at in so many other ways, however, it may be useful to have one chapter that examines what the degrees of significance are, in comparing the many different kinds of lists that have been presented.

PRECURSORS AND SEQUELS TO THE DEUTSCH-PLATT-SENGHAAS PAPERS

Some lists of advances anticipated the papers on "Conditions for Major Advances in the Social Sciences" (Deutsch, Platt, and Senghaas 1970, 1971) [DPS], which have been the reference papers for this conference. Two of the earlier precursor papers, on "social chain reactions" and "social inventions" (Platt 1961, 1964), surveyed "inventions" such as the U.S. Constitution, the atomic-bomb Manhattan Project, standard time, the pay-as-you-go income tax, oral contraceptives, and "multiplier projects." It was suggested that such social management mechanisms could be created by design, like technological inventions, and could have major and rapid effects in solving social problems. A later paper (Platt 1969) broadened this approach, referring to the study than begun with Karl Deutsch, of "some 40 of the great achievements in social science in this century," including:

Keynesian economics
Opinion polls and statistical sampling
Input-output economics
Operations analysis
Information theory and feedback theory
Theory of games and economic behavior
Operant conditioning and programmed learning
Planned programming and budgeting (PPB)
Non-zero-sum game theory.

This article went on to say, "Our cliches about 'social lag' are very misleading. Over half of the major social innovations since 1940 were adopted or had widespread social effects within less than 12 years—a time as short as, or shorter than, the average time for adoption of technological innovations." It concluded with a plea for the formation of social research-and-development teams to study and create new social inventions.

After Deutsch, Platt and Senghaas had published the still more extended list and analysis in the DPS paper in *Science*, this theme was taken up by D. Stuart Conger (1974), who reprinted the DPS paper in connection with a list of over 1,000 historical "social inventions." His interesting workbook contained an eighty-page analysis of the conditions and methods for social inventions, intended for use by Canadian counterculture groups working for a "Newstart." Conger's book seems to have been treated as a piece of political ephemera and has remained unnoticed by academic social scientists.

General Surveys of Advances in the Social Sciences

More recently there have been three general surveys of advances in the social sciences relevant to this conference. One is that of William Kruskal (1982), who edited papers from a 1979 Chicago conference on *The Social Sciences, Their Nature and Uses*; but these were research papers in several fields without any direct comparison of advances.

Daniel Bell did a large survey for *The Great Ideas Today* in 1979 and

1980, with the two sections reprinted together as *The Social Sciences since the Second World War* (Bell 1982). This study starts with a critical exposition of the DPS article and its table of sixty-two "major advances" from 1900 to 1965. Bell says one is "justified in considering the period between 1945 and 1970 as a single period in which a set of promises were made—in disciplines, in methodology and techniques, and in social programs—which indicated that the social sciences had come of age."

Bell emphasizes theories which promised coherence and major codification. He gives high value to a number of developments not listed in DPS, including game theory and decision theory with the work of D. Luce, H. Raiffa, and T. Schelling; symbolism and semiotics in anthropology, with the work of C. Geertz, M. Douglas, and V. Turner; and the welfare economics of A. K. Sen, leading to the *Theory of Justice* of J. Rawls. Others described by Bell include developments in economics by several Nobel Prize winners (discussed later); theory of rational decisions and public choice by A. Downs, J. Buchanan, G. Tullock, M. Olson, and J. S. Coleman; information theory in cognitive psychology with the work of G. A. Miller, S. Papert, and others; artificial intelligence studies from A. M. Turing and J. von Neumann to M. Minsky; social indicators (M. Olson); social forecasting (D. Bell, H. Kahn, and A. Wiener); and social evaluation (J. S. Coleman).

In the second half of his monograph, Bell deals with the 1970s, in which he says "one can identify four major developments in the social sciences" or perhaps, since he is being critical, something more like major *claims*: sociobiology; new paradigms in macroeconomics (H. Simon, H. Leibenstein, and T. Schelling); new schools of neo-Marxism; and structuralism (Lévi-Strauss, Piaget, and others).

In this study, Bell's interest is not so much in the conditions for advances as in "the question whether the dream of a unified social science . . . is possible." He seems to conclude that Comte's hopes of the unity of science have "not been realized [and] there is a sense today that we are probably farther from that ambition than at most times in our intellectual history."

A Contrary View

The third recent survey was done for the National Research Council by a committee of sixteen members headed by Robert McC. Adams, professor of anthropology and director of the Oriental Institute of the University of Chicago. Their findings have now been published in *Behavioral and Social Science Research: A National Resource* (Adams, Smelser, and Treiman 1982).

Chapter 3 reviews "a number of areas in which significant advances in knowledge have been made in recent years." Three-quarters of the references date from 1970–1981; they include: voting behavior (initiators,

P. Lazarsfeld et al. and the Survey Research Center at the University of Michigan); history of the family (S. Kuznets, N. Smelser, E. Erikson, P. Laslett, and others); behavior and health (many areas and authors); primary groups in society (H. W. Zorbaugh, L. Wirth, W. F. Whyte, F. Roethlisberger, and others); status attainment (P. M. Blau and O. D. Duncan and others);information-processing psychology (H. A. Simon and others); origins of agriculture (several reviews); social choice theory (K. Arrow and others); human origins (selected authors); and the social behavior of monkeys and apes (H. F. Harlow, D. Hamburg, and others).

Chapter 4 of this report lists the uses of "social and behavioral research findings." The first section reviews "three inventions that are used to generate information necessary for planning, analysis and decision making: sample surveys, standardized tests, and economic models." It describes sampling and the work of survey-research centers, and the history of testing, and it has a sketch on economic data and older methods of economic forecasting. The second section describes human factors–engineering and psychophysics; learning theory—including Pavlovian conditioning, token economies in hospitals, biofeedback, and computer-aided instruction; organization and management theory; locational analysis; and policy studies. The third section, on "Changes in the Way We Think about Things", discusses "The Changing Conception of Race and Ethnicity" and "The Function of Social Science Labeling."

This is a strange survey. One would hardly believe it is in the same world as that of Daniel Bell or Karl Deutsch. It discusses human origins, the origins of agriculture, and the social behavior of monkeys—but where is systems theory, or game theory of cooperation and conflict, or computer simulation of social systems? For the recent "advances in knowledge" in U. S. social science, what we are offered is psychology without mentioning Skinner, the behavior of monkeys and humans without E. O. Wilson, economics without either Samuelson or Friedman, political science without Schelling, changes in thinking without Kuhn, and social policy experiments without Rawls.

Such a divergent view suggests that many widely discussed "advances" in the social sciences cannot be agreed on, even as subjects for consideration, by different groups of experienced and eminent workers in the field. Elsewhere, R. M. Adams has been explicit about his disagreement with the approach taken here. In "Rationales and Strategies for Social Science Research," an invited paper given before the American Academy of Arts and Sciences (Adams 1981), he concludes by arguing against "one well-known approach in which the general thrust of my remarks implies that we should not have much confidence . . . [that of] Karl Deutsch, John Platt and Dieter Senghaas. . . . Unfortunately, latent in their procedure was the assumption that the discoveries in question were discrete, enduring and generalizable."

Adams's criticism is that "we would be committed by this approach to a metaphor of scientific progress as primarily a chain of major insights or discoveries, while from each major link might descend clearly secondary refinements and applications." The result would be "concentrating resources on the will-o'-the-wisp of creativity and novelty." He says he could concur with

> most of the sixty-two [advances] as highly significant and creative contributions, [but] to offer this listing as a sample of what should be given highest valuation is to parade under false, scientistic colors. We [social scientists] deal instead, as Cronbach insisted, with a closely interwoven network of new concepts, methods, insights, syntheses, and empirical findings. . . . To give such special prominence to the germs of conceptual advance as Deutsch and his colleagues proposed is to misrepresent what the social sciences are, what they are good for, and once more to promise "breakthroughs," a promise upon which we have never been able to deliver.

Adams recommends instead a formulation that was given by Kenneth Prewitt, president of the Social Science Research Council, who said that the disciplines of the social sciences

> are sciences whose progress is marked and whose usefulness is measured, less by the achievement of consensus or the solving of problems than by a refinement of debate and a sharpening of the intelligence upon which the collective management of human affairs depends.

Such a sharpening is of great intellectual importance, but this kind of split in the profession would seem to call for two different professional labels. Perhaps the group that wants refined debate might prefer—and even be proud of—the name of *social thinkers* or *social analysts* in the field of social thought rather than social science, if they feel they have a higher standard of progress than the traditional scientific concerns of predictability, quantitative fit, testable advances, or possible disproof, which were the criteria for the advances in the DPS list.

Nevertheless I myself think it is important to emphasize that some ways of conflict resolution work better than others; some methods of education, some management systems, and some constitutions work better than others; and in human affairs we need to know which, and how to achieve them. Social problems are too important to be left to a social science whose "usefulness is measured . . . by a refinement of debate."

It should be noted however that Prewitt has taken a less purist position at other times. In his President's Report for 1979–1980 to the Social Science Research Council (Prewitt 1981), he emphasizes the "Usefulness of the Social Sciences," and says that the social sciences measure up well against the natural sciences in "productivity. . . . performance, and . . . profitability," and he emphasizes their quantitative and practical applications, including modeling and game theory.

Similarly, in his longer article on "The Five-Year Outlook" (Prewitt 1982), he speaks of social science as the source of social innovations, giving examples that overlap strongly with the DPS list: "econometric forecasting, sample surveys, standardized testing, demographic projections, management strategies in complex organizations, operant conditioning, input-output matrices, man-machine system design, cost-benefit analysis, and many others." Prewitt concludes with the statement that "innovations will become an increasingly important research theme because the social science research community . . . will focus on those issues that are of most concern to the society and its future." This seems some distance from "a refinement of debate" and is certainly not appreciably different from the point of view taken here.

Economics: Comparison with Nobel Prize Evaluations

After ten years,the DPS list and its conclusions may also be judged by other evaluations that have been made in various social sciences. One of the most authoritative of these is the list of Nobel Prizes in economics, which have been given annually since 1969. They represent a recognition of advances by some consensus of leading members of the profession. It was satisfying to see that the DPS communication of May 1970 (in Appendix) already listed seven of the eleven Nobel laureates in economics who received the prize between 1969 and 1975: Tinbergen (1969), Samuelson (1970), Kuznets (1971), Arrow (1972), Leontief (1973), Myrdal (1974), and Kantorovich (1975). Those missing from the DPS list in these years were co-prizewinners Frisch (1969), Hicks (1972), von Hayek (1974), and Koopmans (1975), although Frisch was in DPS as a "forerunner" in econometrics (Appendix, Table 1, Item 54, Column 4). The later Nobelists in economics who were also in the DPS table are Simon (1978) (listed twice), Lewis (1979), and Klein (1980).

The Chicago economist George Stigler wrote a critical Letter to the Editor about the DPS article as published in *Science*, taking issue with the economics entries (Stigler 1971; reply by Deutsch et al. 1971b). In particular, he objected to the DPS inclusion of econometrics (Tinbergen, Samuelson, Malinvaud; and forerunners Moore, Frisch, Fisher) saying it "has no unified theoretical core or methodology" and "has not yet had a major impact on economics." This was not the Nobel judgment: Three of these six have now won the prize in economics. On the other hand, Stigler also noted the omission of several "works of wide and persistent influence," including "Friedman on the consumption function and the demand for money, Hicks and Allen on utility," and others. Today, the Nobel laureates in economics do indeed include Hicks (1972), Friedman (1976)—and now Stigler himself (1982).

Stigler's disagreement with our choices still shows that there is agreement on the standards of evaluation, as well as on what the major advances might be and who has made them—so that even an outsider can find out at least who is in the running for the next prizes. Such a consensus is common in the natural sciences. Typically a physics or biology luncheon group at a major university can predict the next few Nobel laureates with 50–80 percent accuracy. We see that economics, with its quantitative and mathematical base, may have approached the same level of consensus on what new findings are important—despite the violent opposition between "econometricians" and "monetarists" and other schools.

The DPS criteria for an advance in economics seem to have been at least as high as or higher than those of the Nobel committee, with our omission of the monetarists obviously representing a difference in evaluation. After 1933, DPS listed seven areas of advance by living economists in thirty-three years (1933–1965), whereas the Nobel committee gave prizes for fourteen or more (including all of ours) representing a somewhat longer period (1933 to the 1970s); but DPS was not under the same pressure to find distinct advances for annual recognition for fourteen years in a row.

The DPS conclusions about the national or local conditions needed for making advances are also reinforced by this list of Nobel Prize winners in economics. What stands out is a concentration of developments in the United States, associated with major universities—Harvard, Chicago, and Yale—and in research institutes like the Cowles Commission. This commission supported econometrics research, notably after 1942 at the University of Chicago under the leadership of Jacob Marschak, who brought together bright young men such as Koopmans, Arrow, Klein, and Simon. The commission, and Koopmans, moved to Yale under James Tobin (Nobel 1981) in 1953—partly in protest against the new economists being hired at Chicago by Theodore Schultz (Nobel 1979), including Friedman, Stigler, von Hayek, and other conservative free-marketeers and monetarists. Of the thirteen Americans who have now won the economics prize (including Debreu [1983]), nine have been associated with the University of Chicago as students, faculty members, or researchers. Three others were with the Cowles Commission elsewhere, including Tobin and two non-American winners, Frisch, and Tinbergen; and Lewis, a British citizen, was a long-term member of the Princeton faculty.

Unfortunately, the consensus now on more recent advances in economics seems to have declined greatly, as we will see in discussing the economics papers at this conference.

Psychology

For its fifteenth anniversary, the magazine *Psychology Today* (1982) had a section called, "Psychology Today: The State of the Science," in which eleven leading U. S. psychologists wrote on the question, "What have we started to learn about human psychology . . . that we didn't know fifteen years ago?"

It was disturbing to find that few of these authors acknowledged any advances in areas other than their own. Neal Miller and Stanley Milgram spoke of the new knowledge of the brain, psychopharmacology, behavioral medicine, biofeedback, and behavior therapy. Milgram added the subject of his book *Obedience to Authority*, communication with animals (whose reality was denied by Neisser), and sociobiology. Donald O. Hebb praised E. Hilgard's recent findings demystifying hypnosis. B. F. Skinner spoke of "concept formation, creativity, and decision-making" as now being clarified by "an operant analysis of verbal behavior"; and the use of positive reinforcement to improve achievements in school, work, and the family, and in "ethical and intellectual self-management."

The antibehaviorists, on the other hand, emphasized "cognitive psychology." Jerome Bruner praised the movement "away from the restrictive shackles of behaviorism"—with an "earth-shattering" "freshet of new work" on mental processes, perception, memory, problem solving, development, and language. Philip G. Zimbardo said "cognitive psychology has taken the head once lopped off by radical behaviorism and returned it to the body of psychology." Children would now "be taught strategies for more effective studying . . . [and] . . . problem-solving."

Richard S. Lazarus called recent behaviorism "an unproductive, temporary aberration," and referred to his 1966 book on *Psychological Stress and the Coping Process*. Ulric Neisser saw his own 1967 book, *Cognitive Psychology*, as "a rival to psychoanalytically based psychology and to behaviorism"; he also praised the studies of J. J. Gibson and E. Gibson on the development of perception.

The sociologist Bernice Neugarten spoke of the enlargement of "developmental psychology" to include research on aging. David McClelland emphasized studies on people's need for power, and the effects of meditation in reducing anxiety or increasing motivation. The psychotherapist Rollo May said, "The outstanding development in the last 15 years . . . is what I call the populist trend in psychology . . . [with people knowing] a dozen different forms of psychotherapy." Today, he said, with the loss of myths and religion, "psychology . . . is all we have left for coping."

Several of these authors did agree on the importance of the information-processing approach and of computers and the electronic revolution, with electronic games providing "a powerful reinforcer that is transforming youngsters."

There is some consensus among these lists, but it is hard to see in this mixture much evidence of positive and accepted accomplishments—certainly not the kind of testable major findings that a whole profession agrees on and is busy using or refuting. The recent results from the biological and medical side seem the most solid and useful—on the genetics of mental disease, the relation of brain structure to behavior (notably Sperry's work), and the new psychopharmacology and biochemistry that are performing miracles for millions. The use of positive reinforcement for therapy and training is also spreading steadily, and is of course the key to the attractiveness and power of electronic games and computer-assisted instruction [Loftus and Loftus 1983].

"Cognitive psychology," however, except for the information-processing approaches, is not clearly an advance on behaviorism. James G. Miller, who founded the Mental Health Research Institute at Michigan, has said in this conference that "cognitive psychology" has no very distinguished experiments, is "not a discipline," and some of it is "actually no more than a restatement of theses that were accepted in the 1920s and then went out of style in psychology for about forty years" (p. 175).

Besides these disagreements, one notable aspect of these lists, reinforced by other evidence, is the steady disappearance of the Freudian approach and even the Freudian language from psychology and therapy, as it has begun to disappear from the literary and cultural scene today. A generation of disciples is dying off. This may mark the end of that whole era of attempting to practice psychology and psychotherapy by insight and introspective methods that are hard to verify or control, and that have led mainly to ambiguous analyses and sterile polemics.

Political Science

Karl W. Deutsch has published a survey of "Major Changes in Political Science, 1952–1977," prepared for the Twenty-fifth Anniversary Meeting of the International Social Science Council in Paris in 1977. This is a dense review with hundreds of references, to show that in these years "political science has undergone something like a revolution. . . . The total of fields and subfields of active research concern have doubled." Among the many developments he mentions, those that meet the criteria of the DPS list would seem to include: cognitive dissonance (Festinger, Abelson); structuralism (Lévi-Strauss, Piaget); theory of justice (Rawls); theory of democracy (Dahl, Lipset, Rokkan, Downs, and others); political development (Lerner, Almond, Inkeles, and others); and computer simulation and global modeling (Forrester, D. H. Meadows, D. L. Meadows). Conflict theory and peace research are mentioned but not emphasized.

Deutsch's survey has some discussion of neo-Marxist writings; but it may be that Marx's influence in economics and political science, as well as in culture and philosophy, is also going the way of Freud's. Bell's review (1982), cited earlier, noted an "upsurge of Marxist politics and neo-Marxist thought" in the 1960s and 1970s. Recently, however, even among leftist social scientists, there seems to have been disillusionment with the many "revisionist quarrels," as well as with the inadequacy of Marxist theory to explain developing societies, postindustrial societies, or even "Marxist" societies. From a modern point of view, Marxist societies seem to have poor systems design, with a failure to include feedback stabilization mechanisms (Platt 1966), leading to poor incentives, dependence on punishment methods, and inflexible bureaucracies. Bell quotes Leszek Kolakowski (1978), formerly "the most brilliant Marxist philosopher in Poland," as saying, after thirty years of study:

> Marxism has been the greatest fantasy of our century. . . . As an explanatory "system" it is dead, nor does it offer any "method" that can be effectively used to interpret modern life. . . . The influence that Marxism has achieved, far from being the result or proof of its scientific character, is almost entirely due to its prophetic, fantastic, and irrational elements. . . .

We may have come to a turning point in social thought. Of the three towering nineteenth-century figures, Darwin, Marx, and Freud, who produced such transformations in our ideas of the human being and society, perhaps only Darwin's work will retain enough scientific validity to be important after the year 2000. Whatever succeeds the work of the system builders, from Marx to Parsons, may be more technical and more testable—perhaps collectively created hierarchical flow models, with complex interacting feedback loops showing characteristic stability boundaries or locked-in patterns. The focus will not be on history or dramatic conjectures so much as on detailed, ongoing feedback mechanisms of instability or correction.

Frequencies of Alpha, Beta, and Gamma Levels of Advance

Is there any way to estimate the importance of the advances in these various lists? Gerhard Bruckmann has suggested that without too much difficulty, we could make an order-of-magnitude index of "significance" (p. 282), classifying various advances into alpha, beta, gamma . . . levels of importance. He would use alpha for the large Kuhnian changes, like the Copernican or Darwinian revolutions, that might have occurred in a major field only once or twice per century before 1900. In this century the rate of advances at this level have probably speeded up, because of the increase in the level of education and the number of researchers in every field, and the hundred-fold increase in funding since 1940. Advances comparable to the alpha advances of the past might therefore be occurring more frequently now, perhaps every ten or twenty years.

Such a speedup can be seen fairly easily in the natural sciences (Platt

1979), with multiple major revolutions having occurred in the fields of astronomy, physics, chemistry, geology, and biology just since 1940.

A similar acceleration may also be evident in the social sciences. For example, in the DPS list from 1940 to 1965, there are several revolutions in social technologies and in thinking in different fields that have been ranked by various critics as comparable to the greatest ones of the past. These include:

Operations-research and systems analysis, transforming military and industrial operations.
Cybernetics and feedback theory, with applications to goal-directed systems from psychology through all the social sciences.
Game theory, from economic and political behavior to variable-sum games and conflict theory.
Application of computers to complex social data processing, going on to economic and social simulation.
Operant conditioning and behavior modification, with applications to biofeedback, therapy, learning, and responsive social interactions.
Logic and cognitive dynamics of science and the "structure of scientific revolutions."

If we want to make these judgments more quantitative, we might try to measure the "Bruckmann index" of different advances—say, by comparing numbers of citations, or the numbers of times the new methods or results are used by other workers—or even by the level of controversy about them. Of course, what is to some a major advance will seem only a fad or even a regression to others. Someone outside a given field might be unable to judge these substantive issues or to take sides intelligently for or against any of the groups of experts, yet might still be able to detect—by content analysis of such utilization, or of the debates, or by citation clusters like those studied by Derek Price—that some developments or findings differ enormously from others in their "importance" in an advancing field. The differences are not small; they vary by two to three orders of magnitude between Kuhn's 1,000 citations per year over many years, and the 1 to 10 citations to an average book or paper in either the natural or the social sciences.

In the case of the rather subjective lists given here, however, we can use a much simpler procedure to extract some rough rankings. We can do a sort of inverse transformation of Bruckmann's approach, looking not at the number of citations of a given "advance," but at the frequency or number of comparable advances listed per decade in a given tabulation. In such a frequency classification, an alpha development would then be of the sort that an expert regards as the most important in a period of ten to twenty years in a given broad field; beta, the quality that might be seen once per year; and so on. If we look at a field where some 10,000 articles are published per year, a paper with only a median number of citations—say, 10 or so—would then be at the epsilon level or lower, comparable in importance to thousands of other articles in the same year.

This can obviously be nothing but the crudest sort of measure; but since it is also important not to overanalyze the discriminations that are being made for various reasons by various reviewers, such a rough measure may be just what is needed here. By this test, any discussant who singles out one major advance in a twenty-year period could be seen as nominating it, more or less, for alpha status. But if a development is simply grouped with twenty other developments in the same field in a ten-year period, it is not being cited very selectively or praised very highly. And anyone who tabulates 100 developments as being "important" in one field in a given decade, must be thinking of most of them, statistically, as gamma-level. These order-of-magnitude differences in frequency listings are great and obvious; and they immediately distinguish the useful annual or encyclopedic reviews from more critical attempts to single out major new directions.

We can look at our various lists here from this Bruckmannian point of view. For example, in the field of economics, few people would regard more than two or three of the Nobel Prize subjects or the advances on the DPS list since 1933 as being of alpha importance—comparable, say, to Adam Smith or Karl Marx. This means that the rest of the fifteen Nobel awards in economics might be of roughly beta level; and the DPS list in economics, being somewhat smaller, might be called beta-plus, with two or three advances at this level per decade. Nobels that keep up annually with any field will usually be at the beta level or below. Likewise, most of the other items on the DPS list for the 1930–1965 period, which shows one or two advances per decade for the larger fields of psychology, economics, and political science (Appendix, Table 2), would have to be assigned to roughly the beta-plus level, with just a few alphas, by such a frequency criterion.

By this test, Bell's monograph on the social sciences discussed earlier (Bell 1982), is quite selective. Before 1970 his frequency of advances is comparable to the DPS study, suggesting a beta-plus level. But Bell's second section names four major developments or claims distributed over several fields in the last twelve years—sociobiology, macroeconomics, neo-Marxism, and structuralism—so that, to the extent that they are regarded as valid, these would seem to be ranked at the level of alpha advances.

The National Research Council study, despite its disagreement with our approach, has roughly 50 percent overlap with the subjects and authors in DPS; but it adds a comparable number of other developments, so these are either alternatives at about the beta-plus level, or additions at about the beta level.

On the other hand, the *Psychology Today* evaluations add up to twenty or thirty different "advances" in a single field in fifteen years, so most of these would not be higher than the beta or gamma level, even if there had been any kind of consensus among the authors.

In the case of political science, Deutsch's survey for 1952–1977 is intended to demonstrate the growth and vitality of the field by citing hundreds of references, or many every year; but this necessarily means that most of them must have been selected from about the gamma level.

Advances Listed in This Book

By this frequency criterion, the different papers in this book are describing very different levels of advances. The introductory chapter by Deutsch refers mainly to the DPS list; he adds only two or three other advances, such as global modeling and motivation research, so presumably these are being thought of similarly as alpha or beta-plus advances.

Chapter 2 by Inkeles, on sociology, lists for the 1945–1970 period half a dozen primary developments in that one field, plus some fifteen "secondary peaks" of discovery—evidently alpha to beta-plus for the primary ones, and beta for the secondaries. Chapter 3 on the same field by Eisenstadt lists some thirty-five major contributions from 1961 to 1978; this is two per year, or gamma-level. But in the period of overlap of the two studies, from 1961 to 1970, Inkeles lists seven contributions whereas Eisenstadt lists twenty-one—and only four of the names are in common (Inkeles, White, Duncan and Blau, and Goffman). This shows up numerically the difference between their "two modes of inquiry," as noted in the discussions—a difference that is demonstrated again when Inkeles cites sociobiology as "advancing so rapidly" (p. 19), while Eisenstadt calls it "unconvincing" (p. 58).

Chapter 4 by Wildenmann mentions some eight contributions in political science since about 1950—a frequency that might represent the beta-plus level if there were any general agreement by other observers on these names.

Chapters 5, 6, and 7 on economics, by Krelle, Tinbergen, and Fritsch and Kirchgässner, list the largest number of contributions per year. Krelle notes some thirty contributors to nine major fields. He uses the Bruckmann classification of advances explicitly, and says that his five areas of advances between 1960 and 1980—monetarism, disequilibrium analysis, theory of allocation, rational expectations, and new political economy—represent "a sort of delta-progress." This is too low an evaluation; by the yardstick used here, they would be more like beta-plus. They are about four years apart, and he rates them as only slightly less important than the older "four main advances"—the Nobel Prize cluster of game theory, econometrics, general equilibrium theory, and growth theory, which evidently approach the alpha level. He also mentions the "whole school of ethics, started by Rawls"—presumably beta-plus, being ranked somewhat below the game theory he says it is based on.

Tinbergen's chapter lists thirty "innovative ideas" with thirty-six senior authors between about 1964 and 1981, a frequency that puts most of these at the gamma level. Fritsch and Kirchgässner, in Chapter 7, list eight areas of "major trends and developments in economics since 1965," with sixteen subheads of "major contributions" and forty-four contributors. This frequency puts their major areas at the beta level and most of the contributions at the gamma level.

The disturbing thing, however, if we are to believe that this is indeed a field of positive and recognizable scientific advances, is that there is almost no agreement between these three lists in economics. There are only two names in common (out of thirty-six and thirty, respectively) between Tinbergen's list of contributors and Krelle's: Klein (Nobel 1980) and Krelle himself. Six of Krelle's nine areas of advance are found, with slightly different names, in the Fritsch-Kirchgässner list of major contributions; but the two lists have only nine contributors in common (out of thirty and forty-four, respectively). And there seem to be *no* names in common between the Tinbergen list and the Fritsch-Kirchgässner list for 1965–1980. These three European papers on economic science are evidently seeing the field from three very different angles.

Such a divergence seems to confirm that the earlier consensus on advances in economics is now breaking down. Kenneth Boulding has spoken of "Economics in Disarray" and has compared the situation to the blind men and the elephant (Boulding 1980). The 1973 Nobelist Wassily Leontief (1982, 1983) has also castigated economists severely. He says, "Not having been subjected from the outset . . . to the harsh discipline of systematic fact-finding . . .economists . . .avoid or cut short the use of concrete factual information"—with two-thirds of the articles in the *American Economic Review* being mathematical models or analyses without any data. "Year after year economic theorists continue to produce scores of mathematical models . . . without being able to advance, in any perceptible way, a systematic understanding of the structure and the operations of a real economic system" (Leontief 1982, 1983). It will be interesting to see how the Nobel Prize committee copes with this situation.

Chapter 8, by Miller, describes the cross-discipline studies involved in his "living systems theory," which he evidently sees as one of the alpha advances on the DPS list in the last forty years.

Chapter 9, by Bruckmann, is likewise devoted to a single subject, "global modeling," urging that this be added to the DPS list, presumably at least at the beta-plus level. This might be listed as a separate development from the "systems dynamics" computer-simulation method of Jay Forrester on which it is based. Half the discussants seemed to regard global modeling as a real advance, but half opposed it as "a dangerous concept" that had been "devastatingly criticized" by economists.

Chapter 10 by Boudon, on developments in mathematical and statistical thinking in the social sciences, lists some twenty major developments with some thirty major contributors and ninety references in the period 1963–1981. This is about one development per year; but they are not limited to a narrow field, so these are largely beta-level. In the discussion, several of them are singled out as being of special importance.

This brings us to the case of "catastrophe theory," which is particularly controversial. Fritsch and Kirchgässner call it "promising," with "great potential," although the difficulties of applying it to social processes are "formidable." Boudon, however, questions whether it will have an impact on the social sciences. The American mathematician M. Kac has called it "an elegant and profound piece of mathematics created by René Thom," but thinks its social applications are "a flood of claims" and "a temporary aberration" whose "star . . . has begun to fade" (Kac 1982). With such divergence, it may be some years before a final assessment can be made.

Chapter 11 by Kruskal is not a list of advances but an analysis of methods of evaluation of social science research, with useful warnings that can apply to methods such as this one. Chapter 12, by Cohen, also does not add to our list, since its social science references are primarily to the older *International Encyclopedia of Social Sciences*.

In Chapter 13, Weingart discusses the single case of T. S. Kuhn, saying that he "represents the last major advance in both the history and the philosophy of the social sciences." This would upgrade him from his place as just a cocontributor in the DPS list.The discussants afterward largely supported this alpha-level ranking of Kuhn, although one said that his work was a "catalyst" and "not really an advance."

Chapter 14 is an analysis by Rapoport of the concept of advances. In psychology, outside the DPS list, he mentions the experiments of Asch on social conformity; the work on semantic differential of Osgood, Suci, and Tannenbaum; and Bruner's work on childhood development, which Rapoport compared with Piaget's, in the discussion period. In the context, these appear to be at least beta-plus identifications.

In Chapter 15, Bell urges more assessment of failures, and would downgrade many claimed "advances" because of their "contradictions" or "extravagant claims that have not been fulfilled"—notably cybernetics, culture-and-personality theory, Freudian ego theory, and "structural functionalism." This is where Bell says he is opposed to "simply a multiplication of lists," by way of urging more explicit evaluation like his own extensive evaluation of major advances discussed earlier (Bell 1982).

The final chapter, by Deutsch, would also add some further "candidate contributions" to the DPS list: the theory of collective choice by

Olson, and sociobiology by Wilson, both evidently being rated at the beta-plus or alpha level.

Additions to the DPS List of Major Advances

A personal distillation of these analyses and reevaluations is shown in Table 16.1, which extends the DPS list of sixty-two advances to the present time. The numbering starts at No. 63, to follow Table A.1 in the Appendix. The entries are intended to be at the alpha and beta-plus level, mostly from 1965 to 1980, but they include a few earlier ones that seem to have been undervalued in the 1970 DPS articles.

With one exception, there is no thought here of making a major revision of the original DPS list. Reassessment in any of the sciences is continuous, changing with time and fashion and personal criteria of what is important. Other authors can and will make different lists for any purposes they wish, as we have seen; but the original article grew out of our point of view at that time and is here simply reprinted as such, as the place from which the discussion started.

The exception I think most of us would agree to now is a deletion from the DPS list of the political party theorists—Gandhi, Lenin, and Mao—as not meeting the criteria of scientific advances, for reasons that were well discussed in Inkeles's chapter and need not be repeated here.

Most of the new advances listed in Table 1 have been listed in the top rank by several speakers at this conference. Many of them have also been opposed by one or more speakers, as being faddish, unimportant, or even damaging misconceptions. But the greatest advances in history have been similarly criticized at the time or later; this by itself does not prove their eventual worthlessness—or their greatness. Such disagreements, when they have reached this stage of considered evaluation, cannot be resolved by further debate, but only by continued time and test and attempted use.

Table 16.1 has been limited to a list of fields, contributors, and dates, since there has been an extensive discussion here of the precursors and conditions and other aspects of most of these developments. One column has been added to show the DPS criterion of "a new perception or operation" that the advance appears to represent.

Obviously, dozens of beta-level or higher advances that others have proposed in this conference are being omitted. My reasons for choosing this particular group of fifteen additional advances can simply be set against their arguments.

First, three of the first few added items in Table 1 are among those that were already mentioned in the DPS paper as being "borderline cases":

the work of McClelland, No. 63; Festinger and Abelson, No. 64; and Osgood, Suci, and Tannenbaum, No. 66. They now seem to be more important than that, as shown by the many citations in this volume. Multiple citations have also suggested the addition of the work of Dahl, Downs, Lipset, and Rokkan, No. 65; Arrow again, No. 70; Duncan and Blau, No. 73; Bauer, Gross, Russett, and Szalai, No. 75; and Friedman, No. 76.

The rest of the entries in Table 1 are not merely highly cited; they also have internal promise and external implications that make me regard them as alpha-level developments. In fact, I think the 1970s may come to be known as a time of dazzling advances in the social sciences, with achievements such as:

Artificial-intelligence research, No. 67.
Rawls's *Theory of Justice*, No. 68.
The Forrester-Meadows-Meadows Club of Rome study on *The Limits to Growth*, No. 69.
Wilson's *Sociobiology*, No. 71.
Schelling's *Micromotives and Macrobehavior*, No. 72.
Thom's Catastrophe Theory, No. 74.
The Raiffa-Fisher-Ury development of "the science of negotiation." No. 77.

It is true that many of these are controversial, but they demonstrate important things; they turn our thoughts to new problems and solutions; and all of them have potential major applications to social understanding, policy, and design. A summary word on each may illustrate what I think is its major reason to be designated at least a beta-plus advance.

Artificial intelligence research, though often oversold, has already transformed psychology, education, and human-computer interactions in many social applications. "Just as the theory of evolution changed our view of life, so artificial intelligence will change our view of the mind," says Minsky (1983).

John Rawls's "theory of justice," which calls for a bridging of inequalities by giving maximum help to the most disadvantaged ("maximin principle"), may be the most important philosophical theory of social welfare distribution since Bentham and J. S. Mill or Marx in the last century. There has been some opposition from libertarians; nevertheless, Rawls has made explicit and semi-quantitative a principle that underlies the social claims of the most diverse groups today—from capitalist theorists to the advocates of human rights and affirmative action, and even to Third-World groups demanding that we "serve the people" or create a "new international economic order." In the struggles of the next fifty

Table 16.1. Basic Innovations in Social Science, continued from Appendix, Table A.1. (Additions to DPS List of 1970, impacts mostly after 1965)

	Contribution	Contributor	Time	New Perception ["There is . . ." or "If . . . then . . ."] or New Operation
63.	Achievement motivation (Psy)	D. E. McClelland	1953–1961	Measurable dimensions of culture and education
64.	Cognitive dissonance (Psy)	L. Festinger R. Abelson	1956	Dissonance: learning, change; much dissonance: withdrawal, rage
65.	Conditions of democracy (Pol)	R. Dahl A. Downs S. M. Lipset S. Rokkan	1965–1968	Preconditions and stabilized feedbacks in a democracy
66.	Semantic differential (Psy)	C. Osgood G. J. Suci P. H. Tannenbaum	1957	Reproducible dimensions of meaning
67.	Artificial intelligence (Psy)	H. A. Simon A. Newell M. Minsky	1956–1982	Flexible problem solving and learning by computers
68.	Theory of justice (Phil, Pol)	J. Rawls A. K. Sen	1958–1971	Justice as fairness; distribution rules to help the worst-off
69.	Many-variable system dynamics and global modeling (Math)	J. Forrester D. H. Meadows D. L. Meadows	1963–1972	Simulation of complex feedback interactions, showing limits and effects of policies

70. Social choice theory (Math)	K. J. Arrow	1963	Limits on voter choices and democratic processes
71. Sociobiology: kin altruism, genetic components in behavior and culture (Soc)	W. D. Hamilton R. L. Trivers E. O. Wilson J. Maynard Smith	1964–75	Experimental and theoretical genetics of animal and human behavior and social structures
72. Private choice–public action [social traps] (Pol)	M. Olson T. C. Schelling M. Shubik	1965–1978	Micromotives and macroeffects of self versus group interest
73. Stratification, status, and mobility (Soc)	P. M. Duncan O.D. Blau	1966–1967	Dynamic description of status systems
74. Catastrophe theory of jumps in biological and social systems (Math)	R. Thom E. C. Zeeman	1966–1976	Bifurcations and special properties of multivalued surfaces
75. Social accounting and social indicators (Soc)	R. Bauer B. Gross B. Russett A. Szalai	1966–1969	Measures and change rates of many social goods and ills
76. Monetarism (Econ)	M. Friedman	1967–1968	Money supply determines growth, prices, and jobs
77. Negotiation theory (Pol)	H. Raiffa R. Fisher W. Ury	1978–1982	Game and decision theory applied to negotiation strategy

years, the Rawlsian flag may be raised on both sides of the barricades.

As for global modeling and the *Limits to Growth* studies, there have been objections by economists and by establishment thinkers, capitalist and communist and Third-World alike; but these studies started a whole industry, of groups in many centers trying to estimate the feedback interactions of key variables in long-run global survival—a subject that traditional economics never treated. Sociobiology, in turn, has opened up the subject of the ancient evolutionary feedback-loops connecting *Genes, Mind, and Culture* (Lumsden and Wilson 1981), regardless of whether Wilson's animal-model approach turns out to be the most valid one in the long run or not.

The work of Schelling and others formalizing the dilemmas of private choice and collective consequences has shown dozens of practical ways of using feedback—reinforcements, penalties and incentives—to solve large-scale problems by redirecting small-scale choices. These "social traps" "represent all of our most intractable and large-scale urban, national, and international problems today" and this new discipline "could do more than almost any other academic study to illuminate and solve these locked-in collective problems" (Platt 1973).

Thom's "catastrophe theory," in spite of its faddist appeal and questions about how it is to be applied to social problems, has given us a new language for describing evolutionary jumps or revolutions in biology and in social and cultural evolution. It also explains some otherwise puzzling phenomena, such as the suddenness of the jumps (Platt 1970); and bifurcations and dichotomies in a continuous field; and polarized outcomes, locked-in patterns, and hysteresis, in individual and social behavior.

Finally, the new "science of negotiation" (Fisher and Ury 1981; Raiffa 1982) grows out of non-zero-sum game theory findings like those of Rapoport and collective-action theory results like those of Olson, Schelling, and Shubik. It formalizes the negotiation of the mutual benefit of all parties, and has already been used in complex international negotiations with some success. It may be a key element in finding solutions to our great global confrontations of the next few years.

If it is worth analyzing such a subjective list along the DPS lines, it will be found that the distribution of these fifteen advances in Table 1 is much like that in the original DPS list. Psychology is assigned four developments; politics, four; sociology, three; mathematics, three; and economics, one. Of the thirty-eight contributors shown, thirty are Americans, and fourteen have done much or all of their work in Cambridge, Massachusetts; almost all seem to have done their work in university departments or institutes.

It is clear, however, that any such list reflects subjective evaluations and biases as well as considered judgments. It is evidently too personal, too small, and too continuous with the points of view in the older list to give any reliable proof of continuity in the conditions for advances in the last fifteen years; but neither does it give any evidence of striking change. As far as this Table 1 is concerned, the old DPS conclusions about the rates of progress and the conditions for advances would seem to be as valid as ever.

And despite my fine words, Rapoport is right in his pessimism: These are not yet operational solutions to the urgent problem of human survival, which will require the design and adoption of new stabilizing global institutions. Yet I think these advances may give us the intellectual base for beginning such designs, with a new understanding of conflict and cooperation and collective and ethical self-management of our democratic processes.

At this point, however, I cannot end such a comparative study without adding my own conclusion that one of the older developments in social science remains the greatest in this century, far beyond any Nobel prizes: an *alpha-plus*, in its implications for the long-run human and social future. I am referring to Skinner's development of behavioral reinforcement and operant conditioning, with its all-positive or "responsive" methods of shaping behavior (Platt 1972, 1973, 1981).

I know that such an evaluation could call forth a chorus of violent disagreement in many quarters. This is partly due to the fact that Skinner's methods and his results have been widely misquoted and misinterpreted for various reasons. As I have said elsewhere, "Skinner may have had the worst press of any great scientist since Darwin." But the application of these methods—in animal training, in behavioral therapy, in learning, and in personal self-management and group self-management (Platt 1973)—is not a fascist procedure but a system that can be humane, open, and effective. His methods show us how to use immediate personal response and positive reinforcements to close the feedback loops in thousands of social networks. They show us how far we could make learning, work, and play and all the relationships of society more continuously rewarding—without the inhibiting constraints and punishments that for centuries have dominated our methods of learning and social development (Platt 1981). They even show us more effective methods of "controlling the controllers".

I think this reinforcement approach deserves reexamination to see how it would fit into all-positive democratic management systems, in the light of the new social structural findings of Downs and Rawls and Arrow and Schelling and Raiffa. It could transform families and education, religion and the law, toward much more integrative patterns. This would be of far more value to a tortured world than all the discoveries of the natural sciences in this century. The great problems facing us now are not to be solved by developments in energy or electronics or by looking at the mind as a computer, but by looking at the world as a responsive and reinforcing family.

References

Adams, R. McC. 1981. "Rationales and Strategies for Social Science Research." *Bull. Amer. Acad. Arts and Sciences 34* (7), April, pp. 10–34.

Adams, R. McC.; Smelser, N. J.; and Treiman, D. J., eds. 1982. *Behavioral and Social Science Research: A National Resource*, Parts I and II. Washington, D. C: Committee on Basic Research in the Behavioral and Social Sciences, National Academy Press.

Bell, D. 1982. *The Social Sciences Since the Second World War*. New Brunswick: Transaction Books.

Boulding, K. E. 1980. "Economics in Disarray." *Technology Review*, May, pp. 6, 20.

Conger, D. Stuart. 1974. *Social Inventions*, Saskatchewan Newstart, Information Canada, Box 1565, Prince Albert, Saskatchewan, Canada.

Deutsch, K. W. 1978. *Major Changes in Political Science, 1952–1977*. Paper No. PV/78/2. International Institute for Comparative Social Research, Wissenschaftszentrum Berlin.

Deutsch, K. W.; Platt, J.; and Senghaas, D. 1970. "Major Advances in Social Science Since 1900: An Analysis of Conditions and Effects of Creativity". Mental Health Research Institute, University of Michigan, *Communication* No. 273, May. (Reprinted as Appendix to this book, slightly condensed.)

———. 1971a. "Conditions Favoring Major Advances in Social Science." *Science 171*, February 5, pp. 450–459.

———. 1971b. Reply, *Science 172,* June 18, pp. 1191–1192.

Fisher, R., and Ury, W. 1981. *Getting to Yes: Negotiating Agreement Without Giving In*. Boston: Houghton Mifflin.

Kac, M. 1982. "Dehydrated Elephants Revisited." (A Critique of Catastrophe Theory), *American Scientist 70*, November–December, pp. 633–634.

Kolakowski, L. 1978. *Main Currents of Marxism: Its Rise, Growth, and Disillusion*. 3 vols. Oxford: Clarendon Press.

Kruskal, W. H., ed. 1982. *The Social Sciences, Their Nature and Uses*, Chicago: University of Chicago Press.

Leontief, W. 1982. "Academic Economics." *Science 217*, July 9, pp. 104, 107.

———. 1983. "Academic Economics Continued." Reply to Letters, *Science 219*, February 25, p. 904.

Loftus, G. R., and Loftus, E. F. 1983. *Mind at Play: The Psychology of Video Games*. New York: Basic Books.

Lumsden, C. J., and Wilson, E. O. 1981. *Genes, Mind, and Culture*. Cambridge, Mass.: Harvard University Press.

Minsky, M. 1983. "Why People Think Computers Can't." *Technology Review 86* (6), November–December, pp. 65–81.

Platt, J. R. 1961. "Social Chain Reactions." *Bull. Atom. Sci.*, November, pp. 365–369, 386. Reprinted in J. R. Platt, *The Step to Man* (New York: Wiley, 1966), pp. 39–52.

———. 1964. "Research and Development for Social Problems." *Bull. Atom. Sci.*, June 1964, pp. 27–29. Reprinted in J. R. Platt, *The Step to Man* (New York: Wiley, 1966), pp. 132–138.

———. 1966. "The Federalists and the Design of Stabilization." In *The Step to Man*. New York: Wiley, pp. 108–131.

———. 1969. "What We Must Do." *Science 166*, November 28, 1969, pp. 1115–1121.

———. 1970. "Hierarchical Restructuring." *General Systems 15*, pp. 49–54.

———. 1972. The Skinnerian Revolution. *The Center Magazine 5(2)*, March–April, pp. 34–52. Reprinted in H. Wheeler, ed., *Beyond the Punitive Society* (San Francisco: W. H. Freeman, 1973), pp. 22–56.

———. 1973. "Social Traps." *American Psychologist 28* (8), pp. 641–651.

———. 1979. *Eight Major Evolutionary Jumps Today*. International Institute for Comparative Social Research, WZB, Berlin, Paper IIVG/Pre 79–8. Also in A. S. Markovits and K. W. Deutsch, eds., *Fear of science—Trust in Science*. Cambridge, Mass.: Oelgeschlager, Gunn and Hain, 1980, Chap. 13, pp. 149–165. Reprinted as "The Acceleration of Evolution," *The Futurist 15* (1) February 1981, pp. 14–23.

———. 1981. "Can Positive Incentives and Reinforcements Reduce the Punitive Aspects of Society?" In J. Dator and C. Bezold, eds., *Judging the Future*, Manoa: Social Science Research Institute, University of Hawaii at Manoa, pp. 72–85.

Prewitt, K. 1981. "Usefulness of the Social Sciences." Guest editorial, *Science 211* (4483). February 13. From the President's Report, Social Science Research Council, 1979–1980.

———. 1982. "Assessing the Significance of Social Science Research." In *The Five-Year Outlook on Science and Technology, 1981*, Vol. 2: *Source Materials*. Washington, D. C.: National Science Foundation, pp. 553–559.

Raiffa, H. 1982. *The Art and Science of Negotiation*. Cambridge, Mass.: Harvard University Press.

Stigler, G. J. 1971. "Social Science: Identifying Major Advances," *Science 172*, June 18, p. 1191.

CHAPTER 17

Substantial Advances: Real but Elusive

Karl W. Deutsch

IT IS DIFFICULT TO SUM UP the papers and discussions in this book and at the conference that preceded it. What can be offered are the present impressions of one participant, which may differ from those of the other scholars who took part and from one's own later judgment.

The participants differed by country, background, age, field of specialization, and philosophic orientation. A look at the chapters of this book will show that there was no prearranged agreement, and no prefabricated unanimity beyond a willingness to work together on our common topic.

Even so, one result stands out. There have indeed been real and substantial advances in the social sciences during the twentieth century, and no one at the conference denied it. Moreover, these advances were relatively numerous, they were found in all fields of social science, and they often contributed to each other beyond the boundaries of disciplines. Together, they have added up to significant cumulative gains.

Some General Trends

Eight ongoing trends in the social sciences were suggested by the flow of the discussions and by many of the cases listed in the chapters:

1. There are no general eternal secrets; the world, including the world of human beings and their societies and cultures, is coming to be seen in principle as *knowable but not exhaustible.*
2. Instead of thinking of truth as something finite, to be approached ever more closely, we are coming to think of truth as an infinite succession of *new horizons*, surpassing but including the landmarks of the older ones.
3. The social sciences, like other sciences, are moving from a preoccupation with supposedly simple cases to the search for combinations and configurations of a *plurality of relevant conditions* (for examples of this reorientation, see McIver 1942; Kroeber 1944; and Lipset 1956).
4. This in turn has been paralleled by a trend away from thinking in terms of determinism and towards thinking in terms of *probability* (Wiener et al. 1943).
5. Probabilistic thinking itself has moved beyond focusing mainly on the central tendencies of a statistical distribution to the consideration of *variances* and other characteristics of the entire distribution. (I am indebted to I. Richard Savage for having alerted me to this trend in the late 1950s.)
6. Similarly, there has been a trend away from *one-way* images of sequences of cause and effect to analysis of the *two-way* processes of *feedback loops*, since Norbert Wiener's work (1943, 1962).
7. These changes have implied less exclusive emphasis on Popperian "falsification"—that is, possible refutability—of entire theories, and more stress on determining the *limits of the validity* of each (for the implications of this change in the style of debating, see Rapoport 1960).
8. Together with these cognitive changes, we are moving from a single notion of knowledge toward a plural notion, including at least *three kinds of knowledge*—and, corresponding to them, *three kinds of ignorance*:

> First, ignorance of most that there is to be known, as in Newton's image of himself as "a boy playing on the sea-shore . . . whilst the great ocean of truth lay all undiscovered before me".
>
> Second, ignorance of most that we, or any one of us, may wish to know.
>
> Third, ignorance of what we *need* to know, if we are to avoid substantial damage to ourselves or to the persons or things we care about.

Social science, like all sciences, rightly tries to reduce all three kinds of ignorance, but many of us have a special sense of urgency with regard to the third kind.

Two Major Approaches to Social Science

Within this general framework, today we see the emergence of two major kinds of social science.

One of these seeks insights that are largely subjective. It is tied to the personality of the investigator and to his or her ability to reproduce or parallel within his or her own feelings the moods and intentions of the persons, groups, and culture studied—albeit at a certain emotional distance and with a lesser intensity. This approach is *hermeneutic*—seeking understanding—and *heuristic*—seeking to discern new insights, ideas, and reorientations in the investigator's mind.

Successful or partly successful examples of this approach through controlled empathy are found in some works of cultural anthropology, literary analysis, psychiatry, and "understanding" sociology. Many of these insights were not reproducible, but others were. These led to the recognition of new patterns that could be confirmed and reproduced and so became science. Even the insights that remained irreproducible and subjective—or reproducible, or plausible, only for members of a particular culture or social group—often had a pedagogical value. They trained investigators to greater sensitivity and perceptiveness, improved their judgment, and contributed to their mellowness of mind. For many social scientists, including some at this conference, this has remained the model of what social science ought to be (see Dilthey 1927; Hodges 1944; Collingwood 1956; Habermas 1981; and, for a recent classic formulation, Geertz 1982.

The opposite approach, long dominant in the natural sciences, seeks *objective* knowledge, impersonally reproducible by any observer or experimenter capable of performing the relevant operations of test or measurement, and corroborated by many different kinds of such operations. It has been the viewpoint of the unity of science that this kind of verifiable knowledge—within the limits of its particular domains of validity and its relevant operations of observation and measurement—can and should be sought in all fields of human behavior. The goal is not the reduction of the behavior of human individuals and groups to some mechanical models or procedures borrowed from the natural sciences, either past or present. Rather, new models or mathematical methods may have to be developed in many cases; and since new problems and discoveries in mathematics or in the various natural and social sciences may emerge at different times, this asynchrony may create formidable difficulties. Still, what is sought is science, in the sense of knowledge that is sharable and reproducible, retraceable step by step by some system of logic appropriate to the case, and containing *truth* in the sense of Einstein's word, "*Die Wahrheit liegt in der Bewährung*"—"Truth is what meets the test of practice" (see Bridgman

1925, 1980; Charles Morris 1938, 1968; Frank 1950; Einstein 1950; Wiener 1962; and, for a recent classic statement, Simon 1982).

The second mode of science holds for the social as well as the natural sciences. Here one looks for *facts*—that is, for classes of repetitive, observable events. One seeks to arrive at *existential statements*, of the logical form of "there is . . . ," and "if . . . then . . . ," and such statements can be confirmed by the cumulative evidence of mutually independent tests.

In practice, social scientists can then follow three types of pathways. They can start out with insights and attempts at pattern recognition, and then try to make these interpersonally reproducible and derive from them by deduction testable statements about expected facts. Or one may begin with selecting and collecting reproducible facts, and then try by induction to derive patterns from them. Or, finally, one may try to zig-zag between these two approaches, taking some steps within one mode, such as starting with an insight, then select facts relevant to it, then derive a new or a modified insight from the facts so selected and collected, and then look for further facts and testable connections among them. This last is in fact what many social scientists do, but it is not easy, and it leaves abundant room for controversy about the most appropriate proportion of steps to be allocated in each case to each approach.

All three paths are beset with difficulties. The search for insights, emphasis, and emotional understanding may stop short of communicable insights and clear pattern recognition, and may content itself with mere mellowness of mind. Other, more empirically inclined social scientists may think themselves hardboiled and resistant to the temptations of imagination and sentiment, and end up counting trivia—facts that remain trivial in their disconnection. Still other researchers may fail in their attempts to connect the two pathways of hermeneutic insight and empirical verification, so that their research fails to produce results that are cumulative and coherent. Yet, as our lists of advances indicate, many social scientists have succeeded in overcoming all these pitfalls.

Appraising the Importance of Contributions: How Substantial Is "Substantial"?

The original list of sixty-two social science contributions for 1900–1965, published in 1971, included only advances the authors had considered major ones (Deutsch, Platt, and Senghaas 1971). The Berlin Conference of 1982 produced in its various contributions a much higher total of suggestions, with about 100 candidates in economics and about 100 in other fields. Were these new cases, many of them from the 1965–1980 period, all of the same caliber as those on the original list?

One solution, suggested by Gerhard Bruckmann, was to divide the new cases into alpha, beta, and gamma categories. Alpha contributions then would be those with a major impact on at least one field of social science. Beta-type advances would be of lesser but still substantial importance; and gamma contributions would be those small advances that through their accumulations would so do much for a large part of scientific progress and development. Once again, the distinctions between these three types are apt to be hard to agree on in practice.

Some Problems for Further Research: Differences among Fields of Social Science

Which of the two basic styles of social science—the hermeneutic-literary or the empirical and mathematical—predominates in which field? Which style predominates among the recent major contributions to that field, among the teachers and researchers active within it, among its major journals, and among its students and other members of its larger constituency?

What has been the distribution of power between the two styles of science within each particular field? There is a kind of organizational power that shows itself in the editorships, editorial policies, and reviewing policies of professional journals; in the program committees and programs of professional meetings; in the appointment policies of universities and the promotion policies of academic departments; and in the distribution of research funds and research opportunities. This distribution of institutional power often is self-reinforcing, since it is hard for the adherent of one scientific style to advance in a field dominated by its opponents.

There is also, however, another type of power, the power to discover and create. The institutional power of a style dominant in a field may yet become stricken with sterility, and the outsiders developing or continuing the minority style may make the main discoveries of their epoch, partly because of their personal gifts but also—perhaps in larger part—because of the kind of problems becoming ripe for solution at that time within their field. This is why the patterns of dominance of this style or that in one field or another sometimes have been reversed in the past, and may be reversed again.

Underneath this ebb and flow of academic power, however, there has been a secular trend: the advance of mathematical thinking and quantitative analysis in all fields of social science and, indeed, in many fields of the humanities. (For an earlier example in the history of literature, see Burdach 1926; from history, see Mosteller and Wallace 1964; and Clubb and Scheuch 1980; from archeology, see Childe 1982, and generally, Lazarsfeld and Rosenberg 1954, 1955; Deutsch, Platt, and Senghaas 1971; Deutsch and Wildenmann 1976.) But this secular trend toward more mathematicization and quantification will remain barren if it is not linked to continuing acts of insight and recognition of patterns worth counting and analyzing by mathematical and other methods. Here again, despite this common thread, the detailed story will have to be explored in all its diversity from field to field.

Similarly, the frequency of truly major contributions—those one might assign to the alpha class—will differ from field to field, and not only because of the bias of different observers. Some fields may truly have grown through the continuing accretion of small-class gamma contributions, whereas alpha-type breakthroughs may have been crucial in others. The frequent suggestion that social scientists should content themselves with middle-range theories sounds plausible, but whether accretion of small gamma-type steps or of middle-sized beta-type advances, or the repeated occurrence of alpha-type breakthroughs has prodominated in some particular field of social science is a question future empirical research will have to answer.

Applications and Predictions: What Promises Were Fulfilled?

In the course of the conference it was repeatedly pointed out that the development of the social sciences often had been accompanied by promises that had remained unfulfilled. Much had been claimed for coming practical applications, but far less had been delivered. Was it not important for the social sciences to meet the expectations they once had kindled?

As a generalization, the accusation is untrue. The depth psychiatry of Freud, Jung, Adler, and Erikson has been applied widely, and it has alleviated the sufferings of hundreds of thousands of middle-class patients whose culture and education were close to that of the middle-class psychotherapists treating them. (For a discussion of the limited availability—and perhaps the limited validity—of these psychotherapeutic methods across barriers of class and culture, see Hollingshead and Redlich 1958.)

Applications of Keynesian economics in government policies often led to positive results in Western industrial countries during the quarter century after 1945, but far less so under the changed conditions after 1970. Survey research, that child of the development of sampling theory and interview methods, has been widely applied in electoral campaigns, in educational and welfare policy, and in commercial market research. Game theory and linear programming have been applied in a variety of uses, including inventory management. Ideas of circular causation and feedback hierarchies have come in to replace the old quarrels between causality and teleology in the debates among social scientists. (For a crucial impulse to that development, see Wiener, Rosenblueth and Bigelow 1943.)

Yet there remains a feeling of dissatisfaction. If social science has progressed, why does the world contain so much human suffering, unrelieved and often poorly understood?

For one thing, scientific knowledge, even if communicated, does not necessarily make people change their habits; nor does it make societies and states change their practices and institutions. The uncomfortable new information is more likely to be disbelieved or just ignored, and the preprogrammed behavior continues. Medical discoveries about lung cancer have not stopped millions from smoking. Why should social science discoveries in themselves have greater power?

Where habit change occurs, it is most often intergenerational. Freud's and Einstein's age-mates, in the great majority, did not think much of their discoveries. Their widespread acceptance came thirty to forty years later, and their large-scale application later still. Similar lags have been common in the history of the natural sciences. The ideas and discoveries of Copernicus, Galileo, and Kepler had no immediate application in practice. Their full application to more accurate intercontinental navigation came only in the second half of the seventeenth century, with a delay of between 50 and 150 years. Faraday's discovery of the principle of the generation of electricity by rotating wires in a magnetic field came in 1831, but it had to wait another forty years, until after Faraday's death, for its practical application in the dynamo.

Similar delays are common in the social sciences. Adam Smith argued for free trade in 1776; long after him, in 1846, it became British commercial policy. The general economic and social inferiority of the slave system, compared to free labor, was well understood in 1833 when Britain abolished slavery. It took another thirty years and a civil war to end slavery in the United States.

One reason other than inertia is the *limited validity* of most scientific propositions, including those in the social sciences. Their validity, even at best, is limited by the conditions of time, place, history, and culture. To feel this vaguely makes many practical people highly distrustful of some social science findings; but to find the precise limits of its validity may take much more work and time.

Moreover, much of nature and society consists of *countervailing processes*. One of these may push in a particular direction, while another may promote the opposite. The real outcomes then will not be one extreme or the other, but often may oscillate more moderately somewhere between. In the real world, these countervailing processes exist side by side, one perhaps stronger at one time and the other at another. This, as G. K. Chesterton remarked, is why kittens do not grow to the size of elephants. Although opposing processes often work side by side, they are not discovered at the same time. Whichever process a social scientist finds first, he or she must pursue to its full implications, obeying Plato's command to "follow the argument wherever it may lead." But the as yet undiscovered countervailing process may make the real outcome quite different from the predictions.

All these qualifications are well known to social scientists, or ought to be. Why, then, do they so often make excessive promises for their discoveries? One reason may be the normal optimism of many investigators about the potential importance of their discoveries—an optimism that may be an essential motivation for their labors. Perhaps a more weighty reason may be the structural pressures that push them toward overpromising. The larger the scale, the longer the duration, and the higher the empirical content of a social science research effort, the more costly it will be and hence the more dependent on financial support from sponsors, individual or institutional. Almost all such sponsors, however, are buyers in an invisible market; they want to spend little and get much. They want it soon and in practically applicable form. Often they want early applications of new basic knowledge that has been produced on someone else's budget. The scientists who want to work—in their sponsor's interest as well as in their own—will be perpetually tempted to promise them what they want.

These familiar contrasts between promise and early observable performance have led us to regard some recent "candidate contributions" with caution. Thus two such candidate contributions—the theory of collective choice (Olson 1967, 1982), and sociobiology (Wilson 1975)—have remained, in the view of most of the participants at this conference, so far just that—only candidates for the full status of substantial contributions as defined for our purposes.

Another Task for More Research: Conditions Favoring Substantial Advances

The original DPS papers of 1970 and 1971 emphasized various conditions frequently associated with substantial advances, such as interdisciplinarity, use of mathematics and statistics, and work in small teams but location at large centers of learning and research with a plurality of institutions. In the papers prepared for the conference of 1982, and in its proceedings, little was said about these matters, perhaps partly because of the shadow of the more anti-scientific climate of opinion in the United States and West Germany at the beginning of the 1980s (see the essays in Markovits and Deutsch 1980).

The earlier findings, however, survived without challenge. The list of advances from 1900 to 1965 remained open to discussion, but it seems to have been a robust sample. There was no disagreement with the earlier findings that the fascist dictatorships of Italy and Germany had produced no major advance in any of the social sciences and that, although there had been some such advances in the Soviet bloc, such as one version of linear programming, such advances there had been relatively much rarer than they had been in the West.

Broader and more thorough studies of conditions favoring advances of the kind listed in this book remain a task for the future.

More Studies of Meaning and Context

Other tasks remain. Prominent among them is that of narrowing the gap between the two types of social science—the empirical-quantitative and the interpretative-hermeneutical—through the development of a type of communication theory that will be relevant to both scientific approaches.

A great deal of classical communication theory has been channel-oriented. It focused attention on the capacity of communication channels to transmit information; on their configuration in feedback circuits, and their hierarchies, including monitoring circuits processing secondary symbols; and on facilities for information storage and recall. The content and meaning of the messages in all these channels and memories received little, if any, attention (for classic communication theory, see Wiener 1962; Cherry 1978; Shannon and Weaver 1949; Deutsch 1977).

Another approach to the study of the process of communication would center attention on the content of messages, and particularly on their meaning in context. Such an approach could be sketched as a sequence of ten questions.

The first four questions are cognitive:

1. In what *code* is the message formulated? What is its language or form? Can it be understood?
2. What is its *source*? Who is speaking?
3. What is its *context*? What is the message about? Is it a joke, a threat, a love letter, a technical instruction, or a business proposition?
4. What is the *content* of the message? What does it say?

The next four questions deal with the emotional and psychological aspects of any message:

5. Is the message *pleasant* or unpleasant? How is it related to what Sigmund Freud called the "pleasure principle" or the *id* of the receiver?
6. Is the message *true* or untrue? How does it measure up to what Freud called the "reality principle"?
7. Is the message *moral* or immoral? What are the results of its

confrontation with what Freud called the *superego* of the receiver?

8. How would the message, if accepted as true and valid, affect the *self-respect* of the receiver and the respect he or she would be likely to respect from others? In Freud's term, what would it do to his or her *ego strength*?

The last two questions are pragmatic:

9. How does the message fit in with the already existing *intentions*, plans, and commitments of the receiver?
10. What is to be done about it? What are its implications for *action*?

This approach can be carried further. The receiver not only can ask these ten questions but can ask them once more about the intentions of the sender. The sender can ask these same ten questions about the probable interpretation the receiver will make of the message. The more similar the answers to these three sets of questions, the greater will be the probability of mutual understanding. The more different these sets of answers, the greater the likelihood of misunderstanding.

The answers to the questions posed by the receiver depend only partly on the message. They also depend, often much more strongly, on the memory of the receiver, on the information stored there and triggered for recall by the incoming message. Similarly, the intentions of the sender depend partly on the sender's memory and particularly on the sender's image of the receiver's memory, and hence on his or her image of the effect the message will have on the receiver's probable response. In this sense, a content-oriented communication theory must also be necessarily a memory-oriented one.

Whether through this approach or any other, the gap between the two basic approaches to social science must be narrowed. The way to an appropriate synthesis will be long and difficult, for as a real synthesis it will require adding some new, relevant information to the two original positions, the literary-philosophical and the empirical-quantitative. Without such information, only compromises and eclecticism would result. (Deutsch 1980).

In the meantime, social scientists must act as the best physicians have been acting. If society is our patient—as Plato already suggested—with its illnesses in our time threatening to become fatal, then we must seek to apply whatever incomplete and inadequate knowledge we now have. Emergency patients cannot wait for more research results. Yet we must never forget that we need more knowledge if we are ever to do better. We must not forget our task to keep the social sciences moving and advancing, because it is their continuing advances that are indispensable.

References

Alker, H. R.; Deutsch, K. W.; and Stoetzel, A. H. eds. 1973. *Mathematical Approaches to Politics.* Amsterdam: Elsevier; San Francisco: Jossey-Bass.

Bridgman, P. W. 1925. Second ed., 1980. *The Logic of Modern Physics.* Arno Press.

Burdach, Konrad. 1926. *Der Dichter des Ackermann aus Böhmen und Seine Zeit.* Berlin: Weidmann.

Cherry, Colin. 1978. *On Human Communications*, 3rd ed. Cambridge, Mass.: MIT Press.

Childe, V. Gordon. 1982. *What Happened in History*, new ed. Harmondsworth, Middlesex: Peregrine Books.

Clubb, J., and Scheuch, E. K., eds. 1980, *Historical Social Research.* Stuttgart: Klett-Cotta.

Collingwood, R. G. 1956. *The Idea of History.* Oxford: Oxford University Press.

Deutsch, K. W. 1977. "On the Learning Capacity of Large Political Systems." In M. Kochen, ed., *Information for Action.* New York: Academic Press.

Deutsch, K. W. 1980. "Political Research in the Changing World System." In *Intl. Political Science Rev. 1* (1), pp. 23–33.

Deutsch, K. W.; Platt, J. R.; and Senghaas, D. 1971. "Conditions Favoring Major Advances in Social Science." *Science 171* (3970), pp. 450–459.

Deutsch, K. W., and Wildenmann, R., eds. 1976. *Mathematical Political Analysis: From Method to Substance.* 5th Social Science Yearbook for Politics. Munich: Olzog.

Dilthey, Wilhelm. 1927. *Gesammelte Schriften*, Vol. 7. Leipzig: Teubner, pp. 205–227.

Einstein, Albert. 1950. Foreword. In Philipp Frank, *Relativity—A Richer Truth.* Boston: Beacon Press.

Frank, Philipp. 1950. *Relativity—A Richer Truth.* Boston: Beacon Press.

Geertz, Clifford. 1982. "The Way We Think Now: Toward an Ethnography of Modern Thought." *Bull. Amer. Acad. Arts Sci. 35* (5), February, pp. 14–34.

Habermas, Jurgen. 1981. *Theorie des Kommunikativen Handelns.* 2 vols. Frankfurt: Suhrkamp.

Hodges, H. A. 1944. *The Philosophy of William Dilthey.* London: Routledge, pp. 42–51.

Hoffmann, Stanley, ed. 1960. *Contemporary Theory in International Relations.* Englewood Cliffs, N.J.: Prentice-Hall, pp. 50–52.

Hollingshead, A. B., and Redlich, F. C. 1958. *Social Class and Mental Illness.* New York: Wiley.

Kroeber, Alfred Louis. 1944. *Configurations of Culture Growth.* Berkeley: University of California Press.

Lazarsfeld, P. F., ed. 1954. *Mathematical Thinking in the Social Sciences.* New York: Free Press. Reissued New York: Russell and Russell, 1969.

Lazarsfeld, P. F., and Rosenberg, Morris, eds. 1955. *The Language of Social Research.* New York: Free Press.

Lipset, Seymour Martin. 1956. *Union Democracy.* Glencoe, Ill.: Free Press.

Lumsden, C. J., and Wilson, E. O. 1981. *Genes, Mind and Culture: The Coevolutionary Process.* Cambridge, Mass.: Harvard University Press.

Markovits, A., and Deutsch, K. W., eds. 1980. *Fear of Science—Trust in Science: Social Conditions for Change in the Climate of Opinion.* Cambridge, Mass.: Oelgeschlager, Gunn and Hain.

McIver, Robert. 1942. *Social Causation.* Boston: Ginn and Company.

Morris, Charles, ed. 1938, 1968. *Encyclopedia of Unified Science.* Chicago: University of Chicago Press.

Mosteller, F., and Wallace, D. L. 1964. *Inference and Authorship: The Federalist.* Reading, Mass.: Addison-Wesley.

Olson, Mancur. 1967. *The Logic of Collective Action: Public Goods and the Theory of Groups.* Cambridge, Mass.: Harvard University Press.

———. 1982. *The Rise and Decline of Nations: Economic Growth, Stagflation and Social Rigidities.* New Haven: Yale University Press.

Rapoport, Anatol. 1960. *Fights, Games and Debates.* Ann Arbor: University of Michigan Press.

Rastogi, P. N. 1982. *India, 1981–1986: A Forecast on Economic, Political and Social Developments.* New Delhi: Uppal.

Rosenblith, Walter. 1967. Afterword to N. Wiener, *The Human Use of Human Beings.* New York: Avon.

Shannon, C. E., and Weaver, W. 1949. *The Mathematical Theory of Communication.* Urbana: University of Illinois Press.

Simon, Herbert A. 1982. "Unity of the Arts and Sciences: The Psychology of Thought and Discovery." *Bull. Amer. Acad. Arts Sci. 35*(6), March.

Wiener, Norbert 1943. Second ed., 1962. *Cybernetics*, 2nd ed. Cambridge, Mass.: MIT Press.

Wiener, Norbert. 1967. *The Human Use of Human Beings.* New York: Avon.

Wiener, N.; Rosenbluth, A.; and Bigelow, J. 1943. "Behavior, Purpose and Teleology." In *Philosophy of Science 10*, January, pp. 18–24.

Wilson, E. O. 1975. *Sociobiology: The New Synthesis.* Cambridge, Mass.: Harvard University Press.

Appendix

Major Advances in the Social Sciences Since 1900: An Analysis of Conditions and Effects of Creativity[†]

Karl W. Deutsch, John R. Platt, and Dieter Senghaas

THE ENVIRONMENTAL AND GROUP CONDITIONS for creative success in the social sciences are a frequent subject for debate. It is not generally realized how much information about these creative conditions can be obtained from a statistical analysis of creative instances. To examine this question, we made a list of some 62 leading achievements in the social sciences in this century, as shown in Table A.1. Through this list we have tried to explore 12 major groups of questions.

1. Which were the major achievements or advances or breakthroughs in the social sciences in 1900–1965? Are there publicly verifiable criteria by which they can be recognized? Can such

†Slightly abbreviated from Deutsch, Platt, and Senghaas (1970) reference in Chapter 1.

Table A.1. Basic Innovations in Social Science, 1900–65

No.	1 *What*	2 *Who*	3 *When*	4 *Based on Whose Work*	5 *Where*	6 *Type of Institution*
1.	Theory and measurement of social inequalities (Ec)	V. Pareto C. Gini	1900 1908	L. Walras D. Bernoulli A. Lexis B. Czuber	Lausanne Cagliari Padua, Rome	University chairs
2.	Sociology of bureaucracy, culture and values (Soc)	M. Weber	1900–21	W. Dilthey K. Marx	Freiburg Heidelberg Munich	University chair with res. support
3.	Theory of one-party organization and revolution (Pol)	V. I. Lenin	1900–17	K. Marx	Shushenskoe (Siberia) London, Munich	Underground party
4.	Psychoanalysis and depth psychology (Psy)	S. Freud C.G. Jung A. Adler	1900–25 1910–30 1910–30	J. Breuer	Vienna	University Institute of Psychology
5.	Correlation analysis and social theory (Math)	K. Pearson F. Edgeworth R.A. Fisher	1900–28 1900–30 1920–48	C. Weldon F. Galton	London Oxford Cambridge, Eng. Harfenden, Eng.	University chairs
6.	Gradual social transformation (Pol)	B. Webb S. Webb G.B. Shaw H.G. Wells	1900–38	J. Bentham K. Marx	London	Fabian Society
7.	Elite studies (Soc)	G. Mosca V. Pareto H.D. Lasswell	1900–23 1900–16 1936–52	K. Marx C.H. St.-Simon	Turin Lausanne Chicago	University Institutes
8.	Unity of logic and mathematics (Phil)	B. Russell A. N. Whitehead	1905–14	G. Bollo G. Frege	Cambridge, England	University Institute
9.	Pragmatic and behavioral psychology (Psy)	J. Dewey G.H. Mead C. Cooley W.I. Thomas	1905–25 1900–34 1900–30 1900–40	W. James	Ann Arbor Chicago, Ann Arbor Chicago New York	University chairs
10.	Learning theory (Psy)	E.L. Thorndike C. Hull *et al.*	1905–40 1929–40	E.C. Tolman C. Darwin S. Freud	New York New Haven	Teachers Coll. Inst. of Human Rels.
11.	Intelligence tests (Psy)	A. Binet L. Terman C. Spearman	1905–11 1916–37 1904–27	F. Galton L.A. Bertillon	Paris Stanford London	Testing organizations
12.	Role of innovations in socioeconomic change (Ec)	J.A. Schumpeter W.F. Ogburn A.P. Usher J. Schmookler	1908–14 1946–50 1922–30 1924 1966	E. Böhm-Bawerk L. Walras F. Edgeworth J.B. Clark	Vienna New York Cambridge, Ma. Minneapolis	University chair and res. program
13.	Conditioned reflexes (Psy)	I. Pavlov	1910–30	W. Wundt J. Moleschott G. Lewes D. Pisarev I. Sechenow	Leningrad	Imperial Medico-Surgical Academy

Table A.1. (*continued*)

	7	8	9	10	11	12	13	14	15	16	17	18	19	20	21
	Substantial Impact on			*Number of Workers*	*Ages*	*Quantit. Aspects*	*Requirements of*			*Inter disci-plin-ary*	*Stim. by Prac. De-mands*	*Social Practice Related to*			*Years Until Im-pact*
No.	**Theory*	**Methods*	**Results*	†		‡	*Capital§*	*Manpower §*	*Time §*	*	*	**Individ.*	**Group*	**State*	
1.	—	Y	Y	1+N	52 24	QFE	L	L	L	N	Y	—	—	—	25
2.	Y	—	Y	1	36	QPI	L	L	H	Y	—	—	—	—	20±10
3.	Y	—	Y	1+N	30	QPI	L	H	H	Y	Y	Y	Y	Y	10±5
4.	Y	Y	Y	1+N	44 35 40	Non-Q	L	L	H	N	—	Y	Y	—	30±10
5.	—	Y	Y	1+N	43 55 30	QFE	L	L	L	Y	Y	—	—	—	25±15
6.	Y	—	Y	4+N	42 41 44 34	QPE	L	L	L	Y	Y	—	Y	Y	35±5
7.	Y	Y	Y	1+N	42 52 34	QFE	L	L	L	Y	Y	—	—	Y	40±10
8.	Y	—	—	2	33 44	QPE	L	L	H	Y	—	—	—	—	30
9.	Y	—	—	1	46 37 36 37	Non-Q	L	L	L	Y	Y	Y	Y	—	20±10
10.	Y	Y	Y	1+N	31 45	QFE	H	H	H	N	Y	Y	Y	—	20±5
11.	Y	Y	Y	1+N	48 39 41	QFE	L	H	H	N	Y	Y	Y	Y	15±5
12.	Y	—	Y	1+N	25	QPI	L	L	L	Y	Y	Y	—	Y	40
13.	Y	Y	Y	1+N	61	QPI	H	H	H	N	N	Y	Y	Y	20±10

Table A.1. (*continued*)

No.	1 *What*	2 *Who*	3 *When*	4 *Based on Whose Work*	5 *Where*	6 *Type of Institution*
14.	Gestalt psychology (Psy)	M. Wertheimer K. Koffka W. Koehler	1912–32	E. Mach C.V. Ehrenfels	Berlin	University chairs
15.	Sociometry and sociograms (Soc)	J. L. Moreno	1915 1934–43	—	Innsbruck	University chair
16.	Soviet type of one-party state (Pol)	V.I. Lenin *et al.*	1917–21	—	Leningrad	Politburo
17.	Large-scale nonviolent political action (Pol)	M.K. Gandhi	1918–34	H.D. Thoreau L.N. Tolstoy	Ahmedabad	Political movement & instit. (Ashram)
18.	Central economic planning (Ec)	Q. Krassin G. Grinko	1920–26	War economy (German)	Moscow	Government institute
19.	Social welfare function in politics & economics (Ec)	A.C. Pigou K. Arrow	1920–56 1951	M.J.A. Condorcet V. Pareto	London Stanford	University chairs
20.	Logical empiricism and unity of science (Phil)	M. Schlick R. Carnap O. Neurath P. Frank L. Wittgenstein H. Reichenbach C. Morris	1921–38 1921 1936–50	E. Mach K. Pearson B. Russell A.N. Whitehead	Vienna Cambridge (Eng) Berlin Chicago Cambridge, Mass.	Vienna Circle & University chairs University chairs
21.	Quantitative mathematical studies of war (Pol)	L.F. Richardson Q. Wright	1921–55 1936–66	Thucydides	London Chicago	University chair & res. program
22.	Projective tests (Psy)	H. Rorschach H. Murray	1923	E. Bleuler S. Freud C.G. Jung	Herisau, Switz. Cambridge, Mass.	Cantonal Inst. Univ. chair
23.	Sociology of knowledge & science (Soc)	K. Mannheim D.deS. Price	1923–33 1950–60	K. Marx M. Weber	Heidelberg Frankfurt Princeton New Haven	University chairs, Institutes & Programs
24.	Quantitative political sci. & basic theory (Pol)	C. Merriam S. Rice H. Gosnell H.D. Lasswell	1925–36	European political sociology	Chicago	University chairs
25.	Functionalist anthropology and sociology (An)	A.R. Radcliffe-Brown B. Malinowski T. Parsons	1925 1925–45 1932–50	H. Spencer J.G. Frazer E. Durkheim M. Weber	Capetown Sidney Chicago Oxford London Cambridge, Mass.	University chairs & travel grants
26.	Ecosystem theory (Soc)	R. Park E.W. Burgess	1926–38	G. Simmel	Chicago	University chairs
27.	Factor analysis (Math)	L. Thurstone	1926–48	K. Pearson C. Spearman	Chicago	University chair
28.	Operational definitions (Phil)	P.W. Bridgman	1927–38	E. Mach A. Einstein	Cambridge, Mass.	University chair

Table A.1. *(continued)*

No.	7 Substantial Impact on *Theory	8 *Methods	9 *Results	10 Number of Workers †	11 Ages	12 Quantit. Aspects ‡	13 Requirements of Capital§	14 Manpower §	15 Time §	16 Inter disci- plin- ary *	17 Stim. By* Prac. De- mands *	18 Social Practice Related to *Individ.	19 *Group	20 *State	21 Years Until Im- pact
14.	Y	Y	Y	3+N	32 26 25	Non-Q	L	L	L	N	—	—	—	—	25±5
15.	—	Y	Y	1	23	QFE	L	L	L	N	—	—	Y	—	10
16.	Y	—	—	1+N	47	QPI	H	H	H	Y	Y	—	Y	Y	5±5
17.	Y	—	—	1+N	49	Non-Q	L	H	H	Y	Y	Y	Y	—	15±10
18.	Y	Y	Y	1+N	50 30	QFE	H	H	H	N	Y	—	Y	Y	7±6
19.	Y	Y	Y	1+N	43 30	QPE	L	L	L	N	Y	—	—	—	40±10
20.	Y	Y	—	3+N	39 30 39 37 29 30 35	QPI	L	L	L	Y	—	—	Y	—	20±5
21.	Y	Y	Y	1+N	40 46	QFE	L	L	H	Y	Y	—	—	—	25±10
22.	—	Y	Y	1	39 42	Non-Q	H	H	H	N	Y	Y	—	—	15±5
23.	Y	Y	Y	1+N	40 28	Non-Q	L	L	L	Y	Y	—	—	Y	10
24.	Y	Y	Y	3+N	41 39 34 34	QFE	L	H	H	N	Y	—	Y	Y	15±5
25.	Y	—	Y	1+N	44 41 35	Non-Q	L	L	H	N	—	—	—	—	20±10
26.	Y	Y	Y	2+N	62 40	QFE	L	H	H	N	Y	—	Y	—	25±5
27.	—	Y	Y	1+N	39	QFE	H	H	H	Y	Y	—	—	—	15±10
28.	Y	Y	—	1	45	QPI	L	L	L	N	—	—	—	—	15±5

Table A.1. (*continued*)

No.	1 *What*	2 *Who*	3 *When*	4 *Based on Whose Work*	5 *Where*	6 *Type of Institution*
29.	Structural linguistics	R. Jakobson & Prague circle N. Chomsky	1927–67 1957–	—	Brno Cambridge, Mass. Cambridge, Mass.	University chairs & programs
30.	Economic propensities, employment and fiscal policy (Ec)	J.M. Keynes	1928–44	A. Marshall	Cambridge, Eng.	University chair
31.	Game theory (Math)	J.v. Neumann O. Morgenstern	1928–44 1944–58	—	Berlin Princeton	University chairs & Institute
32.	Peasant and guerrilla organization & gov't (Pol)	Mao Tse Tung	1929–49	V.I. Lenin	Kiangsi Yenan Peking	Political movement
33.	Community studies (Soc)	R. Lynd H. Lynd L. Warner C. Kluckholm	1929–62 1941	R. Park W.I. Thomas	New York Chicago	University chairs
34.	Culture and personality & comparative child-rearing (An)	R. Benedict M. Mead G. Gorer A. Kardiner J. Piaget E. Erikson J. Whiting I. Child	1930 1930 1939 1940–60 1950 1953	S. Freud O. Spengler E. Sapir F. Boas A.L. Kroeber	New York Geneva Cambridge, Mass. Cambridge, Mass. New Haven	University chairs, res. projects, travel grants
35.	Economics of monopolistic competition	E.H. Chamberlin J. Robinson	1930–33	A.A. Cournot F. Edgeworth T. Veblen	Cambridge, Mass. Cambridge, Eng.	Univ. chairs
36.	Authoritarian personality and family structure (Psy)	M. Horkheimer H. Marcuse E. Fromm T. Adorno *et al.* A. Mitscherlich	1930–32 1950 1962	S. Freud A. Adler	Frankfurt Stanford Frankfurt Heidelberg	Institute for Social Res. & univers.
37.	Large-scale sampling in social research (Math)	M. Hansen	1930–53	M. Hogg	Washington	Government office
38.	Laboratory study of small groups (Psy)	K. Lewin R. Lippit R. Likert D. Cartwright	1932–36	J.L. Moreno	Cambridge, Mass.	University and res. institutes
39.	National income accounting (Ec)	S. Kuznets C. Clark U.N. Statistical Office	1933 1953	J.M. Keynes League of Nations	Philadel. Cambridge (Eng.) Washington New York	Public Res. Insts. & Univ. chairs
40.	General systems analysis (Phil)	L.v. Bertalanffy J.G. Miller A. Rapoport R.W. Gerard K. Boulding	1932 1953	H. Spencer A. Comte V. Pareto I. Prigogine W. Koehler A. J. Lotka M. Schlick H. Reichenbach	Vienna Chicago Ann Arbor	University research Institutes

Table A.1. *(continued)*

No.	7 Substantial Impact on *Theory	8 *Methods	9 *Results	10 Number of Workers †	11 Ages	12 Quantit. Aspects ‡	13 Requirements of Capital§	14 Manpower §	15 Time §	16 Inter disci- plin- ary *	17 Stim. By* Prac. De- mands *	18 Social Practice Related to *Individ.	19 *Group	20 *State	21 Years Until Im- pact
29.	Y	Y	Y	1+N	31 29	QPE	L	L	H	N	—	—	—	—	20±10
30.	Y	Y	Y	1+N	45	QFE	L	H	H	N	Y	—	Y	Y	6±4
31.	Y	Y	Y	2+N	25 42	QFE	L	L	L	Y	—	—	Y	Y	10±5
32.	Y	—	—	1+N	36	QPI	H	H	H	Y	Y	—	Y	Y	15±10
33.	—	Y	Y	2	37 37 43 42	QFE	H	H	H	N	Y	—	—	—	20±5
34.	Y	Y	Y	3+N	43 29 30 48 44 48 45 38	Non-Q	L	H	H	Y	Y	Y	Y	—	20±10
35.	Y	Y	Y	1	31 32	QPE	L	L	L	N	—	—	Y	Y	10±5
36.	Y	Y	Y	3+N	31 32 32 47 53	QPI	L	L	L	Y	Y	Y	Y	Y	20±5
37.	—	Y	Y	N	25	QFE	H	H	H	Y	Y	—	Y	Y	5
38.	Y	Y	Y	1+N	42 32 35 30	QPI	H	H	H	N	Y	Y	Y	Y	10±5
39.	—	Y	Y	1+N	32 31	QFE	H	H	H	N	Y	—	—	Y	10±5
40.	Y	Y	—	4+N	35 38 43 54 46	QPI	L	L	L	Y	—	—	—	—	15±5

Table A.1. *(continued)*

No.	1 *What*	2 *Who*	3 *When*	4 *Based on Whose Work*	5 *Where*	6 *Type of Institution*
41.	Attitude survey and opinion polling	G. Gallup H. Cantril P.F. Lazarsfeld A. Campbell	1936 1937–52 1940 1942	U. Yule	Princeton New York Ann Arbor	University and res. institutes, commercial organizns.
42.	Input-output analysis (Ec)	W. Leontief	1936–53	F. Quesnay L. Walras	Cambridge, Mass.	University chair
43.	Linear programming (Ec)	L. Kantorovich J.B. Souto G.B. Dantzig R. Dorfman	1938–50 1941 1948 1958	—	Leningrad Buenos Aires Washington Berkeley	University res. insts. & govt. office
44.	Content analysis (Pol)	H. Lasswell I. deS. Pool B. Berelson P. Stone	1938–56 1961–66	—	Chicago Cambridge, Mass.	University institute
45.	Operant conditioning & learning. Teaching machines (Psy)	B. F. Skinner	1938–58	I.P. Pavlov E.L. Thorndike C. Hull	Bloomington Cambridge, Mass.	University chairs
46.	Statistical decision theory (Math)	A. Wald	1939–50	C.F. Gauss D. Neyman-Pearson R.A. Fisher	New York	University chair
47.	Operations research and systems analysis (Math)	P.M.S. Blackett P. Morse R. Bellman	1941–50 1948–59	—	London Cambridge, Mass.	Govt. res. institutes
48.	Scaling theory (Psy)	L. Guttman C. Coombs	1941–54	L. Thurstone R. Likert	Ithaca, NY Ann Arbor	University chairs
49.	Quantitative models of nationalism & integration (Pol)	K. Deutsch B. Russett R.L. Merritt	1942–67	O. Bauer A. Usher R. Emerson N. Wiener	Cambridge, Mass. New Haven	University chairs
50.	Theories of economic development (Ec)	R. Rosenstein-Rodan R. Prebisch R. Nurkse W.A. Lewis G. Myrdal A.O. Hirschman R.F. Harrod E. Domar H. Chenery	1943–58	K. Marx J. Schumpeter A.A. Young	London Santiago New York Manchester Stockholm New Haven Oxford Baltimore Stanford	Government offices, UN regional commission, University chairs
51.	Computers (Math)	V. Bush S. Caldwell D.P. Eckert J.W. Mauchly	1943–58	C. Babbage Y. Boole N. Wiener J. v. Neumann	Cambridge, Mass. Philadelphia	University & govt. research laboratories
52.	Multivariate analysis linked to soc. theory (Soc)	S. Stouffer T.W. Anderson P. Lazarsfeld	1944–54	K. Pearson U. Yule R.A. Fisher E. Durkheim	Washington Cambridge, Mass. New York	Government and univ. research institutes
53.	Information theory, cybernetics & feedback systems (Math)	C. Shannon N. Wiener	1944–58	C. Bernard W. Cannon	Cambridge, Mass. Orange, NJ	University res. inst. & Bell Labs.

Table A.1. *(continued)*

No.	7 Substantial Impact on *Theory	8 *Methods	9 *Results	10 Number of Workers †	11 Ages	12 Quantit. Aspects ‡	13 Requirements of Capital§	14 Manpower §	15 Time §	16 Inter disci-plin-ary *	17 Stim. By* Prac. De-mands *	18 Social Practice Related to *Individ.	19 *Group	20 *State	21 Years Until Im-pact
41.	—	Y	Y	3+N	35 31 39 32	QFE	H	H	H	Y	Y	—	Y	Y	5
42.	Y	Y	Y	1+N	30	QFE	H	H	H	N	Y	—	Y	Y	15
43.	—	Y	Y	1+N	26	QFE	H	L	H	N	Y	—	Y	Y	10±5
44.	—	Y	Y	2	42 36 34 40 28	QFE	L	H	H	Y	Y	—	Y	Y	10
45.	Y	Y	Y	1+N	32	QPE	H	H	H	N	Y	Y	Y	—	15
46.	Y	Y	Y	1+N	37	QPE	L	L	L	N	Y	—	Y	—	15±5
47.	—	Y	Y	N	44	QFE	H	H	H	Y	Y	—	Y	Y	5
48.	—	Y	Y	3+N	38 31 25	QFE	H	H	H	N	Y	Y	Y	Y	10±5
49.	Y	Y	Y	1+N	30 27 30	QFE	L	L	L	Y	Y	—	—	Y	20±5
50.	Y	—	Y	6+N	41	QFE	L	L	L	Y	Y	—	—	Y	10±5
					42 36 28 45 28										
51.	Y	Y	Y	N	43 29 29 53 39 24 36	QFE	H	H	H	Y	Y	Y	Y	Y	10±5
52.	Y	Y	Y	3+N	44 26	QFE	L	L	L	Y	Y	—	Y	Y	5
53.	Y	Y	Y	2+N	43 28 50	QFE	H	H	H	Y	Y	Y	Y	Y	10±5

Table A.1. (*continued*)

No.	1 *What*	2 *Who*	3 *When*	4 *Based on Whose Work*	5 *Where*	6 *Type of Institution*
54.	Econometrics	J. Tinbergen P. Samuelson E. Malinvaud	1935–40 1947 1964	H.L. Moore R. Frisch I. Fisher	The Hague Cambridge, Mass. Paris	Government inst. & univ. chairs
55.	Cognitive dynamics of science (Phil)	J.B. Conant I.B. Cohen T. Kuhn D.deS. Price	1946–64	R. Merton B. Barber P. Frank P. Bridgman A. Koyré	Cambridge, Mass. Berkeley	University chairs
56.	Computer simulation of economic systems (Ec)	L. Klein G. Orcutt	1947–60	—	Philadelphia Madison, Wis.	Research institutes
57.	Structuralism in anthropology and soc. science (An)	C. Lévi-Strauss	1949–66	M. Mauss B. Malinowski	Paris	Museum (government)
58.	Hierarchical computerized decision models (Math)	H. Simon	1950–65	—	Pittsburgh	University research institute
59.	Cost-benefit analysis (PPB) (Pol)	C. Hitch	1956–63	P.M.S. Blackett W. Leontief	Santa Monica	Government-related research institute
60.	Computer simulation of soc. and political systems (Pol)	W. McPhee H. Simon A. Newell I. Pool R. Abelson	1956–66 1958–64	P. Lazarsfeld B. Berelson A. Campbell W. Miller D. Stokes	Pittsburgh Cambridge, Mass. New Haven	University chairs & research instits.
61.	Conflict theory & variable sum games (Psy)	A. Rapoport	1960–	J.v. Neumann O. Morgenstern N. Rashevsky	Ann Arbor	University research institute
62.	Stochastic models of social processes (Math)	J.S. Coleman	1965	—	Baltimore	University & research institute

Table A.1. *(continued)*

No.	7 Substantial Impact on *Theory	8 *Methods	9 *Results	10 Number of Workers †	11 Ages	12 Quantit. Aspects ‡	13 Requirements of Capital§	14 Manpower §	15 Time §	16 Inter disci-plin-ary *	17 Stim. By* Prac. De-mands *	18 Social Practice Related to *Individ.	19 *Group	20 *State	21 Years Until Im-pact
54.	Y	Y	Y	1+N	42 32	QFE	H	H	H	N	Y	—	Y	Y	10±5
55.	Y	Y	Y	3+N	41 53 32 40 39	Non-Q	L	L	L	Y	—	—	Y	Y	15
56.	Y	Y	Y	2+N	27 30	QFE	H	H	H	N	Y	—	Y	Y	5
57.	Y	Y	Y	1+N	41	QPI	L	L	L	N	—	—	—	—	15±5
58.	Y	Y	—	1+N	34	QPE	H	H	H	Y	Y	—	Y	—	10
59.	—	Y	Y	3+N	46	QFE	H	H	H	Y	Y	—	Y	Y	7
60.	Y	Y	Y	2+N	35 40 29 41 30	QPE	H	H	H	Y	Y	—	Y	Y	5±3
61.	Y	Y	Y	1+N	49	QFE	H	H	H	Y	Y	—	—	—	2
62.	Y	Y	Y	1+N	39	QFE	H	H	H	Y	Y	—	—	—	5

*Y, yes; N, no; —, not substantial
†1 + *N*, 2 + *N*, etc; the "+ *N*" denotes a larger number of collaborators with a less crucial share in the work
‡QFE—quantitative findings explicit; QPE, QPI—quantitative problems explicit or implied; Non-Q—predominantly nonquantitative
§L, low; H, high.

advances be called cumulative in the sense proposed by James B. Conant, that successive advances are built upon earlier ones?

2. In what fields did such breakthroughs occur?
3. Did major advances relate mainly to theory, or to method, or to matters of substance? In what fields did such advances occur most often?
4. Are there any changes and trends over time in the incidence and characteristics of these breakthroughs?
5. Who accomplished such advances most often—individuals or teams?
6. What were the ages of the contributors at the time of their achievements? Any special personality characteristics?
7. Were the results quantitative, explicitly or by implication?
8. Did such breakthroughs require much capital? Manpower? Other resources?
9. Where were they accomplished? At what geographic locations? At what types of institutions? Under what social and political conditions?
10. Where did the ideas come from? Were most advances made primarily within existing disciplines or were they mainly interdisciplinary in character?
11. Did the major advances have any close relation to social practice? Were they inspired or provoked by practical demands or conflicts? Were they applied to practice? If so, were they applied by or to individuals, small or middle-sized groups, or national governments and states?
12. How long was the delay between each major breakthrough and its first major impact on social science and/or social practice?

The evidence bearing on these questions is summarized in Table A.1 opposite the 62 achievements in the years 1900–1965. The achievements themselves were selected on the basis of our personal judgment as to their importance for social science in this century. We also called upon the opinions and advice of a number of colleagues in other fields, and we checked each contribution against the relevant entries of the recent edition of the *International Encyclopedia of the Social Sciences*.[1]

The principal findings from this study are three.

1. There *are* such things as social science achievements and social inventions, which are almost as clearly defined and as operational as technological achievements and inventions.
2. These achievements have commonly been the result of conscious and systematic research and development efforts by individuals or teams working on particular problems in a small number of interdisciplinary centers.

3. These achievements have had widespread acceptance or major social effects in surprisingly short times, with median times in the range of 10–15 years, comparable with the median times for widespread acceptance of major technological inventions.

Criteria for Recognizing Major Advances in Social Science

The major achievements or breakthroughs selected for this study were defined as having the following characteristics. First, they either had to involve a new perception of relationships or they had to result in new operations, including scientific operations. That is, they had to help people see something not perceived before, leading to new discoveries (statements of the form "there is . . . ") or new verifiable propositions (statements of the form "if . . . then . . . "); or else they had to create the possibility of doing something that had not been done before.

A second essential condition for any major contribution, whether dealing with perceptions or operations, was that it should have proved fruitful, in producing a substantial impact leading on to further knowledge. Impacts simply on social practice, on the other hand, were treated as interesting but nonessential.

We feel that the 62 contributions listed in Table A.1 are among the most significant achievements in social science satisfying these criteria in the years 1900–1965. We should emphasize that there is no intent to use this list for any invidious bestowal of professional recognition and that other achievements might well be chosen by other criteria of significance or for other purposes.

We omitted purely technical achievements such as television, despite their great impact on society, feeling that so far they have not contributed to social science as much as, say, computers have. We also omitted more purely political and organizational achievements such as the National Astronautics and Space Administration (NASA), the Manhattan Project, the British National Health Service, the European Common Market, the Tennessee Valley Authority, credit cards, "think tanks," the great public and private foundations, the Peace Corps, and the partial Nuclear Test Ban Treaty, although all these have intellectual components that would justify their entry in a broader list. On the same grounds we omitted such primarily practical innovations as Henry Ford's development of the assembly line, the time and motion studies by F. W. Taylor and his followers, the studies of human relations in industry by F. J. Roethlisberger and his associates, the development of such rural organizations as the *kibbutzim* in Israel and the *kolkhosy* in the Soviet Union, B. Ruml's invention of the "pay-as-you-go" income tax, the development of high-information teaching by J. Zacharias and associates, man-and-computer designs as developed by C. E. Shannon and R. Fano and others, and the proposal for a guaranteed annual income (or a negative income tax) by J. Tobin and M. Friedman among other economists. By contrast, the innovations by Lenin, Mao, Gandhi, and the Webbs were included because they were connected with explicit theories.

Several contributions seemed to us to constitute borderline cases. In social psychology, these include the frustration-aggression hypothesis by John Dollard, Neal Miller, and their collaborators (New Haven, Connecticut, 1940); the theory of cognitive dissonance developed by Leon Festinger, Robert Abelson, and others (Stanford, California and New Haven, Connecticut, 1956–1957); the development of cognitive anthropology by Floyd Lounsbury and others (New Haven, 1956–1968); the concept and measurement of the semantic differential by Charles Osgood, G. J. Suci, and P. H. Tannenbaum (Urbana, Illinois, 1957); and the concept and partial measurement of achievement motivation by David E. McClelland (Middletown, Connecticut, 1953, and later Cambridge, Massachusetts, 1961). At the borderlines of psychology we find the discovery of a wider range of mind-influencing drugs; the works of Konrad Lorenz and others on "imprinting" in young animals; the broader explorations in the chemistry of memory; and the work on the electric stimulation of brain centers directing larger sequences of behavior, by Delgado and others. None of these have been included in our present list, primarily because we did not feel sure that until now the impact of any of these contributions on broader areas of the social sciences has been as large and lasting as the impact of those contributions we did include. A future tabulation may well have to include some or all of these present-day borderline cases. In any case, a comparison with our tables in the rest of the article will show that an inclusion of these borderline cases would have strengthened rather than weakened the trends indicated by our major findings.

Clearly, other individuals and other schools of thought would have a different ranking for particular achievements, but one would hope that within the boundaries we accepted there would be a considerable amount of overlap within the academic community in evaluating the top fifty to seventy contributions in this century.

An inspection of our list shows that many of the later contributions were clearly building on the earlier ones, and that they resulted in clear increases in the powers of social scientists to recognize relationships and to carry out operations. Many of the advances had a substantial impact on the subsequent development of several social sciences and on social practice as well. Together, these advances add up to unmistakable evidence of the cumulative growth of knowledge in the social sciences in the course of this century. Statements such as "we know no more about human psychology and politics than Aristotle did" today mainly express the ignorance of those who utter them.

Main Fields of Advances

The assignment of major social science innovations to particular fields is indicated in column 1 of Table A.1, and their distribution among fields is shown in column 1 of Table A.2. The latter table reveals the leading position of psychology, economics, and politics, with 13, 12, and 11 major contributions, respectively. A major advance was made therefore on the average every five to six years in *each* of these three fields.

Several contributions involving the applications of mathematical and statistical methods to these subject fields are included in these numbers; thus linear programming and the computer simulation of economic systems were each coded as contributions to economics.

Another 11 major contributions were primarily mathematical or statistical in nature and were coded in a separate category, even though they may have had applications in various substantive fields. Factor analysis and information theory are two examples of this category. Although these coding rules tend to underrepresent the number of major advances in social science methods, it still appears that a major advance in mathematical or statistical method was made on the average at least once every six years.

Substantive advances in sociology and anthropology seemed to have occurred once per decade, and in anthropology about once every twenty years. These calculations somehow underrepresent, however, the actual rate of progress in these fields, particularly with regard to sociology. Several of the advances in social psychology, political science, and even

Table A.2. Major Social Science Contributions by Field and Focus, 1900 to 1965

Field	Total 1900 to 1965	Major contributions 1900 to 1929	Major contributions 1930 to 1965	Focus on theory 1900 to 1929	Focus on theory 1930 to 1965	Focus on method 1900 to 1929	Focus on method 1930 to 1965	Focus on results 1900 to 1929	Focus on results 1930 to 1965
1. Psychology	13	7	6	6	3	6	6	6	6
2. Economics	12	5	7	4	5	4	6	5	7
3. Politics	11	7	4	7	2	2	4	4	4
4. Mathematical Statistics	11	4	7	2	5	4	7	4	6
5. Sociology	7	6	1	4	1	5	1	6	1
6. Philosophy	5	3	2	3	2	2	2	0	1
7. Anthropology	3	1	2	1	2	0	2	1	2
Totals	62	33	29	27	20	23	28	26	27
	62	62		47		51		53	

economics were almost as important for the progress of sociology, as they were in their fields of origin.

Furthermore, several of the advances in mathematical and statistical methods had a major effect on sociology, though much less in the case of anthropology. Finally, several scholars at the beginning of this century such as Vilfredo Pareto and Max Weber covered in their scholarly activities sociology and various other fields. We coded one of Pareto's contributions—the measurement of inequality—in economics, and another—elite theory—in sociology; and we coded Max Weber's contribution as sociological. In fact, of course, all three contributions had an effect on the progress of sociology.

Another five contributions resemble those in mathematics and statistics in the fact that their primary impact was not in any substantive fields of social science. Since they were not primarily quantitative, however, we coded them in a separate category as philosophy, logic, and history of science. Russell and Whitehead's demonstration of the unity of logic and science, the work of the Vienna circle on the unity of science, and Thomas Kuhn's work on the role of paradigms in scientific revolutions are examples of such entries.

Theory, Method, or Substance?

Important advances typically combine theory, methods, and results, rather than choosing one of these elements as a focus of interest. Our analysis of these factors is given in columns 7, 8, and 9 of Table A.1, and is summarized in Tables A.2 and A.3. As Table A.3 shows, over the sixty-five year-period, about 53 of the contributions, or over 80 percent, yielded substantive results in terms of discoveries or data; 51 contributions produced advances in methods; and 47 produced advances in theory.

Most often such advances have cut across at least two of these aspects of social science and have often crossed all three of them. The distribution between single-focus and multifocus contributions is shown in Table A.3-B. Only five contributions were limited to theory alone, and all these occurred before 1930. In contrast to the history of the natural sciences, we did not find a single major advance in the social sciences in this century that consisted in a purely empirical discovery. The discovery of America by Christopher Columbus, or later the prediction and discovery of the planet Neptune by J. J. Leverrier and J. G. Galle required nothing more than the application of existing theories and methods of observation. But in the social sciences, every major new discovery of substance seems to have required some significant advance in theory or method, or both, as a precondition. In the light of these findings the long-standing quarrel whether to emphasize mainly theory or methodology or empirical results seems ill-conceived and obsolete. All three seem to form part of one pro-

Table A.3. The Main Foci of Major Social Science Advances, 1960–1965

A. Substantial Impact on:

Years	Total	(1) Theory	(2) Methods & Techniques	(3) Results
1900–04	7	5	4	7
1905–09	5	5	2	3
1910–14	2	2	2	2
1915–19	3	2	1	1
1920–24	6	5	6	5
1925–29	10	8	8	8
1900–29	(33)	(27)	(23)	(26)
1930–34	6	4	6	6
1935–39	6	2	6	5
1940–44	8	6	7	8
1945–49	4	4	4	4
1950–54	1	1	1	0
1955–59	2	1	2	2
1960–65	2	2	2	2
1930–65	(29)	(20)	(28)	(27)
1900–65	(62)	(47)	(51)	(53)

B. Single-Focus versus Multifocus Contributions

	1900–1929	1930–1965	1900–1965
Only theory	5	0	5
Only methods	0	0	0
Only results	0	0	0
Total single-focus Contributions	5	0	5
Theory and methods	2	2	4
Theory and results	5	1	6
Methods and results	6	9	15
Theory-methods-results	15	17	32
Total multifocus contributions	28	29	57
Grand total	33	29	62

duction cycle of knowledge, and substantial advances in any one of these phases are likely to lead to advances in the other two.

Trends With Time

Substantial social science advances at the level of importance examined here have been surprisingly frequent, averaging close to one advance per year, as shown in Table A.4. Taking into account the greater difficulty

Table A.4. Major Contributions by 5, 10, 15, and 30-Year Periods, 1900–1965

Years	10-yr	Total	15-yr	Psychol.	Econ.	Pol.	Math.	Soc.	Phil.	Anthr.
1900–1904	12	7	14	1	1	2	1	2	–	–
1905–1909		5		[3	1	—	—	—	1	—
1910–1914	5	2		2]	—	—	—	—	—	—
1915–1919		3	19	—	—	[2	—	1	—	—
1920–1924	16	6		1	[2	1	—	[1	1	—
1925–1929		10		—	1]	2]	[3]	2]	1	1
1900–1929		33		7	5	7	4	6	3	1
1930–1934	12	6	20	[2	[2	—	[1	—	—	1
1935–1939		6		2]	1	1	1	—	1	—
1940–1944	12	8		1	2	1	3]	1	—	—
1945–1949		4	7	—	2]	—	—	—	1	1
1950–1954	3	1		—	—	—	1	—	—	—
1955–1959		2		—	—	2	—	—	—	—
1960–1965		2		1	—	—	1	—	—	—
1930–1965		29		6	7	4	7	1	2	2
1900–1965		62		13	12	11	11	7	5	3

of estimating the full impact of social science contributions after 1950, which drastically reduces the number of such contributions in our account, it seems that this high frequency has remained at least undiminished since 1930. For social science investigators who need to keep abreast of knowledge in several disciplines, this raises serious problems of the partial obsolescence of their information.

A closer look reveals a great deal of variance around this average, in terms of both periods and fields. The interpretation of this variance is made difficult by three conditions. First, our dating of major social science contributions was in terms of first major publication, or of the major writing or experimental work preceding publication where the timing of such work was known to us. By thus tying each contribution to a particular starting year, Table A.4 disregards the fact that the follow-up and development work on each contribution took several years and often decades.[2]

A second difficulty in analyzing starting dates over time rests in the fact that some of the contributions coded under 1900 had been already under actual development from some date in the 1890s; this produces an artificial concentration of contributions at the beginning of our period.

A third problem applies to the recognition of the importance of a social science contribution. Table A.1, column 21 reveals that it often takes a considerable number of years for many social science contributions to have a significant impact on their field, as well as on social practice. If this is so, it should be very difficult for us, writing in early 1970, to identify with confidence any major social science contributions from the 1950s and 1960s, since many of these may not have become visible to us through any significant impact to the present. Indeed, Table A.4 shows that out of 62 contributions coded, only 5, or less than 8 percent, had a starting date after 1950. One possible interpretation of this fact would be that we are living in an age of epigones in which major new contributions have become much rarer than before. A second interpretation would be that social scientists are now so busy with working out the implications of earlier advances that they have less time and motivation to take major intellectual initiatives. A third interpretation would be that new advances in the social sciences since 1950 have been as frequent as before in earlier decades but that the delay in their impact is still preventing us from recognizing them. (See the fuller discussion of this point on p. 418.) At this time the evidence before us does not seem sufficient to decide these questions.

Even so, we can say something about particular periods and fields.

For the half century 1900–1949 the total of 57 contributions yields an average of about 1.1 per year. The same average is found for the first period of the century between 1900–1929; for the next 20 years, 1930–1949, the average is 1.2.

In considering single decades, only one decade, 1910–1919, is far below this average, with only five contributions, whereas the decade immediately following, 1920–1929, with 16 contributions, is the highest of all decades examined. The interpretation seems plausible that a number of gifted individuals were delayed in their work by the impact of World War I but that their delayed contributions then arrived in the next decade. It seems that this war did not inspire directly any large number of contributions.

The decade that included most of World War II, 1940–1949, by contrast, was rich in contributions, with a total of 12. And a number of these were directly related to requirements of the war effort, such as operations research and computers and cybernetics, or to economic planning made salient by the war, such as input-output analysis and the theory of economic development. It should be noted, however, that most of the advances during World War II were made in the United States, which was not a theater of war, and to a lesser extent in Britain, which was only exposed to aerial attacks. Both these countries, moreover, had been enriched by an inflow of social scientists who had emigrated from the European continent. None of these compensating conditions had existed at the time of World War I.

With regard to particular fields, all fields show a certain clustering in time except philosophy of science and anthropology, in which the total number of contributions was small. Nearly two-thirds of all advances in psychology occurred in two decades, 1905–1914 ($n = 5$), and 1930–1939 ($n = 4$), and five-sixths of all contributions fell into the three decades 1920–1949. More than two-thirds of the advances in mathematical and statistical methods were made in the two decades 1925–1944 ($n = 8$). Nearly one-half of the advances in political science were made in the one-and-a-half decades 1915–1929 ($n = 5$), and the same period produced more than one-half of the advances in sociology ($n = 4$). Such periods of concentration of efforts in each field are indicated by boxes in each field.

Owing to the considerable time delay between the making of an advance and its major impact on social science and/or social practice, many of these advances were having their major effects only in the 1950s and 1960s, and further effects may still be to come.

Who Accomplished the Advances: Individuals or Teams

A question often discussed is whether major contributions in science are most often the product of single individuals or of larger groups working in actual collaboration. (This question is distinct from the question of simultaneous or nearly simultaneous discoveries. If two or more scientists, each working substantially alone, should make the same advance or make complementary contributions to the same developments, we should still count each of them as having worked alone, even though the products of their work would eventually contribute to the same development. The independent work of E. H. Chamberlin and J. Robinson on the theory of monopolistic competition would be an example.)

Our first coding of the number of contributions to each advance, insofar as we knew it, is shown in column 10 in Table A.1. The addition "$+N$" denotes a larger number of collaborators or continuators, whose share in the work we deemed less crucial.

For purposes of analysis, we chose a three-category scheme of coding. After trying several alternatives, we included in our first category all those scientists who had worked alone, together with those who had been clearly the principal authors of the crucial element in the new advance or discovery, even if they had significant but less decisive help from several collaborators. Cases of the latter sort were coded $1 + N$ in Table A.1. Max Weber is an example of the social scientist who worked alone; Sigmund Freud is an example who made the decisive contribution even though he was assisted by collaborators and others who developed his work in various directions, such as C. J. Jung or Otto Rank and Alfred Adler.

Our second category includes two-man teams and two-man teams assisted by other collaborators. Such two-man contributions include the work of Russell and Whitehead on the unity of logic and mathematics; and the work of von Neumann and Morgenstern on the theory of games is an example of a two-person effort assisted and continued by other workers. In many of these cases, it is hard to see how the same people, working as separate individuals, could have created the advance in question. This team creativity seems to be an increasingly common modern phenomenon. In a historical survey, it is hard to think of many pairs of thinkers working together as an equal team until we come to Goethe and Schiller, and Marx and Engels, and John Stuart Mill and Harriet Taylor Mill. In the natural sciences and engineering, such teams are also becoming commoner in this century, from the Curies and the Wright brothers to Yang and Lee, and Watson and Crick.

Our final category consists of all work by three or more principal contributors whether or not it was further assisted or continued by still other investigators. Examples are the development of logical empiricism by Schlick, Carnap, Neurath, and others in the Vienna circle, and the work on authoritarian personality and family structure by Horkheimer, Marcuse, Fromm, Adorno, and others at the Frankfurt Institute for Social Research, as well as the development of multivariate analysis in the social sciences by Stouffer, Anderson, and Lazarsfeld. Large-team research is no longer restricted to the research and development laboratories of industry and the government, or to the "big science" areas of modern physics and biology, but is increasingly apparent in the social science achievements of the last few decades.

The distribution of social science advances over these categories, together with their changes over time, are shown in Table A.5. The results suggest that nearly two-thirds of the contributions were primarily the work of individuals, while nearly one-third were produced by teams of three or more persons. Contributions by two-person teams were relatively rare. There was, however, a significant change in these proportions over time. During the period 1900–1929, about three-quarters of all contributions were primarily the work of individuals, in contrast to less than

Table A.5. The Changing Size of Teams, 1900–1965

	Number of Principal Contributions in Each Effort:			
	1	2	3	4
	1 and/or 1 + N	2 and/or 2 + N	3 or more	Total
1900–1929	25	4	4	33
1930–1965	13	3	13	29
Total	38	7	17	62

one-half of the total contributions in 1930–1965. Teams of three or more persons made only 4 contributions during the first period but nearly three times as many—13—during the second. The trend toward team research becomes even stronger if we single out from the category of primarily individual contributions the case of those scientists who seemed to have worked alone. We found 8 such cases between 1900 and 1929, but only one such case in 1930–1965. This single case was the development of the theory of monopolistic competition; and this contribution, as stated earlier, was made twice, by E. H. Chamberlin and J. Robinson working independently from each other.

It should be emphasized that our coding in many of these cases must be considered provisional, and that the results can be used only with great caution. Even so, the trend toward increasing reliance on team research in the social sciences, and the capacity of team research to produce fundamental contributions, seem indicated quite clearly. In view of the cultural lag in some social science fields, where the image of the lonely scholar in the library is still extolled and teamwork is held in disdain, the evidence of social science contributions since 1930 should be given more attention.

Ages and Personalities of the Contributors

The ages of the contributors at the time they made their breakthroughs are shown in column 11 of Table A.1 and the detailed analysis is given in Table A.6. For the entire period 1900–1965, the median age group among 160 contributors was between 35 and 39 years, with a mean age of 37 years. The modal age group, with 41 contributors, was a little older, in the range of 40 to 44 years. Slightly more than 40 percent of all contributors were more than 40 years old at the time of their contribution, but only 6 percent were over 50 years.

Table A.6-B shows that for the period as a whole, psychology was a young man's game, with more than one-third of all contributions coming from people under 35. Modal contributions in economics and political science also fell in the 30- to 34-year age group. Both economics and political science, however, show second peaks for contributors 40 to 44 years old. The modal age for contributors in mathematics and statistics, as well as in philosophy, is somewhat higher—30–39 years; it is still higher for sociology and anthropology: 40–44 years.

To be sure, any attempt to correlate age and achievement in the universe of social science contributions—as in any other scientific universe—is somewhat hazardous. The times of the breakthroughs are at best approximate; the assignment to one individual rather than another may be only approximate; and the step-by-step nature of progress, even in the studies of a given individual, may make the specific dating of the "break-

Table A.6-A. Ages of Listed Social Science Innovators at Time of Innovation

Name	Birthdate	Date of Innovation	Age at Time of Innovation
1. V. Pareto	1848	1900	52
C. Gini	1884	1908	24
2. M. Weber	1864	1900	36
3. V. I. Lenin	1870	1900	30
4. S. Freud	1856	1900	44
C.G. Jung	1875	1910	35
A. Adler	1870	1910	40
5. K. Pearson	1857	1900	43
F. Edgeworth	1845	1900	55
R.A. Fisher	1890	1920	30
6. B. Webb	1858	1900	42
S. Webb	1859	1900	41
G.B. Shaw	1856	1900	44
H.G. Wells	1866	1900	34
7. G. Mosca	1858	1900	42
V. Pareto	1848	1900	52
H.D. Lasswell	1902	1936	34
8. B. Russell	1872	1905	33
A.N. Whitehead	1861	1905	44
9. J. Dewey	1859	1905	46
G.H. Mead	1863	1900	37
C. Cooley	1864	1900	36
W.I. Thomas	1863	1900	37
10. E.L. Thorndike	1874	1905	31
C. Hull	1884	1929	45
11. A. Binet	1857	1905	48
L. Terman	1877	1916	39
C. Spearman	1863	1904	41
12. J.A. Schumpeter	1883	1908	25
13. I. Pavlov	1849	1910	61
14. M. Wertheimer	1880	1912	32
K. Koffka	1886	1912	26
W. Koehler	1887	1912	25
15. J. L. Moreno	1892	1915	23
16. V. I. Lenin	1870	1917	47
17. M.K. Gandhi	1869	1918	49
18. Q. Krassin	1870	1920	50
G. Grinko	1890	1920	30
19. A.C. Pigou	1877	1920	43
K. Arrow	1921	1951	30
20. M. Schlick	1882	1921	39
R. Carnap	1891	1921	30
O. Neurath	1882	1921	39
P. Frank	1884	1921	37
L. Wittgenstein	1889	1918	29

Table A.6-A. *Continued*

Name	Birthdate	Date of Innovation	Age at Time of Innovation
H. Reichenbach	1891	1921	30
C. Morris	1901	1936	35
21. L.F. Richardson	1881	1921	40
Q. Wright	1890	1936	46
22. H. Rorschach	1884	1923	39
H. Murray	1893	1935	42
23. K. Mannheim	1893	1923	40
D.S. Price	1922	1950	28
24. C. Merriam	1874	1925	41
S. Rice	1889	1928	39
H. Gosnell	1896	1930	34
H.D. Lasswell	1902	1936	34
25. A.R. Radcliffe-Brown	1881	1925	44
B. Malinowski	1884	1925	41
T. Parsons	1902	1937	35
26. R. Park	1864	1926	62
E.W. Burgess	1886	1926	40
27. L.L. Thurstone	1887	1926	39
28. P.W. Bridgman	1882	1927	45
29. R. Jacobson & Prague Circle	1896	1927	31
N. Chomsky	1928	1957	29
30. J.M. Keynes	1883	1928	45
31. J. v. Neumann	1903	1928	25
O. Morgenstern	1902	1944	42
32. Mao Tse Tung	1893	1929	36
33. R. & H. Lynd	1892	1929	37
L. Warner	1898	1941	43
C. Kluckhohn	1905	1947	42
34. R. Benedict	1887	1930	43
M. Mead	1901	1930	29
G. Gorer	1905	1935	30
A. Kardiner	1891	1939	48
J. Piaget	1896	1940	44
E. Erikson	1902	1950	48
J. Whiting	1908	1953	45
I. Child	1915	1953	38
35. E. H. Chamberlin	1899	1930	31
J. Robinson	1903	1935	32
36. M. Horkheimer	1899	1930	31
H. Marcuse	1898	1930	32
E. Fromm	1900	1932	32
T. Adorno	1903	1950	47
N. Sanford	1909	1950	41
E. Frenkel-Brunswick	1908	1950	42

Table A.6-A. *Continued*

	Name	Birthdate	Date of Innovation	Age at Time of Innovation
	D. Levinson	1920	1950	30
	A. Mitscherlich	1909	1962	53
37.	M. Hansen	1910	1935	25
38.	K. Lewin	1890	1932	42
	R. Lippit	1914	1946	32
	R. Likert	1903	1938	35
	D. Cartwright	1915	1945	30
39.	S. Kuznets	1901	1933	32
	C. Clark	1905	1936	31
40.	L. v. Bertalanffy	1901	1936	35
	N. Rashevsky	1899	1938	39
	J.G. Miller	1916	1954	38
	A. Rapoport	1911	1954	43
	R.W. Gerard	1900	1954	54
	K. Boulding	1910	1956	46
41.	G. Gallup	1901	1936	35
	H. Cantril	1907	1937	31
	P.F. Lazarsfeld	1901	1940	39
	A. Campbell	1910	1942	32
42.	W. Leontief	1906	1936	30
43.	L. Kantorovich	1912	1938	26
	R. Dorfman	1916	1958	42
44.	H. Lasswell	1902	1938	36
	I. de S. Pool	1917	1951	34
	B. Berelson	1912	1952	40
	P. Stone	1936	1964	28
45.	B.F. Skinner	1904	1936	32
46.	A. Wald	1902	1939	37
47.	P. M. S. Blackett	1897	1941	44
	P. Morse	1903	1941	38
48.	L. Guttman	1916	1941	25
49.	K. Deutsch	1912	1942	30
	B. Russett	1935	1962	27
	R.L. Merritt	1933	1963	30
50.	P. Rosenstein-Rodan	1902	1943	41
	R. Prebisch	1901	1943	42
	R. Nurkse	1907	1943	36
	W.A. Lewis	1915	1943	28
	G. Myrdal	1898	1943	45
	A.O. Hirschman	1915	1943	28
	R.F. Harrod	1900	1943	43
	E. Domar	1914	1943	29
	H. Chenery	1918	1947	29
51.	V. Bush	1890	1943	53
	S. Caldwell	1904	1943	39
	J.P. Eckert	1919	1943	24

Table A.6-A. *Continued*

Name	Birthdate	Date of Innovation	Age at Time of Innovation
J.W. Mauchly	1907	1943	36
52. S. Stouffer	1900	1944	44
T.W. Anderson	1918	1944	26
P. Lazarsfeld	1901	1944	43
53. C. Shannon	1916	1944	28
N. Wiener	1894	1944	50
54. J. Tinbergen	1903	1945	42
P. Samuelson	1915	1947	32
E. Malinvaud	1923	1964	41
55. J.B. Conant	1893	1946	53
I.B. Cohen	1914	1946	32
T. Kuhn	1922	1962	40
D. de S. Price	1922	1961	39
56. L. Klein	1920	1947	27
G. Orcutt	1917	1947	30
57. C. Lévi-Strauss	1908	1949	41
58. H. Simon	1916	1950	34
59. C. Hitch	1910	1956	46
60. W. McPhee	1921	1956	35
H. Simon	1916	1956	40
A. Newell	1927	1956	29
I. de S. Pool	1917	1958	41
R. Abelson	1928	1958	30
61. A. Rapoport	1911	1960	49
62. J.S. Coleman	1926	1965	39

Table A.6-B. Age of Social Innovators at Time of Innovation, 1900–1965

Age of Social Scientists at Time of Breakthroughs	Psy	Ec	Pol	Math & Stat	Phil	Soc	An	Total in Age Group
20–24	—	1	—	1	—	1	—	3
25–29	3	7	3	4	1	2	1	21
30–34	11	8	8	3	4	1	1	36
35–39	9	2	4	6	8	2	2	33
40–44	7	8	8	3	3	7	5	41
45–49	5	2	4	—	2	—	3	16
50–54	1	2	—	2	2	—	—	7
55–59	—	—	—	1	—	—	—	1
60–64	1	—	—	—	—	1	—	2
65–69	—	—	—	—	—	—	—	0
70–	—	—	—	—	—	—	—	0
Totals 1900–1965	37	30	27	20	20	14	12	160

Table A.6-C. Age of Social Science Innovators at Time of Innovation, 1900–1929

Age of Social Scientists at Time of Breakthroughs	Psy	Ec	Pol	Math & Stat	Phil	Soc	An	Total Reported
20–24	—	1	—	—	—	1	—	2
25–29	2	1	—	1	1	—	—	5
30–34	2	1	2	2	3	1	—	11
35–39	6	—	2	1	3	2	—	14
40–44	3	1	5	1	1	3	2	16
45–49	3	1	2	—	1	—	—	7
50–54	—	2	—	—	—	—	—	2
55–59	—	—	—	1	—	—	—	1
60–64	1	—	—	—	—	1	—	2
65–69	—	—	—	—	—	—	—	0
70–	—	—	—	—	—	—	—	0
Totals 1900–1929	17	7	11	6	9	8	2	60

Table A.6-D. Age of Social Science Innovators at Time of Innovation, 1930–1965

Age of Social Scientists at Time of Breakthroughs	Psy	Ec	Pol	Math & Stat	Phil	Soc	An	Total in Age Group
20–24	—	—	—	1	—	—	—	1
25–29	1	6	3	3	—	2	1	16
30–34	9	7	6	1	1	—	1	25
35–39	3	2	2	5	5	—	2	19
40–44	4	7	3	2	2	4	3	25
45–49	2	1	2	—	1	—	3	9
50–54	1	—	—	2	2	—	—	5
55–59	—	—	—	—	—	—	—	0
60–64	—	—	—	—	—	—	—	0
65–69	—	—	—	—	—	—	—	0
70–	—	—	—	—	—	—	—	0
Totals 1930–1965	20	23	16	14	11	6	10	100

through" quite arbitrary. However, we did not have any particular bias in this matter in our selection of dates, contributions, and contributors; and in fact, when we listed our scientists, we had no idea how old most of them were at the time of their contributions. We therefore believe that, with these reservations, the distributions of ages as given by this analysis have at least a first-order significance.

The overall data show interesting differences between the time periods 1900–1929 and 1930–1965. As shown in Tables A.6-B and A.6-C, the modal age of all contributors in the earlier period was 40 to 44 years. In the more recent period, the modal group was much younger, in the range of 30–34 years. The median age group, however, remained the same for both periods. The shift toward younger contributors in the more recent period was marked in psychology, economics, and political science. This might be partly an artifact because of our better knowledge of the earlier stages of more recent developments.

On the other hand, the opposite trend may be noted, though to a weaker extent, in the remaining fields. In mathematics and statistics, the main increase in contributors from 1930 onward occurred in the 35- to 39-year age group, in sociology it occurred among 40- to 44-year-olds, and in anthropology it was spread over the age groups of 40 to 44 and of 45 to 49 years.

Altogether it seems striking that the fields that attracted most contributors and that were also richest in contributions, attracted the largest number of young scientists. By and large, the less frequent the major contributions occurred in any field, the older tended to be the people who made them. This puzzling correlation is more easily noted than explained. It is conceivable that older scientists may have been less creative and more dominant in certain fields, which might then have attracted fewer of the gifted younger scholars. An opposite interpretation of the same data might suggest that in some fields it may have been intrinsically more difficult to make any major contribution and that these more difficult fields required greater experience, and hence greater age, as a condition for success. The question is not trivial, but it cannot be answered without further study.

In applying these results to the always interesting question of the effect of age on creativity, all these figures must be corrected or normalized, of course, for the number of social scientists active in each age group. Details on the total number of scientists of different age groups in the different fields and the different countries for the full time period are not readily available, but older scientists are necessarily less numerous in any rapidly growing field, as Derek Price has emphasized, so that an approximate general correction is possible.[3]

Very roughly speaking, the number of social scientists grew between 1900 and 1965 at an average rate of about 5 percent per year, doubling approximately every 14 years. The proportion of scientists in the age groups 20–34, 35–49, and 50–65 therefore were roughly 4:2:1. Generally any age group of scientists had at least twice as many members as the age group 15 years older, even if we are not counting the effects of biological and professional attrition. If we allow for the fact that the number of scientists over 50 is roughly only one-fourth of the number of scientists under 35 (and was a still smaller fraction before 1940 when the length of life was less), the apparent falling off of contributions in the higher age groups is not nearly as serious. Relative to their numbers (assuming the one-fourth ratio), scientists over 50 still maintained 67 percent of the productivity of those under 35. Adjustments of this kind, however, still leave the peak levels of productivity in the intermediate age range of 35–49 years.

Our findings accord relatively well, on the whole, with those reported by Harvey C. Lehman.[4] The findings for the period 1900–1929 seem to fit Lehman's data for social philosophy, architecture, and "best books" from world literature. The data for the period from 1930 onward are quite similar to Lehman's data for psychology, for "contributions to economic and political science," and for "contributions to education theory and practice." In fact, the downward trend of ages as shown in our data may eventually carry the social sciences toward the young ages found in mathematics and physics, where the highest average rate of major contributions occurs for investigators in the age range of 30 to 34 years.

From the scattered biographical data we have encountered, it is hard to make a quantitative statistical tabulation of personality characteristics. Nevertheless, a number of traits stand out. One is the generally high intelligence of the contributors involved, which one might estimate is generally in the 160 range and up, on the basis of their capacity for information handling, speeds of response, and insight in conversations and lectures, and the brillance of presentation and reasoning in their books, quite aside from any consideration of the importance of the listed achievements.

Other characteristics would include energy and leadership. A large percentage of these contributors started major centers and institutes and even larger national organizations built around their new discoveries, although we did not think we were being overimpressed by the existence of the organizations in our initial selection of the achievements. (A bias of this sort, however, is hard to eliminate, because it is hard to conclude that an achievement is unimportant—at least in methods, results, or practice—when a major organization has made it professionally important for many years to large numbers of workers in the area. Even if it is false or misleading—as some of our 62 examples may well prove to be in the long view of history—an achievement that is socially enlarged in this way cannot help but be important.) People who build successful new organizations obviously must know how to work with disciples or other people, how to support them, and how to get their cooperation and support as well.

From a different point of view, however, this kind of energy, leadership, and decisiveness may be seen as rudeness and dominance, which were frequent accusations against leaders as different as Lenin and von Neumann. The rudeness is often a simple intolerance of fools, critics, and time-wasters, which is seen as intellectual arrogance by those against who it is directed. But qualities like this have often been necessary to turn ideas into action. On the other hand, an enormous number of the people in our list also had to have qualities of intensity, seriousness, and a certain kind of patient effort, especially for those achievements (*H* in column 15 of Table A.1) that took years of work and thought.

There are only 3 percent of women amoung the contributors to these major advances, a figure comparable with the percentage of women who have won Nobel Prizes in the sciences.

The Frequency of Quantitative Results

Throughout the entire period, one-half of the major advances in our list produced explicit quantitative findings. Another one-sixth posed at least explicit quantitative problems, bringing the explicit quantitative work to two-thirds of the total. Still another dozen contributions clearly implied quantitative problems even if they did not pose them explicitly. Altogether, major social science advances that thus contributed to quantitative knowledge, explicitly or by implication, amounted to more than five-sixths of the total. An overview of these data is given in Table A.7, and the details on which they are based are shown separately for each contribution in column 12, in Table A.1.

As these figures show, we succeeded in identifying only nine major contributions that were predominantly nonquantitative in character, amounting to about one-seventh of the total. These included, however, contributions of such importance as psychoanalysis, pragmatic and behavioral psychology, Gestalt psychology, nonviolent political action, Rorschach tests, the sociology of knowledge, functional anthropology, culture and personality studies, and the cognitive dynamics of science. Without

Table A.7. Major Quantitative versus Nonquantitative Contributions In Social Science, 1900–1965

Period	1 Nonquantitative	2 Quantitative Problems Implied	3 Quantitative Problems Explicit
1900–1929	7	8	4
1930–1965	2	4	5
1900–1965	9	12	9

Period	4 Quantitative Findings Explicit	5 Total Quantitative: Explicit	5 Total Quantitative: All	Total
1900–1929	14	18	26	33
1930–1965	18	23	27	29
1900–1965	32	41	53	62

these primarily qualitative contributions, modern social science would not be what it is. Despite their small number, nonquantitative contributions, centering usually on some kind of pattern recognition, have been an essential element in scientific progress and may well continue to be so in the future. Both types of scientific personalities, the quantifiers and the pattern-recognizers—the "counters" and the "poets"—will continue to be needed in the social sciences.

The high proportions of quantitative contributions may well be in part a product of our selective bias. Thus we did not include among our list of advances the rise of several schools of thought such as existential psychiatry and phenomenological psychology and sociology, because we could not identify any specific new discovery or capability that they contributed to the social sciences, nor any major impact they have had thus far on the social sciences. A mere modification of the focus of interest of the investigator was in no case treated as sufficient ground for inclusion in our list, since it would not have permitted us to distinguish, on other than subjective grounds, group changes in intellectual fashions and genuine contributions to the social sciences. Since we have explicitly stated our own criteria and listed the contributions, counted by us on this basis, other investigators may, of course, state different criteria and propose different lists for their own purposes.

The evidence for the quantitative emphasis in modern social science seems more solidly founded, however, than in our biases as investigators. Those biases, insofar as they were effective, presumably would have applied to the entire period which we investigated. A division of the entire period into an earlier part, 1900–1929, and a later one, 1930–1965, as presented in Table A.7, however, shows a clear decline in the frequency of nonquantitative contributions, from 7 in the earlier period to only 2 in the later one. Similarly, the number of contributions where quantitative problems are merely implied rather than stated explicitly declines from 8 to 4. By contrast, the share of contributions with explicit quantitative findings rises from about two-fifths in the first period (14 out of 33) to over three-fifths (18 out of 29) in the second. It seems plausible to infer that, despite the continuing importance of some nonquantitative contributions, the trend toward the predominance of quantitative work in the social sciences has been continuing and may well be rising.

Requirements in Capital, Manpower, and Principal Investigator's Time

The making and testing of any new discovery requires some kind of investment. Some of this investment is in the form of capital equipment. Such capital requirements may be high in regard to such matters as special laboratories, computing facilities, investigating or implementing organizations, and the like. In other cases, capital requirements may be low, requiring only small experiments with cheap equipment, or simply the resources of a university library, or public library, available at no significant additional capital cost.

Another set of requirements involves manpower. Large numbers of assistants, laboratory helpers, poll takers, or tabulating clerks may be required either for pay, or as volunteers, or as students. In other investigations, the work of a single scientist or of a very small number of collaborators may be sufficient. Finally, some contributions require the commitment of long stretches of the principal investigator's time and thought, as did Max Weber's historical and sociological studies, or Freud's development of psychoanalysis.

In other cases, the basic idea may not require much of the principal investigator's time, as perhaps in the case of Schumpeter's notion of the importance of innovations or Bridgman's development of operational definitions. This distinction, however, is relative. Von Neumann and Morgenstern spent a good deal of time developing the theory of games during the early years of World War II, following up von Neumann's early paper of 1929, but we still assume that their effort took them less time than Freud or Max Weber had to spend on their own contributions. Our coding for each contribution in terms of the three types of requirement is given in columns 13, 14, and 15 of Table A.1.

A summary of these data is presented in Table A.8. As the data show, major contributions in the social sciences are likely to require a good deal of the chief investigator's time. Nearly two-thirds did so in the cases we

Table A.8. Requirements in Capital, Manpower and Principal Investigator's Time, 1900–1965

	High Requirements		
Period	Capital	Manpower	Principal Investigator's Time
1900–29	8	14	20
1930–65	18	19	20
1900–65	26	33	40

	Pattern of Requirements					
Period	HHH	HLH	LHH	LLH	LLL	TOTAL
1900–29	8	0	6	6	13	33
1930–65	17	1	2	0	9	29
1900–65	25	1	8	6	22	62

H = High
L = Low
Patterns of Requirement: 1. Capital
2. Manpower
3. Principal Investigator's Time

studied, but it is worth noting that relatively quick insights, with relatively moderate requirements for follow-up work by their author, still amount to more than one-third of major contributions. This relationship remains substantially unchanged over the period 1900–1929, and 1930–1965, respectively.

In contrast to the unchanging claims on the principal investigator's time, requirements for auxiliary manpower have been increasing. For the entire period 1900–1965, more than one-half of all major contributions had been marked by such manpower requirements. But the proportion of contributions dependent on such high manpower inputs increased from less than one-half in 1900–1929 to about two-thirds in 1930–1965. If one excludes from the first period the social science contributions related to mass politics, such as Lenin's one-party organization and one-party state, Gandi's nonviolent political action, Krassin's central economic planning, and Mao's theory of peasant and guerrilla organization of government, all of which required large amounts of manpower, then the contrast between the first and second period becomes still stronger.

The change over time is most clear-cut with regard to capital requirements. Over the entire period over two-fifths of all contributions could not have been made without requiring relatively high amounts of capital. Over time, the share of contributions requiring high capital commitment to research rose from less than 25 percent in the period 1900–1929 to over 60 percent in the period from 1930–1965. In the majority of successful contributions, relatively high capital commitments to research have become not an exception but a rule, not a luxury but a necessity.

High resource requirements in one respect turned out to be strongly correlated to high resource requirements in other respects. In particular, the proportion of contributions of the pattern HHH, requiring high amounts of capital, manpower, and principal investigator's time, was much higher than could have been expected by pure chance. Over the entire period 1900–1965, about 40 percent of all contributions were marked by high resource requirements in all three respects; and this proportion rose from less than one-quarter in the period 1900–1929 to nearly three-fifths in 1930–1965. By contrast, the proportion of contributions with only modest resource requirements in all three categories (LLL) remained at about one-third of the total with but little change over the two periods.

Looked at in conjunction, Tables A.7 and A.8 suggest that the trends towards higher capital requirements and toward a greater emphasis on quantitative findings may be positively correlated. A more detailed tabulation of resource requirements by five-year periods, not reproduced here, corroborates the surmise. The two five-year periods 1925–1929 and 1940–1944, which contained the largest number of contributions with explicit quantitative findings—5 and 8, respectively—also show the greatest concentration of projects with high capital requirements—3 and 5, respectively—and these turn out to be all of the HHH type, which required high inputs of capital, manpower, and investigator's time as well.

Table A.9. Capital Requirements and Quantitative Results, 1900 to 1965. "High" and "low" refer to the level of capital required

Type of result	1900 to 1929		1930 to 1965		1900 to 1965	
	High	Low	High	Low	High	Low
Nonquantitative results	1	6	0	2	1	8
Application to quantitative problems explicit and/or implied	3	9	4	5	7	14
Quantitative findings explicit	4	10	14	4	18	14
Total	8	25	18	11	26	36

If we limit ourselves to contributions with explicit quantitative findings on the one hand, and to nonquantitative contributions on the other, and if we limit ourselves further to the contrast of high capital and low captital requirements, then we obtain the relationships shown in part of Table A.9. Here we find that out of 26 high capital contributions during the entire period, 18 produced explicit quantitative findings, whereas out of 36 contributions with low capital requirements only 14 produced such explicit quantitative results. This tendency may be seen already in the period 1900–1920, when low-capital work predominated; but it becomes considerably stronger in the second period when high-capital work became more frequent.

The perception of social science work as cheap—a notion that is widespread among lay people and some university administrators—seems based on the experiences before 1930, when only one-fourth of all major social science contributions required major amounts of capital. Since 1930 more than three-fifths of all contributions have required relatively large amounts of capital, particularly for survey research and large-scale tabulations, and this proportion seems likely to increase further in the future. (Row 4, columns 3 and 4 in Table A.9) If explicit quantitative results are desired, the requirement for capital support becomes still stronger. Low-budget research, the work of lone individuals or work on nonquantitative topics, may play a smaller and smaller role. The industrial revolution in the production of knowledge has reached not only a large part of the natural sciences but the social sciences as well.

Where the Pioneers Were: Localities and Institutions

Countries and Cities: The Concentration Effect

An analysis of major social science contributions by location is made difficult by four conditions. First, in several cases our information is poor. Second, work on many of these advances extended over a considerable number of years, during which the investigator often moved from one place or institution to another, or successively to several. Third, many advances involved the work of several investigators, with some working during the same period and others in succession, with some or all of them changing their locations and institutional affiliations in the course of their work. Finally, our own familiarity with some countries, institutions, and fields of social science is greater than it is with others; and thus our own biases may have further increased the divergence between our image of the situations and the true state of affairs. At this stage, therefore, our findings must be considered highly provisional and treated with great caution. Even so, however, some relationships may be so strong that it seems unlikely that they should have been produced by a mere combination of such sources of error. We shall present our results in this section, therefore, in the hope of stimulating at least some interesting questions.

Some results of our provisional coding are shown in Tables A.10, A.11, and A.12. In the coding reported in Table A.10, we counted all locations where any of our 62 important advances had been initiated as shown in column 5 of Table A.1. Thus, if a major contribution had been initiated by two scientists working at different locations, each location was counted. Thus part of the work of the Vienna circle in the philosophy of science was also initiated by Hans Reichenbach in Berlin, and Berlin was counted in addition to Vienna; modern computers were initated by teams of scientists in Cambridge, Massachusetts and, in Philadelphia, and both locations were counted.

The mere continuation of an advance initiated elsewhere was *not* counted separately even if the initiator had moved to the new location to carry on his work. Thus game theory was credited to Berlin, where John von Neumann had published his first major paper for it in 1928, and not

Table A.10A. Geographic Locations of Major Social Sciences Advances, 1900–65 (by continents and by countries in Europe)

By continents

	Europe	North America (U.S.A.)	Other	Total
1900–29	33	12	4	49
1930–65	11	41	0	52
1900–65	44	53	4	101

By countries in Europe

	England	Germany	Russia	Austria	France	Switzerland	Other	Total
1900–29	13	8	4	3	1	2	2	33
1930–65	4	2	1	1	1	0	2	11
1900–65	17	10	5	4	2	2	4	44

to Princeton where he continued his work with Oskar Morgenstern in the early 1940s. Similarly, Chicago, where the work of the Vienna circle on the unity of science was continued after 1936, was not added to Berlin and Vienna, where the work had been initiated. (A change in these coding conventions would further increase our finding of the increasing importance of the United States to be discussed later.) Given the coding conventions just reported, we believe that our codings can be reproduced with only minor deviations.

The methods of multiple coding just described produced 100 locations for the 62 major contributions listed. The analysis is presented in Table A.10A. For the entire period 1900–1965, it shows a relatively even distribution of locations between Europe and the United States, and between the pre-1930 and post-1930 periods. It discloses, however, a radical shift in the relationship in the contributions between the Unitd States and Europe in the two periods. In the period 1900–1929, Europe produced 34 contributions against only 12 from the United States; but in the period from 1930 onward, European contributions dropped to 11 whereas those from the United States rose to 40, even though our method of coding tended to favor the assignment of contributions to their first origins in Europe where this seemed indicated by the record. (Of the U.S. contributions in the second period, only 5 could be credited in the main to European-born Americans.)

Within Europe, Britain and Germany were leading in both periods, followed in the first period by Russia and Austria, with smaller contributions from Switzerland, France, and others. In the second period no European country other than Britain and Germany made more than one contribution. In both periods Britain and Germany produced more than half of all the European contributions.

Within the European countries (Table A.10B) we find a similar concentration. One-half or more of all the British contributions came from London. Nearly one-third came from Cambridge. In contrast, the contribution of Oxford was minor. In Germany, Berlin predominated, and Heidelberg and Frankfurt accounted for 2 contributions each. Munich and Freiburg each had only 1 contribution to its credit, and for such famous university centers such as Göttingen and Bonn we found none at all.

In Austria, all contributions came from Vienna. In France all came from Paris. In Russia, more than half came from Leningrad, and 4 out of 5 came from Leningrad or Moscow. Six other European cities each had 1 contribution to their credit.

In the United States Table A.10B shows that most contributions before 1930 came from Chicago, which contributed 7 out of 12. New York contributed another 2; no other U.S. center produced more than 1 at that period. From 1930 onward, Cambridge, Massachusetts, rose to major status, producing 9 contributions out of the total of 40; New York and

Table A.10B. Geographic Locations of Major Social Science Advances, 1900 to 1965 (by cities)

	1900 to 1929	1930 to 1965	1900 to 1965
	England		
London	7	2	9
Cambridge	4	1	5
Oxford	2	0	2
Manchester	0	1	1
Total	13	4	17
	Germany		
Berlin	3	1	4
Heidelberg	2	0	2
Frankfurt	1	1	2
Munich	1	0	1
Freiburg	1	0	1
Total	8	2	10
	Austria		
Vienna	3	1	4
	Russia		
Leningrad	2	1	3
Moscow	1	0	1
Shushenskoe, Siberia	1	0	1
Total	4	1	5
	Others in Europe		
Paris	1	1	2
Turin	1	0	1
Lausanne	1	0	1
Herisau	1	0	1
Brno	1	0	1
Rotterdam	0	1	1
Stockholm	0	1	1
Total	5	3	8
	United States		
Chicago	7	3	10
Cambridge	1	9	10
NewYork	2	5	7
Washington	0	5	5
Ann Arbor	1	3	4
New Haven	1	3	4
Ithaca	0	2	2
Pittsburgh	0	2	2
Philadelphia	0	2	2
Princeton	0	1	1
Orange	0	1	1
Baltimore	0	1	1
Madison	0	1	1
Bloomington	0	1	1
Berkeley	0	1	1
Santa Monica	0	1	1
Total	12	41	53

Washington, D.C., added 5 apiece; Chicago and Ann Arbor, Michigan, each contributed 3; New Haven, Conneticut, Ithaca, New York, Philadelphia, Pennsylvania, and Pittsburgh, Pennsylvania, each provided 2. Taking the period 1900–1965 as a whole, three centers—Chicago, Cambridge, and New York—provided more than one-half of all U.S. contributions; Washington, D.C., Ann Arbor, and New Haven provided approximately another one-quarter.

Since these six centers represent only a small minority of U.S. social scientists (20 percent in the eleventh edition of *American Men of Science*, and probably never more than 30 percent), they evidently achieved an order-of-magnitude increase in effectiveness compared to other centers, as measured in terms of these major advances. (If 20 percent produce three times as many advances as 80 percent do, they are evidently producing twelve times as much per person.) By contrast, centers like Berkeley and Princeton, so eminent in other scientific fields, each initiated only one major social science contribution during these 65 years, whereas such centers as Los Angeles, St. Louis, Stanford, and Minneapolis seem to have none at all. If Festinger's work on cognitive dissonance had been included, however, Minneapolis and/or Stanford would have to be credited for it; and greater Los Angeles could be credited with Hitch's work on PPB (planning-programming-budgeting) at the Rand Corporation in Santa Monica. We will return to the reasons for this concentration effect in discussing the types of institutions responsible for these major advances.

However, it is worth noting that these concentrations of social science achievements in particular countries and particular centers seem to be even more marked than the concentrations in modern physics and biology,[5] and they do not seem directly related to any general factors such as increased war funding or science funding in the fields involved or at the centers in question. We surmise that contributions to social science may be extremely sensitive to external economies, such as the presence of local subcultures with other first-rate investigators and facilities in other fields,

Table A.11. Countries Where Major Social Science Advances Were Initiated 1900–1965 (Single Coding)

	U.S.	Europe:	U.K.	Germany
1900–1929	7	26	7	4
1930–1965	22	7	2	2
1900–1965	29	33	9	6

	Russia and Soviet Union	Austria	France	Other	TOTAL
1900–1929	4	4	1	6	33
1930–1965	1	0	1	1	29
1900–1965	5	4	2	7	62

Table A.12. Language Areas Where Major Social Science Contributions Were Initiated, 1900–1965

	English	German	Russian	French	Other	Total
1900–29	15	9	4	2	3	33
1930–65	24	2	1	1	1	29
1900–65	39	11	5	3	4	62

as well as to an intellectual climate specifically favorable to social science in the country and in the local community.

In order to check on a possible bias implied in multiple coding, we also analyzed the origins of major social science contributions by the single-coding method, crediting each contribution to one country only. The results are shown in Table A.11, and they confirm the major trends revealed by Table A.10. As Table A.11 shows, the United States and Britain together account for more than one-half of all contributions. From 1930 onward the concentration becomes extreme, with the United States accounting alone for more than three-fourths of all contributions.

The concentration of contributions in a few countries is exceeded by the concentration in terms of language areas as shown in Table A.12. Throughout the period 1900–1965, 39 contributions—nearly two-thirds of all the contributions—originated in English-speaking countries, followed by 11 contributions from German-speaking areas, 5 from the Russian-speaking area, but only 3 from French-speaking territories. Most of the German, Russian, and French language contributions originated in the pre-1930 period. For fundamental work in the social sciences after 1930, the knowledge of any language other than English cannot so far be called essential.

Types of Institutions

Another type of location was analyzed, this time in terms of types of institutions where major social science advances were initiated. Here again we used the single-coding method, and the results are shown in Table A.13. For the period as a whole, contributions were almost evenly divided between those made mainly with the support of a university chair or lectureship ($n = 29$), and those made with the support of a research institute or office ($n = 27$). Among supporting organizations of the latter type, university-related research institutes predominated with 18 contributions, as against 9 such contributions from government research institutes or offices. Finally, 5 major contributions were made with the support of nongovernmental political organizations.

During the earlier period, 1900–1929, university chairs predominated, accounting for 19 contributions out of 33. University-related research

Table A.13. Types of Institutions Where Major Social Science Advances Were Initiated, 1900 to 1965

Type	1900 to 1929	1930 to 1965	1900 to 1965
1. University chair or lectureship	19	10	29
2. Institute or project	6	12	18
3. Government research organization	2	7	9
4. Combined items 2 and 3	8	19	27
5. Nongovernmental political organization	5	0	5
6. Other	1	0	1
Total	33	29	62

institutes and direct governmental research played only a minor role, but all contributions from nongovernmental political institutions were made before 1930. Since 1930 no political movement seems to have produced a major new idea or contribution to the social sciences. During the period since 1930, contributions from university chairs shrank to 10 contributions out of 29, while contributions from university-related research institutes and from governmental research institutes at least doubled. Organizations of the research institute or "think tank" type thus accounted for about two-thirds of all major social science contributions since 1930.

This goes far to explain the strong tendency we noted for major advances in social science to be concentrated in particular cities. Several of the more productive cities have not one but several informal or formal centers or institutes or think tanks in the social or behavioral areas. It would be surprising if researchers in such places did not have more time to think about fundamental problems in their areas, and if they were not more effective in such environments where they can combine and criticize and multiply ideas.

It is important to emphasize that this concentration effect is in the opposite direction from the apparent *reduction* of scientific "effectiveness" per man with the growth of the whole scientific establishment, which Derek Price has pointed out.[6] When a larger fraction of the population is being tapped for science training, it is not surprising if the increased numbers of recruits are somewhat less competent than the self-selected smaller fraction of earlier years. And the added centers that these men help to staff are relatively new, and often do not have the emphasis on, or the support for, fundamental new thinking to nearly the degree of, say, the old established London and Cambridge centers. But this tendency to decline in quality with general growth does not contradict the fact that scientists of a given competence and training may gain enormously in effectiveness in creative achievement by being brought together into concentrated intellectual communities of the type we have been describing.

(The power of this method of intellectual concentration for social problem-solving is so great that perhaps we should regard the invention of the "think tank" as the achievement that multiplies all the others, even though it is an organizational achievement of the type we have excluded from our list. Thomas Edison, who is credited with organizing the first research-and-development team, went a long part of the way toward this idea; and Alexander Sachs, who helped to found the Institute for Advanced Studies at Princeton in 1932, should certainly be counted as one of the major contributors to the concept of general centers for concentrated abstract thought.)

It is also interesting to note that the overwhelming majority of social science contributions has been made under constitutional systems of government, and within these the main share belonged to constitutional governments which were democratic. As Table A.14 shows in the period from 1900–1929, countries under constitutional democratic governments were the source of two-thirds of all major social science innovations in the period (21 out of 33), while another 8 such innovations originated under authoritarian but constitutional regimes such as the German, Austro-Hungarian, and Russian monarchies before 1917. From 1930 onward, almost all major social science advances—27 out of 29—originated in countries under constitutional democratic governments.

Soviet-type governments, once they were established in power, contributed remarkably little in the way of major new advances in the social sciences, in contrast to their zeal in applying elements of existing social science knowledge that suited their purposes. Throughout 1900–1965, only two major social science advances seem to have originated under an established Communist regime: central economic planning in the 1920s, and linear programming in the late 1930s, both in the Soviet Union.

One single social science advance originated under an authoritarian non-constitutional regime: Bertalanffy's work on general systems theory in the mid-1930s in Austria, where the local authoritarian dictatorship of Chancellor von Schuschnigg had reduced its own constitution to a piece of paper, but fell short of all-out totalitarian rule. (Although initiated in

Table A.14. Types of Political Regimes under Which Major Social Science Contributions Were Made, 1900–1965

	1	2	3	4	5	6
		Authoritarian		Dictatorship		
	Demo-cratic	With Effective Constitution	Without Effective Constitution	Com-munist	Anti-Commun-ist	Total
1900–29	21	8	3	1	0	33
1930–65	27	0	1	1	0	29
1900–65	48	8	4	2	0	62

Austria, general systems theory was mainly continued in the United States and Canada.) Both before and after 1930, important countries were governed for prolonged periods by anticommunist totalitarian dictatorships such as Fascist Italy (1922–1943), Nazi Germany (1933–1945), and the military regime in Japan (1936–1945). It seems noteworthy that throughout our period not a single major advance in the social sciences originated under any anticommunist totalitarian dictatorship.

Disciplinary or Interdisciplinary?

Interdisciplinary work has been a major intellectual source of contributions throughout the period, rising from nearly one-half of all advances in 1900–1929 to nearly two-thirds of the total thereafter (column 16 of Table A.1 and Table A.15). This growing importance of interdisciplinary work reinforces our finding of the great importance of locating social science work at major intellectual centers in the proximity of many kinds of information and expertise from many disciplines. Locating a highly specialized social science enterprise at some small town or college, "far away from all distractions," seems instead to be a very promising prescription for sterility.

Table A.15. Main Intellectual Sources of Contributions: Within Discipline versus Interdisciplinary, 1900–1965

	Mainly within Discipline	Mainly Interdisciplinary	Total
1900–1929	17	16	33
1930–1965	11	18	29
1900–1965	28	34	62

Relation to Social Practice, Demands, and Conflicts

The role of practical demands or conflicts in stimulating major advances in social science is indicated by the data in column 17 of Table A.1 and Table A.16. The data show that throughout the entire period 1900–1965 about three-quarters of all major social science advances of our list were inspired by practical demands and practical conflicts. Thus Freud's work on psychoanalysis was undertaken in response to the needs of patients he encountered in his practice; the work of J. M. Keynes in economics was clearly related to the economic problems of Britain after World War I and to the problem of mass unemployment posed by the Great Depression.

Table A.16. Major Social Science Advances Inspired by Practical Demands or Conflicts, 1900–1965

	Stimulated by Practical Demands		
	Yes	No	Total
1900–04	5	2	7
1905–09	4	1	5
1910–14	0	2	2
1915–19	2	1	3
1920–24	5	1	6
1925–29	6	4	10
1900–29	22	11	33
1930–34	5	1	6
1935–39	5	1	6
1940–44	8	0	8
1945–49	2	2	4
1950–54	1	0	1
1955–59	2	0	2
1960–65	2	0	2
1930–65	25	4	29
1900–65	47	15	62

In the course of time, the importance of this relationship to practice has been growing. During the period 1900–1929, two-thirds of all major advances were made in response to such practical challenges and needs. During the more recent period 1930–1965, the proportion of such practice-inspired work rose to more than four-fifths of the total. From these data, taken together with our general knowledge of social science, it seems reasonable to infer that the image of the ivory-tower social scientist is a myth, and that close connection to social practice—within the limits of still preserving the intellectual independence of the social scientist—may well be favoring the making of new advances and discoveries in many social sciences.

The growing importance of social practice in stimulation of advances in the social sciences has been matched by the high rate of social science applications that has followed on them. The data are presented in columns 18, 19, and 20 of Table A.1, and in Table A.17-A and A 17-B. They show that about three-quarters of all major advances were followed by substantial applications, and that the proportions of such applications rose from nearly two-thirds of all advances in the period 1900–1929 to more

Table A.17. Applications of Major Social Science Advances, 1900–1965

A. Main Levels of Application

Year	Total	Social Practice: Major Applications Related to Any Level	Individuals	Groups	State
1900–1904	7	4	2	3	3
1905–1909	5	4	3	4	2
1910–1914	2	1	1	1	1
1915–1919	3	3	1	3	1
1920–1924	6	4	1	2	2
1925–1929	10	5	0	5	4
1900–1929	33	21	8	18	13
1930–1934	6	6	3	5	5
1935–1939	6	5	1	5	3
1940–1944	8	8	3	6	8
1945–1949	4	3	0	3	3
1950–1954	2	1	0	1	0
1955–1959	2	2	1	2	2
1960–1965	2	0	0	0	0
1930–1965	29	25	8	22	21
1900–1965	62	46	16	40	34

B. Single-Level vs. Multi-Level Applications

	1900–29	1930–65	1900–65
A. Single-level applications			
1. Only individual	1	0	1
2. Only groups	3	2	5
3. Only state	2	3	5
Total single-level applications	6	5	11
B. Multilevel applications			
1. Individual + group	4	2	6
2. Individual + state	0	0	0
3. Group + state	8	12	20
4. Individual + group + state	3	6	9
Total cross-level applications	15	20	35
Total applications	21	25	46
Total major advances	33	29	62

than four-fifths of all advances in the period 1930–1965. About one-fourth of all social science advances produced applications to problems of individuals. Applications to groups were more frequent, totaling nearly two-thirds of all advances, and applications at the level of the nation-state followed on more than one-half of all advances. The applications to the level of national policies increased substantially, from about 40 percent of all major social science advances in 1900–1929 to about 70 percent in

1930–1965. However, the post–1930 social science advances seem to have been less radical and far-reaching in their applications than the ideas of Freud, Lenin, Gandhi, Mao, and the Webbs, all of which were formulated before 1930.

A further analysis of our data presented in Table A.17-B suggests that most of those social science advances that produced substantial applications did so at more than one system level. If one cares to extrapolate these trends, one should expect a further increase of multilevel applications of social science advances in the future.

The Delay in the Impact of Major Social Science Advances

Like all advances in any science, social science advances take time before they have any identifiable impact on a broader field of scientific activity or on the practical affairs of society. Our estimates of this delay for each of the advances in our list are given are in column 21 of Table A.1, and the results are summarized in Table A.18. For the period 1900–1965 as a whole, the minimum delay of the impact for nearly three-quarters of the major advances was most often less than ten years; the median delay was most often in the neighborhood of ten years; and the maximum delay occurred most often in the neighborhood of fifteen years. These figures

Table A.18. Delay of Major Impact on Science and/or Society by Major Social Science Contributions, 1900–1965

	A. Minimum Delay, in Years				
	0–10	11–20	21–30	31+	Total
1900–1929	20	7	5	1	33
1930–1965	25	4	0	0	29
1900–1965	45	11	5	1	62
	B. Median Delay, in Years				
	0–10	11–20	21–30	31+	Total
1900–1929	7	18	4	4	33
1930–1965	21	8	0	0	29
1900–1965	28	26	4	4	62
	C. Maximum Delay, in Years				
	0–10	11–20	21–30	31+	Total
1900–1929	4	8	12	9	33
1930–1965	12	14	3	0	29
1900–1965	16	22	15	9	62

may understate the true length of the delay for two reasons. First, the seven advances listed at the beginning of our period as having begun in 1900 actually may have begun already some years earlier, so that the time between the start of the intellectual advance and its impact may have been longer than it appears in our coding.

Second, as discussed earlier, we may have omitted from our list several relatively recent advances that we failed to recognize precisely because their impact has been delayed. For the recent period, as for any time-limited period, the achievements with the longer delays are less likely to be recognized and are underrepresented.[7] This effect is more serious than is commonly realized in such studies, and leads to the result that if the probabilities of different delays were equal, at least up to delays as long as the time period of the study, the apparent average delay would not be one-half the length of the study; as might be expected, but is rather only one-third the length of the study. So for a 65-year period, if all delays up to 65 years or more were equally probable, the apparent average delay would be 21.6 years; and for a 35-year period of study, only 11.6 years.

The median delays estimated for the total period of the present study, and for the recent period, (last two lines of Table A.18-B), are substantially shorter than these figures, and closer to something like 12 years and 8 years; so that there is not a constant probability, but evidently a real falling off in frequency of the longer delay times (of, say, 20 years and up) for the kind of advances listed here. As Table A.18 shows, the most frequent median delay time dropped from between 11 and 20 years in 1900–1929 to less than 10 years in 1930–1965; and the most frequent maximum delay time declined from about 25 years before 1930 to about 15 years in the more recent period.

If one wishes to extrapolate from these data, one might surmise that the time lags of impacts might be further shortened in the future, with increasing higher education, speeds of communication, and large-scale development organizations. But the extrapolation is not certain, because this truncation effect of a short time base may be a major reason for the apparently shorter average delay in our recent period (as well as for the apparent decrease in the number of advances in this period.) And there may also be a serious distortion of apparent delay times by social forces; because the increasing share of social science advances aided by the support of research institutions or governments may have increased the proportion of research that is expected to have an early impact on practical affairs, or at least on other work in the social sciences—since projects with an expectable quick payoff are usually much preferred by sponsors, regardless of their perhaps lesser likelihood of resulting in fundamental contributions.

These time data suggest the desirability of extending the support of fundamental social science research efforts in the form of 10- or 15-year programs at clearly favorable locations. Such more sustained support might encounter political and bureaucratic difficulties, but it would seem to be the most promising strategy for making and consolidating advances like those described here in our basic understanding of social relationships and our ability to solve pressing social problems.

The radical increase in natural-science knowledge and its application has produced a radical increase in the problems of coordination in all industrialized societies. To cope with this radical increase in urgent problems, it seems essential to produce an early and large increase in social science knowledge and its constructive applications. The evidence here suggests that the intellectual and organizational means for such an increase are at hand if we care to use them.

Notes

1. *International Encyclopedia of the Social Sciences*, D. L. Sills, Ed., 17 vols. 1968. New York: Macmillan. For specific advice we are indebted to Robert Dorfman, Albert O. Hirschman, Simon Kuznets, Wassily Leontief, Gardner Quarton, Anatol Rapoport, J. David Singer, Guy E. Swanson, and others. None of these, of course, should be saddled with responsibility for our present work.
2. Another table could be compiled, based on the number of major contributions put forward by the data in Table A.1, Column 3, showing the number of major social science contributions under active development in each year. Such a table would reveal interesting information about the general intellectual climate in each period. Since our own interest is centered on conditions for intellectual creativity, however, we have chosen to concentrate on the starting date of social science contributions.
3. D. J. de S. Price, *Nature 206*, 1965, pp. 233–238.
4. Harvey C. Lehman, *Age and Achievement* (Princeton: Princeton University Press, 1953), esp. pp. 324–326.
5. There are some striking historical cases of concentration, in the natural sciences. Evolution by natural selection was proposed in the 1800s *independently* by four men within a forty-year period—Wells, Matthew, Darwin, and Wallace. All were British. But front-line physics today counts breakthroughs from ten or twenty major centers.
6. D. J. de S. Price, *Little Science, Big Science* (New York: Columbia University Press, 1963).
7. This statement can be made more quantitative. In making a study over a limited time-period, T (say 30 years), of developments that have a time-delay, D (say 10 years), between initiation and impact, the developments can only be identified by their impacts over the last $(T - D)$ years (20 years) of the

study. (To say the same thing, developments initiated in the last D years (10 years) will be unidentified.) For developments with longer D , $(T - D)$ is shorter, and more cases will be missed; and obviously the number of cases identified will become zero when $D = T$ or greater.

More specifically, if the probable number of developments per unit time that have delays between D and $D + dD$ is $p_D dD$, then the probable number detected in time T will be $(T - D)p_D dD$, and the apparent average delay, $\overline{D}_{Ap}$, will be given by

$$\overline{D}_{Ap} = \int_0^T D(T-D)p_D dD \Big/ \int_0^T (T-D)p_D dD$$

For the interesting case that various delays, D, are equally probable, at least up to $D=T$ or greater, we have p_D = constant, and we get by simple integration an apparent average delay.

$$\overline{D}_{Ap} = \frac{1}{3}T$$

That is to say, the factor $(T = D)$ is a linear declining function with increasing D, and the mean x-value for such a "triangular area" is one third of the distance to the zero point at $D = T$. If all the delays up to time T were detected with equal probability—that is, without this truncating $(T - D)$ factor—of course the apparent average delay (for p_D = constant) would be $\overline{D}_{Ap} = \frac{1}{2}T$.

ABOUT THE PARTICIPANTS

Ariane Berthoin Antal is a research fellow in the Research Policy and Planning Unit of the Science Center Berlin. She holds a Bachelor's degree from Pomona College and a Master's in international relations from Boston University. She has published a number of research articles on the political economy of the environment, especially land use and food production, and she is also concerned with corporate social reporting.

Daniel Bell is Henry Ford II Professor of Social Sciences at Harvard University. He attended the City College of New York and obtained his Ph.D. from Columbia University. He has taught at the University of Chicago and at Columbia University. He has served on U.S. Government Commissions in the Johnson and Carter administrations, was the chairman of the Commission on the Year 2000 for the American Academy of Arts and Sciences, and is a trustee of the Institute for Advanced Study at Princeton. He is the author of many books, including *The End of Ideology; The Coming of Post-Industrial Society*, *The Cultural Contradictions of Capitalism*, and *The Winding Passage: Essays and Sociological Journeys 1960–1980.*

Raymond Boudon is a professor of sociology at the Sorbonne in Paris. He was born in 1934 in Paris and studied at the Lycée Louis-le-Grand and the École Normale Supérieure. From 1968 until 1972 he was director of the Centre d'Études Sociologiques. He has also been a fellow at the Center for Advanced Study in the Behavioral Sciences at Stanford and a visiting professor at Harvard. Major works include: *Les Méthodes de la Sociologie* (1969), *La Crise de la Sociologie* (1971), *Mathematical Structures of Social Mobility* (1972), *L'Inégalité des Chances* (1973), and *La Logique du Social* (1979).

Gerhart Bruckmann is professor of statistics at the University of Vienna. He studied at the University of Graz, at Antioch College, Ohio, and at the University of Vienna, and has a Ph.D. from the University of Rome. He was in the Statistical Service of the Austrian Federal Chamber of Commerce and became the director of the Austrian Institute for Advanced Studies, 1968–1973. He is president of the Austrian Futures Research Society, and chairman of the board of the Austrian Institute for Socio-economic Development Research. He is a consultant for the International Institute for Applied Systems Analysis in Laxenburg, and is the author of *Auswege in die Zukunft*, and coauthor of *Groping in the Dark—The First Decade of Global Modeling*.

I. Bernard Cohen is the Victor S. Thomas Professor of the History of Science at Harvard University and a faculty member of the Kennedy School of Government of Harvard University. He has an S.B. and a Ph.D. from Harvard. His research includes the history of scientific ideas, the development of science in the United States, revolutions in science, the work of Isaac Newton, and the relations between the sciences and the social sciences. He has published several books, including recently *An Album of Science: From Leonardo to Lavoisier, 1450–1800; The Newtonian Revolution*; and *Revolution in Science: History, Analysis and Significance of a Name and a Concept.*

James S. Coleman is a professor in the Department of Sociology at the University of Chicago. He received his Ph.D. from Columbia University and taught for many years in the Department of Social Relations at Johns Hopkins University. He has been a fellow at the Center for Advanced Study in the Behavioral Sciences, a Guggenheim Fellow, and a Fellow at the Institute for Advanced Study in Berlin, 1981–1982. He has many publications, including *The Adolescent Society, Introduction to Mathematical Sociology, Power and the Structure of Society*, and *The Asymmetric Society.*

Karl W. Deutsch is the Stanfield Professor of International Peace in the Department of Government at Harvard University, and has been the director of the International Institute for Comparative Social Research/Global Development at the Science Center Berlin since 1977. He earned a Dr. Jur. from Charles University in Prague and a Ph.D. from Harvard University, and holds honorary degrees from several universities. Professor Deutsch's publications include *The Nerves of Government, The Analysis of International Relations, Politics and Government*, and *Tides among Nations*. His most recent research involves global modeling, international peace, and the politics of emerging nations.

Yehezkel Dror is professor of political science and Wolfson Professor of Public Administration at the Hebrew University of Jerusalem. He studied political science, sociology, and law at the Hebrew University and Harvard University. He has been a fellow at the Center for Advanced Study in the Behavioral Sciences, a senior staff member of the Rand Corporation, a senior planning advisor to the Israel Ministry of Defense, and a fellow at the Institute for Advanced Study in Berlin. His books incluse *Public Policy Reexamined, Design for Policy Sciences,* and *Crazy States.*

S. N. Eisenstadt is professor of sociology at the Hebrew University of Jerusalem. He has been a visiting professor at many European and American universities, a member of the London School of Economics, a fellow of the Netherlands Institute for Advanced Study in Wassenaar, and a fellow at the Center for Advanced Study in the Behavioral Sciences at Stanford. His recent books include *The Political Systems of Empires, From Generation to Generation*, and *Revolution and the Transformation of Societies.*

Bruno Fritsch is professor of economics at the Swiss Federal Institute of Technology (ETH) in Zurich and honorary president (founding member) of the Swiss Association for Future Research. He holds a Dr. rer. pol. from the University of Basel. He is now teaching and researching international economics and development; interactions between economic activities and ecological systems; world modeling; and the relation between energy, resources, and knowledge. His recent publications include *Growth Limitation and Political Power*; *Wir Werden Überleben*; and articles on social costs, planning, simulation, ecology, growth, and research on the future.

Alex Inkeles is professor of sociology at Stanford University and senior fellow of the Hoover Institution on War, Revolution, and Peace. He was at Harvard University for twenty-two years as professor of social relations, and director of studies at the Russian Research Center and Center for International Affairs. His books include *Public Opinion in Soviet Russia, The Soviet Citizen, What Is Sociology, Becoming Modern*, and most recently *Exploring Individual Modernity.* He is currently analyzing the social structure of the emergent global society and studying convergent and divergent tendencies in various aspects of modern societies.

Bernward Joerges is Privatdozent in the Department of Sociology at the Technical University of Berlin, and working at the Science Center Berlin in the International Institute for Environment and Society. His interests are in the social ecology of energy systems and urban space, and the effects of technological change on everyday life, consumer behavior, and scientific creativity.

Gebhard Kirchgässner is an Oberassistent at the Institute for Economic Research at the ETH Zurich. He obtained the degrees of Diplomvolkswirt and Dr. rer. soc. from the University of Konstanz. He has taught at the University of Konstanz and in political economy and econometrics at the University of Mannheim.

Hans-Dieter Klingemann is professor of Political Science at the Free University of Berlin. He holds a Dr. rer. pol. and earned his Habilitation in sociology at the University of Mannheim. He has taught sociology and political science at several European and American universities. His current research is on the structure and process of political participation, and on crisis factors in the sociopolitical system of West Berlin. He is the author of *Bestimmungsgründe der Wahlentscheidung*, and coauthor of *Politischer Radikalismus, Politischer Psychologie*, and *Political Action.*

Hermann Krallmann is a professor at the Technical University of Berlin in the fields of systems analysis and data processing. He studied at the Technical University of Darmstadt and obtained his Ph.D. from the University of Mannheim, and he held the chair of information technology at the Universitites of Bremen and Berlin. He has managed projects on "Innovation and Investment Planning of Manufacturing Equipment" and "Communication and Information Systems,"and has published numerous papers in the field.

Wilhelm Krelle is professor of economics at Bonn University. He studied mathematics, physics, and economics at the University of Tübingen and holds a Dr. rer. pol. and a Dipl. Phys. from the University of Freiburg. He was a Rockefeller Fellow at Harvard, Michigan, Chicago, and UCLA, and has been a professor at the Hochschule St. Gallen before coming to Bonn.

William Kruskal is the Ernest DeWitt Burton Distinguished Service Professor of Statistics at the University of Chicago, and he is currently the dean of the Division of the Social Sciences. He has been president of the American Statistical Association, and of the Institute of Mathematical Statistics. His primary research interests are on the intersection of statistical method and public policy.

Wolf Lepenies is a professor of sociology at the Free University in West Berlin. He studied at the Universities of Münster and FU Berlin. Major works include: *Melancholie und Gesellschaft* (1969), *Soziologische Anthropologie* (1971), and *Das Ende der Naturgeschichte* (1976). He also has edited a four-volume collection on the history of sociology entitled *Geschichte der Soziologie* (1981).

Andrei S. Markovits is associate professor of political science in the Department of Political Science at Boston University. He held previous teaching positions at Wesleyan University, Columbia University, New York University, and John Jay College of Criminal Justice of the City University of New York. He is the editor of *The Political Economy of West Germany: Modell Deutschland*, and coeditor of *Problems of World Modeling: Political and Social Implications*, and of *Fear of Science—Trust in Science.*

James Grier Miller is president of the Hutchins Center for the Study of Democratic Institutions. He holds M.D. and Ph.D. degrees from Harvard, and was chairman of the Department of Psychology and the Committee on the Behavioral Sciences at the University of Chicago. He was the founder and director of the Mental Health Research Institute at the University of Michgan from 1956 to 1968, and was president of the University of Louisville during the 1970s. He has been the editor of *Behavioral Science* for over twenty years, and is the author of many books, including the general systems compendium, *Living Systems.*

Helga Nowotny, who is currently a fellow at the Wissenschaftskolleg zu Berlin, is director of the European Centre for Social Welfare in Vienna, and Privatdozent for sociology at the University of Bielefeld. She holds a doctorate in law from the University of Vienna and a Ph.D. in Sociology from Columbia University. Her main interests lie in the areas between science, technology, and society, including a sociological perspective on information technologies, the use of social science in conflict situations, and women in the sciences. She is the author of *Kernenergie—Gefahr oder Notwendigkeit* and coauthor of *Counter-Movements and the Sciences.*

John Platt is a former biophysicist working on general systems theory as applied to science and social change. He studied at Northwestern University and has a Ph.D. from the University of Michigan. He taught physics and biophysics at the University of Chicago for twenty years and was associate director of the Mental Health Research Institute at the University of Michigan from 1965 to 1977. He is the editor of *New Views of the Nature of Man*, and the author of *The Excitement of Science, The Step to Man*, and *Perception and Change: Projections for Survival.*

Anatol Rapoport is director of the Institute for Advanced Studies in Vienna. He holds a doctorate in mathematics from the University of Chicago and held professorships of mathematical biology at the University of Michigan and of psychology and mathematics at the University of Toronto. He was guest professor in several universities in America, Europe, and Japan. He is the author of several books on the philosophy of science, semantics, conflict theory, and theory of games, including *Fights, Games and Debates; Strategy and Science; Two-Person Game Theory*; and *Mathematische Methoden in den Sozialwissenschaften.*

Jan Tinbergen was the Nobel laureate in economics for 1969. He was born in 1903 in The Hague and studied economics and physics at the University of Leiden. He was professor of development planning at the University of Rotterdam from 1933 until 1973, and at Leiden from 1973 until 1975. Major works include: *Business Cycles in the U.S.A. 1919–1939, On the Theory of Economic Policy, Economic Policy: Principles and Design, Shaping the World Economy, Development Planning*, and *Income Distribution.*

Peter Weingart is professor of science and science policy at the University of Bielefeld. He studied economics, sociology, business administration, and constitutional law at the University of Freiburg, the Free University of Berlin, and Princeton University, and received an M.A. and a Dr. rer. pol. from the Free University. He is researching topics in the sociology of science, science and education policies, and the philosophy of science. He is the author of numerous books and articles, and the coeditor of the *International Yearbook of the Sociology of Science.*

Rudolf Wildenmann is professor of political science at the University of Mannheim and at the European University Institute in Florence. He studied at the Universities of Tübingen and Heidelberg and has the degrees of Dipl. Volkswirt and Dr. phil. from Heidelberg, and a Habilitation from the University of Cologne. He was the editor of the *Deutsche Zeitung* in Bonn for several years, and later an Ortkolleg of the Federal Agency of Civic Education, and a senator of the O.Fg. for six years. He was a founding member and chairman of the European Council for Political Research, and has published several books and many articles on comparative politics, political-strategy problems, and other subjects.

Eckhart Zwicker is professor of corporate system and planning theory at the Technical University in Berlin. His fields of specialization include system analysis, corporate planning models, and decision support systems. His publications include a book entitled *Simulation and Analysis of Socioeconomic Systems.*

Name Index

C

D

I

J

K

L

M

N

O

P

Q

R

S

T

U

V

W

Y

Z

Subject Index

A

B

C

D

E

F

G

H

I

J

K

L

N

O

P

Q

R

S

T

U

V

W

XYZ